HOLDING THE LINE
AN AUTOBIOGRAPHY

HOLDING THE LINE
An Autobiography

John C. Hermon

GILL & MACMILLAN

Gill & Macmillan Ltd
Goldenbridge
Dublin 8
with associated companies throughout the world
© John C. Hermon 1997
0 7171 2591 2

Index compiled by
Helen Litton

Print origination by
O'K Graphic Design, Dublin

Printed by
ColourBooks Ltd, Dublin

A catalogue record for this book is available from the British Library.

1 3 5 4 2

For
Thomas, Robert, Rodney and Barbara
with love from
your crusty old Dad

CONTENTS

FOREWORD

After an initial spontaneous burst of enthusiasm, writing this account of my life became a slow and very demanding process. The early impetus to write was provided by the deep anger and frustration I felt over the political and media misrepresentation of the truth about a series of shooting incidents involving members of the Royal Ulster Constabulary in late 1982, in which six unarmed men were killed. I felt compelled to set the record straight about the events of that time, and about the subsequent inquiry headed by John Stalker.

At one stage, I was even tempted to write two books: the first relating specifically to the Stalker Inquiry, his book about it and the Yorkshire Television drama-documentary *Shoot to Kill*; the second an autobiography. However, wiser counsels prevailed. After all, I concluded, the Stalker Affair was but a small part of a whole, of almost forty years in the RUC, and should be placed in that context.

Recollection of my childhood and early years in the RUC was cathartic, full of painful reminders of people, events and emotions. In later years, as Chief Constable, I was aware of myself becoming, like so many other officers exposed to the pressures of policing a divided community, a 'casualty' of the turmoil that has beset Northern Ireland since 1968. As I reflected and wrote on my life in the RUC, I recognised that while I had few regrets, many memories of frustration and terrible sadness dominated my thinking. I was reminded of an eighteenth-century quotation by Lady Montagu, which I find most poignant: 'How am I changed! Alas, how am I grown/A frightful spectre, to myself unknown!' While she was describing how smallpox had completely distorted her, I would hope that the pressures of the job as Chief Constable had not gone that far. Changed, yes, more cynical and less trusting, yes; but not completely changed. Readers must judge for themselves.

I should explain that the completion of this book has been possible only because of the assistance of three key people. My wife Sylvia's editorial skills were tested to their limit as she put shape on the raw material of recollection, and supervised the development of several drafts. Her legal training and sensitivities proved to be of inestimable value. My sister, Belle, enthusiastically typed every word of successive drafts, from my first scribbles to the final version. And my publisher, Michael Gill, of Gill & Macmillan, showed considerable patience and provided enormous encouragement during my bleak months of stalemate and indecision. I wish to thank the three of them not just for their practical assistance, but for putting up with me and my shifting moods while this book was slowly taking shape.

I am also grateful to Alistair Graham, Patricia Hannon, Marshall Matchett, Louis McRedmond and the staff of the Linenhall Library in Belfast — all of whom will be aware of their particular contribution.

Regrettably, much of the detail that I wrote about my period as Chief Constable has now been omitted, as a direct consequence of the 1989 Official Secrets Act. This legislation remains a source of irritation to me as it necessitated the deletion of significant information, which I feel should be within the public domain. Nevertheless, our own domestic editorial control, with additional legal advice, meant that when the Northern Ireland Office first read the page proofs, it had 'no suggestions to make' to the text from 'a variety of points of view including confidentiality and national security'. So, while I continue to feel annoyed at the omissions, they were made reluctantly by the author, rather than imposed by the 'establishment'.

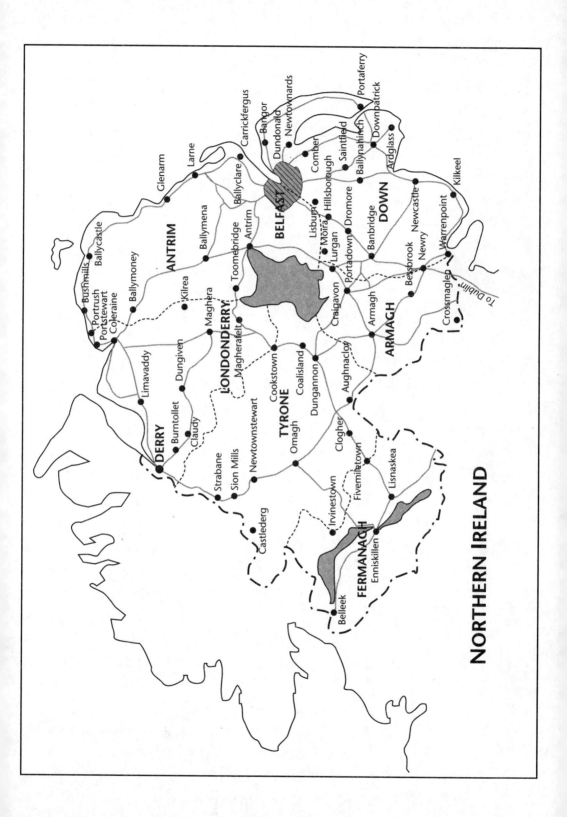

NORTHERN IRELAND

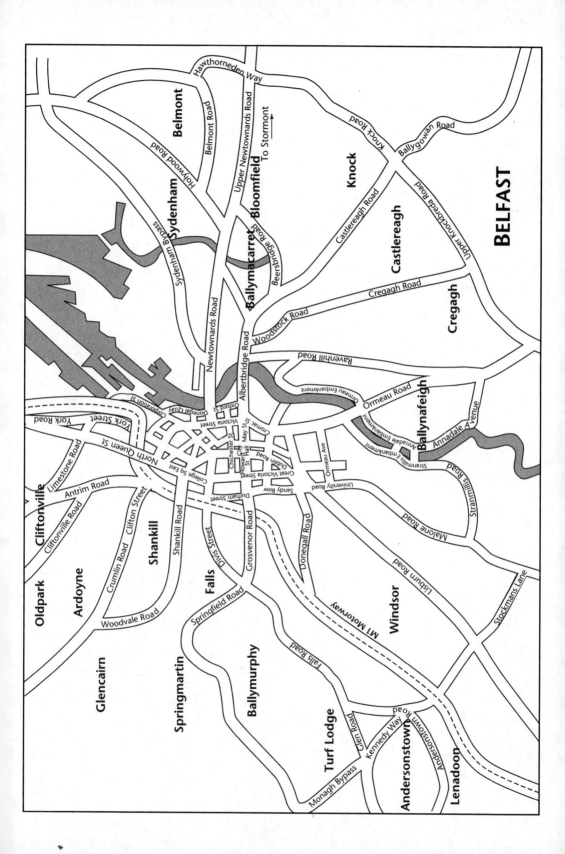

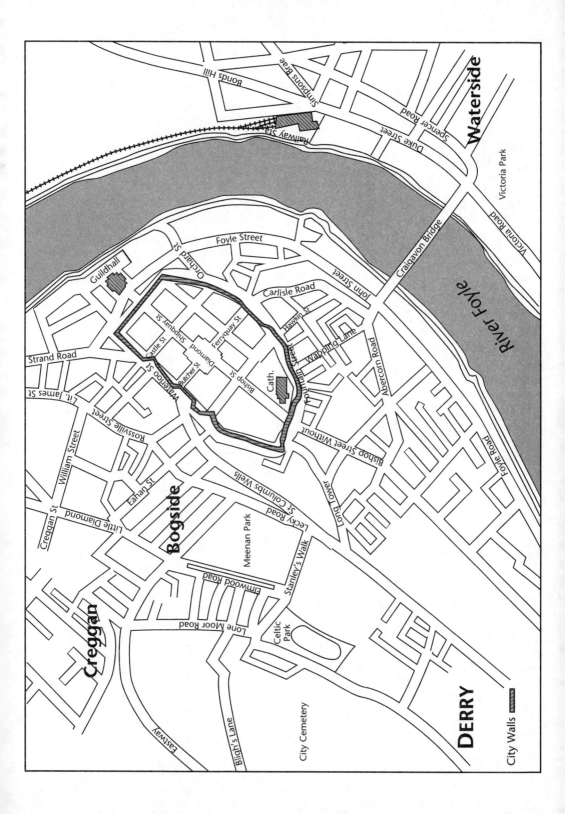

JOINING THE RUC

I feel as though I came alive only when I joined the Royal Ulster Constabulary. It became my life for almost forty years, and yet I had no sense of making it a career; it was enough for me just to be a member. From the outset, the RUC gave me the freedom to think and to develop as a person. It gave me freedom to be myself — a freedom I had known neither as a child nor in my teenage years.

Born on 23 November 1928, and christened John Charles after two of my father's brothers, I was brought up in the townland of Castletown in Islandmagee, on the County Antrim coast. My childhood was not an especially happy one. With a despotic and intemperate father and a religiously inclined mother, I grew up in a family atmosphere too often permeated with parental disharmony and fear. Fear of our father had its effect on all of us, particularly my mother. It was to her that I owed most as a child: protection, church-going, various sports, and such formal education as I achieved.

Possibly as a consequence of my home environment, I felt apart in ways from my own family, and from the local group of boys with whom I played. I was painfully shy and remained so for many years, learning to enjoy my own company and solitary pursuits. I always carried with me a sense of separateness, as if I were an onlooker watching my physical self behave naturally with others while my inner self stayed detached. That innate sense of separateness I still carry with me, and time after time it has been regarded by many — including friends — as aloofness, or even superiority. It is neither, but such judgments are understandable.

My father's unhappy disposition and heavy drinking were attributed by his own family to his First World War experiences. He had been a soldier in the 'Ulster Division' and had fought in some of the worst battles, losing not only several friends but a brother. He himself sustained wounds, but I feel that his suffering was more mental than physical. Whatever the reason, with his aggressive temperament he could not keep workmen, and with little aptitude for management he made a rather poor job of conducting the building contractors business he had inherited from his own father. Nothing in our own house was ever quite finished, despite his line of work.

Living as we did on a hill out in the country, there was no electricity, water or mains sewerage system until after the war. Instead, we had a well from which we pumped water for drinking, and another one, much further up the hill, which met our needs for the toilet and bathing. There was a septic tank for domestic waste. All of these creations were my father's. Oil-burning lamps and battery-powered radios completed the picture within our home, together with a telephone — a real novelty in those days. For a time, my mother had a little shop, providing confectionery, cigarettes, tobacco and some groceries for the neighbours and holiday-makers.

With my mother busy running the shop and my father away working or socialising in his Belfast club, there were few happy family occasions and no holidays. I sought solace from the local countryside, which I grew to love. Above all, literally, there was Blackhead, with its lighthouse, less than a mile from our home. Round about lay the green fields bordered by thorn hedges, and with whins to cap the hill, there was a yellow profusion from spring through to late summer. There were views of Islandmagee to the north, and of Belfast Lough and the Irish Sea to the east and south. The stony beaches, the cliffs and mysterious caves of Blackhead and the rocky face of the romantically named 'Gobbins' gave me hours of fun and adventure. These places, together with fishing from the rocks or boats and occasional opportunities to row, meant everything to me.

The only town of any size in the locality was Whitehead. A summer destination for Belfast people and Scottish and English tourists, it nestled in a hollow on the coast two miles south-west from our home. At night, I would watch the flashes from two lighthouses: one on the Copeland Islands several miles across Belfast Lough, the other Blackhead, with its friendly, familiar beam. In fog, there was the incessant blast of a fog-horn from the Copelands, and the detonation of a rocket from Blackhead every few minutes to alert any vessels entering or leaving the Lough. It was against this landscape that I grew up with, but away from, my family.

I was the youngest of four children, and never knew William, who died of an illness shortly after I was born. Isabella, known as Belle, was my only sister, and my senior by about three years. She was totally devoted to our mother and firmly protective of her during my father's outbursts of temper. With hindsight, I can see that Belle was the most steadfast and stalwart of us all, and, consequently, suffered more. Her experiences, I believe, moulded her and stay with her to this day.

Besides Belle, there was our older brother, Robert, who was asthmatic in his early years, and of a roguish disposition. Having left school at fourteen, he had been employed by a well-known photographer, who had a studio in central Belfast. However, when the Second World War broke out, it was the army which offered Robert both an avenue of escape from home and the prospect of adventure. At first, I envied him, and can remember praying almost nightly, 'God, don't let the war end before I'm old enough.' But it did.

Robert served with the Eighth Army, known as the 'Desert Rats', in North Africa, then in Sicily and Italy. He was grievously injured by shell-fire, taken prisoner by the Germans and later freed by the advancing Allied Forces. By the time he was discharged in 1944, he had been assessed as 85 per cent disabled, and was shattered both mentally and physically. His arrival home came as a great shock. The telephone rang one bright, windy afternoon. It was Robert phoning from the railway station at Whitehead. I ran shouting from the house and along the rough paths through the fields until I saw him in the distance, limping along. How pathetic he looked! His right arm was held upward to the sky by an iron splint, which in turn was encased by plaster of Paris that extended around his chest.

After frequent periods in hospital, Robert left home once more, married and went to work in England. His life thereafter was blighted by a combination of poor health and personal difficulties. During that time, we two maintained little direct contact, which is something I lived to regret. He subsequently divorced, remarried and found a deep Christian faith.

I, meantime, had long since passed through Whitehead Public Elementary School, where I was regarded as a good pupil, although I realise now that I did not apply myself as I should have done. Mathematics, or 'sums' as they were known then, were my forte. It was a rare occurrence if I did not win the penny proffered weekly by the headmaster, Mr Joe Hall, for the fastest pupil to do six sums correctly.

While I have many happy memories from my elementary school days, two unpleasant ones remain with me. Being naturally left-handed, I wrote with that hand for my first year or so. A new teacher, however, brought this to an abrupt end. I was often called to her desk to have my writing ability tested. I would begin using my left hand, until a series of sharp, painful jabs in the small of my back persuaded me to use the other one. With such 'encouragement' to become right-handed, my writing quickly took on the rude, uneven structure it still displays.

The other school experience to make a lasting impression upon me revolved around a geography examination. In final preparation for it, we had to change desks in the classroom. During the exam, Mr Hall observed that several answers to probable questions had been scribbled on the wooden-topped desk where I was sitting. So engrossed was I in the exam that I had not even noticed the scribbles, and denied all responsibility for them. I was summarily caned, quite ferociously, in an effort to make me admit culpability. I would not. I could not.

At lunchtime, it emerged that several of my classmates had seen the true culprit writing on the desk before I moved to sit there. When bullied by the others into owning up, he did so reluctantly and sullenly. He merely received a verbal admonition from Mr Hall. I was dismayed by such mild treatment of the guilty boy, who had witnessed my caning in silence, and, more particularly, by the absence of any apology for the wrong done me. Nevertheless, my admiration of the man never waned.

Because of these two incidents, I suspect, I became much more considerate of people's idiosyncrasies, and certainly slow to fix blame, save on the most compelling evidence. They also made me more self-assertive, as many — including the headmaster — were to discover.

Around June 1941, Mr Hall distributed several scholarship application forms for the best pupils to compete for places at Larne Grammar School. I was most indignant to have been left out, and stayed behind that afternoon to ask for one. At first, he refused, but I persisted until he eventually conceded.

At home, I then faced further difficulty in persuading my father to sign the form. It was only on my mother's surprisingly firm insistence that he did so. I sat the examination and was called for interview. Excited at the prospect of one of her children going to grammar school, my mother dressed me as best she could, and sent me off to Larne by train. There I met the man who, over the next few years, had a tremendous influence on my development.

This was Mr John W. Darbyshire, the headmaster. He was an impressive man, with a stocky frame and exceptionally large, powerful hands. Rumour had it, though never confirmed, that he had boxed professionally in order to pay for his education. I remember little of my interview, except that when asked what I wished to be, I replied, 'A builder, like my father.' His response was, 'Yes, but an engineer to build bridges and buildings and roads.'

Much to the amazement, I imagine, of our neighbours and to the sheer delight of my mother, I was awarded one of the few scholarships to Larne Grammar School for that year. My father had little to say on the matter. I suspect that he was inwardly pleased — even proud, although he would not admit it, possibly even to himself. However, when I commenced grammar school in the autumn of 1941, the Second World War provided too many distractions for me to be expected to devote all my time to schoolwork. Instead, I have vivid memories of watching the convoys of ships as they gathered in Belfast Lough, to lie safely at anchor behind the floating boom which stretched across it. The immediate benefits of their presence were the oranges and grapefruit casually thrown overboard by the American crews. These fruits were often washed up on the beach at Blackhead — great treasure trove for us children to collect and bring home! With food rationed, they were very welcome additions to our basic larder.

The darker, cruel side of the war also affected us. I can vividly recall how the night-time bombing raids on Belfast, especially at Easter 1941, reddened the sky over the city as buildings burned. The sounds of bombs and gunfire some eighteen miles away could be heard clearly above the drone of the enemy bombers passing only a few hundred feet above our house on the hill. Fires started by incendiary bombs at Bangor and along the County Down coast were reflected on our large front windows.

That awful Easter bombing of Belfast was reported to have killed more people than any other single raid on a city anywhere else in the United Kingdom. The next morning, army lorries brought evacuees out to the country. There were whole families, single adults and lone children, who came to stay with relatives or friends, or to occupy vacant weekend cottages. Dozens of people congregated outside our house, waiting anxiously to use our telephone, and hoping to learn that their loved ones in Belfast were safe.

For me, going to school interrupted this 'excitement'. After cycling each weekday morning to Whitehead or Ballycarry, I would travel onwards by train to Larne. School itself was a new, broadening experience, and I found lessons interesting. Although I participated in sport, I was painfully self-conscious and not particularly good. I played rugby without distinction, and other team games — like committee work later — were never really to my liking. The fact that I was the only boy in my age-group from our area to attend a different school only accentuated my feeling of distance from my former friends. At the same time, geographical separation prevented me from making close friends at Larne. The upshot was that I was always happiest at Blackhead, as I still took great pleasure in being alone in the remote countryside. Only 'Tatters', a faithful mongrel, was my regular companion.

Two separate incidents, one at school and the other on a train travelling home, produced a new side to my solitary character: I discovered that I could fight to defend myself! Bullied into conflict on both occasions by boys from the grammar and the technical schools in Larne, I was initially very reluctant — frightened, indeed. Hand-to-hand fighting was not something I had ever engaged in or regarded as a sport to be enjoyed. To my amazement, I soundly defeated both opponents, leaving one in tears. While I took no pleasure in my triumphs, I did gain some self-confidence, simply because I knew thereafter that I had the capacity to fight and win, if pushed to it.

Beyond day-school, my mother ensured that we attended Sunday School, and she, with Belle, frequently attended church. After the bombing of Belfast and the influx of evacuated children, our Church of Ireland rector in Whitehead made an unusual request. Knowing that we had a large open-plan room, he asked my mother if he could hold an afternoon Sunday School there for the evacuees. My father actually agreed to this! With the church providing about thirty collapsible chairs, Sunday School began in our home, and continued throughout most of the remaining war years. Having so many children around every Sunday brought a very exciting dimension to my life, even though it meant the additional chore of placing, and stacking away, the chairs.

It was through the church that I was introduced to a variety of sports, which I enjoyed for years. I joined the church scout troop and badminton club; I also played table tennis and, subsequently, hard-court tennis. Some ability in these sports enabled me to take part in certain league matches later.

After three years at grammar school, my examination results were quite good, and I naturally believed that I would continue for a further two years. This was not to be. My father decided that further education would be a waste of both time and money. Despite the pleading of my mother and the intervention of the headmaster, I had to leave school. The money and parental consent required for me to join the Merchant Navy as a cadet were not forthcoming, even though I had been offered the opportunity by a neighbour, himself a seafaring officer with the Union Castle Shipping Line. Instead of going to sea, I ended up in a Belfast accountancy firm. The owner and my father were friends and had come to some arrangement about my training as an accountant. I, therefore, felt my father's influence at home and at work.

Finally, the break came. My mother and father separated in 1947. Belle and I remained with our mother, who eventually moved to Belfast. We went to live with her brother, Tom, and his daughter, Nan, a music teacher. By this time, Belle had trained as a shorthand typist and obtained a secretarial post in the city.

Shortly before leaving Whitehead, I can remember the local RUC Sergeant, Gerry Mahon, suggesting that I might consider joining the police. He was aware of my difficult home circumstances, but my immediate response was, 'No.' The prospect frightened me somewhat. It certainly was not, I thought then, ever for me!

Instead, I studied to matriculation standard at evening classes and, because of financial necessity, I found work with a different employer, a large textile manufacturer called Cyril Lord. His arrogant and harsh attitude to his staff made me uneasy in his employment and, after some time, I took a job with the Automobile Association. I was instructed on my duties by a pleasant and attractive young lady, Jean Webb. She was rather shy and aloof, but nevertheless, I became totally devoted to her within a few months. For the first time in my life, I was hopelessly in love. A year quickly went past. My scarcely concealed affection for Jean became obvious to other staff, and was the subject of humorous comment, but she did not reciprocate. I was nearly twenty and Jean was a sophisticated twenty-one. What could I do to attract her attention?

Living in Belfast at this time, I had no social life outside work, except for winter badminton in the church and evening classes in modern dancing, which I went to alone. Although self-conscious about my gaucheness, I did manage to make some progress on the dance floor. Cousin Nan, whom I liked very much, also introduced me to a Shakespearean Society, which periodically held readings. I became fascinated by the Bard, a fascination which endures. While Shakespeare, some sport and my bicycle saved me from boredom during my spare time, there was nothing in these with which to woo Jean.

While I had firmly decided we would be married, I seemed powerless to do anything about it. My lack of self-confidence and fear of rejection prevented any direct approach. I also felt that I could not declare myself while we worked together, and so, in October 1949, I decided to change jobs yet again. There it was: in the vacancy columns of the *Belfast Telegraph*, I discovered a rare advertisement for recruits to the Royal Ulster Constabulary, and applied. Even though the pay on offer was a little less than what I was already earning with the AA, I never hesitated. My feelings for Jean had brought about my change of employment, and the fact that it happened to be the police was a happy accident.

In the week before Christmas 1949, I invited Jean to play in an open badminton tournament in my church club. To my delight, she accepted, and we had a most enjoyable evening. In the absence of public transport, I walked her home, a distance of about three miles — and then walked on air for the rest of that Christmas!

On New Year's Eve, an acquaintance from my dancing classes accompanied me to a very popular dance hall at Bellevue, Glengormley. There, on the densely crowded floor, I was very surprised to spot Jean. She was dancing closely with a partner, in whose company she remained for the rest of that evening. My Christmas ecstasy died on the spot! Totally despondent, I set off to walk home. At midnight, along the Antrim Road, I cynically wished myself a 'Happy New Year'!

Only a few weeks earlier I had reported to Chichester Road Barracks, where I was interviewed by a Sergeant Vance, who had some seniority in age and service. This was the beginning of a series of interviews and very detailed form-filling. Finally, I was asked to report to Queen Street Barracks for a physical examination. Of the candidates who appeared that morning, only five were passed medically fit. There followed a final call that afternoon to RUC Headquarters in Atlantic Building, Waring Street, Belfast, for the last interview. Although my interview was fixed for 4 p.m., I arrived about fifteen minutes early to accustom myself to the place. What a drab building it turned out to be, with its confusing flights of bare stairs and dull linoleum along the corridors.

At four o'clock precisely, a plain-clothes police officer escorted me into an office where Sir Richard Pim, Inspector General of the RUC, and District Inspector Cramsie, then Commandant of the Training Depot in Enniskillen, were waiting. (The title of 'Inspector General' was replaced by that of 'Chief Constable' only in 1970.) Sir Richard was a tall, impressive man with strong aquiline features and piercing eyes, while Mr Cramsie was slight and wiry. Both spoke with refined, cultured accents but their manner put me quickly at ease.

The interview took an unusual course, lasting more than twice as long as I had expected. Eventually, I was told that within two days I would be informed in writing whether I had been accepted or rejected. This created a problem; if accepted, I would have to report to the Training Depot in two weeks, which was exactly the period of notice I was obliged to give my employer. With a degree of impudence that came of naïvety, I asked to be told the result there and then, otherwise I would be unable to give the AA proper notice.

Sir Richard repeated that I would be informed in writing. Again, I requested that I be told immediately. A frown crossed his face, while Mr Cramsie, I thought, looked amused. Their eyes met, and Sir Richard, with a faint smile, nodded and said, 'In the circumstances, you may take it that you are accepted.' I left the room exhilarated — or perhaps shocked would be a better description.

The morning of Thursday, 2 February 1950, saw me leave my uncle's home in Knutsford Drive, Belfast *en route* for Enniskillen, County Fermanagh, some ninety miles due west. With a suitcase of so-called 'essential items', including a minimum of £2 cash because we were to be paid one month in arrears, I arrived at the Great Northern railway station at around ten. A small group of men stood together on the platform, conspicuous by reason of their cases, and the 'regulation boxes' at the feet of some. A regulation box, as I later discovered, identified the owner as a policeman's son or close relative, because it was traditionally passed down through generations of police families. I approached the group rather nervously, recognising only two or three faces of those who had attended the medical examination on the same day as me. There was very little conversation between us as we waited for the gate of the railway platform to open.

I slipped away, found a telephone kiosk on the platform and telephoned Jean at the AA office. I gave her the news that I was about to depart for the RUC Training Depot, but it evoked little enthusiasm, let alone conversation, other than a cursory, 'Wish you well.' Her cool response left me deflated and forlorn as I turned back towards the train.

Heading off towards Enniskillen, six or seven of us sat together in the railway carriage. The others chatted but I remained silent, preferring the flash past of the bleak winter landscape, with its bare trees and dull fields. The dullness matched my mood. Immediately before entering Enniskillen, the train passed over the high-arched Weir's Bridge and through a heavily wooded area, alongside fast-flowing water. It was a very beautiful stretch of the narrow river which links the Upper to the Lower Lough Erne, and the sight of it cheered me greatly. I was to visit this particular spot frequently by boat in later years, especially in the autumn, when the hundreds of trees that crowded the steep banks were a blaze of varied colours, and the surface of the water was a mirror for their beauty.

At the railway station, two Morris tenders, driven by uniformed constables, awaited us, and we were swiftly conveyed through Enniskillen to the Depot. It was located within the old part of the town on an island in the River Erne. Bridges at its east and west ends joined the island to the mainland. The Depot was on the western tip, and was bounded by either water or a high stone wall. Driving down Queen Street, I had my first glance of what was to be my home for several months. The main building was impressive, built in pale grey stone and obviously very old. On the grass in front stood a flag-pole with the Union Jack flying. A large parade-ground stretched from the grass to the entrance, with other old buildings on each side.

Within this complex was the headquarters of the most senior police officer in the area, the County Inspector. The Depot was also the RUC's District Headquarters, with a District Inspector in charge. One wing of the main barrack block accommodated both of these senior officers, their staff, and the operational police, then numbering probably thirty men of all ranks. In addition, there were normally three or four squads of between twenty and thirty recruits in training at any one time. Training lasted for twenty-six weeks, and the Depot was guarded by twelve senior recruits, who were held back for a couple of months from the previous, fully trained squad. As raw recruits, we found ourselves the object of much curiosity from operational policemen and from those recruits senior to us. Woe betide the junior recruit who became too forward or familiar with them!

2

MY FIRST TASTE OF POLICE LIFE

Our first day at the Depot was cold, wet, windy and altogether miserable. It was dark before 6 p.m., and since the place was poorly lighted, it became quite eerie in the evening. New faces joined us, having arrived from other parts of Northern Ireland. After a roll-call, dormitories, beds and lockers were allocated. A drill instructor, Sergeant Nevin, was appointed as our squad sergeant and, hopefully, as our mentor and friend for the next twenty-six weeks. There would be no weekend leave for the first six weeks because, as he explained, we were not fit to be seen in public until after then! Our first instruction was on how to make a bed with our dull, grey or fawn-coloured blankets, white linen sheets and pillowcases. The dormitories were stark with six to eight men in each. Women recruits, if any, had single rooms in a separate building.

Finally, the oath of allegiance 'in the office of constable' had to be sworn before a local Justice of the Peace. During my training and subsequent years of study, the awesome nature of that office impressed itself upon me. I felt a great sense of responsibility and a firm commitment to maintaining the dignity of the office of constable, which was to endure throughout my thirty-nine years of service.

When we started our careers in 1950, the RUC had an establishment of around 3,000 and was normally at full strength. Recruits were not difficult to attract, as serving members of the Force were invited to identify young people of good character and sound family background in order that they might be encouraged to join. While many recruits were the younger sons of farmers or the sons of police officers, others were shop assistants and tradesmen. There was also a fair sprinkling of experienced personnel, since ex-servicemen were drawn to police life.

Like other United Kingdom police forces in the early 1950s, the RUC had very few women police officers — about forty in total. Women recruits then had to be unmarried or widowed without dependent children. Upon marriage, a woman member of the Force had to resign: it was May 1969 before the first married woman joined the RUC.

Coincidentally, a rare intake of women recruits had in fact reported at the Depot on 1 February 1950, the day before us. Designated 'V' squad, they underwent the same basic training as the men and were fully integrated with our squad. Initially, there were some murmurings about this because women police constables were viewed with derision by some male recruits, who regarded them as an impediment to their own training. On reflection, I believe that the presence of the women raised our level of behaviour, including our language and manners, and undoubtedly added to the element of competition in written examinations.

On 2 February, our 'W' squad comprised twenty-five men of varying backgrounds, education, experience and age. I could not help but feel insecure. Having to sleep in a dormitory in an unfamiliar environment with five strangers was for me a demanding, even stressful, experience. As the evening progressed and we prepared for bed, conversation began to flow between my companions, with Christian names shared and introductions made. For my part, I said little, and had difficulty in sleeping as subdued chatter continued late into the night. Again and again, I asked myself if I had been wrong to join the police.

The next day, I located the gymnasium, which was marked out for badminton, and later I discovered where we could play table tennis in the recreation block. There was also a 200-yard cinder running-track. At the rear of the Depot, I also noticed a powerful police launch and four or five timber, clinker-built rowing-boats, each about seventeen feet long. With the prospect of using these recreational facilities, I began to relax. I quickly realised, however, that the training staff had other ways of burning up our energy, such as drill, physical training, games and 'fatigue duties'.

Three suits of blue denims were issued to each male recruit, with the worst to be used for 'fatigues'. These duties included cutting grass, weeding and tidying up the Depot. Proper police uniforms, for which we had each been measured by tailors at Queen Street Barracks in Belfast, arrived after six weeks. Initially, these were worn only for the formal weekly parade and inspection on a Wednesday morning. Caps, on the other hand, were issued immediately, as proper saluting of officers was part of our training from the very beginning.

Haircuts were also an immediate imperative. Enniskillen barbers were well accustomed to the correct style for police recruits, if 'style' be the right word to describe it! Little hair was left on the back and sides of the head, which showed below the cap. If a recruit thought he knew better than the barber, he invariably found himself cautioned on return to the Depot and sent back for another haircut. We also had early instruction on how to polish our boots, especially the toe-caps, heels and sole-edges. Until then, I had never worn boots of any sort, and they grazed my ankles and blistered my soles badly. With the passage of time, however, my feet hardened and the boots became tolerable.

This totally alien, bustling, people-intensive environment came as a tremendous shock to me. I am sure many others were as apprehensive of the strict military-type regime as I was, although I never discussed my feelings openly with anyone. It was a case of bearing it in silence, even the boots!

At the time of recruitment, I was almost skeletal in appearance, being slightly over six feet tall, but weighing only 140 lb. During our first fortnight, the Orderly Sergeant suddenly called for silence one evening in the dining-hall. I expected an important announcement, and certainly not what followed. 'Hermon,' he called out, 'you're first for seconds. We have to fatten you up!' I can still recall my awkward and embarrassed progress to the serving-counter, amidst general laughter. I had to get used to it, because this routine continued for several weeks. I even began to look forward to second helpings, as I had a voracious appetite by the end of a frenetically busy daily schedule.

I took to rising early, usually between five and six o'clock. I moved quietly, studying before going out to the running-track to use up some of the energy which seemed to increase by the day. Studying became almost compulsive; I found that I could not learn enough. I read and reread my notes, learned legal definitions and much more besides. I became an avid player of badminton and table tennis. Relishing both the physical and academic aspects of my training, I started to thrive in my new environment. When spring arrived, I frequently took one of the available rowing-boats out on Lower Lough Erne.

While my taste for solitary pursuits carried over from my childhood into the weeks of training in the Depot, I did make friends with several other recruits. Meetings with them down the years were enjoyable, as we could reminisce, not least about the 'Twelfth' of July 1950.

On that particular 'Twelfth' (the traditional day of widespread Protestant celebration) there was to be an Orange parade through Enniskillen town and permission to leave the Depot was refused to all recruits. As some of us were feeling claustrophobic, I suggested after lunch that we take out a rowing-boat. Quickly and surreptitiously, five of us left from the river bank at the rear of the Depot. We later disembarked at the East Bridge in Enniskillen. Warren Wray, who always had a puckish outlook on life, climbed the bank like a mountain goat, and positioned himself on the bridge wall. The rest of us followed suit. Everything went well until, while the parade was passing, Warren made a loud comment about two Orangemen, dressed in sashes and bowler hats, who had slipped behind a hedge to obey a 'call of nature'. We fell about laughing and then panicked. With Warren bringing up the rear, we piled back into the boat and rowed with more enthusiasm and muscle than skill. Suddenly, an oar snapped.

Paddling back with a single oar to the Depot turned into something of a struggle. As we arrived, Sergeant Timoney, the Orderly Sergeant of the day, awaited us. His face told us that he was not one bit pleased. He was a quiet man with little apparent humour, but was dedicated to his job, and known as a stickler for high standards. He told us we would be reported for breach of discipline, and, as I had signed for the boat and the oars, I would have to account for the broken one.

With my previous experience of rowing-boats, I was able to produce an extremely detailed report on why the oar had broken at the point where it rested in its leather sleeve in the rowlock. I pointed out that instead of using copper nails, someone had secured the sleeve to the oar with iron nails, and these had corroded, thereby rotting the wood underneath. A few days later, we were advised that in the circumstances we did not have to pay for the oar. Instead of regarding this as a salutary lesson to end such escapades, I developed quite a liking for nonconformity!

Every weekday for the first four months or so, there was a period of drill and one of physical training. The remainder of the day was devoted to intensive schooling, not just on the criminal law but on the powers, responsibilities and duties of a police constable. Considerable emphasis was put on practical policing. Notes had to be taken in class, and lessons absorbed for the following day.

I particularly recall one school period, which dealt with the Larceny Act 1916. Sergeant Martin Williams asked me to define 'stealing'. A sufficient answer would have been the simple definition within section 1 (1) of the Act. Instead, I recited verbatim the whole of section 1, subsections 1, 2 and 3. It was only when I stopped that I sensed the stunned silence of the class, and saw the look of surprise on Martin Williams's face. A short pause ensued before he spoke. 'Sit down, Hermon. You'll go far in the job.' There was general laughter as I showed my great embarrassment. Unknown to me, this was the beginning of the Hermon myth within the RUC.

After five weeks of training, I took top place in the first written examination. The second, third and fourth exams came, and each time I took first place. In the final one, I was joint first with another recruit. Throughout my studies, I never consciously set out to compete with others. Rather, it was in a purely personal way that I was most competitive, seeking high achievement and excellence from myself. How well others fared in comparison was really of little interest to me. Similarly, running became a source of personal pleasure and achievement. Each week, usually on a Saturday morning, all recruits took part in a long-distance run, varying from two to six miles. I do not remember ever being other than first, either jointly or on my own.

During those twenty-six weeks of intensive training at Enniskillen, I came alive and found myself. Although still inwardly shy, I learned to converse more easily. Time flew by. My formal training finished in August, and was followed by two months of guard duty as a senior recruit in the Depot until 2 October 1950. That day saw a flurry of activity for us, surrendering equipment, saying farewells to staff, packing, attending to a multitude of detail, and all the while we were coping with the excitement of becoming real policemen at last.

For unusual reasons, the young Hermon had made an impression as a recruit. My skinniness was certainly remembered, as were my academic results, supposedly based upon a remarkable memory and dedication to study. Some officers retained a considerably distorted view of my real ability and my commitment to work. In later years, when meeting particular members of staff, I was bemused by their recollections of me, because they seemed to me to bear little resemblance to how I had seen myself.

For my part, I vividly recall the impressions made on me by the staff. The quality of the training I received in Enniskillen imbued me with a sense of service rather than enforcement, and it moulded my attitude towards people over my entire police career. Our instructors, for example, while teaching us the rules and the manner of giving evidence in court, emphasised very strongly that police officers had to be totally impartial. They were not in court as prosecutors. Instead, they had to present all the relevant evidence, whether in favour of or against an accused person.

On 3 October, I rose early and prepared for departure by making a nostalgic tour of the Depot and the boats. With my duck-egg blue bicycle and baggage, I boarded the train in Enniskillen and eventually reached the Waterside railway station in Londonderry. There, the ubiquitous Morris tender was waiting for me, driven this time by a much overweight senior constable, John McCartney. Long afterwards, we became friends, but in very different circumstances. On this occasion in 1950, he was taking me to my first posting, and that was to Eglinton Barracks, just outside Londonderry — or Derry, as it was historically, and is still generally, called.

Eglinton was a small village with one shop, one café (which I had through necessity the misfortune to frequent), a small post office, one public elementary school, one public house, only one church and two very large houses, owned, I guessed, by people of some wealth and social status. As it was October, the leaves on the trees alongside the village road were changing from a faded green to shades of brown, yellow and even red. There was such an air of peace and tranquillity about the village that I took an immediate liking to it, even before the tender had stopped at the barrack gate.

When the barrack door opened, a constable emerged with his hand outstretched and a broad smile on his face, 'Welcome, young fella. Come and I'll help you with your cases.' The barracks were of the standard type, built throughout Northern Ireland in the pre-war period from 1935/6 onward. The rectangular building was set in its own grounds with a low wall at the road, and fencing to the sides and rear. It was divided into two parts: one providing accommodation for the sergeant and his family, the other for the small police party of four constables.

There was no time for a detailed inspection of my new home because the Sergeant-In-Charge, W.G. Grace, appeared within a few minutes. Having welcomed me, he told me to be prepared to accompany him on a cycle patrol at 6.30 p.m. sharp. After an unpalatable tea in the café, I presented myself for duty. I could see that Sergeant Grace viewed my sports bicycle with scepticism, but he made no comment. As we walked or wheeled our bicycles, he asked me about myself and my life before joining the RUC. In turn, he told me about the area and about the unusual problems caused by the local presence of a Royal Navy aerodrome with about 1,300 personnel, including some 200 members of the Women's Royal Naval Service.

After a three-hour patrol, we were again approaching the village when, in the growing darkness, a cyclist suddenly sped past us on an unlighted bicycle. Sergeant Grace immediately directed me to 'Stop him!' I saw the cyclist turn right, and in hot pursuit I turned into the road, but there was no sign of him. As he could not possibly have travelled the whole length of the road in the short time it took me to reach the corner, I concluded that he must have gone into the grounds of a nearby hall. With the light from my torch, I managed to find him hiding behind a large chestnut tree in a pathetic attempt to evade discovery. Together we emerged on to the road. At that stage I felt very embarrassed because I simply did not know what to do with the lad. We just stood there until Sergeant Grace arrived a few moments later to caution him and explain that he would receive a summons.

Back at the barracks, the Sergeant told me to make an entry in my police notebook recording the date, time, place and nature of the offence, together with the name, address, occupation and age of the culprit and any explanation offered. With this came the realisation that I had noted my very first case for prosecution at the local Petty Sessions.

That same evening, I was also introduced to the 'duty sheet', which was completed daily by the Sergeant and set out the tasks to be performed the following day. Each constable in turn had to do a twenty-four-hour guard duty as Barrack Orderly. This meant parading at 9 a.m. and remaining on duty for the next twenty-four hours, except for two hour-long breaks for meals, at 1 p.m. and 5 p.m. respectively. From midnight, one was — if duties permitted — allowed to prepare a makeshift bed in the guardroom. To say that I found Barrack Orderly duty boring would be putting it politely. I hated it! When I left Eglinton, I swore that I would never again do a twenty-four-hour guard, and circumstances were such that I never did!

During the early part of the following year, Sergeant Grace went into hospital for a much delayed operation. I made a point of visiting him when I attended the Petty Sessions in Derry City. He asked me how many detections I had made in his absence. When I identified six or seven, he laughed heartily. It transpired that other visitors from Eglinton had already told him that the new Constable Hermon was very strict and had made about 140 detections! I was genuinely shocked at this, as the reality was altogether different. I had, in fact, found people in the area very welcoming towards their new constable, and this included entertaining me to discreet cups of tea during my patrols. Yet, I was able simultaneously to remain my quiet, private self. I am convinced it was this 'separateness', which I had experienced throughout my adolescence, that created the myth of Hermon as a strict, even severe, disciplinarian.

That said, I was as happy serving in Eglinton as I had been in training at Enniskillen. My inward peace was disturbed, however, by feelings of insecurity or embarrassment when I was confronted with awkward situations. The most challenging of these occurred when, following my return to the barracks after midnight, word came that a serious fight was under way in the village. I left immediately. There, in the forecourt of the shop and licensed premises, were two men whom I knew. Several other locals were standing around, watching and discussing the antics. The smaller of the two on the ground was a slight, wiry farmer, called Donaghy. The much more strongly built man, named Cowan, was sitting astride Donaghy's chest, and striking him forcefully with both fists. The smaller man was gamely fighting back. When I ordered Cowan to stop, he ignored me completely.

Physically, either of them was more than a match for me, and I knew it. I also knew that peace had to be restored. I removed my cape, drew my baton and again ordered Cowan to stop fighting. Again, orders were to no avail. With strength born of the fear of being inadequate to the occasion, and of being humiliated in the presence of the bystanders, I struck Cowan heavily with my baton across his shoulders. He rolled off Donaghy and on to the road. When I prodded him with the baton, he arose dazed. I then ordered him to lift Donaghy and assist him to the barracks, from where both men were eventually released.

Gossip spread that the young constable, his baton flashing in the street lights, had single-handedly subdued the two, known as 'fighting men' when they had drink taken. Even Sergeant Grace congratulated me on handling the incident without assistance. But I was ashamed of the fears I had felt, and concealed them in silence.

Law continued to fascinate me. Indeed, when guard duty permitted, I began to read with enthusiasm not only those Acts of Parliament on issue to the barracks and retained in the Sergeant's office, but the rules and regulations laid down in the RUC Code. This way, I quickly discovered how virtually every facet of life in the police was controlled or guided by written regulations. The growing of vegetables for family use and the disposal of any surplus by a member were regulated, as was the keeping of a cow! The rigidity of the rules was almost always tempered by common sense and humanity. The old adage that 'Regulations are for the guidance of wise men and the blind obedience of fools' was in my view applied within the RUC with considerable success.

My interest in these matters had at least one embarrassing outcome. The Game Amendment Act (Northern Ireland) 1951 decreed that it was unlawful to burn gorse on uncultivated land between 15 March and 15 July. This was designed to protect wildlife during the breeding season. In the spring of 1951, while on one of my cycling patrols in the hills between Eglinton and Claudy, I caught sight of gorse burning furiously in the distance. I could also see a man moving along the edge of the blazing hillside and drew the obvious conclusion that he had set it alight. My knowledge of the recent statute sprang immediately to mind, and I determined to make what would probably be the first detection under that Act.

I raced towards the fire, deposited my bicycle and crept up undetected behind the culprit. 'What do you mean, burning the mountainside at this time of year?' I bawled at him (or words to that effect). Sweaty, smelling of smoke and with soot engrained on his face and hands, he growled back, 'For God's sake, Constable, I've been trying to put it out for hours!'

In my more regular studies, I always had the quiet, unobtrusive support and encouragement of Sergeant Grace. He also began gradually delegating to me tasks which were directly his responsibility, including the filing and indexing of documents and the drafting of short reports. When alone in the barracks, we would discuss local problems and reported offences. Only years later did I appreciate how beneficial it was for an experienced sergeant like him to express his views and seek the opinions of a probationer constable like me.

In many other respects, Sergeant Grace was an unusual man. His four children, three boys and a girl, were then aged between four and twelve. He and his wife must have started their family quite late in life. Young George, John, Charles and Elizabeth tended to frequent the guardroom while I was on duty, plaguing me with their pranks and persistent questions. On one occasion, when they were particularly boisterous and taking some advantage of the fact that they were the Sergeant's children, I threatened to lock them all in the police cell, if they did not calm down and behave. The threat, having failed to produce the desired effect, was immediately executed by my bundling them all into the cell and bolting the door. A little while later, Mrs Grace came looking for them and seemed less than pleased to find them incarcerated!

That incident apart, Mrs Grace and her husband were protective of me, and wished to see me happily married. The same thought was often in my mind; when I was on patrol, my thoughts would drift towards Jean and our slowly, but steadily, deepening relationship. Since both of us were shy, private people, inexperienced in displaying emotion, our special relationship took its time to mature. I hoped that we would eventually marry, although I scarcely dared believe that Jean could return my love. To disclose my feelings would, I feared, end our friendship. Throughout this time, we corresponded regularly and I tried to travel to Belfast to visit her during my monthly leave of thirty-two hours. Occasionally, I took one or two of my thirty days' annual leave in order to see her, and she also came as my guest to the annual district police dance.

While dancing certainly was not my forte, running along country roads remained a passion. Indeed during the spring of 1951, the Sports Officer from the nearby Royal Naval base encouraged me to join the training sessions which he conducted for athletes amongst the sailors. I did so from time to time. When a sports day was organised, I was invited to participate in those events of my choice. I decided on the cross-country race of approximately six miles through lanes and fields up into the hills to the south of the village, and back again.

I set off with at least fifty or so naval personnel of varying non-commissioned ranks. To my surprise, I found myself well to the fore in the run-in and actually finished about 400 yards ahead of the first sailor. The Commander of the base shook hands and heartily congratulated me on my run. When he asked the Sports Officer who I was, it was with obvious embarrassment that the latter replied, 'The local bobby, sir'!

On the more serious side of my time in Eglinton, a certain incident caused me considerable anxiety for the person involved. He was a young, married man with one child, and I knew he eked out a precarious living on a small hill farm. When I stopped him on the road driving his tractor, I discovered that he had neither insurance nor a valid driving licence, because he could not afford to pay for them. Although I felt sorry for him and his family, there was no alternative but to recommend prosecution — no vehicle insurance, in particular, was a grave breach of the law. Some weeks after his conviction, he called at the barracks. He was in good form and presented me with a box of apples from his own trees as a thank-you present for helping him! He explained that if I had not prosecuted him, he would never have bothered to insure his tractor and would now probably have been forced to quit farming, since an accidental fire had badly damaged it. Having been compelled to take out insurance, he could afford the necessary repairs and remain in farming. My initial anxiety about prosecuting him disappeared in an instant.

In September 1951, I was notified of my transfer to the County Police Headquarters at Victoria Barracks in Strand Road, Derry City. Although it was a routine transfer, and I should have expected it, I was disappointed at having to leave Eglinton. I found it especially hard to take my leave of Sergeant Grace. I did not realise for several years the extent to which he had influenced my development as a constable in the RUC. For his part, he was genuinely sad to see me go. Less than two weeks later, he wrote to me. His manner of expression was simple, direct and sincere. I felt unworthy of his praise, wishing I had done more and stayed longer, and yet I drew from his words a degree of confidence in my ability to be a good constable.

My arrival at Victoria Barracks was treated casually. It was the RUC's County Headquarters, and personnel — especially at constable level — were coming and going all the time. The offices, kitchen and dining-room were on the ground floor, with sleeping accommodation upstairs. I was pleased to find one large, albeit sparsely furnished, recreation-room, amongst the rows of offices and dormitories. My own room was on the first floor, at the rear of the building. It overlooked extensive cattle pens, which stretched almost the entire length of a fairly narrow, cobbled street. Beyond them lay the docks and quays of Derry's harbour. The noise and smell of the cattle awaiting live shipment filled my bedroom, especially during the warm summers of 1952 and 1953.

The windows of the spartan dining-room also looked out over the pens. Against the opposite wall of the room were our individual lockers, in which we needed to store supplementary food, as Victoria Barracks had a 'skeleton mess', producing only a cooked midday meal. The main course was predictable, with meat, potatoes and vegetables, except on Fridays, when we had fish to meet the religious obligation of Catholic officers — in truth, it was a welcome variant for us all. Other than that, men in residence were required to provide their own food for both breakfast and tea. Since wartime rationing continued through the early 1950s, basic foodstuffs were still in short supply. Hence, on my cycling trips into Donegal in the Republic of Ireland, where no rationing existed, I invariably returned with my saddle-bag full of food, and cigarettes or tobacco for those constables who smoked. Officers of the Garda Síochána (the Republic's police force) in the border area soon recognised me on my blue bicycle, and allowed me a sensible degree of immunity from search — something I never abused.

Even with such forays into the Republic, I found that my mess bill, together with the cost of extra food, totalled almost £15 each month. This was more than half of a probationary constable's net pay, then around £27 a month. After rail fares to Belfast once a month to see Jean, I had little left for personal savings towards, I hoped, our eventual marriage. Studiously avoiding debt of any sort, it was only occasionally that I could make some financial contribution to my mother.

The strictures of life in Victoria Barracks brought about a very real sense of comradeship between the constables, the majority of whom were young, with only a few older bachelors or married men 'living in'. The small group of men of varying ages who dressed neatly in suits I identified as detectives, either in the Criminal Investigation Department (CID) or Special Branch. The former was responsible for investigating routine crime, including serious assault, burglary and theft, while the latter was, and remains, responsible for uncovering terrorist crime and keeping track of subversive organisations.

Derry has had a long and turbulent history. It is not only Northern Ireland's second city, but, being so close to the border, is the main town for a substantial part of County Donegal. With reliable bus and rail services to and from the Republic, there was always a steady flow of shoppers and business people across the border. Our police Subdistrict itself was principally occupied by business premises and factories for pork processing and shirt manufacturing. Consequently, large numbers of workers from the densely populated urban parts of Derry, and the surrounding rural areas, poured in and out each working day. We found that much of the crime in our Subdistrict was committed by criminals and juvenile delinquents from outside it. Juvenile crime was a very real problem but an understandable one, when there were many children from deprived homes, in a city with high unemployment and few recreational facilities.

Other policing difficulties, peculiar to Derry City, arose from the heavy presence of American and NATO naval forces, as well as British servicemen stationed in camps around the city. When the inevitable fights broke out, we tried to maintain the peace by shepherding those involved back to their ships, or arranging transport to their bases, or delivering them into the hands of their own shore patrols. Members of these patrols could impose immediate restraints, in a manner that was certainly not open to the RUC without breach of regulations or the threat of complaint!

Servicemen apart, it was our duty at night-time to keep in close contact with those people moving about, whether they were late-night revellers, the homeless or workers with unsocial hours. Often there were elderly people, sick children and abused wives in need of help, and many of them turned to the police. In this way, I learned of the massive social service provided by the RUC every hour of every day throughout the year. Seventy-five per cent of our work was then, and for many years continued to be, of that nature.

Even in the busy Victoria Barracks I gradually found time to return to study. By Christmas 1951, I had started a correspondence course in criminal law, evidence and the practical and administrative aspects of policing. My tutor was Mr Terry Kiernan of Inverary Avenue in Belfast. He had joined the Royal Irish

Constabulary, then transferred to the RUC after the partition of Ireland in 1922, and had achieved the rank of District Inspector in the 1930s. During his service, he had met and married a German, with the result that, at the outbreak of war, he had had to resign from the RUC on grounds of national security. He was given alternative civilian employment by the Government, and he renewed his interest in policing by offering a correspondence course, coupled with formal weekly classes, for police officers studying for promotion. I clearly recollect sitting during that winter at a small table in my room at Victoria, wearing my regulation greatcoat and cap, and with a blanket round my knees — all in a vain endeavour to keep me and my hands warm enough to draft answers to Terry Kiernan's searching test papers.

While stationed in Derry, I was also gaining an awareness of the complicated political and religious divisions within Northern Ireland. During my twenty-six months there, I witnessed two incidents that to me reflected more than anything else the dichotomy of views about the British monarchy in Northern Ireland. The first occurred on 6 February 1952, when I was on beat duty, standing on the walls of Derry City and overlooking the Catholic Bogside housing estate. Immediately below were the roof-tops of old Victorian terrace houses. All at once, through the upper half of a sash-corded window, a woman's head emerged. Although a Catholic, she was sobbing uncontrollably when she called up to me, 'Constable, the King's dead!' She had just heard the wireless bulletin about the sudden death of King George VI, and I found her emotion as moving as the content of her message.

The second incident, the following year, was no less memorable. I was again on duty, standing this time in a small confectionery and tobacconist shop. As I was chatting to its owner, a young woman came in, asked for a bar of Fry's chocolate cream, and put two pennies on the glass-topped counter. The shopkeeper duly took the bar from a shelf. She picked it up, but then abruptly threw it into his face. In a raised, excited voice she snapped, 'I asked for chocolate, not for the Union Jack!' Grabbing her two pence from the counter, she rushed out of the shop and was gone. The shopkeeper and I looked at one another in amazement. But as my gaze fell on the rejected chocolate bar, I saw that the paper wrapping bore the red, white and blue of the Union flag in celebration of Queen Elizabeth II's coronation.

At that time, I have to say that I was not at all conversant with, or particularly interested in, the politics of Northern Ireland. In Derry, I detected very quickly a smouldering disaffection, especially within the Catholic working class, towards the 'establishment' generally and, on occasions, towards the police.

The violence in Ireland from the Easter Rebellion of 1916 and the Civil War in the 'Free State' (later the Republic) after the island was partitioned were still within the living memory of many in Derry, and in the folklore of many more. It was to the credit of the RUC, though rarely recognised, that peace and stability pertained in that divided city, with only infrequent exceptions, from the time of partition until the lid flew off the simmering pot of social and political discontent in the late 1960s.

With such a sense of unease between the Protestant and Catholic communities, the RUC in Derry had to be constantly alert. The fact that isolated IRA attacks did occur against military garrisons in parts of Northern Ireland during the early 1950s indicated that the threat of subversion was indeed real. The security of police barracks was given continuous attention. On several occasions during my period at Victoria, sizeable reserves of men were assembled within the barracks to act as a quick reaction force in the event of an anticipated IRA attack. In my time there, none materialised.

At this early stage of my career, I had not experienced any terrorist activity or serious street disorder. St Patrick's Day, 17 March 1952 changed that. There was a bitter confrontation involving a small Catholic parade in the vicinity of William Street and Waterloo Place. It arose from the then illegal carrying of a 'provocative emblem' in the form of the tricolour, Ireland's national flag. Missiles were thrown at the police, who responded by baton-charging the fast-growing and hostile crowd. I soon found myself on the streets along with other constables, and was engaged in several baton charges. Additional police resources were called in from outlying barracks, and Reserve Force Platoons were also brought from Belfast to Derry within a few hours. Rioting persisted into the evening, and to a lesser extent during the following two nights.

During the next St Patrick's Day in 1953, the rioting was vicious, widespread and sustained. The police were for a brief period almost overwhelmed, and a certain amount of panic and confusion ensued. I was extremely disillusioned by our chaos in these situations, as there was precious little evidence of firm command by our superiors during the first hours of violence. From such experiences in Derry, I learned much about riot control, not least the need for clear decision-making in difficult circumstances. A legal adage, 'The law does not speak but to command, and does not command but to compel,' seemed pertinent. In its broadest sense, this principle was to influence my thinking throughout my career. Fairness, generosity and compassion, yes, but always firmness, when necessary, in law and in command.

3

ROMANCE AND ROUTINE

Before being stationed in Victoria Barracks, I had regarded myself as a casual but good poker-player, and continued to do so for a short while after I arrived there. I sat in on several poker schools, for ostensibly 'nominal' stakes. As time passed, these grew, until the day I lost my month's pay, all but £3. That was in a continuing game. With my last £3 I tripled the bet and won the hand. In subsequent games, where the stakes were certainly not nominal, I more than recouped my losses. Although I have no distinct recollection of my total winnings, I do remember that within the month I bought myself a sports coat, flannels, shoes, a shirt and a tie. Even after that spending spree, I was able to clear my mess bill and still have almost a full month's pay in my pocket!

Nevertheless, that was the last occasion I played poker, because I was committed to saving towards my marriage to Jean, even though that matter had not yet been broached between us! Whenever we met, we scarcely had more than a few hours together or a day here and there. Consequently, in the spring of 1952 on one of my monthly visits to Belfast, I suggested to Jean that we should take a holiday together to become better acquainted. To my delight she agreed, having first discussed my suggestion with her parents and obtained their approval.

Jean was an only child and hers was a very close family. I had visited her home on several occasions and suspected that her parents, Roy and Meg Webb, had realised that I was in love with their daughter and that my intentions were entirely honourable. They had no need to worry. Anything beyond holding hands would have been a quantum leap for us! My own reserve ensured that I was uncomfortable in the presence of women, and without experience of any sort. Jean's situation was much the same. Behind her meticulous grooming and veneer of sophistication, she too was shy. Her only other serious boyfriend had been the one I had seen her dancing with that New Year's Eve of 1949. It was exactly two years later that she told me he had made such crude advances to her after that particular dance that she had refused to go out with him again. And so the first time I had seen my rival was in fact the last time she had seen him!

After careful thought, I suggested that Edinburgh in August during its Festival would be the ideal place for our holiday. I had never been; indeed, I had yet to have a holiday inside Northern Ireland, let alone one outside it! By contrast, Jean had already been on many holidays with her parents to England, the Isle of Man and the Republic of Ireland, but fortunately not to Edinburgh. Agreement was reached, and I booked two single rooms in a guest-house situated close to the centre of the city.

We enjoyed that holiday tremendously. The guest-house turned out to be comfortable and well kept, reflecting the efficiency of the couple who owned and ran it. Those two weeks were amongst the happiest and most relaxed of my life, spent as they were in what seemed to us like fairy-tale surroundings with fine architecture and Festival delights. It was there that we really came to understand each other as we walked and talked and laughed together. Our relationship blossomed by the day. There was no doubt in my mind that Jean loved me as I did her.

By the time we left Edinburgh, I had proposed and Jean had happily accepted. We planned to become engaged in September and married within two years, thereby giving us time to save towards the cost of setting up home. Our financial situation notwithstanding, we agreed that Jean would not work after our marriage because we hoped to start a family early. Back in Belfast, I was reassured by the warm reaction of Jean's parents to news of our engagement. Until then, Roy and Meg had not really begun to relate closely to me or relax completely in conversation. That reticence disappeared and I became much closer to both of them, especially Roy. In many ways he behaved more like a father to me than my real one.

Meanwhile, at Victoria Barracks, the good humour of the resident constables continued. There was always a great sense of oneness, comradeship and loyalty each to the other. I suspect the strict discipline, and the shared experience of serving under a rather authoritarian command, forged the bond that welded us together. Our comradeship also meant that pranks abounded.

Several of my own escapades were the subject of peer acclaim. During a period of prolonged confinement to barracks prior to a royal visit, I disappeared. I was in fact sitting on a narrow platform at the top of the out-of-bounds 120-foot-high radio-mast. Oblivious of the concern and intense search below, I was captivated by the view of Derry that night, with the moonlight shining upon the cathedral spires, upon the winding River Foyle, and upon row after row of terraced houses across the river. On descending to reality, I was immediately accosted by an irate and worried Detective Sergeant Lewis, whose normally friendly manner deserted him on this occasion. He strongly suspected me of a few of the worst — or, to some of us, the best — pranks in Victoria Barracks.

Amongst these ranked our spectacular fireworks display, which was neither official nor designed to mark Hallowe'en. We had decided to liven the place up with a carefully co-ordinated plan to let off fireworks, known as 'Mighty Atoms' because of their enormous bang. The detonation of these every five minutes required considerable skill to avoid detection or attribution to any particular individual. Such was the effect of our display that poor Sergeant Lewis left his bed around 3 a.m. to seek refuge in a nearby hotel! Rightly or wrongly, he suspected me of being the organiser. My explanation that I had been 'here and there, doing this and that' did not convince him of my innocence. He was never to know if his suspicions were in fact correct!

For various reasons I also recall moments of great sadness, while stationed at Victoria. Ammunition stocks were replaced in Derry on 31 January 1953, and I seized the opportunity of travelling with the motorised convoy back to Belfast the following day. The Station Sergeant, who knew I wanted to take advantage of every opportunity to visit my fiancée, was helpful and granted me my thirty-two hours' monthly leave of absence for February. Sitting in mufti, inside a canvas-covered police landrover, I travelled along the Glenshane Pass through the Sperrin Mountains. It was a bleak experience on that bitterly cold day. I consoled myself that at least it was a sure way of eventually seeing Jean. As it turned out, the usual happiness of such a visit was completely overshadowed by a disaster that affected many families throughout Northern Ireland.

The previous night had been one of wild storms and persistent rain. While leaving the barracks very early that morning, we had heard some vague talk of a shipping accident. In fact the *Princess Victoria*, a ferry which plied between the ports of Stranraer in Scotland and Larne in County Antrim, had sunk during a violent storm. A massive sea and coastal search for survivors was under way as dawn broke.

On the top of Glenshane Pass, our convoy of police vehicles, landrovers and lorries stopped. All had been travelling slowly because of the snow and icy road conditions. From the vehicle radios we could pick up the messages between those police officers involved in the aftermath of the tragedy off the Antrim coast. News of bodies recovered and the sightings of wreckage were being reported. We learned that the ferocious seas had torn open the stern doors of the ferry, causing it to sink with the loss of most of its crew and passengers. An air of depression descended over us all as we remounted the vehicles, and continued to Belfast.

After my brief leave, dominated as it was by more detailed and gruelling reports of events at sea, I returned to Victoria Barracks. On account of my business experience prior to joining the RUC, I was occasionally detailed for clerical duties in the station sergeant's office during the absence of the Constable Clerk. These duties included responding to requests for leave. I remember receiving one from a senior constable of some thirty years' service, who was a permanent driver for the police vehicles in the transport pool. He asked if I could facilitate a small number of men in having an evening off. With the willing co-operation of other constables and sergeants, this was done without difficulty. I actually knew that their occasion was a Freemasons' dinner.

The following month, the same request was made, but this time the senior constable spoke to me in a way which showed that he assumed I too was a Freemason. Taken aback, I quickly informed him that he was wrong. With a look of surprise, he inquired, 'But aren't you studying?' and added, 'You'll go nowhere in this job unless you're a Mason!' I assured him that if that were so, I did not wish to go anywhere in the job. I thought wryly at the time that, if he had ever considered advancing himself during his long service, his membership of the Freemasons had been of little help!

Even then, the suspicion of Masonic influence within the Force was strong. Mick McKenna was a senior Catholic constable, with whom I worked well while serving in Victoria. He appeared gruff and taciturn. Once, he and I were on duty together protecting the 'Judges' Lodgings', a name given to any building where the Judges of Assize were in residence. Standing at the junction of a cul-de-sac and Bishop Street, I remember Mick nudging me with his elbow and nodding towards the Masonic Hall across the street. 'See there, son,' he said, 'that's where our duty is made out.' I was rather bewildered by the comment, and said nothing.

I knew next to nothing about Freemasonry then, but was often to recall his chance remark. As it happened he was transferred out of Victoria a short time later. On the day of his departure, which was noted by scarcely anyone, he came to my room to say farewell. Handing me a fine table tennis bat, he said, 'Here, son, you'd better have it. I've no use for it now,' and that was all. The bat was obviously a sign of different and better times for him, since I had never even seen him play the game. I was sadder than I expected to see this forlorn figure leave.

As far as membership of organisations like the Freemasons was concerned, the regulations in the RUC Code made it clear that members of the Force were permitted to belong to any society, provided it was not one prohibited by the oath taken upon joining the police. This meant that they could attend lawful society meetings in plain clothes. However, the regulations specifically forbade 'the expression or manifestation of political or sectarian opinions'. It followed that police officers could not privately attend or help organise any demonstration or parade, without having specific approval to do so. They could be members of secret societies such as the Orange Order, Royal Black Preceptory and the Apprentice Boys of Derry, but could not in any way overtly express political or sectarian views. These regulations, inherited from the Royal Irish Constabulary, were based on practical experience during 100 years of policing. Any breach of the prohibition did not reflect weakness in the regulations, but weakness on the part of the individual members or, occasionally, of their immediate commanding officers.

Not being a member of any secret society or organisation, I encountered no problems in this respect. In fact, it was after an incident in Derry that I came to a decision never to join any of them. While off duty and in plain clothes, I had taken shelter from the rain by stepping into the doorway of the Littlewoods shop in Waterloo Place. A number of other people were doing likewise. On the other side of the street, I noticed a constable on beat duty. I knew him better than most as he had been in my squad at the Depot; I was aware that he was in the Orange Order and was also a Freemason. As I stood watching him, I overheard the youth in front of me saying to his companion, 'There's that Orange bastard —', naming him.

Although I knew the man to be an impartial police officer, I suddenly realised that in the eyes of those two youths, he could never be accepted as such. This, together with the other inherent prejudices and fears — even hatreds — that I had already come across within the Catholic community in Derry, convinced me that I should not become a member of any secret organisation with religious or political connotations.

I became much more aware of the feelings of the Catholic minority in Northern Ireland during the celebrations to mark the coronation of Queen Elizabeth II in June 1953. In the village of Dungiven in County Londonderry the Protestant community, mostly from the surrounding countryside, had organised a children's carnival with a fancy-dress parade through the town. Unfortunately, rumours were rife that a loyalist flute band from the neighbouring village of Bovevagh was to lead the parade. The Catholic people of Dungiven were incensed because, some years earlier, there had been a serious confrontation between them and local Protestants over this particular band. Thereafter, an unwritten agreement had been reached between the opposing sides to ensure that Bovevagh Flute Band would never again go beyond a certain road-bridge to the west of Dungiven. As this tradition seemed in jeopardy in the summer of 1953, trouble was anticipated and a contingent of police from Derry was despatched to assist the local members in supervising the parade. I was amongst those despatched. Apart from traffic control, we were required to ensure the free and uninterrupted progress of the children and to maintain the peace. Above all, Bovevagh Flute Band was not to parade in Dungiven that day.

Posted as I was in the centre of the town, I could sense the happy, buoyant atmosphere amongst the local children, parents and onlookers, who thronged the footpaths. But there were outsiders present too, mostly young, hefty men from the country. In threes and fours they stood about on both sides of the long street, and only occasionally did they move along the footpaths behind the throngs of excited people. I felt apprehensive that they were in the background not for pleasure but to prevent any possibility of the Bovevagh band leading the parade through Dungiven.

I particularly recall seeing the local Catholic priest amongst the crowds on the street. Rumour had it that as the parade was going through the village, an angry youth had produced a revolver. This had been quickly taken from him by the young priest. Whether this was true or false, we were never to know.

After the parade had passed peacefully, without the appearance of the dreaded band, we were more than a little relieved. Most unusually, we were given meal-tickets to obtain dinner in a hotel, in the main street of Dungiven. Although it was packed to the door, certain tables had been reserved for RUC members. As the young Catholic waitress served our group of four constables, she whispered, 'You're welcome here today. It's not often that we see you protecting us.' Her casual remark lingered in my mind, and I was to ponder on it long afterwards.

Once crowned, Queen Elizabeth, accompanied by the Duke of Edinburgh, made a series of visits to towns and cities throughout the United Kingdom, including one to Derry in July 1953. There had been strict security in the city for the two weeks prior to the event. The route from the quay, where they were expected to arrive in a Royal Navy frigate, to the Guildhall within the historic walled city had been checked and rechecked by Special Branch and CID.

On the day of the royal visit itself, I had initially begun my duty at the rear door of the Guildhall, where I was unable to see any of the activity going on in Guildhall Square. Suddenly, however, I found myself redirected to a flat roof overlooking the Square to guard against anyone gaining access to it. Early that morning, members of Special Branch had found that the padlock of the trapdoor leading to the roof had been prised open and were most alarmed in case the roof was intended as the site for launching an attack on the Queen. Consequently, I ended up with a magnificent view of the River Foyle, the military guard of honour, the civic dignitaries and crowds of spectators assembled in the Square!

No attack actually occurred. Instead, the Queen's vehicle arrived and she emerged to the playing of the national anthem. At that moment, hundreds of cameras photographed the event, and many recorded an anonymous, matchstick man standing rigidly to attention on a roof above the proceedings. In fact, some time later Edmonson's, a retail shop in Shipquay Street, produced a calendar with a cover photograph of the ceremony. I have often shown that photograph to friends, claiming that I was the most conspicuous person present, but no one could identify the tiny figure on the skyline!

The long hours of duty necessitated by that royal visit had interrupted my studies, but the arrival, on 6 August 1953, of a young single sergeant gave me fresh impetus. When he came to Victoria on promotion, I helped him to carry his boxes and cases to his room. This was Sergeant Michael McAtamney, who came with a reputation for a considerable knowledge of the law. He and I quickly became firm friends. His knowledge exceeded mine, and he helped me greatly with my correspondence course.

Michael McAtamney was to stimulate my thinking, broaden my reading, and sow the first serious seeds in my mind of aspiring to higher rank. Terry Kiernan had mentioned him by name as a star student, who would undoubtedly achieve district inspector rank. He frequently drew comparisons between our approaches, concluding that I tended to be a pragmatist, while Michael tended to be a purist in the interpretation and application of the law.

About that time, two vacancies arose for constable clerks in the offices of the District Inspectors in Limavady and Magherafelt, both in County Londonderry. I applied. While I recall little of the written test, one part stands out. We were required to consider an accident file in order to identify a number of errors. In doing so, I dared to disagree with the recommendation on prosecution and added my own opinion. I was intrigued to learn at my interview that the County Inspector took the same view as I did. When he asked me why I wanted to become a DI's Clerk, I quickly explained that I just wanted the administrative experience before moving on. He was obviously taken aback and told me bluntly that he wished to find good clerks, rather than provide the likes of me with administrative experience! That was the end of that, I thought.

Towards the end of November, I was notified of my transfer to Limavady with effect from 15 December 1953. My appointment was wholly unexpected, because I had so little service and relevant experience. I would initially be required to act as understudy to the existing DI's Clerk, Constable Joe Matchett, who was leaving on promotion to sergeant the following February.

Faced with the news, both Jean and I were saddened that we would not be beginning our married life close to the attractive countryside around Eglinton and Victoria. There were other regrets too, not least the fact that I was leaving the few firm friends I had made in Victoria, like Constable Bobby Killen. He had been my keen opponent at table tennis, with neither of us prepared to acknowledge the other's supremacy. And there was Michael McAtamney, whose friendship I valued greatly. In remarkably different circumstances, which none of us could conceivably have imagined in 1953, both Bobby and Michael were later to join me at senior command level.

At Limavady, the District Inspector, Mr D.A. Walker, was precise in all that he did. From the outset, I enjoyed being clerk to this quietly spoken man with a dry sense of humour. In the DI's absence, Head Constable R.J. Martin would deputise for him. Beneath them in rank were the Station Sergeant, a duty sergeant and about a dozen constables. No detectives were attached to this police District, since it was at that time a tradition of the RUC that the uniformed branch was primarily responsible for the detection of crime everywhere, except in the cities of Belfast and Derry and the main provincial towns. Outside these, detectives were available for investigating only the most serious or complicated crimes.

When I joined the District Inspector's staff in mid-December, I was allocated a single room on the first floor of the barracks. With its large window overlooking the winding River Roe, I had a view that was pleasant throughout the year, and nothing short of superb in the clear evenings of spring and summer as the sun was going down behind the hills between Limavady and Derry. To me, this view compensated for the lacklustre interior, with its indifferent wallpaper and old 'black-out' curtains, a relic from the war.

Although I missed being out and about in uniform on operational duties, I found my new role both interesting and challenging. The financial administration of the District was my most important duty. I had to prepare estimates for the Ministry of Home Affairs, detailing the finances necessary to run every police barracks in our District for the following month. My estimates were based upon information I received from each barracks about pay and allowances for the preceding month. It was my function to check every pay-sheet, every claim for payment or reimbursement, and to ensure all were within the appropriate regulations. Beyond this, it was also my responsibility to ensure that sergeants-in-charge furnished all reports of recordable crimes promptly, correctly and in accordance with Force procedures.

When my office work was finished each day, I had total freedom in the evenings to cycle through the area, visit the beaches some miles away in County Donegal and work on my correspondence course. Since Terry Kiernan continued to hold classes in Derry, I still travelled there each week. He encouraged me to compete in the sergeants' examination in April 1954, but I refused, believing that I needed more experience and a deeper knowledge of the law. While he accepted my decision, he tried to convince me that I was already adequately prepared. On one written paper, his comment was particularly complimentary: 'I think I see another star rising.' Such confidence in me was perplexing, because it seemed to me misplaced.

Gradually, Jean and I finalised our arrangements for our wedding on 14 June 1954. Bobby Killen, still in Victoria, agreed to act as my best man. It was a happy occasion — just a small family wedding in St Peter's Church on the Antrim Road in Belfast. The only hitch was the apparent impossibility of obtaining a home for us once we were married. Accommodation locally was in very short supply, and house purchase was out of the question. Apart from being beyond my small credit balance at the bank, it was not a sensible option, since constables could be transferred at any time, anywhere within Northern Ireland.

By chance I learned that the owner of the place where I ate my meals had relatives who lived in a modern bungalow on a pleasant housing estate in Limavady. They kindly offered us a separate bedroom and parlour in their bungalow, with the kitchen and other facilities to be shared with them. Although my immediate inclination was for Jean to remain in Belfast until something more suitable became available, she felt we should accept the offer, as we would at least be together and she could continue searching for rented accommodation in Limavady.

Reluctantly, I agreed, and so it was that, after our honeymoon, we began married life under the same roof as an unmarried brother and sister. Unlike our earlier fortnight's holiday in Edinburgh, our honeymoon in Scotland had its difficulties. Physical shyness with each other, and Jean's tendency to seek refuge in silence rather than discussion, made for awkwardness. I did not know then how best to show sensitivity and understanding. But at least we were together at last and were confident of our future as a married couple.

It was not long before our shared abode proved unsatisfactory. Once, I forgot some papers, and had to cycle home to collect them. There, I found poor Jean crying quietly in our bedroom. She was terribly unhappy about the lack of privacy and, although she tried to conceal her feelings, she could not relate easily with our benefactors. This in turn made her feel guilty for appearing ungrateful to them. A sense of frustration set in, putting considerable stress on our early married life.

Then, one of the constables, who had been stationed in Limavady for years, was unexpectedly transferred. For years he had rented half of a large old detached house from its owners, who occupied the other half. Upon his recommendation, the owners accepted us as their new tenants, and so, a few weeks later, Jean and I moved in. At last, our problems seemed to have been resolved! We were delighted with our new surroundings and quickly established an excellent relationship with the landlords. Jean and I became relaxed and idyllically happy as our initial sensitivities with each other gradually disappeared. All boded well for us, and we agreed that the time was right to try to start a family.

During this blissful time, Jean quietly registered with a local doctor of her choice. Upon her first visit, he confirmed that she was pregnant, and with great pride she announced this news to me. We discussed our future, and agreed that I should attempt the sergeants' exam in April 1955, before our baby was due. I might just be successful, in which case I could relax from further study during the child's infancy, as it was well known that promotion — if it came at all — could be delayed for some years after the exam itself.

It was a case of 'the best-laid plans of mice and men'. First, my District Inspector was transferred. His successor was Mr T.H. Buchanan, a slight, wiry man with a seemingly debonair, almost cavalier, approach to his duties, and an occasional touch of cynicism towards his superiors. Behind that façade, he was in fact both competent and shrewd. Breezing into my office on his arrival, he first inquired about my length of police service. After that, he asked, 'Do you know anything about police finance?' When I replied that I did, he sighed, 'Thank God, for I know nothing about it'! And that was that. He just breezed out again.

I found that I could work well with Hedley Buchanan. While he encouraged me to express my opinions and discuss matters of practical law enforcement, I also understood that, when he had made up his mind on a point, I had to act fully in accordance with his instructions. I soon observed, as did others, that our new District Inspector and Head Constable R.J. Martin did not enjoy the happiest of relationships. Head Constable Martin was an ambitious and very intelligent man, renowned for his considerable legal knowledge. Differences began to emerge between his recommendations and DI Buchanan's subsequent directions. I particularly remember the Head questioning a decision of Buchanan's, and quoting an alternative legal opinion and textbook source. With a quiet smile, the DI replied, 'I may not know the law, Head, but I do know where to find it.' Tucking the relevant police file under his arm, he left the office, whistling cheerfully as he went lightly down the stairs.

Once, while the DI was away on a short period of leave and Head Constable Martin was acting in his stead, I was given certain instructions, which I believed would be contrary to DI Buchanan's wishes. When I carefully pointed this out to the Head Constable, he abruptly told me to comply with his orders. Somewhat embarrassed, I replied that I was accountable to the District Inspector, and that since the matter was of some importance, it should be held in abeyance until his return in only a few days. With that, he stomped out of my office.

From then on, I felt uneasy and vulnerable to the Head's moods. On occasions, I recognised that he was detailing me for additional uniformed duties to the detriment of my primary role as DI's Clerk. Although I never complained or raised the issue, DI Buchanan himself did on one particular occasion. An election had taken place and he found me in uniform, ready to go to collect ballot-boxes and bring them to the counting centre. I had already been on duty all day at a polling station, and the extra assignment would have continued well into the night. DI Buchanan queried the fairness of this with the Head Constable. When the Head explained that there was no alternative, owing to a shortage of men, the DI retorted bluntly, 'If you can't find anyone else, you may do it yourself.' This only managed to make me feel more uncomfortable; I would have much preferred to carry out the duty than to have a heated confrontation between the two men on my account. As a result of this episode, Head Constable Martin seemed to distance himself further from me, making it even more awkward whenever he was acting in Buchanan's absence. I had a genuine liking and respect for the Head as he was an inherently decent man, but I also had a clear loyalty to my District Inspector.

Without realising it, I was glimpsing for the first time the stresses in personal relationships which can so easily occur at senior levels of command. This uneasiness within the office was exacerbated when someone organised an informal 'book' with nominal sums as bets on whether my colleague, Bob Trueman, or I would perform better in the forthcoming sergeants' examination. Although it was supposed to be light-hearted, the betting was divisive of the police in the barracks, with neither Bob nor I wishing to be part of it.

In these circumstances, Christmas that year came as a welcome respite. Jean and I were able to be at home in Belfast with her parents on both Christmas Day and Boxing Day. As well as visiting my mother and Belle, I had a short meeting with my father to give him a present and wish him a happy Christmas. By this time, he was living alone with his Alsatian dog in the old family home at Blackhead. It was a particularly happy Christmas for Jean, who blossomed as she looked forward to the birth of our first child.

We returned to Limavady in the early evening of 27 December. Just as we were about to retire to bed, a constable called at the house with a message from my father. The Hermon family home had, in his absence, been destroyed by fire and he had lost everything. I was shattered by the news, and felt compelled to travel back as early as possible the next day to view the charred remains of the house. The mainly wooden construction was totally destroyed, and the remaining brick walls badly damaged. My father was already there. I had never seen him so distraught, so disorientated and demoralised. In his fifty-nine years, he had managed to damage the lives of everyone in his family and to lose our respect. For the first time in my life, I felt immensely sad for him: he was vulnerable and in need of help.

In almost total silence, we two walked to Whitehead Barracks, where Sergeant Gerry Mahon, who had originally suggested that I might join the RUC, took notes about what had happened. Before leaving the house on the previous day, my father had apparently banked up the living-room fire with slack, and left a bar of an electric heater burning in his bedroom. We never did find out how exactly the fire had started.

Afterwards, I went back with my father to Belfast, giving him what assistance I could. He arranged to stay with his sister until he obtained more permanent accommodation. Although I had given them up four years earlier, I began smoking cigarettes again when I returned to Limavady later that evening, because my memories and emotions were so jangled by the events of the day.

4

NEW ARRIVALS AND SUDDEN DEPARTURES

The first months of 1955 seemed to pass in a flash as I concentrated on studying for the sergeants' examination. During two days in April, I sat the three three-hour papers. By chance, the invigilator was my own District Inspector, Hedley Buchanan. A considerable number of constables were sitting the examination, alongside a sprinkling of sergeants, who were attempting the head constables' exam.

Afterwards, the inevitable inquests were held on the papers. So many candidates exuded self-confidence and certainty of their success that I was totally deflated, especially when I heard others making points I felt I had overlooked. I felt precariously poised between success and failure. DI Buchanan, sensing my pessimism, commented that 'Anyone who wrote as much as you did is bound to pass.' I saw no logic in that and believed that he was simply being kind.

Soon, however, I became absorbed in nervous apprehension about Jean having our baby. In her advanced state of pregnancy, she was careful not to be too energetic. With increasing frequency, her parents visited us at the weekends, as they too were anxious for their first grandchild. Jean and I thought there was no real need for such anxiety, as her doctor had often reassured us that the pregnancy was proceeding normally.

In the first week of May, Jean began to worry because the baby was not as lively as it should have been. Despite the doctor's calm conviction that all was in order, Jean remained deeply uneasy. Late on the evening of 16 May, she went into labour and, after examining her at home, the doctor admitted her to hospital. The baby was stillborn. After some delay, I was allowed to enter the private ward where Jean lay. Our eyes met. She was crying quietly as she said, 'I'm sorry, Jack. I've lost our baby. I've disappointed you.' If only she knew; my one concern was for her life, her safety, and I told her so. I remember little more of our conversation. All I could do was hold her closely and comfort her, while shedding tears of relief and simultaneous grief. The baby, a boy of 9 lb 12 oz, had been dead before birth, but for how long we never knew.

Although a funeral service for a stillborn child was discretionary, we wanted one, and our rector showed great compassion as he helped to organise it. With Jean still in hospital, it was alone with the rector that I buried our boy in a tiny white coffin in the church graveyard. The days, weeks and months thereafter were terribly sad for Jean and me. Yet we became even closer, drawing on one another. The bonds of love and affection were strengthened by our sense of joint loss and tragedy.

Amidst our personal trauma, I learned in June that I had passed the written sergeants' examination with 84 per cent in all three papers, making me third overall. My success was a fillip to Jean in her grief, and became a focal point for conjecture about our future. Part two of the test followed quickly. On a morning in June, I had to report to Mountpottinger Station in Belfast. (By the mid-1950s, police 'barracks' had become formally known as 'stations'.) There I was examined in foot drill, weapon drill, and my knowledge of weapons on issue to the Force. Although I had little opportunity to prepare, I qualified without difficulty and then attended a final interview.

With only five years' police service behind me, actual promotion seemed very unlikely in the immediate future, and we were confident of remaining in Limavady for quite some time. To our delight, we were unexpectedly notified by the local council that in August we would be allocated one of the new houses in a small estate. What a stimulus that news was to Jean! I encouraged her rising enthusiasm at the prospect of a home of our own with a garden. It seemed to offer a new beginning.

Just as we were starting to feel the sun on our faces again, word came out of the blue that I was promoted to sergeant with effect from 25 July 1955. I was supposed to take charge of Plumbridge Station in County Tyrone, but according to the letter I would first 'spend a month or two in Cookstown', also in Tyrone.

Conflicting emotions welled up inside me. Feelings of achievement and excitement were immediate, but short-lived. Worries crept in so quickly. What about our new house? How would Jean react when I told her? I rushed home to find her. When she heard my news, delight for me showed in her face and in her embrace. But what would we do? Promotion was not all-important to me, especially not then. Instead, I wanted stability for her without our having to move again and search for another house elsewhere, with all the uncertainty that would entail. Unlike mine, Jean's response was positive: 'It's your career, and our future together,' she said. 'You'll accept it. Things will work out.' I was surprised and impressed by her quiet resolution and complete confidence. Those remained her traits in future years, when circumstances for me, or for us both, were hard and sometimes dangerous too. The fast-moving and wholly unexpected events of the summer of 1955 were probably beneficial to both Jean and me in that they inevitably diverted us from the grief and disappointment of our baby's death.

With Jean's loyal support, I left Limavady in July 1955. The reason for my temporary allocation to Cookstown District Headquarters was clarified in due course. The Sergeant there had had a minor heart attack and would be out of work for several weeks, and I was supposed to be his temporary replacement, before going to Plumbridge.

A few days after my arrival in Cookstown, the District Inspector held a formal inspection. Towards its conclusion, he suddenly clapped hands and said sharply, 'There's an attack on the barrack! Take up your defensive positions!' A moment's silence ensued, and then the constables dispersed throughout the building.

At that time of increasing IRA threats, station protection was a top priority and all police establishments had plans for meeting different operational emergencies. I felt, however, that the rehearsal in Cookstown was unreal, too dramatic and chaotic. The presence of so many men bustling about in a building with insufficient key points resulted in much confusion. Surplus men just did not know where to go. This episode served to remind me that, as a sergeant, I had responsibility not only for the efficiency of the constables, but also for their good management.

I actually found it strange to be standing on that first rung of command. I went about my work self-consciously, occasionally asking the senior constables for their views and assistance. All were friendly and helpful, if somewhat guarded until they could form an opinion of me. The three golden chevrons on my right sleeve created a subtle but clear distinction between them and me. It was a strange feeling, almost like wearing a new suit of clothes or pair of shoes; it took time, usage and familiarity before they fitted easily and naturally. Even then, it was difficult sometimes not to slip into an old pair, an old routine — as happened one Saturday, when Cookstown was thronged with shoppers and hundreds of spectators attending a motorcycle scrambling event. To avoid traffic congestion, I found it necessary to do points duty for a short time at a key crossing. As the traffic eased, I was able to return to the kerb, where I was startled to meet my District Inspector, Mr Harry Baillie, and the County Inspector, Mr R.T. Hamilton. They had obviously been watching my 'performance'.

This was my first encounter, but by no means my last, with the 'County'. In his clipped and cultivated voice, Mr Hamilton expressed some surprise at a sergeant doing traffic duty, but, when I briefly explained the position, he seemed satisfied and indeed pleased. As we talked further, he showed interest in my administrative experience as he needed a station sergeant for Strabane in County Tyrone. 'What service have you?' he finally asked. 'Five years and six months, Sir.' His response to that was terse: 'No bloody good! Come on, Baillie,' and off he stalked. Early the next week, a direction was received from the County Inspector's office giving notice of my transfer to Strabane District Headquarters on appointment as Station Sergeant! My appointment to Plumbridge had been superseded.

On 16 August 1955, I went again by Morris tender to Strabane, where District Inspector James Anthony O'Brien introduced himself. I felt completely at ease in the presence of this competent and very knowledgeable officer, who for me was to epitomise all that was good in the senior ranks of the RUC. Head Constable Martin Williams, whom I had first encountered as an instructor in the Depot, also welcomed me that day. He and I shared a large, bright office with a high ceiling on the first floor of the well-run District Headquarters.

Besides these officers, there were probably twenty constables in Strabane Station, including a small number of fully mobilised members of the Ulster Special Constabulary, or B Specials, as they were more familiarly known. (At the time of the partition of Ireland, about 2,000 A Specials had been recruited to serve full-time in support of the police. In addition, men were invited to volunteer as B Specials to serve part-time in assisting the police.) Within our District, there were also five outstations, most of which had a complement of one sergeant and four constables. Being a District Headquarters, Strabane had a District car available in the station for all sorts of police business, as well as a Morris tender and a 'Customs' car for use in the prevention of smuggling across the nearby border with the Republic.

Jean joined me in Strabane, when I had found us a small furnished flat in the home of a delightful lady with whom we had an immediate rapport. Early the following year, to our delight, Jean was again expecting a baby. In September, she was admitted prematurely to the local hospital: it had been discovered that she had a very rare blood group and this was creating problems. A decision was made to induce the birth but, while in heavy labour, she was rushed to Omagh hospital. Such was the urgency that I was not notified until after she had been taken there. Being without any transport at the time, I changed hurriedly and cycled the twenty miles to Omagh.

As the consultant gynaecologist had been fishing when he was summoned to assist Jean, my first vivid impression on arrival at the hospital was seeing him enter the labour ward still wearing his rubber wading boots! After what seemed an agonisingly long wait, he came to tell me that we had a fine baby girl and that she and her mother were well. When I saw them, Jean was crying but this time it was with happiness, relief and fulfilment. Our Barbara was born on 12 September 1956.

Unfortunately, our personal peace and contentment were not matched by events around Northern Ireland at that particular time. During 1955 and 1956, the republican terrorist organisation Saor Uladh (Free Ulster) carried out various attacks throughout the North. This annoyed the IRA — many of whose members were becoming frustrated at the organisation's inactivity — and so it launched a widespread campaign of its own, with the objective of driving the British out of Ireland. Although not yet fully prepared, the IRA was forced to act to take the initiative from Saor Uladh.

The RUC Special Branch had at that time infiltrated the IRA's structures — hence the increasing number of alerts about imminent attacks, including the one planned for Easter Monday, 2 April 1956. The IRA in Dublin had made preparations for an ambitious armed attack, involving more than 100 men, on Gough military barracks in Armagh. However, prior knowledge and pre-emptive action by the RUC prevented any of the attack group from crossing the border. Immediate successes like this one were mainly due to speedy reaction by local Command at District and Subdistrict level in mounting patrols, thereby intercepting or obstructing the movement of terrorists.

Even with this level of awareness, the events of 12 December 1956, together with those which followed throughout that month and for the next two years, were to test the RUC and the Ulster Special Constabulary to their limits.

At 2 a.m. on the 12th, a police patrol in the vicinity of an RAF radar station on Torr Head, on the north County Antrim coast, intercepted a party of approximately twelve armed IRA men *en route* to attack the station. Shots were exchanged, and — although the police were outnumbered — the terrorists made off, with members of the patrol in pursuit. Three of the IRA group were arrested, and weapons and ammunition seized, along with boxes of pepper intended for use against guard dogs.

Other incidents that night included a foiled attempt to blow up an automatic telephone exchange in Armagh city, a bombing at Gough Barracks, the theft of explosives from stores in Fermanagh, attacks on a territorial army centre in Enniskillen and two nearby bridges, and similar activities in Counties Londonderry and Down.

I was unaware of all this until, in the early hours, I was wakened when a police-car patrol called at our house in the Ballycolman estate. I returned to the station to find that all available members had been mustered there, including District Inspector O'Brien and Head Constable Williams. Part-time members of the Ulster Special Constabulary had been alerted, and prearranged road-blocks were being set up. Foot and car patrols were already out conducting road checks, and inspecting key installations. By intensive police and USC patrolling, the IRA's attacks throughout the county were frustrated that night.

From then on, we were placed on an emergency footing. Up to the end of December, a further twenty-five serious terrorist attacks occurred, including one on Derrylin Station in County Fermanagh, in which a constable was killed.

As a result of the ongoing terrorist threat, my role changed abruptly. I had to perform night duty on a weekly rotation system with the Duty Sergeant. I also had to requisition all stores, allocate accommodation, and implement DI O'Brien's directions on enhancing security by mounting extra patrols and arranging protection for vulnerable targets. I was still expected to continue with all of the duties of Station Sergeant, doing those as best I could in the early hours of the morning. The consequence was that I was seldom at home, except for brief meal breaks and to snatch some sleep. The irregular hours were disruptive for Jean, who was left so much alone with our young baby, but she understood the pressures and was totally supportive.

An incident on 1 January 1957 set the tone for that year and proved the need for more sophisticated weaponry. That particular evening, a gang of about fifteen members of the IRA, armed with rifles and machine-guns, crossed the border in a lorry to attack Brookeborough Station, a few miles inside County Fermanagh. The police, alert to the likelihood of attack, had only the previous day borrowed a Bren gun from the local Ulster Special Constabulary, and mounted it inside the station on the first floor, just above the door. As the lorry stopped to rake the station with gunfire, the police officers inside were able to return fire almost immediately. A sergeant had dashed upstairs and, as the lorry drove off, he opened fire with the Bren gun. After a prolonged search of the countryside, two bodies were found abandoned in a disused house. The remaining terrorists escaped back across the border.

The IRA was clearly putting down its marker for another year of violence. And so, about mid-January, British troops were allocated to our District to back up our meagre resources and light firearms. Each evening at 6 p.m., a couple of three-ton army lorries would arrive from Omagh military barracks with between twenty and twenty-four soldiers, commanded by a lieutenant. They provided night patrols throughout the area, and at 6 a.m. the following morning would return to barracks.

About the same time, the Irish Government acted firmly to prevent further IRA attacks being mounted from the Republic. Extra Garda officers were posted to all police stations in border areas, arrests were made and fifteen men were quickly brought before the courts, charged with membership of the IRA or failing to account for their movements. Regrettably, the maximum punishment for such offences was two years' imprisonment on indictment, or six months in prison if — as often happened — they were treated as summary offences. They had, therefore, little, if any, deterrent effect on committed IRA activists.

The IRA's campaign of terror continued unabated throughout 1957 with more than 340 incidents in Northern Ireland. Some of these attacks displayed considerable initiative, such as that on 2 March 1957 in which a goods train was commandeered in the Republic and sent driverless into the Waterside railway station in Derry, where it crashed in spectacular fashion. 1957 actually saw the largest number of incidents in any year, until the IRA called off its campaign in 1962.

The exchange of sound intelligence and practical co-operation between the Garda Síochána and the RUC was given tacit approval by the Irish and British Governments, much to the mutual benefit of both Forces. This relationship, which strengthened over the years, was quickly and warmly extended beyond policing into other areas, including recreational and social activities.

During my earlier service in Victoria Barracks, I had in fact first experienced this co-operation when two itinerants attempted to sell a couple of bicycles in a local shop. Suspecting that the machines were stolen, the proprietor quietly contacted the police, with the result that the itinerants, and the bicycles, were brought to Victoria. It was soon established that identical bicycles had been stolen only a few days earlier in Muff, a village across the border in County Donegal.

Since I happened to be on duty as assistant guard at the time, I donned a civilian raincoat over my uniform and set off. Constable Sam Lindsay, well known to the Gardaí, drove the prison van towards Muff with both the itinerants and bicycles inside under my 'protective custody'. At the border customs post, we were waved through without any formalities whatsoever, and at Muff, two Gardaí, who were on patrol as arranged, took possession of all that was in my custody with scarcely a word spoken!

Similarly, a good working relationship existed between the RUC in Strabane and the Gardaí in Lifford, County Donegal. Sergeant McGowan and the four Gardaí there relied on bicycle or foot patrols, since they had no vehicle transport. Occasionally when Sergeant McGowan felt the need of a car, he would contact me, and one of our drivers, usually Constable J.T. Whiteside, would put on a civilian coat over his uniform and drive across the border. With a Garda member or the Sergeant himself, Constable Whiteside would drive around the area, enabling the other to serve summonses and execute warrants. In light of such incidents, and many more besides, it seems to me that to say co-operation between the Gardaí and the RUC has never been better than at present in the 1990s is a nonsense, based on ignorance of the past. Such informal co-operation between the police and the Gardaí was low-key and discreet.

In the mid-1950s, it became apparent that a determined IRA campaign was under way. Therefore, in January 1957 the Minister of Home Affairs at Stormont decided to introduce internment in Northern Ireland, while in the South it was introduced in March. RUC Special Branch drew up lists of those recommended for internment, and the necessary authority was obtained. As the arrests were made, the men detained within Strabane District were brought to the station. Due to inadequate cell accommodation, some had to be held in station rooms for a few hours, and guarded there by a police officer.

One night as I was working late, I was given charge of one detainee in my office. There was no conversation between us; the only exchange came when I stopped for a sandwich and some coffee, which I invited him to share. This he did. When he was taken at 6 a.m. to prison in Belfast, I thought no more about him.

Some months later, however, shortly after 8 a.m., I was cycling along Barrack Street, where there would normally have been only a few vehicles and pedestrians travelling to work. Outside the Catholic church hall that morning, a crowd of at least 100 people had gathered.

Dressed as I was in uniform and wearing my patrol equipment, I felt uneasy, since it was a predominantly nationalist part of the town. As I approached, the crowd turned towards me. Just then a man stepped out. He was 'my own' internee! The locals were celebrating his early release from prison. His words that morning were unforgettable: 'Here's the man who shared his bread with me the night I was arrested.' At that, the crowd parted and I cycled through to some applause and cheers! To the best of my knowledge, that man is still alive, possibly living in Strabane, and I trust his memory is as long as mine.

Internment did not end the terrorist violence. On Saturday, 17 August 1957, I was on duty late that evening when we learned of a large explosion, wrecking a derelict cottage on the outskirts of Coalisland, a small town in the east of County Tyrone. The local police Sergeant had been killed, while two other constables and two soldiers had been injured. When I arrived home that night and told Jean about the incident, she asked anxiously whether the late Sergeant Ovens had been married, and whether finding his replacement could mean that I would be sent to Coalisland. I reassured her that this was most unlikely, since Strabane itself was a border station under significant threat.

After the Sergeant's funeral on the following Monday, District Inspector O'Brien came to my office and told me the Inspector General, Sir Richard Pim, had directed that a replacement sergeant be found immediately. 'A short list of candidates has already been drawn up,' he added, 'and your name is on it.' Silence descended. 'How many are on it, Sir?' I asked. 'One,' he replied. 'You will report there at 10.30 a.m. tomorrow morning.' Silence again ensued.

Worry about Jean made me cycle home at once to alert her. I broke the news as gently as I could, but she was clearly shocked. Although she appeared to control herself admirably, I knew differently. Leaving the room, ostensibly to prepare our evening meal, she went into the garden to the clothes-line. Our neighbour from across the dividing fence spoke to her and, in the gathering darkness, noticed that Jean was crying. She comforted her when Jean revealed my unexpected transfer. Shortly afterwards, the neighbour, her husband and her mother — all Catholics — went to chapel to pray for us and our safety. The word spread quickly, and others, both Protestant and Catholic, called to express their disappointment and concern.

By 9.30 the next morning, the all too familiar Morris tender was ready to convey me to Coalisland. I never again stepped into that house in the Ballycolman estate, which we had occupied for only eight months.

Many years later, towards the end of my tenure as Chief Constable, I learned that James O'Brien, who had long since retired, was seriously ill in Musgrave Park Hospital. When I entered his small private ward, he insisted on being propped up with several pillows. Our conversation went back to Strabane, and we reminisced over our time together and my sudden departure for Coalisland. Only then did he reveal the full story behind my selection to replace Sergeant Ovens. He explained that after the Sergeant's funeral, Sir Richard Pim had met with other senior officers in Coalisland Station. County Inspector Hamilton had argued forcefully that I would be best suited to take control of that turbulent Subdistrict. While other sergeants had been named and seriously considered, Mr Hamilton's and James O'Brien's own strong recommendation carried such weight that I was chosen. Even in Strabane, he said, he had formed the opinion that I could well become Inspector General of the RUC.

I felt humbled by such comments from a fine and dedicated policeman. James asked me to return to the hospital, and we arranged that I would visit on the following Wednesday. But it was not to be. He died on the Tuesday, and I could only pay my last respects at his funeral.

5

COALISLAND — THE BEST YEARS

A page of life had turned, and Strabane moved quickly into the past. There was no time for farewells, for handshakes or any of the usual formalities. The shock was considerable and the preparation scrambled. Jean and Barbara were left behind to fend for themselves while I went alone to Coalisland Station. This time, I would have sole responsibility for a police Subdistrict, and have it in the most difficult circumstances imaginable.

Mrs Ovens, and her two children, still occupied the married quarters, where I visited her to express my sympathy. This was my first experience of the terrible, special grief associated with terrorist murder. She looked utterly exhausted. The frightened and bewildered children were being comforted by their grandparents, who had come to attend their son-in-law's funeral, and also to arrange for the family to move to Belfast. I felt so ill-equipped to give comfort that I withdrew, and went out to look around my new responsibility.

The station was extremely dilapidated. After the comings and goings of many officers since the murder, the floors were coated with mud. Cutlery and dishes in the kitchen had been washed only when needed; most were abandoned and covered in congealed grease. A stack of unopened correspondence awaited attention in the Sergeant's office. Outside, weeds grew through the security fence of rusty barbed wire surrounding the building. The grass was overgrown and strewn with rubbish. In the yard, a large Alsatian dog, intended to provide protection, had become excited by the influx of strange police officers, and so it barked incessantly. In a small shed lay the blood-stained sock and boot of the late Sergeant Ovens; someone had retrieved them from the rubble after the explosion. With them was the Sten gun he had been carrying at the time of his death. Its barrel was bent almost at a right angle to the handle. These remnants created a truly dismal scene.

The enormity of the task facing me seemed overwhelming, but I knew I had to settle down to it. I immediately issued orders that the station should be cleaned thoroughly over the succeeding days, and that various constables should cut the grass and clear every weed from the protective wire fence. The consequent and quick improvement in the general appearance of the building helped restore the party's pride in its station. As for the much-neglected correspondence, the Senior Constable not only assisted me in dealing with it, but briefed me on the office records.

Satisfied with the improved condition of the station itself, I set about tightening up the human resources within it. While the ongoing murder investigation was the responsibility of a team detailed by RUC Headquarters, I quickly restored an ordered system of duty for coping with routine police matters. In the interests of morale, I ensured that all the men were well dressed, properly equipped and punctual. I reinstated the twice-weekly parades and introduced a brief routine of revolver and foot drill. I occasionally joined the small line of constables on parade, and then required one of the constables to give the drill commands. This stimulated their alertness and interest, and varied their experience of always being at the receiving end of commands.

During the following weeks and months, I reorganised the morning 'schools' for the constables so that tests were included to improve their local knowledge. Quite often, I would outline the ground to be covered on a theoretical patrol through the Subdistrict, and require them to name the houses, farms, premises and occupants that would be passed *en route*. This certainly encouraged greater awareness, and within a short time, the constables knew the vehicle registration numbers, Christian names and surnames of the residents and much else besides.

From the beginning of my service in Coalisland, I determined to apply the law firmly and without favour. To project a firm presence, I maintained a two-man patrol on duty in the town each evening, and as high a level of patrolling in the Subdistrict as manpower permitted. On the Saturday evening of my first week there, I left the station around 9 p.m. to join the patrol. Considerable numbers of people were standing around, and as I approached the post office, I caught sight of two men fighting on the ground. They were quite elderly, and seemed to be under the influence of drink. I ordered the constables to detain the brawling pair, and take them to the police station. Both were well known for their drinking and their mutual animosity. Soon they were fast asleep in the cell. Shortly afterwards, several men called at the station to ask me to release them because, as they explained, the police had never bothered detaining them in the past. Besides, they said, one of them had still to milk his cows! As these friends also appeared to have been drinking, I refused their request and advised them that the other two would receive summonses for disorderly behaviour. When I showed them the two 'sleeping beauties' in the cell, they readily accepted that in their present state neither was capable of identifying a cow, let alone milking it!

Unknown to me, this minor example of an obvious tightening of policing in Coalisland created the image of a young, authoritarian sergeant, who would apply the letter of the law. Quickly, it became known that I did not drink intoxicating liquor, but did attend church quite regularly. This only added to my image and did no harm at all in my efforts to establish the rule of law in my Subdistrict.

With this reputation and with, by now, the support of District Inspector David Johnston in Dungannon (who had originally hoped to be assigned a more experienced sergeant than I for Coalisland Station), I set about the serious task of restoring some normality to this troubled area. To that end, I arranged for better co-ordination between the local Ulster Special Constabulary Platoons and the police. I was able to take the three Platoon Commanders — all shrewd, mature men of moderate views — fully into my confidence, so that our relationship was cemented in trust and friendship. One of our first joint efforts was to replace the half-collapsed sandbag sangar, built by the army, with a more efficient structure to guard the station against attack. This we did clandestinely, without approval, but with voluntary labour and donated materials. On first seeing it, the County Inspector's immediate query was, 'Who's paying for this?' 'Nobody,' I replied. 'Oh, that's alright then,' he said and sauntered on, without giving me the reprimand I expected!

With the formidable-looking sangar completed, and agreement obtained from the District Inspector that I prepare the duty programme for the part-time members of the USC Platoons, we quickly established widespread patrolling throughout the Subdistrict to deny the terrorists easy use of the intricate web of minor roads which criss-crossed the area.

Even so, I still felt that additional manpower was essential, as the police party comprised only six RUC constables and two full-time mobilised members of the USC. I applied to the District Inspector for a seasoned senior constable, as well as two more constables of known ability. I specifically requested that the latter two be Catholics, since all members of the existing party were Protestant, even though the population we served was 85 per cent Catholic. I was delighted with the two very capable Catholic officers who were immediately transferred to Coalisland Station.

The provision of a suitable senior constable took a rather different course. After much thought, I came to a decision which proved controversial with both my District and my County Inspectors. I asked that Constable J.T. Whiteside, whom I had made the subject of disciplinary procedures while in Strabane, should join us in Coalisland. After Strabane, he had been transferred 'under a cloud' to Coagh Station, and again in similar circumstances to Carrickmore, one of the remotest stations in County Tyrone. Nevertheless, I was convinced that, behind his aggressiveness towards authority, there were good qualities, which he consciously suppressed, but which I could call into play.

County Inspector Hamilton's response to my request was blunt: 'Sergeant, you are mad! The man's a trouble-maker! You should know.' Carefully, I explained my reasoning. 'You're mad,' he repeated. 'You can have him but you will accept the consequences.' Thus it was that John Whiteside arrived in Coalisland within a few days. As he was a single man, there were no complications to his transfer, only a sense of relief in Carrickmore Station! John turned out to be an outstanding officer. Ultimately, he was promoted sergeant, gave up excessive drinking and gambling in favour of golf, and further dedicated himself to his elderly mother's well-being until her death.

With Constable Whiteside in my party of men, and with the goodwill and co-operation of the local Ulster Special Constabulary, we policed what was supposed to be the most turbulent of Subdistricts on the shores of Lough Neagh. At that time, its population was probably 8,000, the vast majority of whom harboured nationalist, even republican, aspirations. Yet, two small villages in the area, Newmills and Ballynakelly, were almost wholly Protestant and loyalist. Agriculture was the main occupation, but there was also a surprising number of small industries, including weaving and a linen mill, as well as a coalmine and brick and pipe manufacture using local clay. Of course, Lough Neagh itself provided a full- or part-time living for a long-established fishing community. Unemployment was high, particularly amongst the Catholics. Many registered as unemployed while 'working the double' by having discreet employment on a local farm or, if skilled, in some trade or craft.

There was a warmth and humanity about the area that made my three years there the most fulfilling and, I believe, the happiest time of my police career. The Coalisland people certainly made Jean feel welcome very quickly. Passers-by were accustomed to seeing Barbara's grey pram sitting on the lawn behind the barbed wire with the occupant asleep or sitting up, viewing her new world. They regularly stopped to talk to Jean when she was out in the garden or proudly wheeling the pram through the town. But, of course, there were challenges and pressures too.

Two months or so after my arrival, there was an arson attack on the Coalisland Labour Exchange, from where unemployment benefits were paid. The door had been forced and flammable liquid ignited inside the building. Fortunately, there was an early warning and the only two constables immediately available gave assistance to the fire brigade as its members endeavoured to extinguish the flames. However, efforts to frustrate their good work were made by some youths amongst the crowd which had gathered around the building.

I had gone to the scene, and from my position I could see a tall, thin young man with a fresh red face and fairish hair apparently trying to provoke the youths into either obstructing the police or slashing the fire-hoses. When I ordered those present to go home, this particular man began arguing with me. As the two constables were fully engaged in assisting the fire brigade, the situation was volatile and clearly threatened a breach of the peace. Without the possibility of any additional help, I took firm action by delivering a short sharp clip with my torch to the man's lower cheek and chin. He staggered backwards and, together with the group of youths, disappeared into the darkness.

Shortly after the attack on the Labour Exchange, further serious incidents took place in the Subdistrict, including two unsuccessful attempts to lure the police into booby-trapped locations.

In early November, while on a short period of leave in Belfast, I received a note from District Inspector Johnston asking me to return at once, as Special Branch had succeeded in gaining sound intelligence about the terrorists responsible for these attacks. With my involvement, and with the benefit of the station party's local knowledge, detailed plans for the simultaneous arrest and detention of the suspects were prepared and carried out. Of the men arrested, I particularly remember Kevin Mallon and Francis Talbot, who were eventually charged with the murder of Sergeant Ovens. As Sergeant in the Coalisland area,

I was then required to act in a liaison and administrative capacity at the police office in Crumlin Road Prison, Belfast.

During a lengthy interval between interviewing the suspects, I sat as guard with Kevin Mallon in a small room, and we talked freely on matters unconnected with the crimes. He reminded me of the incident at the Coalisland Labour Exchange, when it was set on fire; and added that he had been the tall young man whom I had struck on the jaw with my torch! Of all people, it was Kevin Mallon who gave me the best insight into how I was perceived, as he spoke candidly of the way in which Coalisland people viewed their local Sergeant.

He also talked about his own life, his family background and education and the lack of job opportunities in Coalisland. The sheer boredom at home, together with the excitement generated by stories of high wages available to builders' labourers in England, had drawn him there. He had worked long hours of overtime and earned a lot of money, which he spent freely, especially on greyhound racing. Restless and without roots, he travelled from town to town and from job to job, wherever the pay was highest. After months of this life, he had returned home, but again had become bored and frustrated. It was then that he became involved in terrorism, for no particular motive other than a craving for excitement.

Months later, I was present at his trial, where I saw a very different Kevin Mallon. Both he and Talbot were well dressed and groomed, respectful to the court and fully compliant with court procedures. They gave their evidence carefully, denying the crime and making serious allegations against the police. Mr Elwyn Jones — then Recorder of Bristol, I believe — was called to the Northern Ireland Bar to lead the defence, with Mr Liam McCollum — then a young Belfast barrister — as his Junior. Elwyn Jones ultimately became the British Attorney-General under a Labour Government, while Liam McCollum became a much respected judge of the Northern Ireland High Court. Together they won the day, and, at the end of July 1958, Mallon and Talbot were acquitted of the murder of Sergeant Ovens.

Anticipating some reaction at Brackaville Crossroads, where the two men lived on the outskirts of Coalisland, I arranged for mobile police reinforcements to be kept in reserve. By the late evening, about sixty people had congregated. With a police landrover about half a mile down each of the rural roads leading to the crossroads, a young constable and I patrolled the area on foot. A few stones were thrown at us, but fell harmlessly. Someone in the crowd suggested that they should recite the rosary, and as they did so, a number of people knelt down. They followed this with the Irish national anthem, and then noisily dispersed, jeering at us as we stood quietly in the shadows. After thirty minutes, I requested that the police reinforcements stand down and that the landrovers be driven away through the crossroads — I wanted the locals to see that I had been prepared for trouble, if it had arisen.

The next morning, I called on Father Geatens, the elderly parish priest of Brackaville Church, and briefed him on the events of the past evening at the crossroads. I asked for his co-operation in helping to prevent further incidents. Father Geatens listened quietly. He assured me that there would be no recurrence and, taking his walking-stick, he accompanied me to the road. As I left, he said, 'There's a place for prayer and it's not at the crossroads,' and he walked off slowly in the direction of the previous evening's incident.

Thereafter, I had no further trouble. This was despite the fact that, upon their acquittal for murder, Mallon and Talbot had been immediately rearrested and charged with other serious offences. These eventually led to fourteen years' imprisonment for Mallon, and eight for Talbot.

It transpired that of the nine men arrested at that time in the Coalisland area and convicted, five were members of the IRA and four of Saor Uladh. With their convictions, to my recollection, all the terrorist crimes committed in my area, except for the murder of Sergeant Ovens, had been accounted for. On the completion of these trials towards the end of 1958, I was unexpectedly contacted by a local resident of the nationalist tradition. He assured me that, while I continued to serve in Coalisland, there would be no further terrorist violence. I was surprised, not to say dubious about the reliability of this unusual assurance, but in fact no further attacks did occur in the Coalisland Subdistrict for the remainder of that particular IRA campaign, which lasted four more years.

Between 1956 and 1962, in the whole of Northern Ireland a total of six RUC officers were murdered, while thirty members of the RUC and Ulster Special Constabulary were injured. Six terrorists were also killed, and six were known to have been injured. Throughout this difficult period, the RUC retained its 1922 establishment of 3,000, but was assisted from 1956 onwards by three RUC Reserve Force Platoons, based in Belfast. Between January 1957 and February 1958, an additional ten platoons were formed and trained. These were comprised mainly of mobilised USC members with a sprinkling of police officers, and were commanded by a head constable and several sergeants. The RUC generally was also augmented by mobilised members of the USC, which at that time had a total strength of approximately 13,000. Irrespective of the dangers involved, people continued to join the USC, and they certainly did not do so for the money. From 1956 to 1961, the basic duty allowance was £7 per annum, with a £2 increase in 1961. Their equipment and clothing were of poor quality, and old-fashioned by police or military standards. Without their assistance, the police could not then have coped successfully with the terrorist campaign. Yet, much criticism has been levelled over the years at the Ulster Special Constabulary by nationalist politicians and extreme republicans. This antipathy had its origin in the violent years of 1920 to 1923, when the 'Specials' were established and when violence was prevalent north and south of the border. Within the nationalist community, there existed an attitude ranging from hostility to unconcealed hatred of the 'Specials'. However, from my experience of them in Coalisland, I developed a great respect for their contribution, which required real sacrifices in terms of time and personal safety, since the majority of them were farmers with isolated smallholdings dotted throughout the countryside.

In the absence of terrorist violence in Coalisland after 1958, I did not have to rely so much on the Specials, and my men were able to concentrate their efforts on what had become known as 'ordinary decent crime' (O.D.C.). At that time, it was 'The Sergeant' whom the local people really wished to see, when they asked for assistance at the station. A constable was not regarded as being in quite the same league, unless he had long service and was well known and liked by the community. Through experience, I learned that clergy of all denominations, local family doctors and school headmasters were accorded considerable respect, and 'The Sergeant' fitted easily into that group.

In 1958, I applied for a motorcycle for use in general policing duties. This was quickly approved, and, throughout my period in Coalisland, I used the motorcycle frequently. The people became so used to the noise of my 250 cc machine that every time they heard one, at night or early in the morning, they assumed it was 'The Sergeant'. Residents would comment that they had heard me passing at a particular time, when I knew that I had been comfortably in bed. Yet, I never denied it. The reputation of being out on patrol all night or being an early riser kept the locals on their toes!

As I grew to know the community better, I recognised that the divisions between Catholics and Protestants, loyalists and nationalists, continued to exist in Coalisland so that, while day-to-day relationships between them were superficially relaxed, there remained a subtle, veiled reserve. 'Live and let live' was the unspoken, but mutually recognised, norm of behaviour. The memories and bitterness of the violence of the early twentieth century rested just below the surface. I realised I had to listen, without commenting, to tales of local incidents of a sectarian nature, like the fatal shooting of a loyalist in Ballynakelly by the IRA as he tried to extinguish a fire in a thatched roof. The murders of two Catholic men, which followed in swift retaliation, were still marked by small crosses on the roadside where they died.

In many such matters, the Catholic curate, Father John Reagan, kept me right. On a number of occasions, I referred to him problems of truancy, of petty theft by young children, and some minor sectarian incidents. We agreed that these could be dealt with by either the temporal or the spiritual 'police', whichever seemed better in the circumstances.

Indeed, quite a lot of what I did in Coalisland was regarded as unorthodox, such as my attendance at the wakes of Catholic residents with whom I had been friendly, and also at Gaelic football matches. Even on duty and in uniform, I was made welcome at the football grounds. Just before the Irish national anthem was due to be played, I would leave quietly in order to avoid having to stand to attention and thereby attract criticism from within the Protestant community.

Such was the good working relationship with the Catholic community in the area that I was the recipient of a unique surrender of illegal weapons one winter's evening in 1959. I was in the married quarters with Jean, when a young man called at the station door. I recognised him and knew that he came from the lough-shore area. He was very obviously ill at ease. Briefly, he explained how he and his family had raised some floorboards that evening, while renovating an old unoccupied house, and had discovered a rifle, a revolver and a large quantity of ammunition.

I received this information with some suspicion, and asked him shrewdly, or so I thought, why he had not brought the whole cache with him, since he had driven directly from the house. His reply made me acutely aware of my naïvety. 'Sergeant,' he said, 'if I had, and the police had stopped me and searched my van, do you think they would have believed me?' No more needed to be said. I returned with him to his home, where I was handed the weapons and ammunition. Although old, they were in excellent condition, as they had been greased and wrapped in grease-proof paper. Within the next few days, I was quietly approached by a man whom I knew and trusted. He said the only other two people alive who knew of the weapons' origins had 'authorised' him to tell me the story behind them.

He explained that around 1922, during the Civil War in the South, relations between the Ancient Order of Hibernians (AOH) and the IRA had been hostile, with the moderate AOH organisation fearful of IRA attacks. Consequently, some of the younger AOH members thought it advisable to have weapons for their own defence. The ones surrendered to me had in fact been brought secretly to Coalisland at that time. On the outskirts of the town, the AOH men were supposed to have overheard the local IRA being drilled in a field by its then Commandant, Master O'Kelly, headmaster of a nearby rural school. Before running away, the AOH members discharged several shots into the air, over the heads of the IRA. In their urgent search for a safe hiding-place for their weapons, the Hibernians remembered an unoccupied house of a Protestant located in an otherwise Catholic area. The weapons were greased, carefully wrapped, and placed below the floorboards of a first-floor room. There they had lain undisturbed for over thirty years, until the recent renovation of the house.

I was intrigued by the story, especially as I had come to know Master O'Kelly's son, Rory, a local solicitor. In time, he became a Crown prosecutor. After a certain court case in Dungannon in the 1970s, Rory had returned to a public house in Coalisland for a drink. Members of the IRA came in and shot him dead. In the very town where his father was said to have been the IRA Commandant many years before, Rory O'Kelly was brutally murdered by a new breed of IRA.

Notwithstanding the difficulties in policing this area at a fraught time, my affinity with many of the local community continued to grow. The people of the western shore of Lough Neagh were to me different from the remainder of the population. Steeped in an Irish republican tradition, and living in a rural area that was often more bog than good land, theirs had been a life of near poverty for centuries. There were some more affluent families, with better farms or small businesses, but they were few. Many eked out an existence with little to sustain their traditionally large families. Extensive emigration of relatives to England, America, Australia or Canada was evidenced by the large numbers of local newspapers posted abroad every week.

I found the people of the lough to be sensitive and friendly, warm-hearted and compassionate towards those even less fortunate than themselves. Many augmented their inadequate income by fishing on Lough Neagh, which was almost as precious to them as their church. Their church, the lough and their land were totally integrated parts of their daily lives.

A major issue for them was the right to fish for eels in the lough. Under an ancient royal charter, the exclusive rights had been granted to an eminent family of that time. The eels could be taken most economically at the weirs in the north-west corner of the lough, where the lower River Bann flowed towards the sea, or at certain points on the river itself. For centuries, the fishing of the lough by local residents had been prohibited, or allowed only if the eels caught were sold to the holders of the royal franchise for a very low price. As a result, the fishermen often took the eels illegally, sometimes using forbidden hooks, and surreptitiously disposing of the catch, perhaps across the border, for much better prices.

More than once the fishermen helped me in policing matters. On one particular occasion, they gave great assistance in recovering the body of an army captain, who had also been an amateur ornithologist, and had fallen into and drowned in the lough, while trying to ring birds on an island. It was on that occasion that I learned of their refusal to fish in any part of the lough where there had been a drowning until the body had been recovered. While many fishermen came to my aid over nine days of searching, no boat-owner would actually allow the body to be conveyed in his craft, a tradition or superstition which probably still exists.

Amongst these fishermen, farmers and business people, Jean and I were building our lives together. We both felt so settled in Coalisland that plans for another child became more than mere talk! Our son, Rodney, was safely delivered in February 1960. Again, the birth had been difficult and demanding for Jean and so, on medical advice, it was her last.

Since we were happy as a family, and as better police relations developed with the community, I had more time available to allow me to move gradually back to studying and to my correspondence course with Terry Kiernan. After little preparation, but with much curiosity, I competed in the head constables' examination. The minimum mark to qualify was 70 per cent. I achieved an overall percentage of 67 in what was a highly competitive exam. Heartened by this and with Jean's encouragement, I again tried the exam in 1960. Despite the domestic upheaval of Rodney's arrival, I felt reasonably well prepared this time.

To my horror, after the papers had been handed in, I found one of my completed answers amongst my scrap-paper. Angry at my own stupidity, I knew it was futile to mention it to the invigilator, but did so nevertheless. His response was as I had anticipated, 'That's your hard luck, Sergeant!' It was, indeed. I failed with a percentage of 68.9. My carelessness had cost me the examination, and I had no one to blame but myself — or so I thought. A year later, I discovered that it had not in fact been the cause of my failure.

By then, Jean and I were reconsidering our position in Coalisland, because we were many miles from Jean's parents, and she wished to be nearer them as the children were growing up. Jean was also concerned that our children would believe life behind rusty barbed wire and sangars was normal. These family concerns, and these alone, made me decide reluctantly to apply for a transfer. As a result, when Sergeant Bill Gray of Bangor Station, County Down was promoted head constable, I was appointed to replace him. On 16 December 1960, I reported for duty at Bangor.

With a resident population of around 25,000, the town had its numbers swollen from spring through to autumn, as it was a very popular seaside resort and attracted many holiday-makers. The hotels and boarding-houses were in popular demand with organised tourist parties, mainly from Scotland and England. By contrast, winters were quiet with the exception of weekends and market-day on Wednesdays. Jean and I found Bangor very different from anywhere else we had lived, and, like all newcomers, we were never really accepted, especially by those residents whose ancestors had lived in Bangor from the nineteenth century. They regarded themselves as 'old Bangorians', as a group apart, into whose status — whether real or imagined — it was never polite to inquire.

Without doubt, my police duties in Bangor were not as complex, sensitive or demanding as they had been in Coalisland, nor, for that matter, was the relationship between the police and the public as intimate as in Counties Londonderry and Tyrone. Certainly, I did not experience the same warmth and kindness, or indeed depth of friendship, within the community as I had known during my service in Coalisland.

Bangor had long been attractive to middle-aged couples as a suitable place to settle after retirement. When one of the pair died, it was commonplace for the remaining partner to remain alone in the house. Sadly, I was to learn from experience that there was a high incidence of elderly, widowed people dying suddenly in their homes throughout the town. Neighbours, milkmen or relatives all too frequently had to notify the police, after receiving no response to telephone calls or visits.

Having dealt with several such reports during my first months in Bangor, I was looking for a constable to deal with yet another call-out of this kind; I wanted to go on a routine supervisory patrol, rather than be bothered with another 'no response' visit. After fifteen minutes of looking in vain for someone else to go, I suddenly realised that the phone message had not mentioned that the person was dead. With considerable self-censure about how conditioned my thinking had become, I cycled as swiftly as I could to the address. With no answer to the doorbell, I went round to the rear of the house and was able to pull down the upper sliding frame of the narrow sash-cord kitchen window and squeeze inside. I went upstairs and found a pitiful sight. An elderly lady lay in bed still alive, but apparently having suffered a severe stroke, as no part of her body — except her eyes — was capable of movement. Those eyes looked at me plaintively, desperately. Within minutes, I had called a doctor and an ambulance and she was quickly removed to hospital. Although she had not died during my initial dithering, I had experienced a powerful lesson in the danger of jumping to obvious conclusions!

In Bangor, Head Constable Jack McNeill kept an efficient station without too much formality or overt discipline. By contrast, District Inspector William Sparrow was generally regarded as fastidious; I also found him to be a worrier and rather excitable. Despite his fussiness, he was professional and astute. When he put pen to paper, he did so to great effect, neither wasting nor mincing his words. I respected and liked both him and Jack McNeill, and worked happily under their command.

I was furious, however, when DI Sparrow told me how he, as one of the officers responsible for marking the recent head constables' examination, had handled my paper. He revealed that my ungainly handwriting had been deemed so erratic and so difficult to read that the examiners had deducted one mark for each question answered! While William Sparrow clearly intended this as advice for the future, I would have preferred not to know that it was punishment for my writing which had cost me the exam rather than my oversight in handing in my answers!

Equally unsettling for me was the inspection by County Inspector 'Dusty' Ferris — so called because of his meticulous insistence on station cleanliness. Normally, assignments would have been shared out between the three sergeants present. Instead, he required me to take the police party through revolver drill, then foot drill, and finally, without warning, to address them 'on all matters of policing peculiar to Bangor District, excluding crime and traffic'. This, of course, meant that our core concerns were excluded. When I finished my talk, the 'County' thanked me formally and added, 'I fully endorse all that the Sergeant has said.' The other two sergeants had enjoyed the easiest ever 'Dusty' inspection, while I felt I had been thoroughly tested under fire! For whatever reasons, the County Inspector had evidently used his own peculiar methods of assessing me that day.

Towards the end of 1961, I had begun to find my duties in Bangor repetitious. This was so even though in June we had finally settled into a newly built police house, and had begun to enjoy to the full the beaches and surrounding countryside of County Down. I had also invested the princely sum of £85 in a completely restored 1949 Vauxhall Velox saloon with a recorded mileage of only 39,000. It had belonged to a bank manager in Scotland and its Scottish registration number, BSN 10, was later to attain unexpected significance. Christened 'Betsy', it was to serve us faithfully for more than five years. For the first time in my service, I had relaxation; the demands and challenges of my first twelve years' service were completely lacking in this seaside resort, and I needed something new to stimulate my mind. Jean sensed it too, and was most supportive when I decided to try the head constables' examination in 1962. A winter of thorough preparation paid handsome dividends when I took first place. Even though there were no vacancies for head constable, and, therefore, no selection board that year, I was content to have cleared the hurdle itself.

By then, Barbara had passed through nursery school, and was enrolled in an excellent primary school within easy walking distance, in the grounds of Bangor Castle. Rodney was a thriving toddler. Jean too was happy in her new home, especially as her parents could often stay with us at weekends and for short holidays. We expected a prolonged stay in the town, and I envisaged myself developing interests within the local community and in our church. To have done so prior to Bangor would have been rather pointless, as our stays in other stations had been of such short duration. Our life-style was completed by our reliable friend, Betsy, allowing us to travel in comfort all over the place, including to Dungannon for Michael McAtamney's wedding to Pat O'Neill in 1962, and for various holidays in the Republic of Ireland.

Just as family life and my career were taking on a more settled pattern and as peace returned to Northern Ireland after the IRA's cease-fire in 1962, another sudden upheaval occurred. Towards the end of that year, I discovered to my surprise that I had been selected as the first RUC officer to attend the British Police Staff College at Bramshill in England. I was reliably informed that it was Sir Albert Kennedy, Sir Richard Pim's successor as Inspector General in 1961, who had selected me for this course. I was also told that it would mean being away from Jean and our children for six months, with weekend visits at six-week intervals.

I cannot honestly claim to have been wildly enthusiastic about the prospect, but, as usual, Jean's immediate response was optimistic and positive. I had to accept, she insisted, since it was in the interests of my career in the RUC. She felt confident that, with the help of her parents, she and our children could manage. In fact, Jean coped very well in my absence, and her letters were always full of reassurance that everything was under control. Yet, I knew that behind the apparent cheerfulness, she did suffer spells of loneliness and anxiety.

As I had received little documentation about the nature of the training, I really did not know what to expect at Bramshill. I was one of more than 200 sergeants from all over England and Wales, who were mixed with a substantial number of police officers of higher rank from Commonwealth countries, and from the diminishing Empire. We were divided into syndicates of twelve, each with one or two overseas students, and a director to guide us in our intellectual travels through a wide-ranging syllabus. This included literature, diverse forms of democracy, concepts of policing, legal history and the role of the British police service. Our professional development was conducted against a background of civilised living, sport and recreation, and discussions with distinguished guest speakers.

While I felt the British officers benefited greatly from association with others from differing cultures, backgrounds and experience, I was intensely irritated by the scarcely concealed prejudice of some British officers towards our colleagues from overseas. I particularly admired the overseas students for the patient way in which they coped not only with this hostility in a strange environment, but with all lectures and discussions taking place in English, which was not their native tongue.

A week or so after my arrival at Bramshill, I had in fact been given a peculiar insight into how the RUC was perceived by some British police officers. Two sergeants from Wales told me how concerned they were that the then Commandant of Bramshill was a Catholic, and how they feared that eventually there would be nothing but Catholic staff in the college. Worse still, they said, they understood that the Commandant was in the process of converting one of the underground cellars of the old Bramshill house into a chapel, where mass could be celebrated for Catholic students. Clearly, they were sure that I, as a member of the RUC with a 'Catholic problem' back home, would be wholly receptive to their views. The fact that the Commandant was a recently retired Major-General of the British army, who had served his country loyally and well, was obviously of no consequence to them. Their concerns were so ludicrous that I could not take them seriously; I could only marvel at the workings of the human mind!

After the Bramshill course, I felt more certain than ever that, as a member of the Royal Ulster Constabulary, I was as professional as any of those police officers I had met, and certainly more widely experienced in harsher circumstances than the vast majority of them. The few abiding and good memories of Bramshill include our final Dining-In, when I tasted alcohol for the first time. With wine at our table, I entered into the spirit of the night, my glass being surreptitiously topped up by my fellow students.

It was a grand, formal occasion with many important guests. Aware that final nights had a reputation for revelry, where a blind eye was turned to most excesses, I procured a large drum from the college engineer. With the drum and a makeshift drumstick, I headed a long chain, mostly of students, but also with the Commandant and his wife, both of whom had been coerced into joining. For some time, we meandered through doors, windows, gardens, and anywhere else to which access could easily be gained. I believe most of us managed to get to bed about 3 a.m. It was with difficulty that I wakened three hours later to pack, before a farewell address from the Commandant. During it, he made reference to a tempestuous Irishman with a large drum, and suggested that such festivities had never been equalled. I suspected that any credibility I may have achieved during my six-month sojourn at Bramshill had dissipated overnight!

Once home, Jean and I agreed that at least another two years of stability in Bangor were necessary for our own good as a family. Indeed, we often debated whether or not to settle there permanently for the children's sake as well as ours. Although we knew there could be no guarantee of permanency in any post, since the 'exigencies of the service' had precedence, Command in the RUC was known to be considerate towards 'deserving cases'. Our private hopes and plans were not to be.

In early August 1963, a selection board was called for promotions from sergeant to head constable. With other qualified sergeants like Bobby Killen, I was called before the board. Afterwards, the selection list was issued from Headquarters. 'Sergeant Hermon, J.C., number 6367' was placed first in order of merit, with 'Sergeant Killen, R.T., number 6627' third. My promotion took effect two weeks later, on 12 September. With promotion came the inevitable transfer, this time to Belfast, where I was to assume command of two sizeable police stations in West Belfast, namely Hastings Street and Cullingtree Road. Never having served anywhere in Northern Ireland's capital city, I realised that this particular transfer presented a significant challenge.

En route to my new stations on Friday, 13 September, I was directed to call on the Commissioner of Belfast, then County Inspector Mr Graham Shillington, under whom I had served as a constable in Victoria Barracks. At Belfast City Police Headquarters, at that time a modern, impressive building at Castlereagh, I was shown into the Commissioner's Office. Our conversation was friendly, but brief. He warned me that policing was different in Belfast to anywhere else in Northern Ireland, and that West Belfast was very demanding indeed. There had been an increase in assaults of a domestic nature and recurring breaches of the licensing laws by publicans. In addition, I would find real problems amongst my new police parties themselves. It was, he explained, my task to effect an improvement in all these matters. I formed an impression that what was required was tact and discretion, backed by firmness. Certainly, I left his office with a clear mandate to make changes.

6

BLUE STREAK'S ARRIVAL IN BELFAST

At the time of my transfer in 1963, Belfast was divided into six police Districts, referred to by letters from 'A' to 'F'. Each was commanded by a district inspector, who in turn was accountable to the City Commissioner and his Deputy, both of whom held county inspector rank. 'B' District comprised the Subdistricts of Andersonstown, Springfield Road, Hastings Street and Cullingtree Road, and was predominantly Catholic. Hastings Street and Cullingtree Road Subdistricts were located between the commercial centre of the city to the east, the Protestant Sandy Row and Donegall Road to the south, the Protestant Shankill Road to the north, and the other two Subdistricts of Springfield Road and Andersonstown to the west — these two also being mainly Catholic.

Generally, the housing of the area was old and poor. Unemployment was endemic, with large families living in impoverished conditions. Over many decades, a tradition of intermittent sectarian conflict had developed between the resident Catholic population and their Protestant neighbours. There was, too, a tradition of Irish republicanism, which provided a natural habitat for the IRA. While there was no recurrence of subversive activity during my tenure, the history and traditions of violence remained, slumbering below the surface, before reawakening at the end of the 1960s. The main problems in my time arose from the very many Protestant parades, which occurred on the periphery of the area, where Protestant and Catholic housing estates were intermingled. Good police relations at ground level with the majority of the residents of whatever persuasion, together with tactful procedures, had kept the peace, albeit uneasily, over many years.

By comparison, republican parades, which were much smaller in number and confined to the Catholic areas, presented few difficulties to the RUC. However, the display of the tricolour, even in a wholly Catholic area, was regarded as particularly offensive by Protestants, as I was soon to learn.

Such political and religious tensions were regularly triggered by the movement of rival football supporters through the District. Not far from Cullingtree Road were the club grounds of two first-division football teams, Distillery and Linfield. The former was supported chiefly by fans from the Catholic community, while the latter was notoriously Protestant. To reach matches at their Windsor Park grounds, Linfield supporters from the Shankill Road area had to traverse the narrow side-streets between terrace houses occupied almost entirely by Catholics, many of whom supported the Distillery team. This created a strong potential for conflict, to say the least!

It was against this background that I took over as 'Head'. My two stations, less than half a mile apart, turned out to be as different as chalk and cheese. In Hastings Street, I found the members of the police party to be open and spontaneous in their attitudes, while those in Cullingtree Road were reserved and wary. With curiosity and some personal amusement, I began to compare the respective sergeants and constables of each station in order to find some explanation for the sharp contrast between them. Sergeant Bill Wilson at Cullingtree Road reflected the attitudes of his constables. Although he was always correct and deferential towards me, I sensed a reserve between us, which I just could not penetrate.

Several months after my arrival, I had to discuss with Bill Wilson the intended closure of the Cullingtree Station (which took place in June 1964), and the implications for the Subdistrict as a whole. How would the two parties integrate when each had such a different approach to policing as well as to discipline? Bill's reply was to ask me probing questions about what I looked for in a station, what I wanted from the officers, and what I thought about the policing of an area like this. We became so engrossed in the discussion that it was several hours and many cups of tea later that we called it a day. As I left, all he said was, 'I think I know now what you're about, Head,' and with that we shook hands. Something had changed that evening. Although it did not blossom fully for some years, there emerged friendship, trust and understanding between us such as I never had with any other colleague.

Within a few weeks, I experienced a noticeable softening and warming of attitudes amongst the party at Cullingtree Road. In this I saw Bill's hand. It was only years later that he told me my reputation as a disciplinarian had preceded me, and that his constables had feared that I would turn the area upside-down by breaking the practices of many years. This is a serious Ulster failing, where people's perceptions of someone, or of an event, too quickly become the truth for them.

With all the constables under my command, I took a very dim view of signs of apathy or slacking on the job. I once found out that a certain constable had left his patrol area, and had gone across the city to borrow a fishing-rod. He returned by trolleybus, and stepped off with the rod in his hand — only to find me standing directly in front of him! The outcome was a nominal fine of ten shillings, coupled with a caution. Not long afterwards, on a bitterly cold morning, he was missing again from his beat, but I found him in the Elizabethan Bar. He was standing in full uniform at the counter, with a hot whiskey in his hand and his cap perched on the back of his head. His explanation was novel if nothing else: he had such a severe toothache that he needed the whiskey to deaden the pain! He immediately reported sick, and actually had a dentist remove one complete row of teeth in a drastic attempt to avoid further discipline! It did not work, and he was fined £3.

The station party knew, as I did, that there was no substance in the constable's excuse. The incident featured in a few apt cartoons on the notice-board. The reaction, however, was not altogether one of amusement, for my approach raised a degree of hostility amongst a very small number of officers in the station, whose comfortable routine was being disturbed. Frustrations grew into malevolence, which festered long into the future.

A particularly nasty episode occurred when a fluorescent tube was stored in the clothes locker in my office. It was one of several such lights from the closed Cullingtree Road Station, which had been approved for installation in various rooms at Hastings Street, including my office. An anonymous letter to the Inspector General had accused me of misappropriating RUC materials, and had indicated that they could be found concealed in my locker! It was easy to explain how the tube came to be where it was. It was more difficult to have to live with the suspicion that one or more of the station party had sent that letter — which proved to have been typed on a Hastings Street typewriter. It was not to be the last anonymous letter on the subject, and this story was even revived during my retirement in an attempt to cause me embarrassment.

Meanwhile, I had to press on with my job. I did much of my patrolling by bicycle, analysing the street patterns to identify which key junctions gave me a view of two, three or even four streets simultaneously. Having related these to the beat and foot patrol areas of the constables, I could almost unerringly locate my officers with the minimum of effort. This in turn allowed me to reduce the time spent on direct supervision, and so I could concentrate on meeting the local residents to develop a closer rapport than would otherwise have been possible. By visiting the many licensed premises in the area, I made it crystal-clear to the proprietors and staff that I frowned upon police officers drinking on duty, or off duty if they were still in uniform.

More generally, police inspections of public houses were tightened, and co-ordinated so that cases of drunkenness on the streets began to drop, as did complaints from wives about drunken, violent husbands. Whatever else, the police and the local community alike understood exactly where I stood on this issue. However, not all publicans presented equally serious problems. Mary Haughey, for instance, ran a good pub with a clientele mainly of pensioners and middle-aged couples, who never caused any trouble. Their only weakness was that they would not leave the premises at the lawful closing hour, preferring instead to stay on for an extra drink and a chat. I tended to reserve supervision of this pub for myself so that I could personally administer severe warnings. Mary and her customers knew, as I did, that any prosecution was most unlikely, but the warnings did at least keep her law-breaking within reasonable bounds.

Well after closing-time one Friday night, as I was passing her premises, someone came out and I very quietly stepped in, closing the door behind me. The two dozen people inside were taken completely by surprise. I duly 'read the Riot Act', chastening Mary and threatening all the customers with prosecution, if I caught them there again. Just as I was about to step out of the pub, an elderly man was standing with his hand raised, ready to give the recognised rap on the door. 'Are you going to knock?' I asked angrily. As quick as lightning, he countered, 'No, I'm going to Lourdes. Are you going to Knock?' The exchange was overheard by those inside, and the story was repeated avidly, losing nothing in the telling!

Time passed quickly at work and at home. Having decided this time to buy a house, we were extremely fortunate to find a suitable one in Dunlambert Park, which was within 400 yards of my parents-in-law in North Belfast. We paid £1,750 for a semi-detached, three-bedroomed house. It was an immense sum of money to us at that time, my net salary as a head constable being £96 per month. From that, our estate agent received £24 each month to pay the mortgage and sundry bills connected with the house.

By November 1963, Barbara was at the primary school which Jean had attended as a child. Rodney was spending much more time with his grandparents, and established a particular closeness with them that lasted their lifetime. We also discovered an excellent swimming pool on the Falls Road, and decided that Barbara and Rodney should learn to swim there. When I discovered that the Catholic proprietor of a local motorcycle-repair shop was a superb swimmer, I asked him to teach them. He willingly agreed. Most Tuesday and Thursday evenings we would arrive at the Falls Road pool, where I sat in uniform if I were on duty. I was relaxed and accepted by all, a fact scarcely believable today. Indeed, in all my time in Hastings Street Station, I never carried a weapon or anything other than my regulation blackthorn stick, the traditional adornment of a head constable.

Living only three miles or so from the station, I varied my means of travel to include cycling, or driving Betsy when the weather was especially inclement. Parked opposite the police station, Betsy naturally became the visible sign of my presence. With its Scottish registration of BSN 10 and its royal-blue paintwork, it was hard to ignore. Years later, I learned from Bill Wilson that within the subculture of constables and sergeants I was referred to light-heartedly as 'Blue Streak'. The fact that I made unexpected supervision patrols around the area only added to the aptness of the title in their eyes. Apparently, whenever I arrived at the station, whether by car or by bicycle, the message 'BSN 10', meaning 'Blue Streak Now In Orbit', was flashed to the stations of the District and to the uniformed officers on duty!

Approaching the first football season of my time at Hastings Street, I studied carefully the question of policing the matches. I raised the issue of manpower many times with the District Inspector, and occasionally — through him — with the Commissioner. While I was convinced that additional resources were needed, tradition dies hard. I was informed that matches had been policed in the past by twenty or thirty officers, and often fewer than that, without any serious outbreak of violence.

That tradition held sway until Easter Tuesday 1964, when Linfield was playing a home match at Windsor Park against another contentious team. Given the sensitivity of Easter itself, and the complicating factor of a Junior Orange parade along Grosvenor Road that same afternoon, I had specifically requested considerably more resources to police the match.

Fortified by a Linfield win, and in many cases also by alcohol, the team's supporters converged on Leeson Street, poured across the Falls Road and surged on towards their Shankill Road base. However, several of them ventured up Raglan Street and, with defiant arrogance, trailed a coat behind them as a provocative gesture to opposing supporters and local residents alike. Unfortunately, the latter rose to the bait and immediately gave chase, with the result that two opposing groups suddenly burst onto the Falls Road. Within seconds, fighting began and damage was caused to property. The traffic flow was immediately disrupted, with shoppers and pedestrians caught up in the turmoil. A brief but violent encounter occurred, before the rioters dispersed. Several arrests were made. Quite by chance, City Commissioner Graham Shillington had decided to visit the area that afternoon, and happened to be sitting in his car, parked on the Falls Road, with a full view of the disturbance.

Back at Hastings Street Station, he congratulated the police on their handling of the disturbance, and revealed his surprise at the incredible speed with which it had developed. Fortunately, it was a case of seeing is believing, as the Commissioner accepted there and then the need for extra police resources to prevent a recurrence of the violence after such matches. In consequence, that was in fact the only really serious confrontation between rival football supporters during my tenure at Hastings Street.

By October 1964, it was not football matches but the British general election, scheduled for the 15th, which was giving rise to sectarian violence in the weeks before polling. The Republican Party had opened an election headquarters in an old vacant shop at No. 145 Divis Street, in a wholly Catholic area. Towards the end of September, three flags had been placed in the shop window, some feet back from the glass so that they could be seen only by passers-by. One of these flags was the tricolour. This resulted in the Rev. Ian Paisley, a fundamentalist Protestant preacher, threatening to lead a protest march from Belfast City Hall to 145 Divis Street, if the flag were not removed. The march was banned, and the tricolour was removed from the window by the local police.

Tension inevitably mounted. The ban on the Rev. Paisley's march did not prevent him holding a rally at the City Hall. Crowds gathered in the vicinity of the Republican Party's office, and police patrols reported an uneasiness and growing hostility amongst local residents, especially the younger ones. The situation was becoming very ugly. Although no serious incidents occurred in Divis Street that particular evening, it was well after midnight before the crowd disappeared, leaving me apprehensive about the rest of the week.

Next day, I had to prepare for a republican parade through my area in the evening. Directions had been given from District Headquarters that police officers were to confine their patrols to the main streets; on no account were they to enter the narrow side-streets leading off Divis Street and the Falls Road. Even though we could hear the breaking of concrete slabs, and cast-iron gratings and other material being prepared as ammunition in the side-streets, we could not take preventive action. That evening proved much more difficult than the previous one, with violence erupting around 10.30 p.m., and spreading along Divis Street into the Falls Road and Albert Street areas. As the lights had been broken in the side-streets, the rioters had the advantage of darkness from which to rain missiles on the police, who were silhouetted against the lights of the main roads.

During the morning of Thursday, 1 October, a second tricolour was placed in the window of 145 Divis Street. This further excited the people who were already standing about outside. Around 4.30 p.m., a contingent of police moved swiftly to the Republican Party's headquarters in Divis Street, cordoned it off and rerouted traffic away from the area. I was in command of Divis Street, and so my party had to cover the entrance to Ardmoulin Street on one side and Percy Street on the other. When the police removed the flag, the crowd surged forward into the road, with the shrieking and screaming of women and children blending with the yelling, booing and swearing of the young men at the back. No batons were drawn, even though several constables were struck by missiles, thrown from behind the crowd.

Suddenly, all hell let loose. A mob emerged from Ardmoulin Street and from further up Divis Street. Missiles were hurled at us and at the few vehicles still on the road. I had no alternative but to order my party of police to draw batons and disperse the rioters. All of us were wearing raincoats and helmets, without the sophisticated riot gear of more modern times. As the numbers of rioters increased, so too did the quantity of broken bricks, pieces of metal and stones thrown at us. I found myself leading baton charge after baton charge, regrouping my officers and encouraging them to greater effort. Many of them were struck again and again by missiles. Some hobbled, or were assisted, to the station and, if necessary, conveyed to hospital for treatment; others filtered back to rejoin the fray.

At the height of the rioting, a forceful baton charge was made, driving demonstrators from Divis Street into Ardmoulin Street, where all the street lights had been smashed. As the crowd dispersed, the police ran back to regroup in Divis Street, before the rioters emerged again. One weary constable had the misfortune to stumble into a drainage trap, the metal grating of which had earlier been used for making missiles. The advancing mob grabbed him, and beat him severely about the head. At the last moment, while deeply unconscious, he was seized by a group of older residents in Percy Street and dragged into the centre of the road. In despair, one of them shouted to us, 'For God's sake, take him!'

When he was finally rescued, I saw his smashed and beaten head completely covered in blood. A local woman insisted that the constable be carried into her home, where she tried to help him until an ambulance arrived. Some days later, I called to thank her for her kindness and discovered that her husband had been convicted several years earlier for possessing ammunition. Although she belonged to a republican family, her Christian charity transcended all else the evening of the Divis Street riot.

Eventually, order was restored in Divis Street, and after calling briefly at Hastings Street Station, I set off on foot to the junction of Northumberland Street, Albert Street and Falls Road, where severe rioting was continuing. The only route open to me was via the Shankill. There, I was extremely concerned to see hundreds of Protestant residents on the streets, chiefly congregated at the junction with Northumberland Street, but also in smaller groups at other minor junctions, leading towards the Falls Road.

I slipped past quietly, conscious of the grave danger that extreme sectarian conflict would break out if the Catholic and Protestant crowds were not confined to their respective areas. Down Northumberland Street, by now virtually deserted of traffic, and round the curve at the Linen Mill building I witnessed an awesome sight. Precisely twenty-four police officers lined the street, 200 yards back from the crossroads formed by Northumberland Street meeting with Divis Street on the left, the Falls Road to the right and Albert Street straight ahead. At that crossroads stood a massive crowd of people, which overflowed into the adjoining streets. Between the crowd and the line of officers were rioters, throwing missiles with impunity. Apart from their batons and helmets, the policemen were defenceless. More than half of their original number had at that point already been injured, and taken to the casualty ward of the Royal Victoria Hospital.

Just then, I watched the rioters surging towards the police line. The attackers had added a new weapon to their armoury: large slivers of plate glass from broken shop windows. Police officers were jumping and weaving as best they could to avoid them, but some invariably reached their intended targets — I, by now, among them. Both my blackthorn stick and my body were scraped by missiles, and the pain from being struck at the base of my spine was increasing steadily.

Something had to be done, and quickly. I advised the officers present that they should arm themselves with three missiles from those littering the street. On my word of command, and with the rioters well within range, we would throw three co-ordinated volleys. Of the sixteen or so policemen left, not one demurred, as they too knew the hopelessness of our position. My decision was calculated and resolute, and I was prepared to accept the consequences of it.

The effect was devastating. Our order and discipline and three good volleys won the day, as rioters went down like ninepins, some screaming and yelling, some bleeding from their wounds, some partly or completely unconscious. Chaos reigned in their ranks, and, in fear, they pushed and shoved one another to effect their escape. A sharp baton charge followed. It was the first time in the ten hours of rioting that I managed to get closer than twenty-five feet to the rioters, such was their advantage through the use of missiles. For the next hour, we stood firm, until the night-duty police arrived as reinforcements.

With sixty extra officers, I was able to form three ranks across the road, with a left flank, right flank and centre. I told each officer to grasp the leather belt of the man on his left, and hold his baton in his right hand. Standing in front of them, I instructed that on the command 'At the double', we would advance towards the throng at the crossroads. The left flank would turn into Divis Street to secure it, the right into the Falls Road and the centre into Albert Street. All stood ready for my order.

Suddenly, there was a loud roar from behind me as a landrover was set on fire by a petrol bomb, causing its occupants to jump out, their uniforms already alight. At this sight, my serried ranks charged. Had I not turned at that moment and run ahead with my blackthorn stick aloft, I would have been trampled underfoot by my own officers! The rioters dispersed into the side-streets.

Snatch squads, mainly from the well-trained Reserve Force Platoons, were then detailed to arrest rioters. Fifty-seven people were arrested and brought to the Belfast Police Office, where they were charged with various offences. But hundreds more rioters roamed the darkened side-streets, where the police had not yet ventured. Consequently, I took a personnel carrier and filled it with volunteers willing to venture into these streets. While we were travelling along one, I saw a bottle curling through the air and glistening in the reflected lights of our headlamps, as it came towards our vehicle. That night, the flight of missiles through the air, the movement of rioters, and the swing of police batons all happened at speed, but, strangely, I had visualised them in very slow motion. Similarly, I remember thinking that the bottle was coming in slow motion directly at me, and would hit me in the face. At that, I jumped up. The bottle smashed through the windscreen and hit me on the chest, with particles of shattered glass entering my right eye. Through all this, our driver had maintained full control of the vehicle and driven on. I quickly took out my handkerchief to cover my eye, and told him to make for the casualty ward of the Royal Victoria.

I was shocked by what I saw there. Dozens of injured police officers and injured rioters stood, lay or sat in the corridors, side wards and waiting areas. Nurses and doctors worked with clinical speed and professionalism. A doctor removed the glass particles from my eye, and a few moments later I was back in the vehicle with my party of volunteers, driving off to resume our skirmishing patrol.

We drove slowly to the bottom of Panton Street, where we disembarked. The rioters were outflanked. I grasped one man, who immediately began to struggle and kick wildly, stopping only when another police officer came to my assistance. My prisoner, still with pieces of broken ironwork and stones in his pockets and with his clothing smelling of petrol, protested his innocence. He claimed he was 'an Orangeman from Oldpark', and knew Head Constable McAtamney well! I detailed two officers to convey him to the Police Office to have him charged with disorderly behaviour.

That Thursday evening and early Friday morning saw the worst and most intensive rioting I ever witnessed in my entire police career, not equalled by later disturbances, when Northern Ireland became submerged in sectarian conflict. Throughout the Divis Street rioting, my only weapon was the formidable blackthorn stick obtained for me from County Armagh in August 1964, by a pawnbroker on the Falls Road.

Those living in the Divis Street area must have been as deeply affected as the police officers by the rioting. An eight-year-old girl who lived with her family in Ardmoulin Street was later to serve as a member of the Police Authority for Northern Ireland. Our working relationship ended unhappily, after an abrasive discussion about these riots and the RUC's tactics in handling them.

My experiences of that time greatly influenced my thinking in later years and, most certainly, my efforts towards anticipating events and their consequences. I was to put into practice Deputy Chief Constable Moffett's advice about the responsibilities of command: 'Do the work the day before, and you will have little to do on the day.'

An analysis of those arrested and charged after the events in Divis Street revealed a high number with previous convictions, and home addresses from areas all over Belfast. Obviously, the riot had attracted hundreds of people from many parts of the city. They had scant regard for the suffering that would be inflicted upon law-abiding residents of the Divis Street neighbourhood, and upon the fragile relations between those residents and the police. With the general election over, the station settled down to routine duties for the remainder of 1964, but our relations with the local community had been seriously damaged.

I again returned to study. I recall a conversation with a senior district inspector from Headquarters who, during the spring of 1965, suggested that I enter the district inspectors' examination later that year. At the time, I really had no intention of doing so, and forgot about it until Bill Wilson more or less dared me to accept the challenge. I studied and passed. My promotion to District Inspector took effect from 29 April 1966, and Michael McAtamney was — to my great delight and by my expressed wish to the promotion board — promoted six days before me.

This time, I was to be transferred to Cookstown, where I had gone temporarily eleven years earlier on promotion to sergeant. Jean and I received the news with mixed emotions, not least because of the upset to the children and the financial pressures the transfer would cause. Jean would again be far from her parents, while Barbara and Rodney would have their schooling disrupted, and would lose their friends.

The last few weeks of my service in Hastings Street proved so eventful and sensitive, however, that I had to force these personal concerns to the back of my mind. As 1966 marked the fiftieth anniversary of the Easter Rising in Dublin, the republican element in Belfast announced its intention to have widespread celebrations on and around Easter Sunday, 17 April. This was happening in the aftermath of friendly overtures to the Republic by the northern Prime Minister, Terence O'Neill. These included an invitation to Sean Lemass, the then Taoiseach (Irish Prime Minister), to Stormont in January 1965, and O'Neill's reciprocal visit in February 1965 to Dublin. These events had incited Ian Paisley to vehement denunciations of Prime Minister O'Neill, and the Unionist Party generally. The various anniversary celebrations planned to mark the Easter

Rising served only to anger him — and many members of his Free Presbyterian Church — still further.

Behind all of this lay the loyalist population's fear of renewed republican violence, a fear made the more real by events such as the blowing up of Nelson's Pillar in Dublin, and talk in the Republic of an alliance between communists and the IRA. The result was the growth of 'Paisleyism', which I would describe as a mixture of extreme evangelical Protestantism and political bigotry. Paisleyism increasingly divided the unionists, until finally, in 1971, the Democratic Unionist Party burst on to the political scene, in opposition to the traditional Unionist Party — now the Ulster Unionist Party, as it is familiarly known.

Tensions preceding the 1966 Easter celebrations had mounted steadily in Northern Ireland. It was decided that all police leave, and all trains between Dublin and Belfast, would be cancelled on Easter Sunday, and that a massive mobilisation of the USC would take place. Widespread patrolling by the police was also maintained on all roads leading from the Republic.

Meanwhile, Ian Paisley and his supporters decided to hold a parade on Easter Sunday afternoon through central Belfast to the Ulster Hall, where a 'thanksgiving' service for the defeat of the 1916 rebels would be held. With this parade, as in his threat to march to Divis Street in 1964, we were seeing the first use of Paisley's tactic of counter-demonstration.

The newly formed Ulster Constitution Defence Committee, created early in 1966 by one of his supporters, received so many applications for membership that another organisation, the Ulster Protestant Volunteers (UPV), was immediately formed to marshal the applicants into a cohesive and structured force throughout the North. Membership was restricted to those born into the Protestant faith, and specifically excluded RUC officers because of the number of Catholic members at all levels within the Force. It was the use of the UPV which, I believe, caused serious problems in various parts of Northern Ireland during the following two years.

Ian Paisley scheduled his parade to coincide with the main republican parade, which was due to march from Hamill Street, within my Subdistrict, along Divis Street and the Falls Road to Casement Park.

On Easter Sunday itself, I was oblivious to all else that was going on in Belfast, and was aware only of the enormous influx of people through my area to join the republican demonstration. They were quietly and carefully controlled by their own marshals, who operated in accordance with our discreetly given directions and advice. The unspoken but acknowledged decision by both the republican organisers and the local police was that the event would be peaceful and orderly.

As the parade of many thousands was forming up, I was walking unaccompanied along Divis Street, carrying only my sturdy blackthorn stick. A young man with a hurley stick in his right hand passed close to me and, as he did so, he flicked it expertly with his wrist. It landed on the blackthorn stick, right beside my knuckles. I walked on without even breaking my pace. To have done otherwise could have caused the spark I wished to avoid. Mercifully, sparks were avoided in my area, if not elsewhere, and at the end of an arduous day I was able to record in my duty diary, 'No untoward incident.'

Anxiety, however, was kept alive by a seizure of weapons by Gardaí in Dublin that evening, and a remark in an address by the Irish President, Eamon de Valera, at the close of the commemoration ceremonies in the Republic. He declared that 'Not much remains to be done to bring about a United Ireland.' Coupled with the strident voices and provocative antics of the extreme loyalists in the North, this declaration and other sinister events south of the border served to heighten northern fears of a revival of violence in their midst.

7

TURMOIL ERUPTS

In the early evening of Friday, 29 April 1966, I left Belfast on promotion to Cookstown as a District Inspector, Third Class. I knew that it normally took a DI about nine years to move from Third to Second, before eventually becoming a First Class DI. Any advance to higher rank could not occur in less than ten years, and so Jean and I were able to look forward to a more settled and predictable future from a family viewpoint. A significant aspect of district inspector rank was that plain clothes were normally worn, while uniform was reserved for special occasions such as attending court and making formal inspections. With one tailored uniform ready before my departure and another due in a few weeks, I was well prepared for my new post.

My first full day in Cookstown as District Inspector started with a feeling of freedom, but it certainly did not end that way. I rose early and walked to the police station so that I could absorb the atmosphere of a provincial town, instead of the city bustle. I was received with considerable deference and formal saluting by junior ranks.

My predecessor welcomed me, gave a resumé of the District, and casually mentioned a matter that had been reported on the previous Wednesday. Apparently, the proprietor of a confectionery and newspaper shop had alleged that a police constable had stolen goods from his premises. The man's daughter and some friends, who happened to have been in the living quarters at the rear of the shop at the time, were supposed to have seen what had happened.

Along with Detective Sergeant Peter Flanagan, I interviewed the complainant, his daughter and other witnesses. Their evidence so impressed me that I left a message at the home of the County Inspector, Mr G.R. Lansdale. This was a man I knew only by reputation, and there was I, a newly appointed District Inspector on my first day in his county, wanting to suspend one of my own men from duty! When he phoned back, I explained that I had already suspended the constable and sought his approval. He gave it tersely, adding that he had arranged a formal inspection of Cookstown Station for the following Tuesday, when we could discuss the matter further.

That first meeting with Roy Lansdale I found interesting, to put it mildly. His height, more than six feet, and strong build combined to make him an impressive figure. In my office, he scanned the report about the alleged theft and returned it to me, saying that he fully supported my suspension of the constable. Peter Flanagan's thorough investigation resulted in the prosecution of the constable, who elected to go for trial by jury. In the event, following a robust defence by his counsel, the jury returned a 'not guilty' verdict. Since there was no residual discipline to be invoked, RUC Headquarters directed that the constable be restored to duty in Cookstown.

Before he was, I arranged for him to report to my office, where I outlined the complete background to the case, and repeated the comments of several reputable traders about his conduct. I also reminded him of the high standards which had to be met by all members of the RUC. Finally, I asked that he reflect seriously on all I had said, on the truth as he, more than anyone else, knew it to be, and then consider his position. He left the room, and fifteen minutes later the Station Sergeant telephoned me with the news that the constable had tendered his resignation.

Almost twenty years later, in a crowded room at a formal function in Belfast City Hall, I was approached by a fine-looking man who asked, 'You don't know me, do you?' I replied that I did, in Cookstown in 1966. He was my ex-constable, who had obviously been successful in a new occupation. 'No hard feelings?' he asked. 'None,' I replied and we shook hands.

I had spent most of that first month in Cookstown travelling around the District, visiting stations and renewing my knowledge of the countryside — from the poor land bordering Lough Neagh around Stewartstown and Coagh, and the wild hill country of turf banks and heather around Pomeroy and Carrickmore, to the fine agricultural land around Cookstown itself.

All the while, I was becoming increasingly aware of the threat to peace posed by Ian Paisley's Ulster Protestant Volunteers, who were recruiting widely in rural areas like mine. His criticism of the traditional Presbyterian Church in Ireland caused much anger and division within families and congregations. Worse followed on 6 June, when Paisley and his supporters paraded through Cromac Square, a Catholic area of central Belfast, where loyalists had not paraded for some thirty years. In my opinion, it was a considerable error of judgment by the RUC to have granted permission for that march. The police were totally unprepared for the intense violence that followed.

Rioting went on for several hours while Paisley's procession remained in the centre of Belfast. By unfortunate coincidence the Presbyterian Assembly was also being held at the time. As the past and the newly appointed Presbyterian Moderators exited from the Assembly Building, along with the Governor of Northern Ireland, then Lord Erskine, the Lord Chief Justice and many other dignitaries, a rowdy mob hurled abuse at them. People of all persuasions throughout Northern Ireland were greatly shocked by this and regarded it as outrageous behaviour. Before long, it would pale into insignificance compared to other events.

If there was any time at which the rising threat of Paisleyism might have been halted, it was, I believe, following that evening of 6 June 1966. By 1968, the divisions within the traditional Unionist Government, the emergence of the

Civil Rights Movement, and the capacity of the IRA to infiltrate it, made conflict inevitable.

On Sunday morning, 26 June 1966, a shooting occurred outside a public house in Malvern Street in the Protestant Shankill Road area of Belfast. Four men from the Falls Road, all Catholics, had just emerged from the pub when they were fired upon. One of them, Peter Ward, was shot dead and two others were injured.

The next morning, I was directed by a telephone call from RUC Headquarters to return to Brown Square Station in Belfast in order to assist District Inspector Sam Bradley, who was leading the investigation into the murder of Peter Ward. When I arrived, we agreed that Sam would concentrate on the criminal investigation, while I took over the routine running of the District. Within days, two members of the extreme loyalist paramilitary organisation, the Ulster Volunteer Force, were charged with the Ward murder, and also with that of another Catholic. Later, a third man was similarly charged.

I remember the anxiety aroused that same week by the news that petrol bombs had been thrown at the Apprentice Boys' Headquarters in Derry, known as the Memorial Hall, and at Presbyterian churches in both Derry and North Belfast. Nevertheless, with the arrests made in connection with the Ward murder, I was permitted to leave Brown Square Station on Saturday, 2 July, for the relative peace of Cookstown.

An Operational Order awaited my return! RUC Headquarters had again directed me to report for duty in Belfast — this time on 4 July. The reason was a visit by Queen Elizabeth and the Duke of Edinburgh to Northern Ireland. On the Queen's route to the city centre from Aldergrove Airport, I was going to be responsible for a sector from Cliftonville Circus to the New Lodge Road and, after lunch, for Howard Street and Great Victoria Street as far as Hope Street.

The 4th was a beautiful day. The crowds were happy and all went well until the afternoon. I watched the cars go down Great Victoria Street to a wave of cheering and knew that, after another 200 yards, they would be clear of my sector. Then, just as the royal car passed a ten-storey building still under construction, I saw something suddenly spring out from its roof. To my horror, silhouetted against the brilliant blue sky was a concrete breeze-block, which briefly circled outwards before dropping straight down towards the cavalcade. To me it seemed to move in slow motion, just like the bottle coming towards my face during the riots in 1964.

I began running towards the scene. The brick struck the front of the royal car, but the noise of its impact was drowned by the continuous cheering and applause. A momentary wave of shocked silence followed. Then a roar of anger rose from the crowd; joy had died, and was replaced by instant rage under the hot sun. The image of that block curling through the air, and the memory of a carnival atmosphere being wiped away in seconds, remain etched in my mind.

The cavalcade swept off, gathering speed as it passed and disappeared from my view into Hope Street. RUC detectives dashed to the roof of the building, where they were helped by workmen to identify the culprit, a teenager. He was taken to the Police Office beside the Belfast Magistrates' Court. The following day, John Francis Morgan, aged seventeen, was charged under the Treason Act with throwing missiles at the Queen 'with intent to injure or alarm Her Majesty or to break or injure the public peace'. Asked if he had anything to say, he had replied, 'Nothing, except I had no intention of harming anyone. I just done it for protest.' He was ultimately imprisoned. I was profoundly disturbed by the incident, but contented myself that it had at least been dealt with effectively on the ground.

I returned to Cookstown, where the rest of that summer of 1966 passed reasonably quietly apart from the taunting of each community by the other during the traditional 'marching season'.

More serious problems arose from the disappearances of some weapons held by part-time members of the Ulster Special Constabulary in the area. Despite thorough police investigations, the missing equipment was never recovered nor was any culprit ever identified. When this became public knowledge, it gave rise in some quarters to veiled allegations that the weapons had been handed over to a Protestant extremist group, such as the Ulster Volunteer Force or the Ulster Protestant Volunteers.

The Subdistrict commandants made strenuous efforts to find the missing equipment, knowing that its loss cast suspicion on their entire platoons and provided a golden opportunity for their critics to denigrate the USC. However, similar unresolved disappearances of weapons elsewhere merely added to the growing doubts about the trustworthiness of some USC members.

By this time, Jean and our children had been able to join me in Cookstown. We took a fairly ordinary, three-bedroomed detached house situated at a minor crossroads, about a mile from the police station. Barbara, now ten years of age, and Rodney, approaching seven, went to an excellent primary school in the town. Barbara found friends of her own age and Rodney had a special chum, whose black Labrador dog he adored. The stability we had hoped for seemed certain now.

Nonetheless, as we moved into 1967, I became increasingly aware of community tensions even in my rural District. A large republican demonstration of several thousand was notified for Carrickmore on Easter Sunday, and I anticipated trouble when the organisers refused to co-operate with the local RUC. The organisers intended to steward the parade themselves without police help. The consequence, inevitably, was complete chaos as scores of vehicles carrying demonstrators and spectators converged on Carrickmore from several roads leading into the village. I had arrived and was observing the confusion when County Inspector Lansdale appeared. Enough was enough. With a signal to local police officers, order was quickly restored so that the parade could begin, albeit late.

Special Branch was anxious to obtain as much information as possible about the participants in the parade, particularly about those seen to be prominent around the colour-party. Since few technical facilities were available to us at that time, the local Sergeant had arranged for a privately owned eight-millimetre cine-camera to be mounted on a tripod in a bedroom of his married quarters in order to record the entire parade as it marched past the station. Such recordings were almost unheard of then, and so it was with some trepidation that I advised the 'County' about our plan.

When Lansdale saw the camera in position with all but the lens hidden behind a lace curtain, he suggested that we should instead pull back the curtain and open the window. Surprised, but pleased, at his attitude, we did so and kept the camera tipped forward for all to see. It was immediately spotted by the demonstrators, and attracted such curiosity that we obtained an excellent film of the procession, with clearly distinguishable faces staring up into the camera! The humour of the situation was still talked about long after the event.

However, a Saturday morning brought a much more serious incident. I was advised that a man's body had been found, immersed head first in an old, disused, stone-lined well near his home. With every avenue of investigation exhausted, we were satisfied that his death had been accidental. Even when sober, the deceased was known to be unsteady on his feet and, since he had been drinking excessively the previous evening, we concluded that he had probably toppled over into the well. When the jury at the inquest brought in a verdict of 'accidental death by drowning', I believed the matter closed.

Some weeks later, I received an unexpected phone call from the Inspector General, Sir Albert Kennedy. His opening remark was devastating. 'How would you like to be Deputy Commandant of the Training Centre?' My response was immediate. 'I would not, Sir.' He delayed before asking a further sharp question: 'Do you refuse to go?' 'Sir,' I replied, 'I cannot refuse to go where my authorities send me. I'm sorry, Sir.' Obviously taken aback, Sir Albert snapped, 'Do you think you are capable of doing the job?' Without hesitation, but with equal firmness, I retorted, 'With respect, Sir, I am the least qualified to assess my ability. I believe that to be the function of my superiors.' After a short pause came the memorable words, 'You're not being very helpful, Hermon. You will be notified of my decision within forty-eight hours.' With that, the telephone fell silent.

I just sat there, feeling extremely perturbed. Within half an hour, there was a second phone call from Headquarters. This time it was Sir Albert's chief administration officer. The conversation with him was very brief and almost entirely one-sided. He spoke, while I listened. I was told that I would be transferred to the Training Centre (the former Depot) in Enniskillen as Deputy Commandant with effect from 15 May 1967. When I inquired about choice, he said abruptly that I had none. I made an appointment to see Roy Lansdale in his office to tell him that I was being transferred to Enniskillen. I thanked him for his trust in leaving the running of the District so completely to me. 'You gave me no trouble, and I gave you none,' he replied. We shook hands and I left. Only a few weeks later, his support and trust were once again given to me, at a time I desperately needed them.

Jean was shattered by the news of my transfer to Enniskillen! Without any warning, all our dreams for ourselves in Cookstown had vanished. Barbara and Rodney were so happy with their school, and their friends. We had started decorating our home, had bought new carpets and furniture to suit it . . . and we suddenly had to leave it all.

The disappointment of being transferred so soon from Cookstown was made worse by the knowledge that once again I must uproot my family. Little did I suspect that this transfer to Enniskillen as Deputy Commandant would in fact remove me finally from on-the-ground operational policing, where I had derived a constant sense of fulfilment. By working with the ordinary, inherently decent people of Northern Ireland I had found that the vast majority of policing was like a social service for people in need, and it was undoubtedly this aspect which I found most rewarding.

In my new role I would be responsible for training civilians to become constables, who would maintain the very high standards within the RUC. When I applied my mind to the implications of it, I was encouraged by the prospect of an entirely different experience from my previous seventeen years' service. Clearly, I had to listen, learn and be guided by the Commandant and the staff. My guiding hand, mentor and friend for the first few months would be the Head Constable Major, James Johnston. The Commandant, County Inspector Tom Crozier, had a wealth of practical common sense and experience. Always an operational officer himself, he had been Commandant for several years and was also the County Inspector for Fermanagh. The latter post was not at all an onerous one in times of peace, but, when terrorism raised its head, Fermanagh became a very difficult, sensitive and dangerous area for police officers.

Not everything went smoothly at the beginning. In my first few weeks at Enniskillen, I received a wholly unpleasant surprise. David Johnston (formerly my DI in Coalisland), by then a First Class District Inspector and on Headquarters staff, called to see me. He formally advised me that a serious, albeit anonymous, complaint had been levelled against me in relation to a Catholic man's death in Cookstown. The allegation was that, because of the influence of Freemasonry and the Orange Order upon me, I had suppressed the fact that James Hemphill, the man found drowned in the well, had in actual fact been murdered. The only possible suspect was a Protestant. Although in retrospect the very suggestion seems ridiculous, it did not seem so at the time. I still remember that sense of chill in my spine, and of shock. I accepted the manila folder containing the written notice of the allegations and inviting my response. I have no recollection of my conversation with David Johnston except for his warning that 'If there is anything in it, you're out!'

Shortly afterwards, I received a phone call from County Inspector Roy Lansdale. 'What's all this about?' he asked. 'Suppressing a murder?' He too had received a copy of the relevant Headquarters file. I assured him that, based on the inquest file and the detailed investigations by Detective Sergeant Flanagan, Head Constable Desmond O'Brien and myself, a comprehensive report on Hemphill's death could still be prepared without the need for any further inquiry. With that reassurance, Roy Lansdale expressed his confidence in me and asked me to get on with it.

I contacted Head O'Brien and Peter Flanagan, and arranged to rendezvous with them the following evening at the Ballygawley Road roundabout between Cookstown and Enniskillen. It was a bright sunny evening and, with total informality, we relaxed on the grass verge beside the roundabout. When I revealed the allegations surrounding Hemphill's death, their reaction, like mine, was one of surprise for they had been even more closely involved in the investigation of Hemphill's death. Both were highly professional and competent police officers and, coincidentally, both were Catholic. Neither of them was remotely influenced by Freemasonry or Orangeism, or likely to condone it in anyone else. Our Ballygawley rendezvous turned out to be the last time I saw Peter Flanagan alive, as he was murdered by the IRA in 1974.

That sunny evening, however, it was agreed that each of us would augment the already comprehensive inquest file by adding to it details of every aspect of our investigation. All of this was sent to Roy Lansdale and, ultimately, the file was examined by the Attorney-General, who in his decision referred to our 'voluminous and comprehensive report'. He dismissed the complaint, so far as I remember, as being unjustified and frivolous.

With this serious allegation put to rest, I could concentrate on my tasks as Deputy Commandant. Amongst the first of these was a particularly novel and unexpected one. A contingent of some sixty recruits, comprising the two senior squads and a number held back from their stations to supplement the group, was in the advanced stages of preparing for a public display of drill and physical training in Enniskillen, then Bangor and at the RUC Annual Sports. The march through each of the towns was to be led by the RUC band with me in front!

The complex displays of drill club swinging had been carefully planned by the instructors, all of whom were former army drill instructors, mainly from the Irish Guards. My own foot and sword drill had to be brought up to a high standard in the course of my first few weeks there. I put myself under the tuition of one of our instructors and, in privacy and by dint of hard work, I managed to achieve a reasonably high standard.

Although the displays were successful, with the one in Bangor being particularly well received by many thousands of spectators, I was convinced that the demand in valuable training time could not be justified and resolved that this should be the last of them.

At almost the same time, yet another tradition in the Training Centre was abruptly ended. In July, Tom Crozier informed me that a leading organiser of the Fermanagh County Show had contacted him regarding the availability of the usual fifty police recruits to assist at the Show. I was surprised and rather irritated that aspiring police officers should be expected to attend to the fences used for the horse-jumping events, and to sell programmes, and other routine matters at the County Show. The fact that the person making the request was a prominent member of the local aristocracy caused me concern.

To me, being a police officer was a profession and being a constable, of whatever rank, was holding an office unique in its independence within the law. As I saw it, the menial functions my police recruits were expected to perform at the County Show could have no positive part in their training or duties. Tom was quite upset when I voiced my objections; he advised me that it was for one day only, and had been a custom for many years. It was with some embarrassment that I told him I would act only on his formal direction. I received no such direction.

Instead, the County Inspector departed on three weeks' leave, which encompassed the date of the Show. Shortly after his departure, the organiser telephoned, and sought confirmation that the recruits would be made available. My reply was brief, but at all times respectful; before the Commandant went on leave, I had received no direction to provide them and I did not think it a proper function for recruits, whose training schedule was very intense.

Clearly, my response greatly perplexed the caller, who protested vigorously that the Show could not be held without the recruits. After a somewhat strained conversation, I agreed that we might be able to find a volunteer sergeant and ten volunteer recruits, but only on the understanding that this would be the very last occasion that they would be involved. Reluctantly, and with discernible constraint, my offer was accepted. I immediately contacted the Head Constable Major and requested him to find me eleven 'volunteers' for the Show.

Once it was over, police recruits were never again requested by its organisers! Unrecognised as such, this was my first major innovation at the Training Centre; I saw it as a commitment to a police force that would be independent of political and other influences. When Tom Crozier returned from leave, he called me into his office and asked about the outcome of the Show. I gave him a brief resumé of what had happened, and received a nod of the head, and the shadow of a faint smile.

With these awkward episodes over, I was able to concentrate on the more pleasant tasks of Deputy Commandant, including the personal rapport I was able to build up with individual recruits, since I had to interview them on their arrival, then again halfway through their training and also at the end of it. Memories of one particular youth remain.

As I was travelling to work one morning, I saw a lonely young man standing with his suitcase, on the footpath. Stopping beside him, I asked if he was lost. 'Could you direct me to the RUC Depot?' he asked. I offered him a lift, and in he climbed. As usual I was saluted by the guards as we entered the Training Centre, and the young man was visibly taken aback by this. A few days later, when I interviewed him, we laughed about it. I also learned that he so enjoyed playing Gaelic football for his village team that he wanted to continue playing on leave weekends. While I made it clear that the police authorities could have no objection whatsoever, I also pointed out to him that objection might come from elsewhere. Several weeks later, when again being interviewed, he revealed that when the Gaelic committee discovered that he had become a police recruit, he was told that he was no longer welcome, nor indeed eligible to play under GAA rules.

Time and again since then, I have been made aware of the sacrifices in terms of family and social life that Catholic members of the RUC must make in order to fulfil their career ambitions. I strongly believe that these pressures operate as powerful deterrents to Catholic recruitment into the Force. Consequently, I often urged political parties, particularly individual members of the largest nationalist party, the Social Democratic and Labour Party (SDLP), and the hierarchy of the Catholic church to take a much more positive role in encouraging their members to join the RUC, thereby redressing the imbalance of its Protestant membership. Regrettably, such encouragement was seldom offered unreservedly.

Similarly, I quickly identified other changes needed in RUC training, the most important of which was the size and structure of the Training Centre itself. About the time of my arrival, land immediately outside the walled perimeter of the Centre became available for purchase. Much needed recreational and other training facilities could have been provided on the additional ground. Although I had the Commandant's support, the proposals were rejected out of hand. The owners of the land had no desire to provide it for police purposes, and yet they were the very same people who most vehemently resisted attempts to move police training out of County Fermanagh some years later.

I had also identified that the lack of adequate training courses for sergeants was a weakness within the Force. Consequently, early in 1968, I decided to structure a three-month course for them, loosely along the lines of the six-month Bramshill course, although more practically orientated. In this I had the enthusiastic approval and support of Tom Crozier, but unfortunately he was soon to retire. Beyond that, political events in Northern Ireland were becoming not only unpredictable, but increasingly volatile. It was not the time for such an innovative venture and, although I had almost finalised it for submission to RUC Headquarters, I deferred it. Events were never to allow me, while Deputy Commandant, to resurrect that venture.

Problems of a domestic nature were also troubling me. Although, for once in our lives, finding accommodation for Jean and the children was not a problem, I had some difficulty in settling them in Enniskillen. As Deputy Commandant, I was allocated 'The Firs', a most attractive and well-appointed house. It was situated outside the Training Centre, on the main road to Belleek and in a very desirable residential area. The rear garden extended approximately 200 yards or more to the River Erne, which links the Upper and Lower Loughs. The two lakes are approximately 300 square miles in area and are dotted with 180 islands. My lifelong love of messing about in the water made this an irresistible place to live! That said, Jean and I soon found ourselves with problems, once we took occupation. The basic one stemmed from the fact that our new home was more than twice the size of our previous one. Scarcely any fittings and furnishings from our previous homes were suitable for this one. Consequently, our small cash reserves were engulfed by a bank overdraft in preparing this, our tenth home in thirteen years of marriage.

More serious problems began to emerge. Enniskillen's Model Primary School was Barbara's fifth school in six years and with the qualifying examination in November, 1967, the disruption of yet another move was particularly severe for her. She had been working diligently in Cookstown, and achieving excellent results, but news of my transfer had unsettled her. Disappointment at losing her friends was evident in her school work and attitude. I, therefore, decided that for the last few weeks of her school term she should stay in Enniskillen with me and attend her new school to become accustomed to her teachers, different routines and, hopefully, make other friends. This actually worked well. Barbara passed her qualifying examination, and began the Girls' Collegiate School in Enniskillen with more enthusiasm than we ever dared hope.

Rodney, however, posed problems of a different sort. The move to Enniskillen proved a traumatic experience for him. He found difficulty in settling into his school, in finding friends and in sleeping at night, for fear of imaginary noises in the roof space. Often he wakened, terrified by his dreams. Not unnaturally he became morose, introverted and erratic in both his eating habits and his behaviour, with frequent outbursts of temper.

Our concern was such that Jean and I resolved to buy him a dog in an effort to give him companionship, and also a distraction. Seeing a newspaper advertisement for the sale of Airedale pups in Strabane, some fifty miles away, I immediately arranged to go there very early the next morning, a Sunday. Jean brought the children to the door as I arrived home, but of course they were totally unaware of my purchase. When I set the pup on the grass, it wandered about aimlessly. For a second or two Rodney was transfixed and then, with absolute delight, he began running towards it. Kim, as we called the pup, was just the tonic young Rodney needed. Never again did we acquire a dog with such therapeutic qualities! We still have the old photographs of Kim, who proved to be a great sailor, and joined our family outings on a recently acquired old clinker-built motorboat. Whenever possible, even during the winter months, we escaped to the lakes, and in particularly inclement weather we drove the car to other beautiful parts of the county. With the family and the additional commitment of becoming District Scout Commissioner in Fermanagh, I found myself busy both on and off duty.

After Tom Crozier retired on 13 March 1968, County Inspector David Corbett became Commandant. David had been my first DI as a probationer in Limavady District, and the Assistant Commissioner of Belfast while I was Head Constable at Hastings Street. As Commandant, David seldom involved himself in my activities, except for formal duties and responsibilities. Consequently, we enjoyed an excellent working relationship.

At this time, tensions had continued throughout the Protestant 'marching season', with disorderly behaviour at several of the focal points of Orange parades. The Unionist Party, under Captain Terence O'Neill, was increasingly seen to be in a state of disarray. Ian Paisley and his extremist supporters were able to exploit this conflict to their benefit, and simultaneously they were directing much of their time and energies towards arranging counter-demonstrations in the face of the growing number of parades organised by the Northern Ireland Civil Rights Association (NICRA). The Association has been best described, I think, in the book *Paisley* by Ed Moloney and Andy Pollak, as

> a coalition of Republicans, the Campaign for Social Justice, left-wing activists, the Communist Party and middle class Catholics. Initially, NICRA attempted to be broad based and moderate in its methods and demands. It even included a member of the Unionist Party on its executive.
>
> But eventually, NICRA, which at first was uneasy about mounting street protests and worried about a Protestant backlash, succumbed to Catholic pressure for action. (p. 154)

NICRA wanted, *inter alia*, the disbandment of the B Specials, one man one vote in local government elections and the fair allocation of housing, irrespective of religious belief.

I certainly sensed the uneasiness aroused within the community by the Civil Rights march from Coalisland to the Market Square, Dungannon on 24 August 1968. Since I had served in Coalisland, I took a particular interest in how the police handled the march and the loyalist opposition, encouraged mainly by Paisley's Ulster Protestant Volunteers. The latter were incensed by the fact that this nationalist parade was allowed by the police to enter the town square, something that had never before been permitted. Such was the threat of imminent violence that the local RUC rerouted the Civil Rights march. This, I felt, was regrettable because, if more police resources had been committed to duty in Dungannon, they could have ensured the safety of the march into the square, despite loyalist resistance. The RUC had never before been faced with such emerging social turmoil and, with the Stormont Government itself in internal turmoil, a proper lead was not given at this crucial time.

County Fermanagh experienced its share of Civil Rights marches, mostly, but not exclusively, at weekends. I occasionally volunteered to take control of the policing of them in Enniskillen, but by and large they passed off virtually without any serious confrontation. This, I maintain, resulted from doing the unexpected, by refusing to be provoked and, above all, by bringing a degree of humour to bear whenever possible.

One such incident still springs to mind. Civil Rights marchers held a sit-down protest in the main street of Enniskillen, after being halted by the police because of a large counter-demonstration by loyalists in the town centre. It was late afternoon on a cold, bleak winter's day. Complete stalemate prevailed between the police and the Civil Rights protesters, who vowed to remain until permitted to continue their march. As darkness gathered, I ordered that the RUC chuck wagons should be brought forward to the front lines of static police so that hot soup, sausage rolls, sandwiches, tea and coffee could be distributed. With this, the stalemate quickly ended! As the smell of the hot food wafted over the heads of the cold impatient protesters, their determination to continue sitting on the road wavered, and off they went, presumably for their own hot meals. The loyalist protesters quickly followed suit.

The effects of the Civil Rights activities, increasingly influenced by republican elements, and the stridency of the extreme loyalist response brought to the surface such bitterness and alienation between Catholics and Protestants in the Fermanagh area as I would never have believed possible. Sadly, this was mirrored in most other areas of Northern Ireland.

In retrospect, it was in the latter months of 1968 that it should have become apparent to RUC Command that the escalating pressures of parades and counter-parades were becoming more than could be effectively policed. With its strength still around 3,000 as set in 1922, the RUC was numerically inadequate for the violent challenges facing it. Isolated voices at senior operational Command were already expressing this view, but were ignored. As Sir Albert Kennedy had predicted in a letter to the Minister of Home Affairs at Stormont, in November 1968, 'the position to-day is fraught with more danger because . . . a number of people on what I may call the loyalist side are confused and are not making any distinction between the IRA and Civil Rights marchers and those belonging to similar organisations. This is resulting in opposition to peaceful marches, demonstrations and meetings of such a nature as could lead to armed conflict, with the IRA stepping in to take advantage of the situation . . . '

Later, I gleaned that the emerging differences between the Prime Minister, Terence O'Neill, and his Minister of Home Affairs, Bill Craig, adversely affected the RUC Command at Inspector General level. The public unrest necessarily required close communication between the Inspector General, his Deputy, Tony Peacocke, and the Minister of Home Affairs. It would have become apparent to members of the Unionist Government that Sir Albert and Mr Peacocke held strongly differing views as to the nature and policing of the Civil Rights marches. I believe that the conflict between the doves and hawks within the Unionist Cabinet encroached upon the realms of law and order to the extent that it affected Sir Albert's decision to retire, and also the subsequent appointment of Mr Peacocke. The latter had expressed the belief that the RUC could alone handle the growing unrest and should do so by firm means.

It was only in private conversations with Sir Albert many years later that I became aware of all this. From his remarks I suspect that he regretted his absence on leave in October, 1968, and that political pressures had influenced his premature retirement. Be that as it may, Sir Albert had arranged to be abroad at an Interpol Conference in Cairo and to avail himself of simultaneous leave from the end of September well into October, 1968. Before his departure, he was aware of the nature of an intended Civil Rights parade to be held on Saturday, 5 October in Derry City. It was planned to commence at Waterside railway station on the predominantly Protestant east bank of Derry and terminate in the Diamond, the heart of the old walled city and mecca of the Protestant Apprentice Boys of Derry. Consequently, the Apprentice Boys gave notice of their intention to hold an Annual Initiation Ceremony along the same route as the Civil Rights march and, by no mere coincidence, this was scheduled for 5 October. A less propitious march could scarcely be imagined, or engineered.

Sir Albert advised me afterwards that his instructions about policing the parade did not include the use of violence against the demonstrators. Although his insistence on taking leave during that most contentious parade may appear unusual, I understand that when asked to remain, he refused because of certain differences of opinion with the Stormont Government. It may have preferred him away, with Mr Peacocke in his place.

It was obvious that serious trouble lay ahead and I still recall the warnings sounded by various politicians in the preceding days. At a Labour Party conference on 2 October, Gerry Fitt, subsequently Lord Fitt, actually forecast civil unrest in Northern Ireland unless there were urgent political reforms, and warned that 'it might break out on Saturday at a Civil Rights march in Derry'.

The following day, Bill Craig announced that, on police advice, he had banned all processions and meetings in certain parts of Derry. Explaining this decision he said that 'The NICRA, despite its high sounding name, is essentially a republican nationalist organisation.' Quite contrary to usual practice, he went on, 'they proposed to move into an area which, by tradition, it had long been agreed they didn't move into . . . similarly it is agreed that there are areas into which loyalists don't go. The Civil Rights marchers will have plenty of room elsewhere. If they want to hold meetings it would be proper for them to have them in their own quarters.'

Not surprisingly, that same day members of the Labour Party in Derry issued a statement condemning 'this scandalous denial of freedom by the Minister of Home Affairs', adding that they 'intended to defy the ban' and that 'The citizens of Derry have a right to march through their own town [and] tomorrow the Labour Party will assert that right.'

With apprehension mounting about what would happen on Saturday, I remember being struck by the foreboding tone of the 'Viewpoint' column in the *Belfast Telegraph* for Friday, 4 October 1968. It commented that:

> Mr Craig's ban on the Londonderry Civil Rights march may have avoided the possibility of trouble in the streets, but it has also ensured that a protest that might have been of purely local interest has become the focus for wider discontent with the restrictionist nature of some aspects of Stormont Government . . . the Minister weakens his case when he dismisses the Civil Rights Movement simply as a 'Nationalist-Republican' front. The Unionist Government operates a system that differs from the norm in Britain, on franchise and housing allocation, and he is unfair to those who disagree with this system by labelling them in anti-British terms . . . In some ways, it is the movement's misfortune that it is so

closely associated with such strident personalities as Mr Gerry Fitt, who can often be accused of exploiting a situation for his own political ends, but that it is founded in sincerely-held grievance is undeniable.

On the Saturday itself, the Acting Inspector General, Mr Peacocke, directed County Inspector William Meharg to take control of the policing of the parade. Bill Meharg, a widely experienced police officer, had been in CID for a number of years rather than on operational duties. His clear direction from Tony Peacocke was to ensure that the Minister's ban was enforced and that the parade was to be kept firmly within the confines of his orders. To describe the RUC as 'ill-prepared' for the demonstration is no understatement. It was ill-prepared in its training, in its equipment and certainly in its understanding of the underlying social, religious and political issues involved.

On that fateful Saturday, I was actually off duty at home in Enniskillen. Aware of the tension within police Command over the march in Derry, I was extremely anxious about its outcome. I was dependent upon radio news reports during the day. I recall that same afternoon that David Corbett asked me to pilot a powerful speedboat for him the next day, because he wanted to go water-skiing, and so I suggested that we rendezvous at Tamlaght Bay about four o'clock on Sunday.

As news of the disturbances in Derry was broadcast that Saturday, my anxiety for future Civil Rights marches inevitably rose. Worse still was the television coverage of water cannons and baton charges being used to control the demonstrators. I remain convinced that if the army garrison within Northern Ireland, between 2,000 and 3,000 strong, had been called out in aid of the RUC in dealing with contentious parades and threatening disorder early in 1968, the events of the following twenty-five years might well have been entirely different. There was ample precedent for such support for the constabulary. Just as in 1966, when the RUC was not in adequate strength nor properly prepared or equipped for the Divis Street and Cromac Square riots, neither was it in 1968 or in 1969. RUC Command and the Stormont Government should have seen that. Never before had such political pressure been applied to the police in Northern Ireland, bringing its members virtually to their knees, before thousands of British soldiers were eventually sent into the North in August 1969. By then, it was already too late. It was from that time onwards that I evolved in my mind a firm and lasting commitment that the RUC should always be adequate for whatever task was demanded of it.

I had no premonition that the events of that day, Saturday, 5 October 1968, were the beginning of a series which would bring Northern Ireland and its grievously divided community into world focus for future decades. It seems incongruous now to recall how the Commandant and I, as Deputy Commandant, reacted in the aftermath of the violence in Derry. On Sunday, we and some neighbours met David Corbett at Tamlaght Bay as arranged. Along with Barbara, I set off in the speedboat with David behind on his skis. Had it not been for my lack of appreciation of the boat's power and speed, I would probably have been less rash in my handling of it then.

In the narrows of the river I drove the craft at speed while David, a competent skier, enjoyed himself. It was a quiet still autumn afternoon, when the placid water reflected the lines of golden rushes and many trees. I loathed the din of the boat's engine, and hated its wash for distorting the beautiful reflections on the water.

Suddenly, David fell off his skis on a sharp turn. With our great speed on the narrow, twisting river this was inevitable. As I slowed down and turned back to pick him up, the ski rope became tangled in the propeller. I had misjudged it in the turbulence of the water. The engine seized, and stopped instantly. David shouted precise instructions on how to restart it. Having advanced the throttle to full, I raised the engine from the water, released the rope from the propeller, and returned the engine to the water. 'Push the button to start,' David shouted, and as I did so, the engine exploded into life. David and I had, however, forgotten that the throttle was fully advanced. The massive thrust of the engine kicked the stern of the boat to the side, with the result that the gunnel struck me behind the knees, tossing me forcefully overboard. Barbara, who had been in the front passenger seat, was thrown like a rag doll over the back of the seat into the stern.

I remember my head hitting the soft muddy bottom of the river and swallowing mouthfuls of water before I surfaced, flapping the saturated sleeves of my woollen pullover, then stretched well beyond my hands. As I did so, I saw the speedboat turning in a sharp circle at frantic speed before it straightened up and shot up the river bank into a tree about ten yards from the edge. The deafening roar of the engine stopped abruptly. Everything was silent, except for the noise of my splashing. Barbara lay still and shocked in the bottom of the boat. I remember little else apart from being pulled ashore by David Corbett. Whether or not I would have made it alone, I shall never be sure.

Amazingly, I felt quite calm and David, although concerned about the damage to the boat, was remarkably contained. Having decided to cut across land to where my boat was moored, we set off only to see the eighteen-stone Derek Norton rowing my little aluminium, orange punt towards us. He had anticipated a problem when he heard the engine's roar cut out suddenly, and came searching for us. Derek's weight together with David's, Barbara's and mine in this little boat presented a strenuous row back to Tamlaght Bay. Suddenly, the police auxiliary boat appeared, crewed by Special Constables Grey and Coulter. Pulling alongside, Bill Grey said quietly to David Corbett, 'We are looking for your body, Sir.'

Apparently, an urgent message from RUC Headquarters had been received at Enniskillen Station, instructing County Inspector David Corbett to report immediately to Derry to assist Bill Meharg in controlling the serious rioting, which had continued from the previous evening. It was entirely fortuitous that they had arrived just as David and I reached Tamlaght Bay looking like drowned rats! Within the week, the first RUC member was murdered in the

'Troubles'; on 11 October 1969 Constable Victor Arbuckle was shot dead during loyalist rioting on the Shankill Road in Belfast. Loyalists were incensed by the recommendations of the Hunt Report, submitted to the Stormont Government on 3 October by the Advisory Committee on Police in Northern Ireland.[1]

Note
1 Cmnd. 535 (Belfast: HMSO 1969).

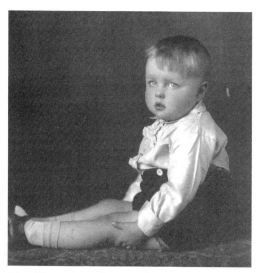

Myself in 1930 at the age of two.

At age nineteen in Belfast, during my short-lived career as a trainee accountant.

My father (centre) and mother in Donaghadee on holiday at the seaside with Mr Turkington, a family friend.

With my brother Robert (right) while on holidays from the RUC Depot in 1950.

As Deputy Commandant of the RUC Depot, Enniskillen, accompanying Bill Craig, Minister of Home Affairs, during a Passing-Out Parade in February 1968.

During the fiftieth anniversary of the RUC, June 1972, accompanying Lord Grey of Naunton, then Governor of Northern Ireland. This was the last Passing-Out Parade taken by the Governor before that office was abolished.

On holiday at Land's End in August 1973 with Rodney, after his illness, Barbara and Jean.

With Jean in 1976 on my appointment as Deputy Chief Constable.

After receiving my knighthood at Buckingham Palace in February 1982.

With Jean after being sworn in as the new Chief Constable of the RUC on 2 January 1980. On the right is my newly appointed Deputy Chief Constable, Michael McAtamney, with his wife, Patricia.

With two good friends: Dick Lawson in the operations room of HQ, RUC (above) and with Bob Richardson, Dick Lawson's successor as GOC (below).

Receiving, on behalf of the RUC, the Freedom of the City of Belfast from the Lord Mayor, Billy Bell. Deputy Chief Constable Harry Baillie is on the right.

Viewing an arms cache with Prime Minister Margaret Thatcher, her husband, Denis, and Tom King, Secretary of State for Northern Ireland.

8

PARALYSIS AMIDST PROMOTIONS

In mid-November 1969, a Directive was received from RUC Headquarters to say that David Corbett's dual role as County Inspector of Fermanagh and Commandant of the Training Centre would cease. With immediate effect, I was appointed the new Commandant. David, who broke the news to me as soon as he heard it, was obviously gravely disappointed. There had been no warning, but I had to cope with this unexpected responsibility.

Shortly after my appointment I called all Training Centre staff together and outlined the progress of change within the Force since October, which had brought with it the Hunt Report on the reorganisation of the RUC and the Ulster Special Constabulary. To help implement the Report's recommendations, Sir Arthur Young, formerly the Commissioner of the City of London Police, was appointed by the British Prime Minister, Harold Wilson, as Inspector General. The Hunt Report made radical suggestions at a time of increasing violence; its main recommendations included the transformation of the RUC into an unarmed police force, the disbandment of the B Specials and their replacement by the Ulster Defence Regiment (the UDR), under the control of the British army. Protestants generally viewed these changes with hostility, while Catholics welcomed them. Emphasising the need to retain discipline, morale and the high level of training, I said that if any of them did not feel willing to continue in this area of police work, or felt they could not accept the dramatic changes still to be faced, I would fully accept their application to move elsewhere. I received no such applications.

The pressures on me at that time of sudden change were enormous. It was only at weekends that I gained some respite from the constant demands of my work. Through all the changes, Jean carried on running our home quietly and efficiently. Barbara, in her third year at the grammar school, was getting on well and had made a number of friends. With our antiquated motorboat and an excellent canoe, she enjoyed the lakes to the full. As for Rodney, his passion was swimming. Although somewhat ponderous at athletics, he could more than hold his own with all comers in the swimming pool of Portora Royal School. He had a tendency towards tantrums and fierce tempers whenever thwarted or irritated. His headmaster drew my attention to Rodney's occasional outbursts in the classroom, and explained that his teachers were concerned about him.

Our local doctor, being unable to diagnose anything specific, arranged for

Rodney to be examined by specialists at the Royal Hospital for Sick Children in Belfast. They identified a minor problem with his foot insteps, which slightly affected his agility and balance, and also what was described as a 'quirk' of temperament for which they could not find a cause. They were sufficiently interested to see him periodically throughout 1969 and 1970, by which time Rodney's condition was giving us much anxiety.

Worries at home were matched by others at work. The herculean efforts during November and December 1969 by the training staff, led by the Head Constable Major, Mr Sam Hamilton, and Head Constable Bill McAllister, had dismantled the whole structure of training in order to reorientate it towards a recruit-training syllabus lasting twelve weeks. With what seemed to be unlimited finance, additional sleeping accommodation and classrooms were provided. I had set target dates for the fast recruitment of candidates by a new streamlined and centralised recruiting system. My targets had initially seemed impossible to my staff and Headquarters alike, but all were met. From November 1969, we were accepting squads of recruits, alternating between fifty and seventy-five, every seven weeks. And so by the end of 1970, we had accepted and trained 560 recruits, a net gain of 433.

This period also saw an influx of advisers from Britain, with several senior British police officers seconded to the RUC to assist in the implementation of the Hunt Report's recommendations. They included Commander Jack Remnant, who became a good friend, and Deputy Chief Constable Robert Boyes. Wilson Hill, who hailed from Northern Ireland and had served for a short time in the RUC in the late 1940s before transferring to the Kent Constabulary, also returned in an advisory capacity.

Bob Boyes's function was to carry out a survey of the establishment, organisation and structure of the RUC. During a chance meeting at Headquarters, Bob told me that serious consideration was being given to my appointment as the new Force Training Officer. I dismissed his casual remark, as the creation of that post was one of so many changes being mooted at the time. These included the restructuring of the existing operational Command units of the six counties and Belfast into sixteen divisions, with six in Belfast and ten throughout the remainder of Northern Ireland. The rank structure of the Force was also to be changed to match that of police forces in Great Britain.

In effect, Bob Boyes's report on the *Establishment and Redevelopment of the RUC*, presented on 7 January 1970, recommended the total transformation of the Force from its previous format. It had been based largely on the Royal Irish Constabulary model, but the organisation was now to become that of an English provincial police force. Clearly, the British Government was convinced that fundamental changes within the RUC, the complete removal of the B Specials, and the political and social reforms — introduced belatedly by the Unionist Government at Stormont in 1969 — would lead to positive political progress within Northern Ireland, as well as the cessation of violence on the streets. It was also hoped that the replacement of the B Specials by the Ulster

Defence Regiment, a locally recruited regiment of the British army, would introduce a fully professional auxiliary force that would be representative of the whole community. In 1970, these were steps into the unknown.

It was a very difficult time. Although the army had firmly assumed control throughout Northern Ireland on its arrival in August 1969, its members were by the end of the year showing signs of fatigue and stress. Violence in the streets was again escalating, with increasingly serious clashes between hostile elements from the Protestant and Catholic communities. Army riot 'snatch squads' were already operating. CS gas was being used in certain riot situations, but street violence kept spreading.

The RUC Reserve Force Platoons were being fully committed, often without an army presence, and demands on police manpower were unremitting. Army operational Command was becoming more dependent on the experience of RUC officers and on the local knowledge of the police, who regularly accompanied army patrols. By December 1969, twelve civilians, as well as the one police constable, had been killed on the streets.

Bob Boyes advocated an establishment of 4,490 members by 1975 in order to meet his sweeping changes of the structures within the RUC. His advice on training was that 'a comprehensive programme of training should be devised which will incorporate training periods throughout the whole career of a police officer and provide specialist and technical instruction where necessary'. He also recommended that there should be a Training Officer with a staff of forty. In mid-March 1970, my appointment as Training Officer was announced. Almost immediately, I was transferred to RUC Headquarters in Belfast, while Bobby Killen, a District Inspector since 1969, was appointed Commandant of the Training Centre.

On 1 June 1970, the Police Act (Northern Ireland) changed the rank structure unique to the RUC, so that former ranks such as Inspector General, County Inspector and Head Constable became Chief Constable, Chief Superintendent and Chief Inspector, respectively. By 16 June, I was, in effect, promoted from Third Class District Inspector to Chief Superintendent. I had no sense of achievement, only the recognition that my job as Training Officer would be demanding. That said, I felt strongly that I had a great opportunity of contributing in a meaningful way to the development of the Force.

At home in Enniskillen, I found Jean, Barbara and Rodney upset at the prospect of yet another move of house. Initially, Jean was very disappointed, but she came to the view that with both the community and the RUC in such a state of flux, there was no certainty anywhere, and therefore no point in refusing my new post. By this stage, our future had lost any semblance of constancy and stability.

I also detected an emerging anxiety within the Force that it would not survive beyond a year or two. With this knowledge, I took stock of my position as Training Officer. I quickly made three decisions, not revealed to anyone. First, I knew I had to be unorthodox and radical in my approach; normal police practices and procedures towards 'getting things done' would not work.

Secondly, I would do all within my power to prevent interference with the development of training from any external agencies or organisations of whatever nature. Thirdly, all training staff would be found from within the RUC itself because my experience over the previous three years had convinced me that the quality and potential within our own membership could not be surpassed.

Jack Remnant from the London Metropolitan Police was a significant help to me in achieving my aims in police training. He had a shrewd understanding of my motivation in maintaining the independence of the Force from political interference. Jack had a puckish sense of humour. When we visited Derry for the formal establishing of a unit of the part-time RUC Reserve in June 1970, we left the city in the mid-evening. As we had nothing further to do that evening, Jack suggested calling at the Naval Base on the east side of the city for some refreshments. Realising that only commissioned officers could enter the mess, Jack and I solemnly promoted our driver to the rank of superintendent so that he could accompany us. On leaving, we formally and ceremoniously reduced the driver back to the rank of constable!

Shortly after his return to London, Jack became ill and died within months of cancer. Nevertheless, Jean and his widow kept in contact for several years thereafter. His replacement to the RUC was also a Metropolitan Police Commander, called Stanley Coates. When his appointment was being discussed in the senior officers' lounge at RUC Headquarters, someone asked what Coates was like. 'He's the finished article,' someone said, 'You know . . . Remnant . . . Coates!' Stanley was in fact a quiet, unassuming man, who adapted easily to the RUC as Jack had done before him. Each of them quickly developed a sound understanding of the realities of policing a grievously divided community, and each made a positive contribution during his attachment.

The Hunt Report had also called for the creation of a Police Authority for Northern Ireland (PANI). This was done by the Police Act (NI) 1970, and the Authority held its first formal meeting on 29 June of that year. It was intended that PANI's membership 'should reflect the proportions of different groups in the community [and] . . . should be responsible . . . for the establishment and maintenance of an adequate and efficient police force . . .' .[1] Its first Chairman was Sir Ian Frazer, an eminent surgeon who had a decisive and penetrating mind. He exercised considerable influence and control over his Authority, which comprised a diverse group of individuals appointed from all walks of life. The Authority enjoyed a good working relationship with its first Chief Constables: Sir Arthur Young, until he retired in November 1970, and then Sir Graham Shillington, until his retirement in November 1973.

As Training Officer, I found that PANI had the will and ability to provide the resources so urgently needed for the development and expansion of the Force. This it did quickly, and with the minimum of bureaucracy, once it was persuaded of the need.

Much of my time had to be spent in persuasion, not only of the Police Authority but of my own superiors. One incident remains in my mind. The reduction in the length of our initial training course, and the escalating numbers of probationer constables, put impossible pressures on our small Driving School. Its primary job was to test the ability of all recruits to drive police vehicles. Those who did not meet the required standard had to complete a four-week basic driving course. I was satisfied that the existing Driving School complement needed to be doubled, with commensurate increases in training facilities and, most importantly, vehicles. This proposal met firm resistance at a meeting in RUC Headquarters on 3 October 1970, especially from Chief Superintendent Wilson Hill, who insisted that the basic two-week driving instruction he had received as a recruit in the 1940s was still perfectly adequate! His comment inadvertently swung the whole argument round. After little further discussion, my request was approved!

Those present at that meeting were not to know that on that particular day I was under extreme family pressure. We had yet again moved to Belfast, and had settled into a fairly small detached bungalow. After the disruption of the move, Jean grew fond of the area. Barbara was happy too, having obtained a place in Strathearn College, a nearby girls' grammar school. As Rodney was due to sit his qualifying eleven plus examination in November 1971, we had decided to enrol him in Cabin Hill school, the preparatory department of Campbell College, which was also near our home. While Barbara experienced no problems at all, the wider curriculum at Cabin Hill was stressful for Rodney. This was reflected in his obvious difficulties with homework, but Jean and I took a relaxed view, preferring him to go at his own pace without the pressures of parental expectations.

When he returned home on the afternoon of 30 September, he told us that in the swimming period that afternoon he had managed seventy-five lengths of the pool. He was obviously extremely fatigued. The following day, he collapsed in school and fell into unconsciousness. A brain scan at the Royal Victoria Hospital the next morning confirmed our worst fears. Rodney had suffered a severe attack of encephalitis, a very serious viral infection of the brain for which there was no known cure. We just had to wait while the infection took its course. The prognosis given us was that our son, still in a coma, could die within a forty-eight-hour period. If he survived beyond that time, there would be increasing, albeit slender, hope that he would pull through. Survival entailed the accompanying high risk of permanent mental and/or physical disability.

Needless to say, Jean was shattered. For her sake, I could not show my own distress. I simply told my immediate superior, Martin Williams, that I required a few days' leave to deal with an urgent family matter. Jean and I decided to confide in no one outside our immediate family circle and the very sympathetic rector of the church we had recently joined. My only concession to duty during the three or four days following Rodney's collapse was to attend that Headquarters meeting on the expansion of the Driving School on the 3rd.

Rodney's progress was painfully slow. Over the first two weeks, there was a gradual improvement until he regained consciousness, but with a temporary loss of speech and rationality. His limb co-ordination and his memory were almost non-existent. There were times when he became very aggressive, not only towards the nursing staff, but towards Jean and me. This would come to a frenzied climax in profanities, which we could not believe had been part of his vocabulary. I felt very frustrated at my inability to help him, but then hit upon an idea.

Pets were not allowed inside the hospital but, from his ward window three floors above ground level, I knew there was a clear view of the hospital's boundary fence and the field beyond. Kim, our dog, was accustomed to travelling in the car and so Jean went up to the ward, where she and a nurse held Rodney up at the window. Meanwhile, I lifted Kim over the fence and took him to the precise spot in the field where Rodney could see him from his window. His reaction was immediate. Recognising Kim, Rodney wept for joy. The dog then became the focal point of his garbled conversation.

Some weeks after Christmas, he was allowed home. His recovery continued as he began to walk, but with a limp, and he found mental stimulation in playing draughts. A pedal-car helped him to strengthen his wasted muscles, and by Easter 1971, Rodney was able to make a tentative return to school. The pupils at Cabin Hill and Campbell College showed remarkable sensitivity, compassion and concern. Boys from his class accompanied him everywhere within the school, even at the swimming pool as he laboriously regained some ability and confidence in the water.

With perseverance and further treatment, Rodney in time worked his way through his school years, and he gained a place at the University of Ulster at Coleraine, and subsequently graduated with an honours degree in Psychology and a teaching diploma in Education. He developed as a quiet, thoughtful young man, with such compassion for others less fortunate than himself that he chose to make a career in social work.

Before then, Jean had suffered much from depression during the worst months of Rodney's illness. With medical assistance, her own determination and with frequent weekends at a caravan we kept in Enniskillen, she eventually recovered her laughter, the spring in her step and renewed interest in her family.

One consequence of these family pressures was recognition by all of us that our house was inadequate, and so in the summer of 1971 we moved once again, to a detached, flat-roofed house on the King's Road in Belfast. However, the loyalist paramilitary Ulster Defence Association was formed three months later, and with many of its members living in a housing estate near us, we were eventually obliged to move — for the fourteenth time in our married life.

The year 1971 also brought with it an accelerating deterioration of law and order within Northern Ireland. Eleven police officers were killed, as were 48 soldiers and 115 civilians. Indictable crime increased by 24.1 per cent, with a reduction of 8.7 per cent in the detection rate. Those figures were almost entirely accounted for by the large increase in the numbers of murders, attempted murders, armed robberies and other crimes in which firearms or explosions were used. With their weapons and their guerrilla-style tactics, the advantage always lay with the terrorists unless sound intelligence was available. At that time, however, the only intelligence structure that existed, the RUC Special Branch, had broken down almost completely as its traditional parameters were changed out of all recognition by the upsurge in terrorism.

New recruits were flocking to join the IRA, but its failure to deal 'adequately' with loyalist mobs caused divisions within the organisation and disappointment amongst extreme republican elements. Consequently, the IRA split at the end of 1969, with the dissidents forming the Provisional IRA. By early 1971, the 'Official' IRA and the Provisionals were in conflict with each other. This resulted in an almost total void in the field of intelligence, which contributed significantly to the downward spiral into death, destruction and mob rule on the streets. Between 1969 and 1973, it also led to the greatest panic-inspired movement of population in any European country since the end of the Second World War. This movement affected both Protestant and Catholic communities, but the latter suffered more severely.

The lack of intelligence had a further, wholly disastrous consequence. Such was the escalation of terrorist activity and the breakdown of law and order that internment was introduced on 9 August 1971. This was the spark which ignited the flame of absolute resistance by extreme republicans in Northern Ireland. In response, equally extreme loyalists, already formed into vigilante groups, came together under the banner of the Ulster Defence Association.

None of this made it a propitious time to develop a training programme within a beleaguered police force. Although much had been achieved, the rising number of applicants for full-time duty and the growing strength of the part-time RUC Reserve put impossible pressures on our limited training facilities and existing accommodation. Since the end of 1970, I had been making repeated requests for an In-Force Training Centre to be established in Belfast. Finally, Headquarters lost patience with my constant demands. 'There's none available and none to be found,' I was told. 'Go and find it yourself!'

That same morning, I placed a constable beside a telephone, gave him a copy of the *Yellow Pages* telephone directory, and instructions to contact estate agents for information about office or other premises available for renting in Belfast. Within a few hours, he presented me with a list of possibilities. A quick reconnaissance by car allowed me an external inspection of the most suitable sites and, on the second or third attempt, produced the solution to my problem — a former rope factory!

The Belfast Ropeworks, at one time the biggest manufacturer of ropes in the world, had been forced by competition and new technology to close its administrative headquarters and its main factory on the Newtownards Road in East Belfast. These had occupied a large nineteenth-century building with eight spacious offices, high ceilings and a catering capacity for light meals. I made an immediate report to my superiors, and they in turn contacted the new Secretary of the Police Authority, Victor Morrison, who promptly came to the Ropeworks to meet me.

Having explained my urgent need for accommodation, I asked Victor for an instant decision. He agreed, but on the understanding that he would have to have it formally approved by the Police Authority and the lease negotiated. As Victor left, he added, 'But it's much too big. What will you do with the other half?' I knew very well what I would do with it! The accommodation became available within a few days, leased initially for five years 'to cater for short-term general force training requirements'. This new training centre became known as 'Connswater', because it was adjacent to the river of that name.

By the end of 1971, the training staff had increased to one Chief Superintendent, one Superintendent, three Chief Inspectors, seven Inspectors, fifty-two sergeants and twenty-three constables. Bill Wilson, of Cullingtree Road days, was amongst them and it was his idea that a Higher National Certificate in Police Studies be offered through the Ulster Polytechnic. Regarded as a 'stormy petrel' by some of my superiors because of my predisposition to challenge their decisions, I found myself moved out to the Connswater site, ostensibly to release my office at Headquarters for other use!

If 1971 had been a difficult year for the Force, none of us was prepared for the veritable blood-bath of 1972. The stage for what was to be the most horrendous year of the 'Troubles' was already set by 'Bloody Sunday', 30 January, when British soldiers shot thirteen civilians dead, following a Civil Rights Association march in the Bogside, the republican heartland of Derry. The following day, John Hume, who later became the leader of the SDLP, said that it was now 'a United Ireland or nothing'. The rhetoric and actions of several local politicians over the following weeks simply added fuel to the flames of violence.

The car bomb, devised by the Provisional IRA early in 1972, has left its legacy world-wide since then. In one day alone thirty bombs exploded in Northern Ireland. Two women, out shopping for a wedding dress, had their legs blown off, and the bride-to-be also lost an arm and an eye. The horror of that was soon swallowed up by repeated horrors. Mere statistics could never convey the impact on a community of the slaughter of 467 people in one year by indiscriminate bombings and shootings. The response of the Conservative Government at Westminster was to prorogue the Stormont Government on 24 March 1972 and impose direct rule, appointing Mr William Whitelaw as the first Secretary of State for Northern Ireland.

Throughout these desperate days, I held to the firm belief that, far from being impossible, finding a solution to the 'Irish problem' was inevitable, no matter how long it might take. Many colleagues, however, were convinced that civil war was unavoidable, that the RUC would be disbanded and that my efforts to develop training were a lost cause. The majority of police officers felt a loss of stability and of status within the community at that time. There was also concern within the Force about the erosion, even destruction, of the constitutional position of Northern Ireland within the United Kingdom. This concern was not often articulated, nor was it universal, but it was experienced by too many to be wholesome within a disciplined Force, and it worried me.

Even so, as 1972 marked the fiftieth anniversary of the RUC, formed on 1 June 1922, it was decided that a golden jubilee event should be held. I was summoned to the office of the Deputy Chief Constable, Mr Jamie Flanagan, and handed the plans for the event. I also was directed to assume responsibility for their implementation. An hour or so later, after I had time to study them, I requested to see him again urgently, because I considered the plans totally unrealistic and impractical; I told Jamie that if they were to be adhered to, then someone else would have to be given responsibility for implementing them. With admirable restraint, Jamie listened to my criticisms.

They must have been persuasive, because he made a snap decision. Tossing the rejected plans onto his desk, he declared, 'Very well, get on with it. Arrange it yourself!' I did. Despite the sudden absence through illness of the Chief Constable, then Sir Graham Shillington, and of the Secretary of State, through 'pressure of business', our jubilee was celebrated in style on 12 June, with a large Passing-Out Parade taken by the last Governor of Northern Ireland, Lord Grey of Naunton. The march past was expanded to include a total of some 176 personnel, drawn from all divisions and units within the RUC, the RUC Reserve, the recruits and the cadets; I was proud to command the parade.

The following day, I returned to Connswater and my normal duties. There, speculation was rife. Would Sir Graham survive the heart attack he had suffered and return to duty or would Jamie Flanagan, a Catholic, succeed him? With Jamie the Acting Chief Constable, conjecture also grew about who would act as Deputy. Without a separate Northern Ireland Government at Stormont, the political environment was extremely volatile and senior RUC appointments, therefore, took on unprecedented significance.

The next day, 14 June, Jamie Flanagan again summoned me to his office, where I learned that the full extent of Sir Graham's illness had not yet been established. Jamie felt it best not to rearrange his chief officers until the position was clarified. He then stunned me with the declaration that I was to become his 'executive assistant', an entirely new phenomenon, pending the return of Sir Graham.

And so it was that on 15 June 1972, Jamie Flanagan occupied the Chief Constable's office, while I occupied Jamie's. It was to be an interesting experience, giving me a much finer insight into the workings of ultimate Command in the RUC, the army, and especially the Northern Ireland Office, with its recently acquired status and Secretary of State. In the senior officers' coffee-room, I was the subject of much good-humoured banter and leg-pulling by my fellow officers. I was not fool enough, however, to fail to recognise the interpretations of my new role in the minds of my peers, most of whom were considerably senior in service to me.

The best way to proceed, I decided, was to apply myself fully to the endless administration attached to the Deputy's job. I bothered Jamie Flanagan as little as possible, although I would see him several times each day to receive his directions. Within two or three weeks, Sir Graham returned to duty and I happily resumed my Training Officer role. I had the private satisfaction of knowing that Jamie Flanagan would draw his breath on several occasions when he became aware of some of the decisions I had made in his name! But he had, and knew he had, my undivided and energetic loyalty.

It was during this period that my brother, Robert, died. I attended his funeral on behalf of our family and met his widow, a devout Christian, who impressed me with her obvious devotion to him. She was coloured, and reserved with a dignified bearing, and I felt happy for Robert that, in his final years, he had found contentment.

By a sad coincidence, my mother also died at this time, after a lingering illness in hospital. My father was not present at his wife's funeral, nor had he been at Robert's (or my wedding, for that matter). He himself died less than a year later in hospital, where I had visited him frequently. He left no estate and I retain only a pair of his cuff-links and his birth, marriage and death certificates. Within a short time, we were attending yet another family funeral, that of Jean's mother, Meg. With Roy Webb retired and alone, we kept him wholly integrated within our family circle, while at the same time respecting his desire for independence.

Despite the traumatic events of 1972, I was content with the progress made within the Force Training Branch that year. It had been protected from undue demands on the use of the training staff for operational duties. Most significantly, the Higher National Certificate in Police Studies commenced on schedule in September at the then Ulster Polytechnic. Twenty-one officers, from constable to superintendent rank, began a two-year programme, which included compulsory studies in police systems and procedure, organisational psychology and social services in the community.

While other training projects went ahead, my staff were already analysing our requirements for the future. A priority amongst these was a police college, and so the local authorities within Northern Ireland were invited by the Police Authority to advance proposals on where it might be sited. The majority responded enthusiastically, offering a total of fifty-seven possible locations. There was enthusiasm too within the Authority, especially amongst those members of the committee with specific responsibility for buildings; they worked extremely hard on the proposal.

My vision was of a numerically strong Force, which would be increasingly representative of our entire community, and of a central training college to serve recruits as well as offering in-service developmental and refresher training. If it were sited in reasonable proximity to our universities, we could also have access to their academic courses in areas like sociology, psychology and law. I envisaged a group of specialists, including RUC members, monitoring the changing needs for policing Northern Ireland, and thus providing essential information to police Command. This, in turn, could be translated into a continuous training programme.

Beyond that, I envisaged the construction of a unique course for police officers from Great Britain and elsewhere, who could learn from our experience of coping with a divided community, which public disorder and terrorism had polarised still further. This dream of the growth in RUC training stayed with me from the early 1970s, through the 1980s and into my retirement.

During the following fifteen years of service, I watched the RUC steadily develop its professional skills, but remain hampered by the lack of adequate buildings and the absence of a comprehensive training facility. It has been hinted to me that there is a hidden motive behind its absence. It has to do with the ultimate acceptability of the RUC itself, which is always subject to the pressures for constitutional and political change within the community it serves. I make this comment objectively, and with some awareness of the political diplomacies which have emerged, submerged and re-emerged over the past two decades. The RUC is regarded as part of Northern Ireland's problem, not its solution.

Since no proper college materialised, Connswater Training Centre remained in operation, not just for its initial lease of five years but for approximately fifteen years, before alternative accommodation and special facilities were provided. Like the historical hedge-schools of Ireland, which produced some outstanding results, RUC Training Branch, when pressed, had done the same!

As our work went on, so too did terrorist violence. Mercifully, the death rate dropped significantly to 250 in 1973, down from 467 in the previous year. A greater degree of stability was achieved, with the army and police working in closer harmony. An indirect consequence of the violence in the 1970s was a rapid rise in intimidation throughout Northern Ireland. With 3,656 reported cases in 1972, 3,096 in 1973 and 2,453 the following year, it became extremely difficult for the security forces to act as an effective deterrent and give some sense of security to the population.

When Sir Graham Shillington did retire in November 1973, he was succeeded by Jamie Flanagan without controversy. Jamie was both popular within the Force and respected by the law-abiding community, for whom his religion was of no consequence. It was, however, relevant to the Provisional IRA, which tried on several occasions to assassinate him, but thankfully without success. There were other changes at senior Command level, whereby Harry Baillie, a serving Assistant Chief Constable, was promoted on 1 November to Deputy Chief Constable, and a junior Commander of the Metropolitan Police, Kenneth Newman, became Senior Deputy Chief Constable. The necessity for two Deputies was recognised and accepted by the Police Authority. The fact that Kenneth Newman had served only one year in the rank of Commander, the lowest in the five-tiered chief officer structure of the Metropolitan Police, caused surprise to most senior RUC personnel. His appointment was generally regarded as a political one, made by the British Government with the endorsement of the Northern Ireland Police Authority and with the intention that Newman would succeed Jamie Flanagan as Chief Constable.

My own sense of security within my post as Training Officer was shaken early in 1974. Two vacancies arose at Assistant Chief Constable level as a result of an increase in the overall membership of the RUC. I decided that I would not apply, as I was content with my job, and my family had settled well into our new home. Unexpectedly, the Chief Constable telephoned and asked me quite tersely if I had applied. When I replied in the negative, he unleashed a blast in true Jamie style. The precise tirade evades me, but it was to the effect that I had a duty to the Force and to the community; if I had anything to offer, I should apply. He said much more, all of it quite aggressively, and then hung up. Over lunch at home, I told Jean about the conversation, and she found it most amusing. It was a decision for me, she said.

That afternoon, I had a guarded discussion with two senior members of my staff about impending changes within the administration of the Force. They made me recognise that, while a good deal had already been achieved, much more remained to be done, and if what I had been trying to do meant anything, then I had to take part in running the RUC to the extent that I was permitted. Consequently, I completed my application and despatched it that day to the Secretary of the Police Authority.

A day or so after the selection board meeting, it was announced that Frank Lagan, my District Inspector while I had been in Hastings Street, and I were to be promoted to the rank of Assistant Chief Constable with effect from 1 April 1974. I would assume responsibility for a new Personnel and Training Department, where my duties would specifically include recruiting procedures, training, manpower planning and forecasting, personnel appraisal and career planning, welfare and internal communication.

In that post, I related directly to Kenneth Newman. Energetically and enthusiastically, he contributed considerably to the creation of a new dynamism within the Force. It was, however, Chief Constable Jamie Flanagan's depth of experience at chief officer level, his intimate knowledge of the RUC and, above all, his subtle but sound political sense, which were the crucial influences during his two and a half years at the top. I believe his tenure of office would have been all the more valuable had he held it for another year.

On the political scene, 1974 also witnessed tremendous upheaval. William Whitelaw had been replaced as Secretary of State in December 1973 by Francis Pym. I recollect meeting Francis Pym once, when I accompanied Jamie to Stormont Castle to brief him. I have a clear recollection of the SOS reclining in a large upholstered chair, Jamie Flanagan on a settee and me on a nearby chair. I was intrigued by Jamie's intense attitude, and the way he leaned forward, determined to press home his point. There flashed into my mind an image of the Indian Raj, with Francis Pym as the British Governor and Jamie Flanagan in the character of a compliant prince. The thought did neither of them justice, but it remains with me whenever I think of Francis Pym as Secretary of State. His stay was abruptly ended within three months by the Westminster election on 28 February 1974. It resulted in a defeat for the Conservatives, and the creation of a minority Labour Government. Consequently, Pym was replaced by Mr Merlyn Rees, who took up his post on 5 March 1974.

Merlyn Rees was quite different in character from his predecessors. I attended a dinner party at Stormont Castle one evening, not long after I had been appointed Assistant Chief Constable. Possibly a dozen people were present. I found myself chatting to the SOS across the table and, afterwards, over coffee. Conversation was easy; I could talk spontaneously and frankly on matters relating to Northern Ireland and the RUC. I left Stormont that evening with a feeling that here was a sensitive man who cared.

Subsequently, it was Merlyn Rees who had to cope with mounting opposition to the power-sharing Executive and Northern Ireland Assembly, which had replaced the old Stormont Parliament. It was hoped that the sharing of power between the majority and minority political parties would win widespread community support for the Assembly. In the first Assembly elections, held on 28 June 1973, the Unionist Parties still had a clear majority, with fifty out of the seventy-eight seats. Nineteen seats were won by the Social Democratic and Labour Party, led then by Mr Gerry Fitt, while the moderate Alliance Party took eight, and the Northern Ireland Labour Party only one. The new power-sharing Executive had its first meeting on 31 December 1973, and the following day it officially commenced its duties. The real bugbear for the unionist population was not the Executive, but the proposal for a Council of All Ireland as envisaged in the Sunningdale Agreement of 1973 between the British and Irish Governments.

Resistance to the proposed Council of All Ireland forged a bond between reasonable, moderate unionists and the hard-core extremists. The consequences were immediate and drastic. The Ulster Workers' Council initiated a general strike throughout Northern Ireland. It was supported by Protestant paramilitary organisations, and co-ordinated in its activities by a committee of some eminent unionist politicians and paramilitary leaders.

Since that successful strike of May 1974, which did bring down the power-sharing Executive, I know that several politicians, especially Conservatives, have alleged that the Labour Government was not firm enough in dealing with it. I could not disagree more. In 1974, the army still had primary responsibility for public order, with the RUC playing a secondary role. Had there been primacy of the police with the army in tactical support, it might have been possible to suppress the strike in its first few days, but it would have been a close-run thing. The army, in any event, had no desire to be in direct confrontation with the loyalist population on the streets at that time. As Jamie Flanagan put it in one of his light-hearted moments, 'It wasn't a national strike; it was a national carnival. The bulk of the loyalists were behind it.' Light-hearted and amusing, yes — but with a level of shrewd reality to it also. In 1984, I was to say, somewhat arrogantly perhaps, 'If I had been Chief Constable in 1974 with the resources, training and ability of the RUC in 1984, and the army in support, that strike would have been lost by the UWC.' I believe this to be true! But in 1974, the RUC really did not have adequate resources to cope with disruption on such a scale.

After the collapse of the power-sharing Executive, and the chaos of the UWC strike, the political scene was in disarray and the people were fearful. Violence was widespread, extreme and varied. There were rumblings within the loyalist community, supported by their politicians, that some new 'force' was required to deal with terrorism. There were rumours that ex-members of the Ulster Special Constabulary had been performing patrols in rural areas, while members of Protestant paramilitary organisations were known to be acting as vigilantes. Meanwhile, the SDLP was calling for an acceptable police force for Catholic West Belfast.

On 24 July 1974, a statement on behalf of the Secretary of State was issued to the media encouraging the population to 'accept and support the police'. The statement revealed that Merlyn Rees had received a number of representations from various sources advocating the creation of a local Home Guard, or some form of what had been imprecisely called a 'Third Force'. It was suggested that this would be in addition to the RUC Reserve and to the Ulster Defence Regiment, and would 'enable the ordinary people of Ulster — some of whom are not able to join these forces — to play a greater part in the protection of the community'. Although consideration was being given to the creation of such a force, no conclusions had yet been reached, but if a way forward could be found, any new scheme of auxiliary police units would be under the overall control of the RUC. The statement also revealed a growing Government concern about the British army's leading role in Northern Ireland:

> If a way could be found, it would also enable the Army to make a planned, orderly and progressive reduction in its present commitments, and subsequently there would be no need for the Army to become involved again in a policing role.

Merlyn Rees thus highlighted the two main issues: the need for prompt action to avoid the threat of vigilante or other unlawful 'policing' groups operating on an *ad hoc* sectarian basis, and possibly influenced by paramilitaries; and the need to reduce the army's strength in Northern Ireland.

The Secretary of State then wrote to the Chief Constable, outlining his suggestions for a community-corps type of organisation to be loosely under the RUC's control, and capable of working without threats or obstruction from the IRA and other paramilitary groups. He asked that an RUC Working Party be formed to examine his proposals and produce a viable scheme — within two weeks! Additionally, he suggested that I chair it!

I was unaware of these proposals, until briefed by the Chief Constable at the end of July. He asked me to select a group of officers for my Working Party, and this I proceeded to do at once. We set to work on the afternoon of 2 August, with a deadline of Tuesday, 6 August to complete and deliver our report to Jamie Flanagan. The brainstorming began and ideas, queries, criticisms and every conceivable thought on the matter poured out of the group. These were recorded on flip-chart sheets which, when full, were taped to the walls until most of that space, in a generously proportioned office, was covered. It was a volatile and demanding, indeed exhausting, experience. Rank was ignored, except when I occasionally had to call for order! Our hours were from 9 a.m. until late evening, with short breaks for sustenance.

Our conclusions were radical in comparison to the Secretary of State's original suggestions. In essence, we rejected the notion of a Third Force, Home Guard or Local Service of whatever nature because, as we concluded, there was no possibility of any such organisation being acceptable to the whole community. Our alternative recommendations were set out in detail and well supported by rational analysis.

Having presented our findings to Jamie Flanagan, I was surprised at his immediate reaction. It was one of irritation, almost disbelief, that we had brushed aside the Secretary of State's suggestions and substituted our own. However, there was no time left for changes, as the report was required for the next day. After prolonged discussion between us, Jamie eventually endorsed our report fully and, in a carefully worded letter, commended it to the Secretary of State.

Throughout the rest of August, much debate ensued between the Northern Ireland Office, Army Headquarters, the Police Authority and the Chief Constable. The Authority and army Command had been aware of the Secretary of State's proposals and had advanced their own views, but our report dropped a sizeable spanner in the works!

The urgency of the situation was brought home to me on 1 September 1974, when the Catholic Ex-Servicemen's Association announced publicly that it was drawing up plans under which 10,000 members could be mobilised, with branches in all parishes throughout Northern Ireland. About the same time, the predominantly Protestant Ulster Special Constabulary denied that its members were unofficially mobilising, but said they would offer their services if called upon to do so by the British Government.

To counter the danger of such opposing vigilante groupings, the Secretary of State adopted the substance of our report. In so doing, he abandoned the idea of a Third Force, and instead he announced a policy involving 'the gradual extension of normal policing services into all areas of Northern Ireland . . . to harness the widely expressed desire of men and women in Northern Ireland to play a part in ensuring the security of their own areas'. This, he said, could be done within the existing framework of the police service.

As a result, new local police centres were established and staffed by members of the RUC Reserve, who worked in their own home areas and were linked into police stations and the emergency services. To fulfil its new duties the Reserve was expanded, with the number of male part-time constables raised from 2,000 to 4,000, and that of part-time female constables raised by 1,250. Full-time women Reserve constables were recruited for the first time, with an establishment of 400, while the number of full-time male Reservists was increased from 350 to 1,000. Similarly, the establishment of the RUC itself was expanded from 5,000 to 6,500, with the women's section going up to 750. The Ulster Defence Regiment was also strengthened, with a greater opportunity for members to be deployed regularly in their home areas.

Although this comprehensive initiative placed additional demands on my department, I regarded the rejection of Merlyn Rees's original concept of a voluntary citizens' police corps as a significant achievement, because it had been so fundamentally flawed. As it happened, 1975 was a particularly turbulent year, with 220 civilian deaths and the emergence of internal conflicts within loyalist and republican terrorist organisations. No citizens' force could, I believe, have survived in such a vicious environment.

Given the increasing demands of my office at that time, Jean and I decided to purchase a small wooden bungalow in Islandmagee, County Antrim, as a sort of retreat at weekends. It was not far from my old family home, and stood right beside the coastal path between Whitehead and Blackhead. Although it was without facilities of any kind, we loved the place. Well built from pitch-pine, it had withstood the battering of many storms in wintertime. With a reputed 'holy well' on the beach just beyond it, we enjoyed pure spring water except at high tide, when the well became submerged. With the addition of an outdoor chemical toilet, oil lamps, a gas cooker and a pot-bellied stove, we found it an ideal spot at weekends. There was ample scope for walking, boating and swimming in the sea. So keen were we on the area that I obtained planning permission for a proper block and brick bungalow to be built on the site for our retirement home.

Apart from our blissful weekends at Blackhead, the most pleasing event of 1975 was certainly being made an Officer of the British Empire in the Queen's Birthday Honours. Jean and I attended Buckingham Palace on 4 November for the investiture ceremony. For Jean, in particular, it was a momentous occasion. We were the first guests to enter the palace that day, and so she secured a prime viewing position. As the first Northern Ireland representative on the Prince's Trust, set up by Prince Charles, I had already visited the palace on several occasions for its meetings. Nevertheless, the honour of having my award bestowed upon me there, with Jean present, was indeed very special. My one regret was that Her Majesty spoke very quietly on my left side. With slight deafness in my left ear since 1952, when five Bren guns were fired in practice and simultaneously beside me, I just could not make out what she said. I often wonder what she thought of my failure to reply; all she received was a smile!

Other memories of 1975 are not at all happy. Some twenty-six police officers were murdered in the 1974/5 period. In most cases, the murder was followed by a formal police funeral headed by the RUC band. As I was responsible for the Personnel and Welfare Branch, I attended virtually every funeral. Since Sergeant Ovens's death in 1957, I was privately most distressed by that hopeless grief which descends upon those bereaved by terrorist murder, most frighteningly by a bomb, where families are left without identifiable remains to put in a coffin. The grief and pain caused by killing, whether by bomb or by bullet, were to have an increasingly profound effect on me in later years.

Meanwhile, with the family settled in the same house for the longest time in our twenty-one years of marriage, I thought we had found stability at last. Others had very different ideas. I was sounded out on whether I would be willing to attend the twelve-month developmental course at the Royal College for Defence Studies. It was primarily intended for officers from the armed forces of the UK and many other countries. For those who attended, it was virtually a guarantee of promotion to the highest echelons of their particular service. It was certainly a prestigious and rare posting for a police officer.

I declined spontaneously, as I had in fact done when the same proposal was put to me on an earlier occasion. I saw my career as having peaked at the rank I then held. I was not an officer of the type even then emerging, who pursued a planned course of academic and professional training, too often resulting in prolonged absences from the reality of policing. I continued to believe that, while academic and professional achievement undoubtedly made already reliable and capable people better, they made those less reliable more dangerous. Many quite mediocre individuals with academic ability and professional knowledge could conceal their inherent weaknesses behind a façade of rhetoric and borrowed ideas, until faced with the pressures of reality.

I had, therefore, no desire to be separated from my family by the formality and general nature of the Royal Defence College course. The fact that Assistant Chief Constable David Johnston was going to attend the course and that Harry Baillie, the second Deputy Chief Constable, had already been attached to the Metropolitan Police Force for seven months meant nothing at all to me, although others seemed impressed by these portents of their further advancement.

It was towards the end of September 1975 that I learned to my surprise and disappointment that Kenneth Newman had applied for the post of Chief Constable in the Northumbria Constabulary and had been short-listed for interview. A hard worker with an ordered mind, Ken had applied himself diligently to his role as Senior Deputy and had introduced a number of administrative improvements within the Force. When he called me to his office to discuss some routine matter, I expressed my regret that he would not be remaining with the RUC for a longer period. I gathered from him that there had been an 'understanding' when he was appointed Senior Deputy Chief Constable of the RUC, but since it had not been realised, his short-listing for the Northumbrian post had been the means of bringing matters to a head. The fact was that he had withdrawn his application that day!

Within twenty-four hours, the Police Authority announced that Chief Constable Sir Jamie Flanagan, 'who on his appointment had expressed the wish that his tenure of office should not extend beyond 1975', had agreed to the Authority's request to remain in office until the spring of 1976 to enable his successor to be appointed. The truth was that Sir Jamie had had no intention of resigning. Although the media were very critical of this totally unexpected development — as was the RUC — Jamie maintained a dignified silence throughout it all. I felt bitter and angry that he should have been forced from office in this manner, and made my views known at the time. Nevertheless, Merlyn Rees was later to write that, 'the allegation that I sacked Jamie was another piece of conspiratorial nonsense'.[2]

Be that as it may, the Police Authority advertised for the post of RUC Chief

Constable on 9 October 1975. A selection board was duly held, and Ken Newman was chosen to take over the position on 1 May 1976.

In the years ahead, and most particularly in 1980/81, when I faced difficult operational decisions, I used to seek guidance by asking myself, 'What would Jamie have done?' To my mind, he had over many years made an outstanding contribution to the RUC in so many ways that I, when personally confronted by tricky situations, never sought to emulate any other Chief Constable apart from him. On his last day in office, he left RUC Headquarters by helicopter, the pilot making the machine 'curtsy' to those waving farewell, before it rose swiftly to disappear.

Notes

1 Cmnd. 535, Hunt Report (Belfast: HMSO 1969), paragraph 183 (2) and (3).

2 Merlyn Rees, *Northern Ireland: A Personal Perspective* (London: Methuen 1985), p. 334.

9

KEEPING THE HOME FIRES BURNING

The outcome of the Ulster Workers' Council strike in 1974 appeared to have greatly influenced Secretary of State Merlyn Rees's thinking, in that it confirmed for him that:

> The police must lead, not follow, and [he] needed to reverse the decision taken in August 1969 to put the GOC in overall charge of security. We needed more policemen and less soldiers.[1]

This consideration obviously inspired Rees's House of Commons statement in January 1976, when he declared that plans for the maintenance of law and order in Northern Ireland would include how best to achieve 'the primacy of the police . . . and the progressive reduction of the army'.

A Ministerial Committee was immediately set up and prepared a programme of work for an official Working Party. Its mandate was broad, embracing such areas as the threat to law and order, the need for police acceptance, and the time-scale for change. John Bourn was appointed by the Secretary of State to chair the Working Party and keep the Ministerial Committee informed on its progress. During the latter part of 1975, I had met John, a civil servant from London, who was attached as an Assistant Secretary to the Northern Ireland Office at Stormont. I had found him to be a reserved, even shy, person who spoke little, but when he did, what he had to say was clear, concise and discerning. The army was represented on the Working Party by a Brigadier and the RUC by me.

During January, John Bourn asked me to consider the manner in which I saw the RUC developing to fulfil the role now advanced by the Secretary of State. This, of course, was a task right up my street, given the time and thought I had already spent on the question and my experience in chairing the earlier Working Party on the proposals for a 'Third Force'. I outlined my ideas to John, flew to London to elaborate upon them and then tidied them up in the light of our discussions and his sound advice.

The Working Party's report, *The Way Ahead*, followed, and on 2 July Merlyn Rees presented its recommendations to the Westminster Parliament. These accorded closely with my proposals to John Bourn in that there would be another significant increase in the strength of both the regular RUC and the full-time Reserve. There would also be an increase in the number of our special patrol groups, while other specialist investigation teams, such as murder and fraud investigation squads, would be introduced. The methods of collecting and collating information, including criminal intelligence, were also to become more sophisticated, centralised and co-ordinated.

Above all, *The Way Ahead* identified the future role of the army as one of support, with the RUC in the lead. At the final meeting of the Working Party, I told the Brigadier how satisfied I was. With evident emotion, he replied, 'And so you should be. You got everything you wanted!'

At this stage, Ken Newman had been several months in post as RUC Chief Constable. With Ken's promotion, the post of a Deputy Chief Constable had become vacant. On this occasion, I had no hesitation in applying. My experience since 1970 had given me confidence in myself. Nevertheless, I felt my chances of success were remote, especially since personal relations between Ken and me had cooled noticeably, possibly because of my anger at the manner of Sir Jamie Flanagan's departure.

From within the Force, there were five other candidates for the vacancy as Deputy. All were ACCs and all considerably senior to me in service and age. Frank Lagan, Martin Williams and David Johnston I knew particularly well. Of the other two, Charles Rodgers had been my immediate predecessor as Deputy Commandant in Enniskillen, while Sam Bradley was then sixty-two years of age.

After the selection board interview, Ken Newman called me into his office and told me that I had been successful. Harry Baillie was made Senior Deputy with responsibility for administrative and support services, while I was to have charge of operational matters. I was surprised, but believe I showed no sign of it, or indeed of any emotion at all. I remember that I ended the brief conversation by assuring Ken that, as his Deputy, I would give him my complete loyalty.

On the announcement of my promotion, Sam Bradley at once resigned, announcing that he was not prepared to take orders from a man who used to be his junior and who had been appointed over his head — apart from that, 'he had nothing against Mr Hermon personally'. His resignation caused a stir, but more heartening for me were the very many messages of congratulations. Amongst them came a letter from James Anthony O'Brien, my former District Inspector in Strabane, whom I held in such high regard. He wrote:

> I was as glad to hear of it as I would have been if I had earned it myself. In saying so I must hasten to add that it was not unexpected as I was convinced from when I first met you in Strabane that you had all the qualities for leadership. I felt somewhat guilty on being responsible for your going to Coalisland but at the time I felt you were the one person who could restore normality in that place. Later when I heard high praise of you from several persons there I was satisfied you were on the high road to success and gratifyingly heard of your various promotions. It remains now for you to be chief constable.

My immediate preoccupation was with the successful implementation of *The Way Ahead*. There were sensitivities within the Police Federation about the reversal of the roles of the RUC and the army. When the Federation was established during Sir Arthur Young's tenure as Inspector General, I believe it was his desire that the Federation be given sufficient independence to enable it to resist the types of influence and control exercised by his predecessors and Ministers of Home Affairs over the former RUC representative body. Consequently, the structure of the new Police Federation in Northern Ireland mirrored very closely that of its equivalents in England and Wales, and in Scotland. There was, however, one significant difference. Within the Federations for Scotland and England/Wales, the chief inspector and inspector ranks had their own separate representative structures, which facilitated a wider, more mature and better-informed decision-making process. The fact that such arrangements did not exist in Northern Ireland allowed the constable rank, in particular a small hard core of radical constables, to exercise undue influence in the Federation's Central Committee. This was especially true in respect of issues which could too easily be interpreted as reflecting extreme loyalist sympathies. It was no coincidence that these few held posts where they were seldom, if ever, exposed to the risks of operational duties. My dealings with this group tended to be brisk and, upon reflection, less than tactful.

Upon promotion, I had also inherited a very different function from that of liaising with the Federation; I assumed direct liaison with the Garda Síochána in the Republic. My opposite number was Mr Larry Wren, then a Garda Deputy Commissioner. Our meetings were on a monthly basis, with the venue alternating between Garda Headquarters at Phoenix Park in Dublin and RUC Headquarters in Belfast. Larry and I chaired the meetings jointly, with the border Divisional Commanders from the North and South in attendance. An unspoken, but shared, objective was the maintenance of good working relations between us. Substantial progress was made on many matters of mutual benefit, including more secure and improved cross-border telephone and radio communications.

That said, the real problem remained in that the RUC was under attack from republican terrorists, whose senior leaders and bulk of resources were located in the South of Ireland. The IRA did not wish to be in conflict with the Irish Government or the Gardaí. The role of the latter, within the Irish Constitution and in the service of their community, was not the same as that of the RUC in the North. Therefore, co-operation between the two Forces could not be unqualified, although this was not overtly acknowledged.

Despite our efforts, 1976 proved to be another very violent year, with twenty-three police officers murdered, as well as thirty-nine soldiers and sixty-four civilians. Street violence by both loyalist and republican extremists escalated at the slightest annoyance to either side. The Peace People, a movement created after the tragic deaths of three children knocked down by a terrorist vehicle fleeing from the army, gave cause for hope. The Parades for Peace throughout Northern Ireland, and especially in Belfast, gathered momentum for a time before fading away. I actually attended several of the marches informally, and was much impressed by the courage and enthusiasm of many participants, but was concerned that they seemed badly led and poorly organised.

As the violence continued, the army found it hard to come to terms with its new role. Merlyn Rees described it succinctly:

> while the army agreed in principle with police primacy, it was difficult for them to accept it in practice, particularly given the determination of the new Chief Constable, Ken Newman, that the police were to be the prime force. Personalities mattered.[2]

While Kenneth Newman dealt directly with the General Officer Commanding (GOC), then Lieutenant-General Sir David House, their directions on implementing the *Way Ahead* initiative were referred to the Commander Land Forces (CLF) at army level, and to me at RUC level. Happily, from our first meeting, the CLF, Major-General David Young, and I established a friendship and trust which were never to be shaken during those crucial months of change.

Much reorganisation and restructuring of the RUC commenced immediately. A surprising number of study groups sprang up and the feeling grew within the Force that there was a surfeit of paperwork and over-planning, a feeling I shared on occasions. I learned that the English tended towards verbosity, whereas the tradition of the RUC was to be terse in written reports. Nevertheless, an understanding developed between the army and the police at all levels of command. The army's excellence in operational staffing and expertise in administrative procedures had rubbed off on the RUC. Similarly, police operational experience in handling street disorder, parades and demonstrations was recognised by the army. Its commanders gave the lead to the RUC in maintaining peace on the streets, and became increasingly adept at providing close back-up and fast response when required.

Merlyn Rees was quite right of course when he wrote that 'Personalities mattered.' David Young left Northern Ireland early in 1977, and was replaced as CLF by Major-General Dick Trent. Initially, we related well, but we ran into problems after the arrival of a new GOC, Lieutenant-General Sir Timothy Creasey, on 1 November 1977.

Although pleasant and gracious socially, Tim Creasey was an aggressive soldier and had difficulty in accepting the army's role of support to the police. Whatever the reality of his and Ken Newman's professional relationship, it was perceived by third parties as strained. Certainly, I found my role more difficult and sensitive after Creasey's appointment.

As well as sorting out its relations with the army, the RUC was coming under fierce criticism and intense scrutiny for entirely different reasons. As the Chief Constable's Report for 1977 records, 'It is naturally a matter of concern that there are so many allegations of assault on persons in police custody or associated with arrests.' The number of complaints alleging assault during interview rose steadily from 180 in 1975 to 384 in 1976 and to a peak of 671 in 1977, before dropping back to 327 in 1978. The Force generally and Sir Kenneth Newman (by then knighted) came under increasing pressure to assuage these allegations.

Since I was operational Deputy, my involvement in this particular matter remained very limited indeed. It arose only once, when Sir Kenneth was unavailable to meet a deputation, which wished to express concern about the alleged abuse of republican prisoners from its locality. The members of the deputation were mostly from East Tyrone, particularly the Coalisland area, and I knew several of them. From the outset, therefore, conversation flowed easily. What impressed me was their obvious and sincere anxiety about two issues. First, there was a growing number of complaints from prisoners that they had been pressurised by the use of physical force whilst in custody. The measures employed were said to include arm-twisting, wrist-bending and blows to the body. Secondly, there was the problem of innocent young men being arrested for interrogation and detained over several days before release.

So reasonable was the delegation's approach that I assured it I would brief the Chief Constable fully, and ensure that every effort would be made to prevent improper behaviour by investigating officers. I also took seriously its three subsidiary grievances: that families were often not notified of a person's detention or were notified only after considerable delay; that the person's location in custody was frequently not disclosed; and that even when it was, a solicitor was not given access to the detainee on request.

Afterwards, I briefed the Chief Constable about the meeting, and he immediately saw to it that the group's criticisms were dealt with. The complaints about location and visits were quickly resolved. The question of access by a solicitor was more complicated, but a partial solution was arrived at, subject to the timing and circumstances of an investigation.

Nevertheless, complaints about alleged assaults on prisoners during police interrogation continued, as did a series of self-inflicted injuries by prisoners. Eventually, in 1978, the Secretary of State, by then Roy Mason, appointed a Committee of Inquiry into Police Interrogation Procedures in Northern Ireland. The Committee was chaired by His Honour Judge Bennett.

It was only by good fortune at this time that my family and I did not become early casualties of the Northern Ireland 'Troubles'. From the time we purchased our little wooden bungalow in Islandmagee, Jean, Barbara and Rodney would travel down most Friday evenings for the weekend. When possible, I joined them, sometimes staying overnight but always managing a few hours on Saturday or Sunday. I had purchased a small ten-foot sailing dinghy, a versatile craft which could be used with an outboard engine or easily rowed. Although it had been bought for Barbara and Rodney's benefit, I began to enjoy sailing it myself.

On the second weekend of March 1977, none of us was able to stay in the bungalow; various engagements kept us at home. On the Friday, a trial of twenty-eight members of the Ulster Volunteer Force had concluded in Belfast. It was, I believe, then one of the longest criminal trials in the history of British justice. Bitterly contested, the charges ranged from a series of murders to robberies and possession of weapons. Twenty-six of those charged were convicted and sentenced to a total of more than 700 years' imprisonment. Many of the crimes had been committed in South-East Antrim, and many of those convicted had resided in that general area, where our bungalow was located. After midnight, I received a telephone call to say that our wooden bungalow was burning furiously in a strong breeze. The fire brigade had arrived, but too late.

Forensic examination and local inquiries suggested that the fire had been malicious. Although no one was charged, it was established that the arson attack was in retaliation for the conviction and sentencing of the UVF members the previous day. Rumour had it that, because of my rank and my knowledge of the area, I had probably been instrumental in effecting the arrests of some of those found guilty. This, of course, was completely untrue. Nevertheless, a local resident, whom I had known as a boy, advised me that it might be best if I did not return to the area. In the years ahead, I had to be satisfied with quiet walks around Blackhead, the place I had loved so much as a child. Jean, however, never wished to return; her fear of the alternative outcome, if any of us had been in the bungalow, was too disturbing.

Even my time for walking had to be curtailed by May 1977, because extreme loyalists were organising yet another strike, modelled on that of 1974, which had brought down the power-sharing Executive. An aspect of their new scheme was the institution of the Ulster Service Corps, mostly comprising former members of the Ulster Special Constabulary. Ian Paisley and the newly formed Ulster Unionist Action Council promoted the strike as a protest against the alleged inadequacy of the British Government's security policy, and also as a demand for the return of devolved government with majority rule for Northern Ireland.

The RUC's existing Civil Emergency Plan was carefully studied in the light of information that the majority of law-abiding citizens were opposed to a strike. We also knew, however, that a substantial and reckless minority, supported by paramilitary organisations, would attempt to compensate for that lack of support by using all forms of coercion. We decided that the thrust of the RUC's policy would be towards maintaining normality, with a firm presence on the ground to enable people to travel to school, to work, and to conduct business more or less as usual.

The RUC Headquarters Emergency Committee met daily, every morning at 7.30 a.m. for the duration of the strike, which commenced at midnight on 2 May 1977. It was more of a close-run thing than the Government, or the media, were prepared to acknowledge. I became directly involved in two incidents either of which, if they had gone in favour of the strikers, would, in my opinion, have given them total victory.

The first incident related to the efforts of the strikers, led by Paisley, to persuade the work-force at Ballylumford power-station to strike *en masse*. Situated on the northern point of Islandmagee, this was Northern Ireland's biggest producer of electricity, and its closure would have brought misery to thousands in their homes and at work. Its shut-down in 1974 had, above all else, gained victory for the strikers on that occasion.

Until Friday, 6 May, most of the power-workers had been reporting for duty, but were doing so in an atmosphere of great unease. This was due to severe pressures from certain Protestant militants within the power-station while the workers were on duty, and subsequent intimidation by more extreme Protestants outside work. In response, I posted extra police patrols on the roads leading to the power-station, and also on the main routes used by its personnel travelling to and from their homes. All pickets were kept not less than 440 yards from its main gate.

About ten o'clock on Saturday morning, I was at my desk in RUC Headquarters, when I received an urgent phone call from a senior civil servant at the Northern Ireland Office. He told me that Ian Paisley and Ernest Baird, one of his chief supporters, had arrived at Ballylumford and that a walk-out by apprehensive power-workers seemed very likely. 'Was there anything I could do?' he asked anxiously.

I promised additional uniformed police at Ballylumford and in the areas where the workers lived, with special plain-clothes units assigned to patrol around their homes. I even undertook to go personally to the power-station to brief the police on the spot. Just as I was about to leave Headquarters, the same civil servant telephoned again. Apparently, the Ballylumford management had just advised him that a walk-out was imminent. 'Could I possibly do more?' he pleaded. I knew that the normal work-force at weekends was approximately 60, compared to about 450 during the week. I, therefore, gave an immediate assurance that, if the workers wished, each would have a police officer to accompany him home and while off duty. I arrived at Ballylumford in record time — I had an excellent driver!

Ian Paisley and his companion were sitting in their car twenty yards from the main gate, where the media described them as having 'kept vigil'. It was a miserable day with heavy rain. I told my driver to park our car across the road from Paisley's. I then lowered my car window so that he, and everyone else, would be aware of my presence. It was a stand-off situation. There was no exchange of words between us. A short time later, a group of power-workers emerged through the gate. Paisley walked over and spoke to them for a while, before returning to his car and driving away. Despite his efforts, work did continue at Ballylumford. After an hour or so, I returned to RUC Headquarters, where I hurriedly had to find the manpower to keep my promise of escorts for the sixty workers!

The location of every power-station worker's home was charted on a map, and each worker contacted and reassured that there would be a twenty-four-hour presence of mobile, uniformed or plain-clothes police officers in his area. In addition, individual contact was to be maintained, with lines of communication by telephone established so that any case of intimidation could be reported to the police and dealt with immediately. All of this seemed to work. My offer of 'a policeman each' was not taken up, nor was I asked for it again.

On the morning of Monday, 9 May, more than 50 per cent of the work-force reported for work, and the extra police deployment remained in position until the strike ended. There was no further threat of a stoppage at Ballylumford; but I encountered Ian Paisley again at the second incident, this time at Ballymena, a predominantly Protestant town in County Antrim.

It had been taken over by loyalists, who had blockaded and cordoned off the town centre by using lorries, tractors, trailers and slurry tankers. Businesses had been forced to close down, as supporters of the strike were patrolling the streets in considerable numbers. It was quickly agreed at RUC Headquarters that I should travel there and take command. This time, I was persuaded to go by army helicopter, in case the roads were blocked. We landed at the Ballymena Ulster Defence Regiment Depot, where my car and driver were already waiting! As I entered the police station in the town, which was at the very heart of Paisley's home territory and electoral base, I was booed and loudly jeered by strikers.

Inside the station, the Divisional Commander and Assistant Chief Constable David Johnston briefed me fully on the situation. I discovered that the barricades and vehicles were solidly pushed together across streets, and that police officers outside the cordoned area had been warned that any attempt by them to break the barricades would result in their being sprayed with slurry. Nothing, it seemed, could move into or out of the area, except for pedestrians with permission. Many of the strikers carried sticks. They were confident and determined.

My plan was simple. There would be a pincer movement by police officers, approaching the cordoned area from opposite directions. Each arm of the pincer movement would comprise a sizeable group of officers, commanded by a superintendent. The heavy grappling equipment would follow, to drag the vehicles used in the barricades over to the side of the road. Behind that there was to be a large contingent of police, commanded by an assistant chief constable and a chief superintendent. A further large reserve of police would be held in readiness to be committed, if required.

Planning for this operation went ahead at Ballymena Station throughout the evening and night, while I travelled to Headquarters in Belfast for a personal discussion with the Chief Constable. I voiced my grave concern that, if force were used by the police in Ballymena and violence erupted, a number of prominent Protestant towns throughout Northern Ireland would very probably, out of anger, follow Ballymena's example. I warned that such a concerted spread of violence would have catastrophic consequences for the containment of the strike, because neither the police nor the army would have sufficient resources to deal with it — it was taking twenty-four hours to assemble the equipment and manpower to deal with Ballymena alone! Nevertheless, Ken

Newman was adamant that what force was necessary would be used to break the barricades in Ballymena. Seemingly, I had no discretion in the matter.

I returned to Ballymena, where a final meeting with the strikers' committee, headed by Ian Paisley, was arranged for eight o'clock the next morning. At it, he repeated that the barricades would stay and any attempt on our part to remove them would result in violence. When I advised him that the police would clear the obstructions from the street using whatever force was necessary, and that those who resisted would be arrested and charged, I noticed a slight change in his expression, in his eyes especially. He asked me to confirm what I had said; I confirmed that those who resisted would be arrested. The meeting ended.

At 11.30 a.m., with the police contingents in position, I told the officers to move forward 200 yards. The two arms of my pincer movement approached opposite sides of the barricaded area. At one side, Paisley and eight supporters stood across the road. The group of police, in disciplined formation, stopped some yards from him; by good fortune, the other arm of the pincer was a little further back, about a minute away, and still advancing slowly. By radio, I directed the Superintendent heading the stationary group to move his men further forward. He did so, and requested Ian Paisley and his party to move aside or face arrest for obstructing the police. When Paisley refused, the Superintendent told his officers to remove them all. The situation was very tense, even in the control room, where I was observing the whole scene.

At that moment, Ian Paisley turned to those manning the barricades to tell them that he and the others were being arrested. The gist of his oration was that they would be martyrs, taken prisoner for their cause, and that thereby they had achieved their goal. With that, he ordered everyone to disperse peacefully and remove the barricades. He and his group were led to a police personnel carrier and driven away. Immediately, the tension eased. Within fifteen minutes, many of the vehicles had been removed, allowing the traffic to flow again. Tired demonstrators went home, and many scores of police officers relaxed.

Shortly afterwards, I gave instructions that those arrested should be released, the circumstances of the arrests reported, and any legal action processed by summons. Paisley was again free to pursue his politically motivated strike, but it was failing.

Nonetheless, the situation throughout Northern Ireland remained tense for several more days. During this period, intimidation of key workers was a very serious concern, 1,830 cases being reported. A particular threat was the intimidation of petrol-tanker drivers, the majority of whom continued to make deliveries until Thursday, 12 May. That morning, an attempt was made on the life of a tanker driver on the Donegall Road in Belfast. Normal deliveries ceased, while a committee of drivers negotiated with Don Concannon, a Minister of State at the Northern Ireland Office.

The following day, the Commander Land Forces and I became involved in these discussions, and in keeping the drivers good-humoured and relaxed, lest the talks should break down and they should join the ranks of the demonstrators. 'What about tea?' someone asked. I believe it was Don Concannon's idea that everybody should have 'fish suppers', and some staff were duly despatched to buy them. This was a deliberate attempt to filibuster: eating fish and chips kept the drivers there even longer. I still maintain that those fish suppers greatly helped to break the strike, prolonging the negotiations at Stormont, while the demonstrators outside lost their nerve or determination. The strike was finally called off on that Friday, 13 May.

Secretary of State Roy Mason, the police and the army had stood firm with no concessions made. Our detailed planning and determination had won the day, but during the eleven days of strike action, three people had been murdered in the violence emanating from it, and forty-five RUC officers injured. One hundred and twenty-four people were also charged with offences, ranging from murder and attempted murder to hijacking, intimidation and rioting. A clear signal — if one were needed — had gone out from the RUC that, even though its members were predominantly Protestant, it would not kowtow to Protestant extremists and their paramilitary allies.

Notes
1 Merlyn Rees, *Northern Ireland: A Personal Perspective* (London: Methuen 1985), p. 91.
2 *Op. cit.* p. 302.

10

CROSSING BRIDGES

Terrorist violence and street disorder continued apace throughout the summer of 1977, but at a much lower level than in previous years. Despite the violence, a royal visit was planned to celebrate the silver jubilee of Queen Elizabeth's accession to the throne. It was arranged that the Queen and Prince Philip would spend 10 and 11 August in Northern Ireland. Whoever recommended these dates must have been living in a different world! The anniversary of internment is 9 August, and 12 August is the annual date for the Apprentice Boys traditionally to march through Derry. Apart from the week of the Twelfth of July, it would have been difficult to think of another time in the year when both republican and loyalist emotions would be running so high, or when major precautions — involving around 30,000 security force members — would be needed. The particular week was to be the most dramatic and stressful of my period as Deputy Chief Constable!

By virtue of my post, I had operational responsibility for the royal visit and, therefore, more than a little anxiety about it! Mercifully, it passed off without any serious terrorist incident. The one minor bomb explosion, on the periphery of the university campus at Coleraine, did not injure anyone, nor did it cause much damage. My relief can only be imagined as I watched the Queen and her party leave Portrush harbour and board the royal yacht, on the evening of 11 August.

The next morning, I travelled to Derry to take command of the policing arrangements for the Apprentice Boys' parade. Delicate negotiation was needed here, not only with the parade organisers but with the Chief Constable himself. For 1977, it had been decided at security or political level that members of the Apprentice Boys would be prohibited from marching from the predominantly Protestant east side of the city across the Craigavon Bridge, into the old walled part of Derry City at the west side. I was deeply worried about this decision, as was the Divisional Commander and his officers, considering it a sure recipe for disaster. Chief Constable Ken Newman had given me a firm direction: the parade was not to cross the bridge and I was expected to stop it. The organisers of the march refused at first to meet me, apparently because my arrival from RUC Headquarters to take command had aroused grave suspicions.

I had detailed briefings from the local police, upon whose knowledge, professionalism and sensitivity I was fully dependent. Alone, in the privacy of the Divisional Commander's office, I telephoned Ken Newman. I was certain the ban on crossing the bridge could not be enforced without provoking violence so extreme that the police would be unable to contain it; almost certainly there would have been many injured, even killed. Ken was, I believe, with the General Officer Commanding and the Secretary of State, when I phoned. After putting, as forcefully as I could, my arguments against the ban, I was asked to 'hold on'. I have no doubt that during the next few minutes, hasty discussions took place. He then came back on the line to give me authority to 'act within my own discretion'.

I immediately seized the opportunity to avoid bedlam, working quickly in the remaining time available. I again discussed the options with the Divisional Commander and his officers, and we agreed a compromise solution, by which the Apprentice Boys would make a number of concessions about the route to be followed that day, and in the future; with these concessions, they would be permitted to cross the bridge. I again asked the parade's organisers to meet me, and this time they did. I managed to secure their agreement to observe the specific directives about the route and conduct of the parade. I detected a genuine sense of relief from them, as they readily agreed to the terms. With that, the parade went ahead without any incident of consequence. Late in the afternoon, the GOC, Sir David House, and the Commander Land Forces, Major-General Dick Trent, flew into the city by helicopter. 'I don't know how you did it and it was never intended, but it worked,' was Sir David's opening remark to me!

By 14 August, I was glad to depart on annual leave. As the two children had decided to holiday with friends, only Jean was with me. Our destination was Scotland for three weeks. We were both tired and Jean's year until then had been difficult, and had not been helped by a recent anonymous phone call.

One Saturday morning, I was in my office at Headquarters when my opposite number in the army, Major-General Trent, telephoned me. Something I had done or said had upset him; I believe it had to do with a public comment attributed to me. Wishing to avoid confrontation, I listened calmly to his tirade. The only interruption came when my direct-line telephone rang. It was Jean, in tears and very upset. She managed to explain that she had just received an obscene and threatening call from a loyalist paramilitary group. I had to choose between two very upset people, one on each phone. I made the wrong decision. I decided to tell Jean I would ring her back immediately, because I had another important call, and hung up. Without being offensive, I quickly terminated my conversation with the CLF, and rang home at once. There was no reply. I dashed to the house, but Jean had already gone.

It was two hours before she returned, during which time I tried in vain to locate her. She was more composed, but clearly shaken and also angry at my response to her call. She had been driving aimlessly around for more than an hour before stopping, rationalising her position and returning home. Thereafter, it was arranged that passing police patrols would pay attention to our house. Subsequently, however, I was advised that we should move. The area was no longer considered suitable, and my profile as operational Deputy Chief Constable made it dangerous for my family to remain there. We began the chore of looking for yet another house, in another area, which Special Branch would approve.

Before returning from our holiday in Scotland, we visited the Princess Margaret Rose Hospital in Edinburgh, where we arranged for Rodney to be admitted in July or August 1978 for surgery to his left hand to enable him to use it more effectively. By then, eight years into his illness, it was to be the final step in our efforts to restore him as far as possible to physical normality. I believe it was during those years and through our efforts that Rodney, Jean and I subconsciously developed a particularly close affinity, which was to be a special source of strength throughout the years ahead.

Immediately following my return from leave, Ken Newman told me that the GOC had suggested that the Commander Land Forces and I should give individual presentations on how the RUC and army saw their respective roles within the policy of police primacy. The presentation had been scheduled for the following Tuesday. This was Thursday. The next day, a friendly source within Army Headquarters advised me that I was being 'set up'. Aware of my period of leave, the army had apparently decided on the presentation and had been busy with its preparation for several weeks. I suspected that army Command at very senior level, presumably piqued at my implementation of police primacy, had determined to make me draw in my horns.

I did not advise Ken Newman or anyone else of this inside information; to have done so would not have helped police/army relations one jot. My solution was simple. That weekend I read myself in about events which had occurred while I had been away on leave, but on the Monday I told Ken that a weekend's preparation was inadequate to do justice to my presentation. I, therefore, suggested that Major-General Trent's presentation should continue as arranged, with my own postponed for two weeks. In this way I had the army's, or rather the GOC's, views on the policy plus two weeks to prepare my response. To my surprise, this proposal was accepted, and a fortnight later I delivered my presentation. At the end of it, the GOC rose and abruptly suggested to Ken that they adjourn to his office. Afterwards, I was told that the GOC thought I had sounded like Moses delivering the Ten Commandments!

It was perhaps no coincidence that shortly after this a Working Group was established to examine what steps had been taken towards implementing the policies laid down by the Bourn Report. The findings of the Group were very positive on the progress made by the RUC in all aspects of operational policing, including community relations and public support. The army's acceptance of change was also favourably commented on, subject to the need for a clearer understanding on its part of its 'support role' in aid of the police. However, the harmful effects on the RUC of the continuing accusations of brutality towards suspected terrorists in police custody were noted as a grave counterweight to the RUC's otherwise positive achievements.

Just about this time, in early 1978, I was informed that Ken Newman would shortly be leaving the RUC for a post in England. The information came not from Ken, but from a senior civil servant at the Northern Ireland Office. This person also asked me informally whether I would accept an attachment to the Metropolitan Police for twelve months, as my refusal to attend the Royal Defence College left me unqualified to be considered for the post of Chief Constable, when it arose. Fairly bemused by all of this, and wondering about the integrity of the Police Authority's role in appointing Chief Constables, I made no direct reply to his question.

Ken Newman did indeed subsequently announce that, with my agreement, he would seek Police Authority approval to have me attached to New Scotland Yard for a year, from 1 January 1979. This attachment would be part of a programme to improve the quality of senior management within the RUC. After an initial doubt, I decided to accept the proposal. With that decision, I was later to recognise, I had stepped into a new world of diplomacy and the 'establishment' politics which governed Northern Ireland.

Jean was very taken aback, her response confused and less than positive. I thereupon determined that if I went to London, she would come too. Belle, who had by now moved in with us, would be at home if Barbara and Rodney needed help. I was convinced that the year in England would benefit both Jean and me.

My secondment caused much debate and conjecture within the RUC and the media. By December, it was agreed that Assistant Chief Constable David Johnston would act as Deputy Chief Constable in my absence. Immediately after Christmas, I travelled to London alone and moved into a furnished house off Queensway, Bayswater Road. It was owned by a Brigadier, who was on an overseas tour of duty. I took up residence there on 2 January 1979. The next morning, I reported to New Scotland Yard to begin a completely new policing experience.

I was delighted to meet Maurice Taylor again there: as sergeants, we had attended Bramshill Police College together, in 1963. He had been given the task of preparing an outline of my programme, which required me to study the departments, branches and specialist units within the Metropolitan Police. He also briefed me generally on the Force, its history, evolution and present organisational structure.

I found the routine within the Metropolitan Police totally at variance with my previous experience within the RUC; the dynamism, the urgency and the unceasing operational pressures were missing in London. I soon realised that the conflict within Northern Ireland was light years away from the constancy pertaining in London. The RUC was seen as different, separate almost, from the police service in Great Britain, although we were respected for the hazards with which we had to cope. There is no question in my mind that I did benefit substantially from my twelve months with the Metropolitan Police, and even more so from my other attachments during that period — to the Home Office, the Ministry of Defence and the intelligence services. Through them, I established a number of contacts, which proved mutually beneficial after my return to Northern Ireland.

My assignment to the Metropolitan Police extended to include Imperial Chemical Industries (ICI), where I was briefed on management systems, career development programmes, executive management and decision-making processes at the highest level. To my mind ICI was much better than the Metropolitan Police in these areas. My several requests to study the policy-making processes at the highest level within the Force were side-stepped. I could see no co-ordinated management at commissioner, deputy commissioner or assistant commissioner level. I was reminded of a light-hearted, but perceptive, comment made by Ken Newman during his first years with the RUC that 'A monkey could run the Metropolitan Police.' It was so large, so institutionalised and so ponderous that no Commissioner, in the time available to him, could change it to any significant degree.

While somewhat disillusioned by senior management structures within the Met, I was most impressed by 'the bobby on the beat' and his immediate superiors, who seemed to retain their humour and sense of perspective.

One particular incident stands out in my mind when I recall arriving in London during the so-called 'winter of discontent', which eventually cost the Labour Government the general election in May 1979, with the Conservatives winning under Margaret Thatcher. On account of the strike by the National Union of Public Employees, litter and rubbish were piled high in the streets. Union members had travelled from all over England and Wales to assemble, 35,000 strong, in Hyde Park before marching in protest to Westminster. I happened to be standing beside a police constable outside the underground public conveniences at Hyde Park, when a number of demonstrators descended to use the toilets. Exasperated to find them locked, they complained bitterly to the young constable, who nonchalantly replied, 'They're on strike today'!

This humour was typical of those with whom I worked most closely at the Met. I had acquired the part-time assistance of a sergeant and a constable, who guided me through the culture of the Metropolitan Police, its command and its problems. Although highly intelligent and capable of holding higher rank, they were either content with their lot or the system had not picked them out. Their unsolicited personal loyalty to me bordered on protectiveness, and I remain indebted to them for the depth of their friendship. After considerable difficulty and a little delay, I managed to acquire a small office in New Scotland Yard, where I could have a desk and telephone. I was close to the Yard's library, where I did considerable research into many facets of policing.

By 14 January, Jean was with me in London, far away from the social demands associated at home with my rank. Our evenings and weekends were free, with few social involvements. Jean displayed a remarkable competence and confidence at driving through London. From early spring, she frequently collected me at New Scotland Yard and we would drive to one of the many parks or historical attractions in and around the capital. Weekends were spent walking or driving as two free spirits. For the sheer sense of freedom that we both enjoyed so much in London, 1979 remained a notable year in our rather sheltered lives.

One evening, we suddenly decided to go to the theatre. Studying the London evening newspaper, I made several phone calls before managing to obtain two seats at a theatre in Rosemary Avenue for a musical called *Oh! Calcutta!* I ignored the diminutive small print in the advertisement, which stated 'The nudity is stunning,' putting it down to exaggerated advertising. We arrived early at the theatre. It was a cold, damp night, and so I was not surprised to see several gentlemen in overcoats with the collars turned up, and with their caps or hats well down over their eyes.

Jean and I were totally unprepared for what happened next. The nudity was indeed stunning! We looked at each other and at the reaction of some of the old, and not so old, men in the front rows of the stalls. To ease our discomfiture, we laughed loudly, and sat on. As the dancing and music turned out to be most impressive, we swallowed our embarrassment, and really enjoyed the show, apart from the gratuitously vulgar skits between scenes.

Other occasions were equally memorable, like our chance visit to the impressive Methodist Central Hall. The main doors were open as we were passing, and so I suggested to Jean that we go in. The foyer and stairways were empty. Unexpectedly, a deep male voice from behind us offered assistance, and we turned to face a strongly built black man, dressed in formal evening wear. So warm and sincere was his invitation to the concert that we accepted, and were escorted into the hall. It was filled to capacity and I could not see any white faces. It was so warm inside that most of the women seemed to be using their programmes as fans.

We stood, and later sat just inside the door, intrigued by the variety of sights and sounds — Bible readings, instrumental music, choirs and soloists. A gentle murmur of whispered conversation and the patter of children's feet running in the aisles permeated the entire evening's proceedings. We later discovered that it was a charity concert to raise money for Prisoners' Aid. As Jean and I walked home, impressed by what we had seen and heard, I reflected how much it would have benefited the police service in London to have experienced that evening.

During this period, I had the luxury of time and the right environment to allow me to relax, read widely and converse with all sorts of people on the broader and deeper aspects of policing. I made short visits to provincial police forces, such as those of Surrey, West Midlands, Devon and Cornwall, and also to Greater Manchester, where I first met James Anderton, then Chief Constable. In the years that followed, we met more often, and I came to understand and greatly like Jim and his wife, Joan.

At the Devon and Cornwall Police Headquarters in Exeter, I met John Alderson, the Chief Constable. As he had just received the final proofs of his book, we had several lengthy and animated discussions about his philosophy of policing. In my opinion, John had overlooked a fundamental reality of policing everywhere: that there would be circumstances where it would be necessary to use a degree of force, including recourse to firearms — whether to deal with a mad bull, a dangerous wild animal, a hostage/kidnap situation or armed criminals. I insisted that the community had to be protected, and that it expected the police to have the capability to perform this role. To drive home my point, I recall saying, 'If the public wants bacon for breakfast, someone has to cut the pig's throat.' It was a trenchant remark, which I repeated elsewhere when some journalists happened to be present, and thereafter it, and I, have been often misquoted.

We were not, however, allowed to forget the continuing conflict within Northern Ireland during our London year. Early on, I received a phone call from Chief Inspector Stanley Hanna of the RUC. He explained that he had been offered promotion to superintendent rank, and would take command of the Bessbrook area. This included the notoriously dangerous Crossmaglen and other border stations. He asked me for my advice. Having reminded him of his contribution to the Force to date, I assured him that I was convinced he still had much to contribute. A transfer on promotion to Bessbrook would, I said, be of limited duration and he could expect to be moved to a less dangerous area after a period of about two years. My advice clearly leaned towards his accepting the offer of promotion.

Some months later, RUC Headquarters telephoned me in London around midnight on 3/4 June. Superintendent Stanley Hanna and a constable had been murdered by an IRA bomb. It had been buried at the side of a narrow road close to the border, and detonated by remote control. Both officers had died instantly. Jean and I were deeply shocked. The next morning, as I walked to New Scotland Yard through Green Park, the full impact of Stanley's death struck home. I had pangs of conscience over the advice I had given him and could not come to terms with it. I retain a sense of loss and regret.

Some time after those murders, I was invited to a reception at the Ulster Office in London, where I first met Humphrey Atkins, appointed Secretary of State for Northern Ireland to replace Roy Mason after the Conservatives' general election win in May. We talked together for a short period, but it was a social occasion and I had no awareness of being assessed. I took an immediate liking to the man; he seemed rather different from what I had come to expect of politicians.

Ken Newman's retirement as Chief Constable of the RUC was announced, I believe, about the end of August, or early September, 1979. Without any reservations whatsoever, I applied to replace him as head of the RUC. My experience as Assistant Chief Constable, but most particularly as Deputy, and my perception of the manner of Jamie Flanagan's departure had changed me considerably. So too had my attachment to New Scotland Yard. I had become more pragmatic in my approach to policing and also rather cynical about the motivation, and at times the integrity, of certain politicians. By this stage, I had also the confidence to believe that I had still more to contribute to the RUC and the community of Northern Ireland.

The meeting of the selection board for the new Chief Constable was arranged for Friday, 28 September. We travelled to Belfast on Thursday evening, collecting Maurice Buck *en route*. I knew him well as Deputy Chief

Constable of the West Midlands Police Force. He had also applied for the top RUC post, as had Harry Baillie. I left Maurice at his hotel and arranged to collect him the following morning and bring him to meet the Police Authority for interview. Our attitude of 'letting the best man win' allowed us to be relaxed in each other's company. I had — and have — no idea as to Harry Baillie's attitude, but it would have been completely natural for him to be enthusiastic, even anxious, for the post. I was junior to him in service, and had been his subordinate in command on several occasions.

I remember nothing of my interview, except that I dealt with the questions frankly, expressing firm views on all. Afterwards, I took Maurice out to lunch before a brief visit to RUC Headquarters, where he visited our Intelligence Units, and later he left for England.

On Sunday, a senior member of the Northern Ireland Office staff in Belfast, whom I knew well, came to our home for lunch — an engagement which had long been arranged. He told me that during my absence in London, serious problems had arisen over the army's attitude to the 'Way Ahead' policy, and outlined a number of differences between the RUC and army Command. As a result, the Prime Minister had in August 1979 appointed Sir Maurice Oldfield, formerly head of MI5, as Security Co-ordinator in Northern Ireland. My friend also explained the intended role of the Co-ordinator and the extent of his authority *vis-à-vis* the Chief Constable and the General Officer Commanding. I was advised that an RUC Assistant Chief Constable and an army Brigadier would be appointed as his Deputies. As for the vacant post of Chief Constable, it was mentioned only to confirm that the person selected would have to be approved by the full Police Authority and by the Secretary of State.

By Monday morning, 1 October, I was rather tense. I had heard nothing . . . no words whispered in confidence about who would succeed Ken Newman. Whatever the decision, it would have a significant effect on my future role. I immersed myself in strenuous gardening all day, taking a series of phone calls from RUC Headquarters and friends. It was 5 p.m. before Sir Myles Humphreys, Chairman of the Police Authority, broke the news that I had been selected for the post. Apparently, it had been the unanimous decision of the Authority. He then asked me to remain in Northern Ireland for the time being.

Strangely enough, the certainty of my promotion to Chief Constable disorientated me somewhat. Gone was my earlier self-confidence. I said a quiet prayer that evening for the strength, compassion and wisdom to fulfil my new role. Praying became something I would do alone many times in the years ahead, praying for strength to sustain me when in doubt over my decisions and actions.

On Tuesday, I called by arrangement on the Deputy Under Secretary, Jim Hannigan, at the Northern Ireland Office, and immediately afterwards on the Secretary of State, Humphrey Atkins. He too briefed me on the role of Sir Maurice Oldfield and reassured me about the independence I would enjoy as Chief Constable. Later that morning, I also went to see Ken Newman to discuss in general terms how we would handle the interim period, before I assumed command. I agreed to Ken's request to refrain from giving interviews or making any public comment until after 31 December.

It was not difficult to detect that Ken and his wife, Eileen, were sorry to be leaving the Force. She had displayed great concern and sympathy for those bereaved or injured by terrorists, while Ken had come to recognise the true calibre of the Force and the dedication of its officers. In a relaxed moment, he even joked with me that he would be happy to see the Bramshill Police College staffed entirely by RUC officers!

The appointments of Sir Maurice Oldfield as Co-ordinator and me as RUC Chief Constable were publicly announced at 5 p.m. on Tuesday, 2 October 1979. My appointment was controversial. I was only the third of the nine Inspectors General/Chief Constables in the RUC's history to have progressed right up through the ranks, from constable to head of the Force.

Back in London, I had to have the remainder of my programme recast to facilitate my permanent return to Northern Ireland by the beginning of November. That last month with New Scotland Yard passed in a flurry of activity, with lunches and dinners, farewells and office drinks. It was time to go home, home to the unknown challenges and problems that were inevitable in my position as Chief Constable.

11

A NEW DECADE,
A NEW CHIEF CONSTABLE AND
A NEW GENERAL OFFICER COMMANDING

On 2 January 1980, Michael McAtamney and I were sworn in as Deputy Chief Constable and Chief Constable, respectively, by Lord Chief Justice Lowry at the Belfast Law Courts. Only our wives accompanied us. It was an informal, relaxed and brief ceremony.

Before taking up the office, I had attended a meeting in Dublin with the Commissioner of the Garda Síochána, Patrick McLaughlin, and some other chief officers. That meeting had decided little if anything, but I was quietly advised that we should defer serious issues until we met again in the New Year. I was left in no doubt that they welcomed the appointment of an Ulsterman as Chief Constable. That follow-up meeting took place on 9 January in Dublin, and I was delighted at the friendly atmosphere between us. Pat McLaughlin and I formed an immediate bond of friendship and trust. The operational Divisional Commanders from all border Divisions, North and South, were already well known to each other. It was quite a festive occasion and augured well for the future.

I believe it was the same afternoon that the new General Officer Commanding, Lieutenant-General Sir Richard Lawson, called on me at RUC Headquarters. He had arrived to take up his appointment as of 8 January. I knew virtually nothing about him, except for a comment by his predecessor, Tim Creasey, which simultaneously identified both their personalities. 'If Dick's progress were obstructed by a mountain,' he declared, 'Dick would charm and melt it away,' while he himself 'would blast it away'!

After our initial conversation, which was more like a verbal sparring match, I saw Dick Lawson out of my office and remarked casually, 'Have fun.' 'Why did you say that?' he asked. 'Because I've been saying it for years,' I replied. 'So have I,' he retorted with amusement. That broke the ice and we went on to develop an excellent working relationship. Our friendship was quickly noticed at all levels within the RUC and army, and was to have a dramatic effect on relations between the two security forces. The fact that we openly indulged in good-humoured repartee and the odd practical joke became widely known, and inevitably exaggerated. Unfounded tales are still floating around!

Two true ones do, however, still surface. The first was when Dick and his wife, Ingrid, came with Jean and me to a pipe-band competition in Portrush.

Afterwards, we decided to treat ourselves to large cones from Morelli's ice-cream parlour in Portstewart. As this was a very popular venue, it was difficult for our separate cars and tail cars to find parking spaces. When Dick and I emerged from Morelli's, each carrying two large cones, our drivers were being cautioned for improper parking along the promenade. The woman constable and the traffic warden suddenly recognised me, and beat a hasty retreat. Apparently, they were shocked to discover the truth of our drivers' story that the Chief Constable and the GOC were in Morelli's for ice-creams; they had thought it was a joke to evade being cautioned!

On the second occasion, Dick sent me a humorous card and a baby's rattle to emphasise the fact that I was the younger of the two of us, since our birthdays were on consecutive days, but a year apart. I swiftly replied in kind on his birthday, which happened to coincide with a formal dinner attended by Sir Humphrey Atkins and a dozen or so others. When Dick opened the official-looking package which I had arranged to have delivered to him during the meal, sweetie cigarettes and jelly babies fell from it on to the dining-table. Laughter and applause erupted, to Dick's obvious embarrassment. Afterwards, Margaret Atkins was obviously not amused by our pranks, and asked me if they were not rather childish, to which I replied, 'Is it not better that the GOC and I joke together, rather than quarrel?'

At the beginning of our tenure, Dick Lawson and I discussed the role of the Co-ordinator, Sir Maurice Oldfield, appointed because of RUC/army difficulties in the time of our immediate predecessors. We were agreed that we did not really require such a post. When Sir Maurice left in June 1980, he was replaced by Sir Francis Brooks Richards, but our clandestine pact continued, and so after some time in the job, Sir Francis was withdrawn without a replacement being made.

With excellent relations between the RUC and the army, I could concentrate on the further development of the Force. One of the most important and sensitive issues was that of allegations of brutality by those Special Branch and Criminal Investigation Department (CID) officers who interrogated suspected terrorists in police custody. The Bennett Report, commissioned by the Secretary of State in June 1978, had been presented to the Westminster Parliament in March 1979. By the time I took office, many of its recommendations had already been implemented and others were being processed. The major recommendation still outstanding was the introduction of closed-circuit television cameras with monitor screens for viewing by uniformed supervisory staff and additional monitors for senior officers.

I had read and reread the full Bennett Report, and regarded its recommendations as a considerable, but not total, vindication of the RUC. The phraseology of the Report intrigued me, not least because it had been drafted by a judge and Sir James Haughton, previously Her Majesty's Chief Inspector of Constabulary. I had met Sir James a few times, including once towards the end of my year with New Scotland Yard, when I had been impressed and reassured by his comments on the Report's findings.

My meetings with the RUC's CID and Special Branch officers had, however, revealed a despondency and deep concern, in particular over the effect the Bennett recommendations would have on their ability successfully to interview terrorists in custody. I was also well aware that the Police Federation, in correspondence with my predecessor in October/November 1979, had been vehemently opposed to many of the recommendations, especially those relating to closed-circuit television.

I was convinced that these measures would serve to protect interrogating officers against false allegations of improper behaviour. I also believed that the strict new procedures would act as a deterrent to those prisoners who sought to inflict injuries on themselves in order to make such complaints. Beyond that, I believed that the proposed measures would discourage the isolated and clandestine abuses, which I suspected a very limited number of police officers did commit, to the detriment and discredit of the entire Force.

I managed to convince many of my senior Command officers, and a majority of the detectives, of the advantages emanating from the Bennett Report, which was fully implemented by June 1980. That month, at the Police Federation's annual conference, I was pleased to be able to reveal that in the five months since 1 January, complaints from known or suspected terrorists in police custody had dropped by 55 per cent, while the overall number of complaints against the RUC had dropped by 14 per cent. Sadly, the year did not end on a similarly positive note.

The last months of 1980, the least violent year since 1970, were marred by the commencement of a hunger-strike by convicted republican prisoners in the Maze Prison's H-blocks, so called because the buildings were shaped like the letter H. They began with their 'Dirty Protest', during which they had smeared their excreta on cell walls. On 27 October 1980, seven prisoners went on hunger-strike in support of a number of demands for special treatment. The strike continued throughout November and December, with a further twenty-three prisoners joining it. Hunger-strikes are one of the most emotive and powerful weapons traditionally used by republicans to whip up sympathy and support throughout Ireland. Tension mounted daily, while diplomatic activity between London and Dublin escalated, with a series of statements by both sides before direct talks were held in Dublin between Prime Minister Margaret Thatcher and Taoiseach Charles Haughey.

Although police and army planning for the containment of the predictable street protests was finalised, I was still not happy about our ability to deal with widespread violence should a hunger-striker die. On 17 December, the condition of one of the first seven prisoners deteriorated so much that local news bulletins reported that he was likely to die at any time. A dreadful sense of foreboding enveloped the community and the security forces alike, all anxiously awaiting what seemed the inevitable fatal outcome.

On this occasion, disaster was averted. Dr William Philbin, Catholic Bishop of Down and Connor, had asked to see me about the safety of seven Catholic families under threat in North Belfast from Protestant paramilitaries. At that meeting in his home, he asked my opinion about a series of constructive proposals to end the hunger-strike. I suggested that his contacts at Government level were inadequate and so I put him in touch with more influential people, and I was also able to assure him that I was taking steps to guarantee police protection for the particular seven families. How far this contact contributed to the outcome of the strike I do not know, but word came to RUC Headquarters on 18 December that 'in response to the pleas from the Cardinal and the Bishops, all seven hunger-strikers at the Maze have come off the hunger-strike'. Unfortunately, the reprieve was temporary; I had not seen the last of hunger-strikes during my tenure of office.

The year 1981 began badly. My Senior Deputy, Harry Baillie, had retired. Deputy Chief Constable Michael McAtamney was not keen to see a successor appointed, and I was well aware that the system of having two deputies had scarcely been a success due to the manner of its introduction in 1973. I decided, with Police Authority approval, to relinquish the second deputy post, but instead, it was eventually agreed that I should have three Senior Assistant Chief Constables. In retrospect, I recognise that this was a mistake. If I had maintained that second deputy's post, it might have avoided the terrible operational problems of November/December 1982, which culminated in six deaths and the subsequent Stalker investigation.

Seven people lost their lives in January 1981 as the result of terrorist activity. These included Sir Norman Stronge, an octogenarian and former Speaker of the Stormont Parliament, and his son James, who were murdered in their home near the border, before the building was set ablaze. It was a terrible scene. Unionists were outraged, in particular that an elderly man could be killed in such a cruel manner. Criticism was levelled at the existing security measures and calls went out for tougher ones.

Criticism and unremitting media attention became hallmarks of my time as Chief Constable. I reckoned that if extremists on both sides, Catholic and Protestant, were complaining about me, then I must have been doing something right or nearly right. Even visiting injured people in hospital could become a source of criticism, as was the case when I spoke to Bernadette McAliskey (née Devlin) after she had been seriously wounded in an attack by the Ulster Volunteer Force (UVF) in January. I had known Bernadette previously, when she was prominent in the Civil Rights Movement, and had been present on one occasion in Dungannon when, at my request, she managed to avert a potentially serious conflict between the police and civil rights demonstrators.

After the UVF shooting, she had been conveyed to the secure wing of the Royal Victoria Hospital, where patients at risk from terrorist attack could be treated. While visiting several RUC officers there, I learned she was in an adjoining room, and looked in for a few minutes to congratulate her on her escape and to inquire about Coalisland, as she lived nearby. Her other visitors were obviously uncertain how best to respond to my presence, but loyalists were not. When news of my brief visit appeared in the local papers, a number of them took grave exception to it, as she was well known for her republican sympathies.

In March that year, I again managed to stir up loyalist wrath after a visit to Belfast by the Lord Mayor of Dublin and a number of Dublin councillors. They met the Lord Mayor of Belfast and fellow councillors at a function in the Europa Hotel. Despite a considerable police presence, an unexpectedly large crowd of Protestant demonstrators, led by the Rev. Ian Paisley, forced its way into the hotel and proceeded to shout abuse at these people from Dublin. Although the protesters were quickly evicted, I was so concerned that I left Headquarters in order to speak to the delegation as it was travelling to the Belfast shipyard. Boarding the bus, I asked if anyone had been molested by the demonstrators, and apologised for the incident having been allowed to occur. Thereafter, we had a light-hearted, indeed humorous, conversation and, as I left the bus, I was pleasantly taken aback by a warm round of applause from its occupants. Once again, my gesture did not endear me to the Protestant protesters, or their leader, as was evidenced by that evening's publicity!

Ian Paisley and his supporters had been particularly irritated when, in December 1980, Margaret Thatcher and several of her Cabinet ministers, including Geoffrey Howe and Humphrey Atkins, had travelled to Dublin for a meeting with Charles Haughey and the Irish Minister for Foreign Affairs, Brian Lenihan. There, an agreement had been reached 'to consider the totality of relationships in these islands', and a structure of meetings drawn up for joint Anglo-Irish studies. Paisley, incensed by this development, met Margaret Thatcher eleven days later, but their meeting was aborted after thirty minutes, apparently because of a conflict of minds!

As a result, Ian Paisley embarked in 1981 on a campaign in which he seemed to be seeking to emulate Sir Edward Carson's successful rallies, earlier in the century, against Home Rule in Ireland. Consequently, a study of Carson's activities was undertaken by Special Branch, and also by me. This proved to be of real benefit in anticipating, and then countering, Paisley's eleven demonstrations throughout 1981 on what became known as his 'Carson trail'.

Paisley's series of demonstrations was interspersed with clandestine gatherings of large numbers of men in the most unusual places, including remote hilltops. They would stand, reportedly waving their firearm certificates for legally held weapons, to indicate how well armed and ready for battle they were if Margaret Thatcher dared to sell their loyalist heritage down the Irish river. Here we had Paisley's 'Third Force' in the making. In isolation, these displays of strength could all have been regarded as comic, even pathetic. However, against the background of a revival of the republican hunger-strike, which the IRA would use to harness the support of the Catholic community, Ian Paisley's disruptive efforts compounded an already ominous situation.

As the hunger-strike commenced, my senior Command and I decided that the RUC's strategy was to be one of containment, linked with continuing appeals to the population as a whole not to be drawn into conflict with the security forces. This meant that unlawful parades and demonstrations, held to protest against the British Government's refusal to make concessions to the hunger-strikers, would be kept within republican areas to avoid loyalist retaliation.

Police resources were, therefore, deployed in strength at interfaces between Catholic and Protestant housing estates. Intensive patrolling was also maintained so that main roads were kept clear of demonstrators to enable traffic to flow smoothly. We anticipated the worst. It was only April 1981, and already in that year twenty-five people had died as the result of terrorism (thirteen members of the security forces and twelve civilians).

On 1 March 1981, the republican prisoners' 'Dirty Protest' ended, but Bobby Sands, a convicted IRA terrorist, started a hunger-strike. Within four days of Sands going on hunger-strike, Margaret Thatcher, on a routine visit to Northern Ireland on 5 March, made abundantly clear her determination not to yield to this type of pressure to gain political status for republican prisoners. On 15 March, another republican prisoner joined Sands, followed by two more on 22 March and, thereafter, by many others.

Less than a month after winning the by-election for the Fermanagh–South Tyrone parliamentary seat at Westminster, Bobby Sands died in the early hours of 5 May 1981. Within an hour, serious and widespread rioting developed in West Belfast. His death had been anticipated, and so the police and army were already on full alert. The ensuing violence throughout that month, when two more hunger-strikers died, was the worst since that of 1969. Nevertheless, our containment strategy succeeded, even though more than 100,000 people lined the route for Sands's funeral.

While I understood and agreed fully with the Prime Minister's firm stance, I also knew that it was interpreted by Catholics as stubborn, unfeeling intransigence. I recognised that hatred, with a frightening vehemence, was emerging in republican and even in less extreme nationalist areas. Clearly, this was to the benefit of the Provisional IRA, the Irish National Liberation Army — another republican paramilitary organisation — and Sinn Féin; doubtless it was also an incentive to the hunger-strikers themselves and those closest to them.

Both the GOC, Dick Lawson, and I were extremely concerned about the inevitable consequences for our people on the ground. We believed that there had to be room for some recognition of the feelings of the Catholic community, which could not accept that rejection of the prisoners' demands for 'special status' justified them being allowed to die. Secretary of State Humphrey Atkins's position was sensitive and extremely difficult, but he listened to our views and our worries about our members.

On Tuesday, 26 May, with little advance notice, Dick Lawson and I, together with our Staff Officers, accompanied the Secretary of State to a meeting with the Prime Minister. Bill Wilson, my close friend from my Cullingtree Road days and now a Superintendent, had been my Staff Officer since shortly after my appointment. We flew from Aldergrove Airport to RAF Northolt, where cars were waiting to whisk us off to the Prime Minister's country residence at Chequers.

It was an interesting experience, particularly the format of the meeting. We were gathered into a large, comfortable lounge. A number of secretaries were present, as well as Cabinet ministers, including the Home Secretary. Our Staff

Officers had to remain outside the room. I was struck by the aura of authority which Margaret Thatcher projected as soon as she entered the room, and by the deference shown to her. I was later to reflect on how subdued they all became in both their manner and their speech. She certainly controlled, indeed dominated, the ensuing discussion.

I contributed to a briefing on the security situation. There followed a detailed discussion about the hunger-strike. Four prisoners had already starved to death, and although none of the other hunger-strikers was in imminent danger of dying, I left the Prime Minister in no doubt about their determination to continue the protest.

I repeatedly made the point that, while totally supporting the principle behind the British Government's stance, I thought it necessary to recognise the human tragedy behind the deaths of people by starvation, and in street disturbances; the Government had to be seen to care about this aspect of the strike. I also emphasised my view that there was a hardening of attitudes, and a resolve growing amongst Catholics in Northern Ireland against the British Government, even though the vast majority of them did not support the prisoners' terrorist activities. There were times during the meeting when I felt only the Prime Minister and I were talking, but this cannot have been so. Some time later, I was told by one of those present that it was interesting to see two stubborn people in conflict!

After three hours of intense discussion, Margaret Thatcher suddenly announced, 'I must go to Ireland! Where is my diary?' A man disappeared and returned with it. 'You are fully committed for two weeks,' he told her, scanning her schedule. 'Too late,' she replied. 'What am I doing this week?' After being told, she said, 'Cancel my engagement for Thursday. I will go then.' Her decision to go was indeed dramatic. I was delighted with the outcome. The fact that the GOC was there too, and clearly in support of me, was reassuring and, I suspect, greatly strengthened my hand.

The Prime Minister did indeed come to Northern Ireland that Thursday. After some routine visits, she gave a press conference at Stormont Castle, during which she expressed her understanding and her sympathy for the relatives of dead hunger-strikers and of those intent on a similar fate. The fact that she showed she really cared what became of those young men in the H-blocks came through to the population of Northern Ireland, as did her outright condemnation of terrorism and her total support for the security forces. To this day, I am convinced that her visit and, more importantly, her words of concern marked a turning-point in that hunger-strike.

On the following Monday, 1 June, I asked my chief officers for an assessment of Margaret Thatcher's visit. It was the unanimous view that the public generally was reassured, especially by her expression of sympathy. More significantly, several officers thought there was a growing division between the Provisional IRA and the Catholic community as a direct result of the visit.

Another eleven people were murdered in July; one was a soldier, the rest civilians. I find it difficult now to portray the constant state of alertness required of the police at that time. So many of their armoured vehicles had been damaged in rioting that repair work could not keep pace. Armour-protected vehicles had to be transferred from places considered to be minimally, or moderately, at risk to areas of intense, and potentially lethal, disorder. The RUC's need for more finance to repair vehicles and bombed police buildings, and to fund our massive expansion programme, became an increasing problem, as the Conservative Government sought to cut back on public spending.

August 1981 brought with it a widespread rejection by the Catholic community of the hunger-strike. At the same time, the already strenuous efforts of Catholic clergy, especially of Cardinal Ó Fiaich, to end it were further intensified. By then, members of the Provisional IRA were also desperately trying to find a way of terminating the hunger-strike, because they knew that Margaret Thatcher was resolute that no concessions would be granted while the strike continued. Despite attempts from all these quarters, four more prisoners died before the efforts of distraught families and the Catholic clergy brought the hunger-strike finally to an end on 3 October 1981.

In all, ten republican prisoners had starved themselves to death. The intense grief and distress caused by such futile deaths was only exacerbated by the IRA, which endeavoured to manipulate the men's funerals. It sought what Thatcher had termed the 'oxygen of publicity', especially at a time when journalists from around the world were giving extensive coverage to the strike and to human rights issues in Northern Ireland generally. Because of the IRA's tactics, RUC officers had to act in strength before and during the ten funerals to prevent paramilitary displays and the illegal use of firearms at the gravesides. This was a most distasteful duty for the police.

By this time, Humphrey Atkins had left Northern Ireland, replaced as Secretary of State by James Prior on 13 September. For Jim, it was to be a case of being thrown 'in at the deep end'. Shortly after his arrival, the murder of a Westminster MP, Robert Bradford, who was a member of the Ulster Unionist Party and a Methodist minister, sent shock waves through a population already shaken by the violence emanating from the hunger-strike and the intensity of continuing terrorist activity. Rev. Bradford had been shot on 14 November by the IRA, while he was holding a constituency 'surgery' in South Belfast. The caretaker of the building was also shot dead, presumably having been mistaken for a bodyguard. When the Secretary of State attended Robert Bradford's funeral, police on duty had difficulty in protecting him from the loyalist mourners, who displayed considerable hostility towards him on the street and in the church.

In response to the deteriorating situation, Ian Paisley called for a day-of-action on Monday, 23 November, commencing with a mass rally at Belfast City Hall and culminating in a massive parade of his so-called 'Third Force' in Newtownards, County Down that evening. There was to be a stoppage of work from midday, with a tractor and car cavalcade in all major towns throughout Northern Ireland, before the Newtownards parade.

I immediately issued a public statement and made media appearances in which I stated bluntly that no third force would be tolerated or permitted to usurp the role of the police or army. Such was the state of agitation and fear amongst the public that I ordered the implementation of the Civil Emergency Plan, on lines similar to those adopted during the hunger-strike. Meetings of the Chief Officers' Group were convened daily, and the Command Room was operated on a twenty-four-hour basis from 17 November. Maximum manpower was deployed throughout Northern Ireland, with an additional battalion of troops flown in from Britain.

The Police Federation Chairman, Constable Alan Wright, and its Secretary, Sergeant David Bennett, were informed of the situation. They had previously requested, and been given, my permission to convene a meeting of the Federation's Central Committee on 18 November. I had no inkling of any sensitivity within that group. Indeed, I believed our relations were good, and was completely unaware of any problems between us. I knew that they had Federation business to discuss, and that they particularly wished to consider the implications of the operational pressures then being experienced by the Force. On the invitation of the Chairman, I agreed to meet the Central Committee on the 18th at 11.45 a.m., before going on to a long-standing engagement to speak at a Rotary Club lunch at 12.30 p.m. I went, therefore, with a maximum of forty minutes allocated to the Federation.

Its meeting had commenced at 9.30 a.m., with all the Committee members in attendance. According to the Minutes of the meeting, which were subsequently sent to me, many strong statements were made prior to my arrival, including a motion of no confidence in me as Chief Constable. It apparently was defeated by ten votes to nine.

It was against this heady background discussion, then unknown to me, that I joined the Central Committee meeting and was welcomed by the Chairman. In the short time available, I identified the problems faced by the Force, outlined the policy and dealt briefly with many of the points raised. I also suggested that they should create a small committee, whose members could talk to me 'at any time in relation to any matters during the current high-risk security situation'.

At a specially convened meeting of the Police Authority that afternoon, I briefed members fully, not only on the current problems but on my meeting with the Federation earlier that day. On 20 November, two days later, the Authority issued a press statement in which its members 'unanimously expressed their confidence in the Chief Constable and in the RUC and its Reserve whose members themselves have suffered so grievously from terrorist attacks'. The statement continued, 'The Authority urges all right-thinking people in the Province to give their full backing and support to the RUC and the other security forces.'

That same day, I received notice of the Federation's newly formed committee, which I had proposed. Its agenda contained a series of routine matters, all of which proved possible to resolve quickly and amicably without recourse to the emotional conduct of the Central Committee on the 18th. After that unfortunate episode, I directed that there be the closest possible contact between regional Federation representatives and operational Command at Subdivisional and Divisional level in order to keep them informed about policing problems and strategy in their immediate areas. This, however, came too late. The full consequences of the Central Committee's loss of stability and sense of discipline had yet to be experienced. The Committee's meeting on 18 November had given rise to intense controversy and speculation within the Force itself, only five days before Ian Paisley's day-of-action.

On 23 November, two separate demonstrations took place at the City Hall in Belfast; one by the Ulster Unionist Party immediately preceded that led by the Rev. Paisley. As I had arranged for an army helicopter to be available to me, I left Headquarters around 3.30 p.m., and flew over the main provincial towns within a forty-mile radius of Belfast. Although traffic was well below that of a normal day, I was much reassured by the absence of unusual activity beyond the city. Only the big evening rally in Newtownards remained.

By coincidence, it was my birthday, and I had in fact invited the General Officer Commanding, Dick Lawson, Secretary of State Jim Prior, and a number of other senior people to dinner at Headquarters that evening. There was a television monitor linked from our Command Room into the dining-room, so that information about all incidents could be displayed instantaneously. A system of operational and intelligence reports had been arranged to keep me totally up to date during the evening.

After a march by about a thousand men of the 'Third Force' through Newtownards, and speeches by Ian Paisley and Peter Robinson, Deputy Leader of the Democratic Unionist Party (DUP), the evening ended peacefully. Thereafter, sightings of Paisley's thousands of men 'on the march in Ulster' rarely materialised.

Conversation at the dinner table reflected events outside; after the march, we could relax without any sense of tension. As they departed, Jim Prior thanked me for having him to dinner and allowing him to be at the hub of things. I assured him that there was no need for thanks, because my purpose in having him and the GOC there was 'to enable me to keep a close eye on them until the events of the day were over'! In truth, the dinner had nothing to do with my birthday!

In a public statement on 26 November, I made it clear that the RUC would not be diverted from its duty by factional groups or political pressures from whatever direction; no republican or loyalist paramilitary organisation, nor any private force activity outside the law, would be permitted to usurp the RUC's authority.

The events about to unfold in early 1982 were all the more poignant to Jean and me because of my award of a knighthood in the Queen's New Year's Honours List, announced on the evening of 31 December 1981. While every RUC Inspector General and Chief Constable, except one, had been knighted, I nevertheless received the news with pride. Jean was evidently delighted for me, and looked forward with excitement to the investiture at Buckingham Palace.

At the very beginning of January 1982, I was informed that the Rev. Ian Paisley intended to call a press conference at his DUP headquarters at 10.30 a.m. on Monday, 4 January. It was strongly rumoured that he would refer to my knighthood and reveal the Minutes of that unfortunate Federation meeting on the previous 18 November with its unsuccessful no-confidence motion in me.

On the morning of Saturday, 2 January, with the involvement of my senior Command, a letter was drafted from me to the Secretary and Chairman of the Police Federation. In it I expressed my concern over the behaviour of the Central Committee at its November meeting. I directed that the Chairman and Secretary each be shown the draft letter before it was officially delivered to them. Both expressed full support for its content after one slight amendment, which they proposed and which further strengthened my criticism of the Central Committee. The final letter was balanced and reasonable; it was certainly not in any way threatening.

Final copies of my letter were delivered by my drivers to each of the men on the Saturday evening. Both telephoned to confirm their acceptance of it. For his part, the Chairman undertook to issue a press statement, attacking political interference and supporting Force policy and me as Chief Constable. It was specifically suggested by Constable Wright that my letter could with advantage be published by the media to outmanoeuvre still further the small minority of dissidents in the Central Committee. I agreed. Copies were duly given to *The Newsletter* and *Irish News* for publication on Monday morning, while release to Radio Downtown, the BBC and the Press Association was under embargo until five o'clock on Monday morning. The intention was to pre-empt Ian Paisley's press conference and throw him on to the defensive. A meeting of the Police Federation's Finance and General Purposes Sub-Committee was called for 10.30 a.m. on Monday.

The Newsletter led with my letter on the front page on Monday, but added little comment. The *Irish News* also published it in full, while the radio carried extracts in various news broadcasts.

The Sub-Committee remained in discussion all of Monday morning and afternoon. Two dissidents, by force of oratory, carried the day. After drafting a statement, most damaging to me personally as Chief Constable, they obtained agreement from the Sub-Committee that it be issued by their Chairman late that afternoon.

Meanwhile, at his scheduled press conference, the Rev. Paisley did, as expected, reveal the contents of the Minutes of the Federation meeting on 18 November. Except for condemnatory remarks directed at me, he merely observed that the Federation had plainly been proposing the re-creation of the Ulster Special Constabulary, not the setting up of a separate force. His comments were, if anything, mild by comparison with the subsequent Federation statement.

This statement expressed the Federation's concern that its Minutes had been 'circulated in an unauthorised manner', and deplored 'the use of a confidential document for a political purpose or to be used as a weapon to embarrass the police service'. It continued by criticising my interpretation of the Minutes and denied that 'there was a calculated attempt by any group of persons to act in an improper manner or without a mandate from their membership without regard for the consequences'. The statement ignored the fact that, without consulting those whom it supposedly represented, the Central Committee had endeavoured to procure a vote of no confidence in the Chief Constable, and had expressed opinions on matters either on which it was uninformed, or which were outside its mandate. Beyond that, neither the Federation Chairman nor Secretary revealed in this statement that they had prior knowledge of my letter, that they had expressly asked for it to be published, or that they had totally supported its content.

Knowing that he had failed to honour his undertakings of the previous Saturday, the Federation Chairman endeavoured to 'go to ground'. I felt that his misrepresentation of the facts had rendered my position as Chief Constable totally untenable and that, unless this matter was resolved, I must consider resignation.

I requested that my chief officers and Deputy assemble in an office close to mine, while I remained at my desk, determined that the issue would be settled one way or the other before I left it. The Chairman was eventually located and came with the Federation Secretary to my office. There, the Chairman apologised and expressed his regrets. He explained that he had been unable to control the two dissidents within the Finance and General Purposes Sub-Committee. They, it seemed, had won over the other members and virtually dictated the contents of the Federation's final statement on 4 January.

I debated releasing to the media all information about my actions since the previous Friday, including the Chairman and the Secretary's behind-the-scenes involvement. I felt that the former's weakness as Chairman and his apparent lack of integrity in associating himself with the press statement of the 4th was unconscionable. I made it abundantly clear to him that there was no alternative but that he should resign as Chairman of the Police Federation, because unless the stigma attached to me by its statement was removed, I would certainly resign. After considering his position, the Chairman advised my staff of his intention to resign his chairmanship. I then joined my chief officers in the adjoining office, where the tension amongst them was palpable. In his statement of resignation, he admitted that:

> A totally wrong impression has been created that I and the Federation are in opposition to the chief constable . . . I can no longer be a party to what is happening. I have the utmost personal respect and professional regard for Sir John Hermon and I cannot permit his name and the office of chief constable to be sullied by people who do not truly have the interests of the RUC at heart.

This unequivocal wording resolved my personal and professional dilemma. It simultaneously enhanced the ex-Chairman's own image to such a degree that he duly received a unanimous vote of confidence from the Central Committee, and there was a stupendous groundswell of opinion within all ranks to back Alan Wright and reject the Central Committee's dissidents. With that, he was swept back into office post-haste as the Federation Chairman!

Throughout this very difficult time, I was most encouraged by the absolute loyalty of my chief officers and of the Superintendents' Association, whose President called to convey the Association's full support for me as Chief Constable and for my policies. I sincerely hoped that it would not be necessary to take any further action to prevent the Federation again behaving in such a manner. There remained a careful 'stand-off' position between the Central Committee and me. In the light of its conduct, this was perhaps the best stance to adopt. That said, in the area of welfare, where the Police Federation excelled, it had my full support. Between us we developed many innovative and imaginative programmes relating to disabled police officers, and to the dependants, widows and families of deceased members.

The Federation's November meeting of 1981 had yet one more, albeit strange, ramification. In due course, I discovered that a serving chief inspector had been nominated as a unionist candidate for election in 1982 to the new Northern Ireland Assembly, and so I ordered a disciplinary investigation into his nomination. When the Chief Inspector denied all knowledge of this and affirmed that he would not have agreed to it, a recently retired sergeant provided a statement substantiating his account. In the statement, the ex-sergeant disclosed that he himself had been a member of the Unionist Party for twenty-five years, and had held several executive positions within it. As I recollect, his posts included vice-chairman of a unionist association, treasurer of a constituency unionist association, and executive member of the Ulster Unionist Council! He omitted to mention that, while he had been serving as a sergeant, it was he who had proposed the creation of a 'Third Force' at the Federation meeting on 18 November 1981! Even though that proposal was heavily defeated, I felt very strongly that it was manifestly wrong and highly damaging to the standing of the RUC that such a matter should have been introduced at the Federation's meeting.

Because of those experiences with the Federation, and because of the findings of an external investigation into leaks by police officers to journalists, I developed within Special Branch a very discreet screening process to identify subversive elements within the RUC itself, and also any officers whose associates might pose a risk to the integrity of the Force or a threat to our intelligence systems. Although no more serious breaches occurred during my tenure as Chief Constable, occasionally the need arose to caution a few officers about their friendships outside the Force, and even to transfer some out of the way of temptation. It came as no surprise to me to find that the few who fell within this net were almost invariably of the loyalist, Protestant persuasion.

12

KINCORA AGAIN, AND AGAIN

The year 1982 is still marked in my memory by two different types of celebration — one family, the other professional. Our daughter, Barbara, was quite determined to marry the young American whom she had met on holiday only a few months earlier. She had invited Kevin to stay with us during Christmas 1981, and by the end of June 1982, they were married. Jean and I were privately very concerned at the pace of events, but Barbara seemed happy and very sure that she had made the right decision.

On the professional side, 1982 was a special year for the RUC since it was the sixtieth anniversary of its creation. Memories of its fiftieth anniversary were still fresh in my mind, and I was determined that our diamond jubilee would likewise be a year to remember. Despite the ongoing terrorist campaign, services of thanksgiving, concerts, mobile displays and open days were held right across Northern Ireland to mark the RUC's jubilee. Through the events we organised, many thousands of pounds were raised for various charities.

On 2 June 1982, sixty years since the formation of the RUC, I formally received, from the Chairman of the Police Authority, the first standard ever presented to the Force. Four days later, the flag was dedicated at a special service in St Anne's Cathedral, Belfast. At our interdenominational service a loyal friend of mine, the late Canon Hugh Murphy, represented the Catholic church by reading the first lesson, while I read the second. The Church of Ireland Bishop of Connor dedicated the RUC standard, while senior representatives of the Methodist and Presbyterian churches took the prayers and sermon.

By contrast, the pipe-band contest to mark the jubilee was a noisy affair at Balmoral showgrounds in Belfast. The Pipes and Drums of the RUC, which I had helped to found in 1977, were joined by bands from the North and South of Ireland. As Chieftain of the Day, I took the salute as they marched off. One particular band from Dublin, when tuning its pipes in preparation for the competition, had been encouraged by me to play a few bars from old republican tunes amidst the disjointed, scrambled noises of other instruments tuning up in the marshalling-area. One of the Irish pipers, in his seventies I believe, took my suggestion very much to heart, and played with considerable gusto. Later, during the march past, as I saluted his band, he gave me a broad wink. From the saluting dais, I winked back!

At quieter times, I had an opportunity to study a tangible memento of 1982 in the form of a non-controversial, pictorial history of policing in Ireland from 1822 until 1982. Carefully researched, and written by Chief Superintendent Sinclair and Detective Superintendent Scully, *Arresting Memories*[1] was published in November of that year. Only three leather-bound copies were ever produced; one is with Queen Elizabeth, the second copy was presented to Secretary of State Jim Prior, and I proudly hold the third.

I have to say that from my attendance at so many RUC jubilee functions, I noticed a perceptible confidence and stability emerging within the Force. However, that confidence and maturity were soon tested more than any of us could have foretold. The last three months of 1982 left the RUC with a legacy of tragedy and errors of judgment, including my own, which dogged us for years ahead.

Before we entered those dark months, my friend Dick Lawson was promoted and replaced as General Officer Commanding on 1 June 1982 by Lieutenant-General Sir Robert Richardson. Bob was a Scot with a lively mind and great common sense. From the very beginning, we two were at ease with one another; he was a man who said what he meant, and meant what he said. Consequently, the excellent relations between the police and army continued.

It was also a source of personal satisfaction that the Commissioner of the Garda Síochána kept in regular contact with me. Following the appointment of Assistant Commissioner Joe Ainsworth, there was a noticeable increase in the attrition rate against terrorists in the Republic of Ireland. Within the resources available to the Gardaí, which had been considerably enhanced by Commissioner Patrick McLaughlin in 1980/81, co-operation between the two Forces was extremely good. Bobby Killen, since his appointment as head of RUC Special Branch, had skilfully consolidated those mutually beneficial relations.

Despite the RUC's celebrations and good cheer of the early part of 1982, the year actually came to be dominated by much more sensitive matters, including Kincora . . . a name which still manages to conjure up images of scandal and skulduggery in high places.

Back in January 1980, just three weeks after my appointment as Chief Constable, an article written by Peter McKenna appeared on the 24th in the *Irish Independent* under the headline 'Sex Racket at Children's Home'. McKenna was the paper's chief news reporter, and the article related to allegations circulating about an official cover-up of the recruitment of boys for homosexual prostitution at a boys' home, known as Kincora. A member of its staff was also alleged to have been involved with a loyalist paramilitary group called 'Tara'. The home had been opened at 236 Upper Newtownards Road in East Belfast in January 1958 by the Belfast Welfare Authority Department. It was a hostel for boys in the fifteen to eighteen years age group, and could accommodate up to a dozen of them. The building itself was a detached house with living and dining areas on the ground floor, and also an office with a door from it into a one-bedroomed flat.

The Warden of the home, Mr Joseph Mains, occupied that flat from 1964 until the home was closed in 1980. Another staff member occupied a different bedroom on the first floor, beside the bedrooms of the boys. Peter McKenna's newspaper article alleged that individuals employed within the social services were well aware that serious sexual abuses were taking place at the home, but that 'reports on certain cases were destroyed under orders from a senior member of the Social Services Department'. Yet, throughout its twenty-two years, no victim of abuse at Kincora had ever made a complaint to the RUC.

With such serious allegations raised in this article, it was clearly a matter requiring immediate police investigation, and the day after the article's publication, a small team of officers, led by Detective Chief Inspector George Caskey, began an urgent investigation into the allegations.

Initial inquiries by the Caskey team did find sufficient evidence to justify the suspension of three members of the Kincora staff, namely Joseph Mains and the Assistant Warden, Raymond Semple, and also William McGrath, who was described as the 'Housefather'. On 16 December 1981, all three, having pleaded guilty to various offences including indecent assault, gross indecency and buggery, were sentenced to several years' imprisonment: Mains for six years, Semple for five years and McGrath for four.

The meticulously thorough RUC investigation also resulted in the detection of four other men, whose behaviour in two other boys' homes in Belfast and one in Newtownabbey led to their convictions for similar crimes in May and December, 1981.

Far from assuaging the public and media concern, these convictions opened a veritable Pandora's box of allegations, based on the suggestion that Kincora had been a focal point of a vice ring involving senior Government officials over a period of years. It was suggested that facts had been suppressed by the RUC, and that there had been cover-ups to protect public figures and high-ranking officials. The revelation that William McGrath had been involved in the small loyalist paramilitary group 'Tara' gave rise to further speculation that he was blackmailed into reporting to the British security service, MI5. It was alleged that MI5 knew about the criminal abuse at Kincora, but had used that knowledge for intelligence purposes to intimidate prominent politicians and others believed to have been implicated.

The suggestion that dirty tricks were being played by MI5 to disseminate black propaganda against politicians and others meant that stories about an RUC cover-up of Kincora frequently appeared in local newspapers. Realising the damage that unsubstantiated rumours could do to the community's confidence in the investigative integrity of the RUC, I decided that these allegations should be thoroughly examined by the same team of detectives, led again by George Caskey.

Simultaneously, I announced in a press release on 18 February 1982 that I had asked Her Majesty's Inspector of Constabulary to appoint an independent chief constable to investigate allegations about a police cover-up. I made plain that 'The appointed Chief Constable will have full access to all the papers past and present and in addition will have general oversight of the continuing investigations. In due course he will forward a report to me and his conclusions will be made public.'

Secretary of State Jim Prior made a comprehensive statement about Kincora that same day in the House of Commons at Westminster. He explained that when police investigations had been completed and any criminal offences processed through the courts, he intended to appoint a Committee of Inquiry under the chairmanship of a High Court judge, sitting in public, to investigate the past management of children's homes, to find out why malpractices had not been identified earlier and also to make recommendations for the future administration of such homes. He was 'anxious that there should be no lasting cause for public disquiet that the truth has not been wholly discovered'.

Sir George Terry, then Chief Constable of Sussex, was proposed to me as the investigating officer. I was happy to agree to his appointment and also to his Terms of Reference, under which he was 'to investigate allegations about the way in which the Police (RUC) have conducted their enquiries and in addition to have general oversight of the continuing investigations'. This he and his team did by tracing all known victims, as well as those past hostel residents and material witnesses whom they could find or who had been located by the RUC. They were all reinterviewed by the Terry team. Many other individuals were contacted in order to check their verbal account of events against the newspaper reports of them. Also interviewed were those journalists whose articles about Kincora suggested that they had information. The three main offenders — McGrath, Mains and Semple — were also reinterviewed on two occasions in prison by Sir George's inquiry team.

Sir George commented that the reporting by some sections of the media, and especially lurid headlines in the press, conveyed the impression that Kincora was virtually 'a male sex brothel'. However, the RUC inquiry and his own came to no such conclusion. In his Report of 27 May 1983, George Terry made it very plain that what he found was:

> nothing more than a number of separate, very secretive and nefarious relationships. These relationships were, with only one exception, between the staff of hostels and the inmates, and the latter knew well the identity of their assailants or where appropriate their buggerers. This entirely gives lie to the media assertions that the boys were made over to a variety of other males of unknown identity through the medium of any 'prostitution ring'.[2]

Moreover, the Terry Inquiry could not:

> establish the existence of any paramilitary organisation connected with the homosexual misconduct in any boys' home or of any attempts to recruit persons to a paramilitary organisation through residents in a boys' hostel. No such viable paramilitary organisation exists beyond an

ideological concept of a few ineffectual individuals.[3]

I was reassured not only by the findings, but by the comment in the Terry Report that throughout his inquiry Sir George had received 'the utmost co-operation' from RUC officers and that there had been 'no question at all of concealment or avoidance of liaison or supply of information whenever required'.[4] By comparison, he was scathing about the performance of those media reporters who had failed to substantiate their allegations of a 'homosexual ring', or to inform Sir George 'of anything which they considered the RUC's team had not discovered'. He concluded that there was:

> absolutely no evidence that residents of any children's home were involved in anything remotely resembling homosexual 'rings' as asserted by the media or the latter's contentions that this so called ring involved Police officers, civil servants, military personnel, Justices of the Peace or legal people. There was no cover-up or concealment of evidence or disciplinary breaches by the RUC personnel.[5]

Referring to press articles which implied 'that nothing was done despite the evidence they claim was available', Sir George remarked that he was 'bound to conclude that they had no such evidence'. He was satisfied that 'no further evidence in fact exists and the stories that were produced for public consumption for whatever reason fall under that well known guise of investigative journalism'![6]

Although Peter McKenna's original article in the *Irish Independent* on 24 January 1980 contained inaccurate details, allegations about sexual abuses at Kincora were substantially correct. His article had been based on information given by social workers 'whose integrity and dedication compelled them to do something that might ensure the matter was ventilated'.[7] Although Sir George Terry's remit did not entitle him to enquire into the shortcomings of the social services, it was obvious to him that some social workers had been guilty of 'a high degree of naïvety, incompetence and in some instances an avoidance of responsibility' — all of which had to be remedied internally.[8]

It was established that at a time of intense terrorist activity and public disorder in early 1974, and again in 1976, 'vague information' had emerged which, if it had been pursued thoroughly then, might well have revealed what was finally brought to light in the 1980 investigations. Sir George recognised that in normal circumstances of policing, this situation could never have continued for so long. The Terry Report, however, drew attention to the intense pressures of the 1970s, when a police station near Kincora was already inadequate for its own purposes, and yet it had to house a battalion and company headquarters of the army. That station and its officers were being shot at, while dealing with a litany of serious crimes, and these conditions had stretched police resources well beyond their capacity. If circumstances had been different and some of the social workers had been able to take action, much additional suffering and humiliation to the boys at Kincora would have been avoided.

I concluded that after the convictions and the subsequent Terry investigation, the whole sordid episode had begun and ended with a small number of perverted Kincora staff degrading some unfortunate disadvantaged boys placed in their care. None of those convicted, even when in jail and with nothing further to lose, ever alleged that they had been blackmailed or coerced by MI5 or military personnel.

In 1983, I was able to state publicly that the reports from the further RUC investigation and that of Sir George Terry had been forwarded to the Director of Public Prosecutions for Northern Ireland, and he had decided there was nothing in them to warrant the institution of criminal prosecutions.

The final chapter in the Kincora saga was added in February 1986 by the publication of the report of His Honour Judge William Hughes, and his two colleagues on the Committee of Inquiry, first announced by Jim Prior in 1982. They had looked into the management deficiencies in children's homes as exposed by Kincora.[9] Their Report made fifty-six recommendations, ranging from better selection techniques for staff to the right of children and parents to complain to outside bodies, including the police, and the provision of a formal complaints procedure in booklets for children in language they could readily understand. With such improvements implemented, it was hoped that nothing akin to the deplorable behaviour at Kincora would ever reoccur in Northern Ireland.

Notes
1 R.J.K. Sinclair and F.J.M. Scully, *Arresting Memories (Captured Moments in Constabulary Life)* (Coleraine and Ballycastle: Impact Printing [of Coleraine] Ltd 1982).
2 Terry Report, paragraph 42.
3 *Op. cit.* paragraph 51 (d).
4 *Op. cit.* paragraph 11.
5 *Op. cit.* paragraph 51 (a).
6 *Op. cit.* paragraph 51 (e).
7 *Ibid.*
8 *Op. cit.* paragraph 51 (f).
9 Report of the Committee of Inquiry into Children's Homes and Hostels (Belfast: HMSO 1986).

13

THE DOWRA AFFAIR

During the latter half of 1982, while the Kincora Affair was rumbling on, incidents occurred which gave rise to two totally separate investigations into the RUC. As far as the Force and I as its Chief Constable were concerned, both will be long remembered. I refer to the so-called Dowra and Stalker Affairs. In reality, both were of far less significance than the traumatic events following the deaths of the ten republican hunger-strikers in 1981, or the violent aftermath of the Anglo-Irish Agreement of 1985. Yet Dowra and Stalker were the subjects of a disproportionate degree of public interest, and of political sensitivity at Westminster and Dublin. Chronologically, the first of the two was Dowra, which began for the RUC in the fourth week of September. Unknown to us, however, it had in fact been festering for nine months in a parochial manner in County Cavan, in the Republic of Ireland.

It all started in a public house, the Bush Bar, in Blacklion, a little village just across the border from County Fermanagh. James Francis McGovern, a single man in his thirties living in Fermanagh, entered the pub late on the evening of 15 December 1981 and, in less than an hour, he drank several beers. He left around 11.30 p.m., but returned a few minutes later, looking for change of a pound note. At the bar, he found himself innocently in the centre of a dispute between an off-duty member of the Garda Síochána, Garda Thomas Nangle, and Vincent McGovern, the son of the proprietor. Thomas Nangle had already had a little too much to drink, but was looking for more. Seamus McGovern, the proprietor and no relation to Francis, thought that Nangle had had enough and refused to serve him.

Unfortunately for Francis McGovern, he spoke when he might better have kept silent, and received for his trouble a blow, however delivered, from Garda Nangle. In his defence later, Nangle claimed that Francis McGovern seemed to bump into his fist as he, Nangle, made to ward off an anticipated blow. In military parlance, Nangle claimed to have made something of a pre-emptive strike! As a result, McGovern lay unconscious on the floor, before being admitted to the Erne Hospital in Enniskillen for the remainder of that night. Fortunately, he sustained no serious injury.

At the time, nothing of this minor fracas in the public house caused the slightest ripple outside Blacklion village, or even within Garda circles. Shortly afterwards, Francis McGovern made a statement to the local Garda sergeant about the alleged assault.

Subsequently, Francis McGovern was apparently approached by another Garda member in an effort to persuade him to drop the case. It seems he agreed to settle out of court for £400. McGovern then formally wrote to the Gardaí in Blacklion to advise them that he wished to withdraw his statement of complaint against Garda Nangle. During the following months, McGovern claimed that he did not receive the £400 as promised.

Despite Francis McGovern's withdrawal of his complaint, a Garda from Blacklion served a witness summons on him to appear at Dowra Court on Monday, 27 September 1982. Since there were other witnesses to the assault, including the proprietor of the pub and his son, the charge could not be allowed to drop just because McGovern did not want to proceed with it.

By coincidence, within the RUC, Assistant Chief Constable Bobby Killen, who had been head of RUC Special Branch for almost two years, had notified me in August of his unexpected decision to resign with effect from 30 September 1982. I was irritated and bitterly disappointed with Bobby for leaving, not least because senior officers with similar command experience were, at that time, in short supply and terrorist violence was again increasing, after a lull in the months of June and July.

I appointed Trevor Forbes to be his successor, and placed him in post from 1 September so that he would have a little time to gain knowledge of his duties, before taking over full responsibility. Although he had no CID or Special Branch experience, I selected Trevor because of his recognised energy and enthusiasm. As a seasoned operational officer, he had proved himself in the difficult border Division around Newry, when he served as deputy to the Chief Superintendent, then Michael McAtamney. Subsequently, Trevor Forbes had been outstanding in his work in Community Relations and also Traffic Branch. He had, however, little or no experience of working with the Gardaí, other than at Divisional level, and had yet to establish a close working relationship with officers at Garda Headquarters in Dublin.

It was from within the Intelligence and Security Branch of Garda Headquarters on 17 September that a Detective Chief Superintendent made a telephone call to RUC Headquarters. His request was for any information which the RUC might have in relation to a man called 'Terry' McGovern of 'Laurencetown', near Enniskillen in County Fermanagh.

Much later, it was established that the Detective Chief Superintendent's inquiry had been triggered by a request from a civil servant within the Department of Justice in Dublin. There was, in fact, no McGovern with the Christian name of 'Terry' known in County Fermanagh, nor was there a place called 'Laurencetown'. It subsequently emerged that 'Laurencetown' was probably an error for 'Florencecourt', close to the splendid Marble Arch Caves in Fermanagh. Francis McGovern came from Florencecourt.

It transpired that in the week commencing 20 September 1982, an RUC Special Branch Chief Inspector had obtained specific intelligence relating to terrorist activities in County Fermanagh. This information raised a question concerning the possible involvement of James Francis McGovern. Both he and his brother, Philip, were believed to have been on the periphery of republican activities for some time. Careful local inquiries and limited surveillance were carried out in the area, with a view to ensuring that both men could be arrested early on Monday, 27 September. Three other Fermanagh men, suspected of being involved in terrorist crimes in that locality, were also scheduled for arrest the following morning.

Over the weekend of 25 and 26 September, when the local Special Branch Inspector in Enniskillen was informed that a certain 'James McGovern' was due to be arrested, he initially believed that it referred to a man whom he knew to be eighty years of age. Immediately, he queried this instruction with his superiors, only to be advised that the direction to arrest related to the two young McGovern brothers. This proper and legitimate check by the Inspector was seized upon later by a newspaper reporter, who depicted it dramatically as an objection to the arrest of James Francis McGovern. This was typical of ill-founded and often opportunistic reporting on the whole of the Dowra Affair.

The full arrest and interviewing operation had been directed and co-ordinated by the Regional Detective Superintendent in Armagh. On Sunday, 26 September, when all the arrangements were ready for implementation the following morning, this particular Detective Superintendent received the tragic news that his mother had died unexpectedly. Consequently, he had to take leave immediately. Control of the arrest operation was passed to his subordinate, and it went ahead as planned for Monday, 27th.

However, when McGovern's home was entered by uniformed RUC officers early next morning, it was quickly established that Francis was not there. Only his brother, who was at home, was arrested. A section of the police unit was quickly despatched to Belcoo, a village on the border, where it was known that Francis occasionally stayed at a certain house. He was, in fact, found there and was arrested.

At Belcoo, he advised the RUC that he was due to appear at Dowra District Court later that day. In view of this information, the RUC officer-in-charge stopped at Enniskillen police station *en route* to Armagh, and asked the police there to ensure that the Gardaí were informed of McGovern's arrest and that Dowra District Court was made aware of his inability to attend. The arresting party with the McGovern brothers then continued to Gough Holding Centre in Armagh.

There, Francis McGovern again raised the matter of his expected appearance in Dowra Court that morning, and on this occasion RUC Detective Sergeant 'A' telephoned Cavan Garda station. He spoke there to Detective Sergeant 'W' and asked him to pass on a message to the Gardaí at Dowra that McGovern was in the custody of the RUC and could not, therefore, appear as a witness that day in a case of assault by Garda Nangle on him. It later became apparent that this telephone call was the first in what became a distorted flow of information.

By coincidence, Detective Sergeant 'A' had grown up in Belcoo as a boy because his own father had lived and served there as a member of the RUC.

With his intimate knowledge of Belcoo and nearby Blacklion, the Sergeant began talking casually about the area to Francis McGovern, while interviewing him. McGovern ultimately chose to put a sinister interpretation on the Sergeant's reference to Blacklion, which McGovern felt implied prior information about the court appearance. Although this inference was totally false, one can with hindsight understand McGovern's reasoning.

Meantime, south of the border, Detective Sergeant 'W' in Cavan had noted the message as it was given to him by Detective Sergeant 'A' from Armagh. 'W' then rang Dowra Garda station and spoke to Garda 'X', asking him if he would deliver a message to the court. 'W' read the message as he himself had understood it. It was easy for 'X' to deliver the message, as the Garda station and the court shared the same building in Dowra.

The message Garda 'X' gave his Superintendent 'Y' was that McGovern would not be attending court that day, and that this information had come from the Gardaí at Cavan, after a message from the RUC at Lisnaskea in County Fermanagh, phoning from Armagh He omitted to mention to Superintendent 'Y' that McGovern had been arrested by the RUC.

Aware only of McGovern's non-attendance at court that day, not the reason for it, Superintendent 'Y' went on into the courthouse. There, he joined the State Solicitor, who was presenting the case against Garda Nangle. 'Y' gave the State Solicitor the concise message as he had received it from Garda 'X', and this of course did not contain any reference to McGovern being detained by the RUC. Neither the Superintendent nor the State Solicitor considered it necessary to advise the Presiding Judge about McGovern's inability to attend court. Consequently, the whole purpose of the series of RUC telephone calls early that Monday morning had been defeated at the last hurdle! The State Solicitor even proceeded to call the injured party, James Francis McGovern, to come forward. He did not, and could not, appear. If the judge had known of the main witness's detention by the RUC, he might have felt obliged to adjourn or postpone the case until McGovern was available.

At the conclusion of the hearing, the judge commented on the increasing frequency of assaults on Gardaí, and said that many of them were committed by so-called 'patriots'. He added that since the court required the best evidence, which was not available to him in this prosecution because of McGovern's non-appearance, he would dismiss the charge against Garda Nangle.

On 1 October 1982, only four days after the Dowra Court hearing, Superintendent 'Y' made a formal statement to a senior Garda officer explaining the message he had received from 'W' and why he had not told the judge. Although this vital statement was made by the Superintendent early in October 1982, it was not made available to the RUC by Garda Headquarters until July 1984. By then, the damage caused by the Dowra Affair to relations between the Garda Commissioner and me was immense. The ins and outs of this alleged assault, and the events of 27 September 1982 both outside and inside Dowra Court, were destined to spread far beyond the confines of that remote rural border area.

On 29 September 1982 the Police Complaints Board (PCB) for Northern Ireland received a written complaint from Father Denis Faul, an outspoken Catholic priest from Dungannon, County Tyrone. In essence, it asked whether there had been 'collusion between the RUC and people in the Republic to pervert the course of justice', when James McGovern was arrested at 6 a.m. by the RUC on the very day he was due to appear in Dowra Court, and then released that evening, after the case against Garda Nangle had been dismissed for lack of the main prosecution witness. In his complaint, Father Faul also drew attention to the fact that Garda Nangle was the brother-in-law of Sean Doherty TD, the Minister for Justice in Charles Haughey's Fianna Fáil Government.

This information was unknown to me at that time, and I believe it was also totally unknown then at RUC Headquarters. Judging by his letter of complaint, Father Faul had no knowledge of the efforts made by RUC officers at different levels to notify the Gardaí promptly of McGovern's detention, and thereby notify Dowra District Court. Had there been less haste and more careful examination of the sequence of events, I believe much unnecessary aggravation might have been avoided.

The following day, the PCB forwarded Father Faul's complaint to RUC Headquarters for investigation. Assistant Chief Constable Trevor Forbes, then only a few weeks as head of Special Branch, immediately checked the background to McGovern's arrest and satisfied me that he could find absolutely no evidence in the case of any collusion between the Gardaí and the RUC at any level. On his return from compassionate leave after his mother's death, the Regional Detective Superintendent, who had originally been in charge of the arrest operation, confirmed Trevor Forbes's findings and also rejected completely any question of there having been collusion.

The kind of rumour put into circulation at that time has been preserved in many publications, including *Operation Brogue*, a book by the late Captain Sean Feehan, head of the Mercier Press. In it he suggested that there was a plot to destroy the Fianna Fáil party and Charles Haughey's political career:

> one of the worst pieces of venom directed against Sean Doherty was the Dowra affair — when he was accused of squaring the RUC to have a witness, James McGovern, arrested in the six counties, a witness who was to give evidence against Mr Doherty's brother-in-law, Garda Nangle, in a court in the Republic . . . the arrest of McGovern was a ploy to discredit Mr Doherty and was planned and carried out by the RUC Special Branch under the supervision of the British Secret Service.[1]

I talked the situation through with Garda Commissioner Patrick McLaughlin on our secure telephone line, and gave him the result of my own inquiries, along with a reassurance that our internal investigation was being pursued urgently. As the RUC Deputy Chief Constable has a statutory duty to oversee disciplinary matters, I left it to Michael McAtamney to investigate, while I carried on with my own duties. With an escalation of terrorist activity in the autumn of 1982, and the six fatal shootings of unarmed men by the RUC, I had much more serious problems than Dowra to worry about.

However, the Northern Ireland Office and Secretary of State Jim Prior began to show a keen interest in the Dowra Affair, as did the Police Authority. I reassured them that there was no evidence or suspicion of any collusion emerging from our inquiries, and that everyone had to await the outcome of full investigations both north and south of the border.

As it happened, the time and the mood were right for rumours of a put-up job, of a scandal. In the political world of the Republic of Ireland, 1982 had already been a tempestuous year, with allegations of unlawful telephone tappings by the Garda Síochána at the behest of the Fianna Fáil Government, and the situation was only exacerbated by charges of improper interference in Garda matters by the Minister for Justice, Sean Doherty. The arrest of Francis McGovern by the RUC and the dismissal of the case against Garda Nangle, Doherty's brother-in-law, were used by journalists and certain politicians to stir the plot in the South. It was hardly surprising that Fianna Fáil lost the general election in November, leaving Fine Gael and the Labour Party to form a Coalition Government, headed by Garret FitzGerald.

Into the plot were thrown all sorts of ingredients, including the following, from *The Boss*:

> On the same Saturday (18 December 1982), an unusual meeting took place at Garda headquarters. The chief constable of the RUC, Sir Jack Hermon, and his Assistant Chief Constable in charge of the RUC Special Branch, Trevor Forbes, had discussions with their opposite numbers in the Garda Síochána — McLaughlin and Ainsworth. It was unusual for such meetings to take place on Saturdays and the agenda was quite extraordinary. There was just one item: any issues which might arise with the advent of the new government in the Republic.[2]

In fact, it was not 'unusual' for such meetings to take place on Saturdays. Since the Garda Commissioner and I both had numerous commitments during December, a weekday meeting proved impossible. As weekend working was part of my normal pattern, I had suggested that we meet on that Saturday morning, to which Pat McLaughlin willingly agreed, as he knew of my deep concern over the escalating terrorist activity in the North. I had just returned from five weeks' leave of absence in America, and there was an urgent need for an operational review of the position with the Gardaí; to have delayed it into the New Year was unacceptable to me. I clearly recollect the purpose of that meeting on 18 December 1982, and remember well the occasion.

I had returned from holiday early on 6 December, only hours before seventeen people were killed in an INLA no-warning bomb in the Droppin' Well Inn, a dance-hall in Ballykelly, County Londonderry. The shock of such a multiple murder reverberated throughout Northern Ireland and world-wide. Those who died were a local boy of seventeen, five young women, and eleven off-duty soldiers. Many others, civilians and soldiers, suffered grievous and lasting injuries. Such terrorist atrocities were causing great community anxiety and tension. Northern politicians were in their customary strident, often irresponsible and excitable mood, and I had James Prior, a relatively new and still somewhat perturbable Secretary of State.

Consequently, I had initiated the Saturday meeting with Pat McLaughlin to discuss co-ordinated preventive security measures across the border, and specifically the need for overt and covert patrolling in the North and South to inhibit the movement of terrorists, their explosives and weapons. The meeting was intense and continued over lunch. To my mind, therefore, the comment in *The Boss* was sheer nonsense. Other media hype about possible collusion could equally be so described.

Nothing emerged in our ongoing investigation to establish or arouse suspicion of any collusion between the Gardaí and the RUC. I heard nothing to suggest that the RUC's involvement in the arrest of McGovern was anything other than a routine and entirely proper initiative. From past experience, I knew that if there had been collusion as alleged, even if our investigations could not establish it, it would eventually have come to my notice. It never did. To the present day, I have been sustained by this fact, and by the knowledge that my actions in relation to Dowra after 27 September 1982 were correctly undertaken.

The matter was really of little consequence to me until the resignation of Commissioner Pat McLaughlin and his Deputy, Joe Ainsworth, in February 1983, as a result of the phone-tapping controversy in the South. Larry Wren was appointed by the Coalition Government as Commissioner. McLaughlin's departure and Wren's appointment were the subject of considerable comment in the Republic, but its problems were not ours, nor should we have been involved in them. While disappointed that Pat McLaughlin was leaving, and that we would lose Joe Ainsworth's enthusiastic and successful efforts to curb terrorist crime, I had no qualms about Larry's appointment, having worked well with him in the late 1970s.

The fact that the Coalition Government was disturbed that the course of justice might have been perverted in the Dowra Affair was first conveyed formally to the RUC early in January 1983 by a request from the Republic's Director of Public Prosecutions for detailed information. The Gardaí had, at an early stage in the investigation of Father Faul's complaint, been asked by the RUC to provide statements from those Garda officers involved in receiving and passing the information about McGovern's arrest to Dowra District Court.

On 8 February 1983, Larry Wren came as Garda Commissioner to RUC Headquarters. Such visits between Commissioners and me were by then routine, and alternated between Belfast and Dublin. My recollection is that he was accompanied by Steve Fanning, who was then, I believe, a Chief Superintendent in the Intelligence and Security Branch of the Gardaí. As a shrewd, capable and dedicated policeman, Fanning commanded great respect and liking within not only his own Special Branch but that of the RUC.

Michael McAtamney was not at that meeting with Larry Wren and Steve Fanning because he had, at the end of January, departed on a planned six-month sabbatical visit to the United States to study police methods. The Commissioner raised various aspects of the McGovern case. During our discussions, it became clear to me that the methods adopted within the Gardaí to investigate complaints against the police differed totally from those within the RUC. As far as the RUC was concerned, its system of investigation was practically identical to those pertaining in England and Wales. Although the Police Authority for Northern Ireland was not itself directly involved in individual complaints, it did have responsibility to overview our procedures to ensure that they were fully and properly carried out. Above all, the Chief Constable of the RUC had to remain aloof from any detailed disciplinary investigations, as he might in the end have to preside over disciplinary hearings and adjudicate on the guilt, innocence or punishment of police officers.

By comparison, the Garda Síochána itself conducted all investigations into internal disciplinary matters, with the Commissioner being accountable to the Minister for Justice. Without a police authority as a buffer between the Gardaí and the Minister, political influence could obviously be brought to bear. In essence, the Gardaí adhered to a system which had in the main existed since the pre-1922 era of the Royal Irish Constabulary.

As our discussions developed, I came to the conclusion that Larry Wren failed to grasp the fact that our respective procedures bore no compatibility with one another. He advised me that there was a belief at lower levels within the Gardaí and the RUC that an Assistant Chief Constable had a knowledge of McGovern's arrest, and indeed had directed it. This, he agreed, could well have been created by irresponsible and unwarranted media statements. He concluded, however, that they had 'not one iota of evidence to sustain the belief'. This point lodged in my mind because of the considerable pressure which I felt he ultimately attempted to exert on me. I advised Larry that, as Chief Constable, I could initiate action for investigating any chief officer only if I received a formal complaint based on some evidence or reasonable suspicion.

For the next routine meeting between us, held on 19 April 1983 at Garda Headquarters, I had prepared an agenda with security questions, as well as more general subjects, which would allow me to brief Larry about the significant reorganisational changes taking place within the RUC. I kept this particular agenda. Jean accompanied me to Dublin that day to do some shopping. I found the atmosphere with the Gardaí invariably relaxed and warm, with plenty of Irish wit in evidence. At bottom, there was a good understanding between us, as had been evidenced at the sixtieth anniversary celebrations of the creation of the RUC and the Garda Síochána.

As the finale to our celebrations a concert had been organised in the Ulster Hall in Belfast on the nights of 7 and 8 October 1982, ten days after the court case in Dowra. The RUC bands and its two choirs contributed to the programme, as did a full choir of An Garda Síochána.

At a reception for them afterwards at RUC Headquarters, a Garda, known as the Bard, presented me with a poem to commemorate our anniversary year. It ran:

> We salute you, gallant colleagues,
> on your Diamond Jubilee.
> You've won yourselves an honoured place
> in Ireland's history.
> Your bravery in times of trial
> Is recognised by all.
> You have not failed whate'er the cost
> To answer duty's call.
> Some have paid the highest price,
> Their deaths caused grief and pain.
> Together we will show the world
> They did not die in vain.

I asked the Bard to read his poem as he would wish it to be heard, and he did so to a hushed audience. At its end, there was a long burst of spontaneous applause. When silence was finally restored, I thanked him for his sentiments, but added that I had one criticism. Silence and some embarrassment followed. Quietly, I began with the second line, 'On your Diamond Jubilee,' but pointed out that 'It's the Gardaí's too. We are pups of the same sire. Would you consider changing the word "your" to "our"?' Laughing, the Bard said, 'Give me a pen, somebody,' and made the change to more enthusiastic applause.

The meeting of 19 April 1983 with Larry Wren, though, took on a completely different tone. The fourteen items on my prepared agenda were all, except one, relevant to our joint thrust against terrorist criminality. However, in the privacy of his office, the Commissioner immediately raised the Dowra issue with a vehemence which surprised me. It was not even on my agenda, because I had not judged it an appropriate subject, since our internal investigations were still ongoing.

To the exclusion of all else, and to my scarcely concealed annoyance, he briefed me in some detail on the problems which had arisen over alleged Fianna Fáil interference with the Gardaí in 1982, during Sean Doherty's tenure of office as Minister for Justice.

It was without doubt the intensity of Commissioner Wren's manner which struck me. Some of the information which he disclosed related to purely internal administrative and financial matters, and had no bearing on the Dowra Affair. I concluded that the Commissioner was being subjected to some considerable political pressure over the Affair. I carefully confined my remarks to the identified and recorded efforts of RUC officers of various ranks to ensure that the Gardaí and Dowra District Court were fully informed of McGovern's arrest and detention.

Such was my anxiety about this meeting with Larry Wren that I recorded my recollections of it while we were making the return journey to Belfast. At RUC Headquarters, I had my notes typed for permanent record. By coincidence, the following week, on 25 April, the Republic's Director of Public Prosecutions lost his appeal in the High Court against the dismissal of the Nangle case at Dowra District Court.

After that particular meeting with Larry Wren, I wrote to him formally, referring to our discussions on Dowra and asking him to let me have a report of everything concerning the possibility of involvement by RUC officers in the case. I recognised the significance, indeed seriousness, of any such involvement, and was more determined than ever to have any allegations emanating from the Gardaí thoroughly investigated within our existing systems. I was equally determined that the RUC should not be drawn into the problems, intrigues and obvious bitterness between the main political parties in the Republic of Ireland. Instead, I wanted the Force to have the goodwill and maximum co-operation of the Gardaí, so that terrorists whose roots were firmly planted in the Republic could be prevented from fulfilling their constitutional aspirations through bloodshed.

Early in May, I received Wren's reply, which properly confined itself to those aspects of the case that had some connection with the RUC. That letter contained comments which, in my view, made implications, if not allegations, about a chief officer of the RUC. I was so concerned by this that I arranged to visit the Chairman of the Police Authority's Complaints and Discipline Committee, who at that time happened to be a practising solicitor. I called at his office and showed him Larry Wren's letter. Having confirmed my views about it, he advised me to tread warily by putting in writing any subsequent discussion of the Dowra Affair with the Commissioner. Reluctantly, I accepted his advice as sound.

Oddly enough, a few years after he had relinquished that post as Committee Chairman, he professed no recollection whatsoever of our meeting or his words to me on that occasion. My two drivers, however, have not forgotten the visit, as it was the only time I ever went to his office.

Since it is the statutory duty of the Police Authority to deal with complaints against chief officers of the RUC, I briefed its Chairman, Sir Myles Humphreys, about the references in Larry Wren's letter. I followed that up by sending a comprehensive letter of my own, with a copy of Larry's letter attached. Later, I telephoned the Commissioner to update him on my actions in relation to his letter, and also confirmed that conversation in writing.

On Thursday, 16 June, Commissioner Wren rang my office at 8.25 p.m., while I was hosting a dinner at Headquarters for a group of senior Australian police officers. The message from the Commissioner was noted and brought to me. It was terse. He needed results.

On 20 June 1983, I received a letter from the Police Authority confirming my view about the Commissioner's letter. It also asked me to request the

Commissioner to forward such evidence as he had in support of his complaint, so that the matter could, if necessary, be investigated. Consequently, I wrote again to Larry in an effort to clarify my position by enclosing copies of the procedures governing the investigation of complaints against chief RUC officers, and explaining what was deemed to be a complaint within those procedures.

A letter of 25 July 1983 from Garda Headquarters, however, included a firm statement that the Commissioner had not made any allegation against any member of the RUC, and recognised that the manner in which this matter was dealt with was a matter absolutely for me and my Police Authority.

I acknowledged receipt of the letter and forwarded it to the Police Authority. It then requested me, under section 15 (2) of the Police Act (NI) 1970, to provide it with a formal report regarding the grounds for the arrest of James Francis McGovern on 27 September 1982, and also the investigation file into Father Faul's complaint. These requests I complied with fully, and to the satisfaction of the Police Authority.

Early in October 1983, the case suddenly took a different twist. I received a letter from Larry Wren advising me that he had taken another look at the correspondence in the McGovern case. Larry emphasised that the Gardaí had not made any 'complaint' against the RUC, but instead wanted some assistance in answering a long list of very detailed questions about McGovern's arrest. To assist Larry, I ordered the preparation of a comprehensive response to his request; this was supplied in a report of 2 November 1983.

Father Denis Faul's complaint had automatically launched a full investigation, during which every officer involved with the detention and interrogation of the McGovern brothers was interviewed after caution. Not a shred of evidence of RUC collusion with the Gardaí ever emerged. I was satisfied that no more thorough investigation was possible, and I was certainly not going to depart in any way from its findings in order to satisfy the expediencies of the moment or unjustified pressures from the South.

Wearied by the manipulations over the Dowra Affair by the Republic's authorities, I issued a public statement on 6 December. In it, I declared that I had 'no desire other than to continue the same cordial co-operative relationship with the present Commissioner' as I had enjoyed with Pat McLaughlin. I also noted that Larry Wren had stated in writing that he had 'no complaint against the RUC'.

Even the resolution of our inquiries did not change Larry Wren's position. The criminal investigation file into Father Faul's complaint was forwarded by Michael McAtamney in mid-December 1983 to the Director of Public Prosecutions for Northern Ireland. In early March 1984, the DPP directed no prosecution, because there was no evidence to justify one.

In April 1984, the inquiry and report into the complaint were forwarded to the Police Complaints Board for Northern Ireland. After thorough scrutiny, there followed requests for further information on a series of detailed and pertinent questions, including a specific request for the statement of

Superintendent 'Y'. Although it had been made in the South on 1 October 1982, unlike all the other statements of Garda officers it had not been made available earlier to the RUC inquiry. His statement was crucial, because it made clear that Garda 'X' had not given him the full message — omitting to say that the RUC had arrested McGovern — and also that 'Y', together with the State Solicitor, had decided not to tell the Presiding Judge that McGovern would not be attending Dowra District Court that day. In light of all the evidence, the Police Complaints Board agreed that no disciplinary charges should be preferred against any RUC officer.

Despite the findings of the DPP and the PCB, on 13 January 1984 Francis McGovern initiated a civil action jointly against the Chief Constable of the RUC and the Secretary of State for Northern Ireland for damages for wrongful arrest and false imprisonment. In May that year, at a Police Authority meeting, I made it absolutely clear that I would contest McGovern's claim and in this I had the total support of the Police Authority, which was concerned lest there be any attempt to settle the case out of court. His legal action lumbered on for several years, fitfully pursued by Francis McGovern. Then, quietly, while I was in America in January 1989, it was settled out of court with a payment of £3,000 agreed damages and costs for McGovern. If I had known of the Northern Ireland Office's intention to settle his claim, I would have certainly resisted it and insisted on airing the whole saga in open court. I feel irritated with the NIO that I was never given that opportunity.

Meanwhile, the Commissioner's refusal to meet me was much publicised during 1984, and late into 1985. I believe the absence of meetings between the two of us had no discernible impact on the level of effectiveness of RUC/Garda co-operation against terrorism at Divisional and District level. If anything, what was missed was the dynamism of Joe Ainsworth's thrust against terrorism and other serious crime in the Republic. Throughout this unpleasant and unnecessary affair, I was immensely reassured that the sound working relationship, affinity indeed, between the main body of the Gardaí and the RUC had remained steadfast. The Bard's poem of October 1982 proved to be no mere flight of fancy.

It was only when the Anglo-Irish Agreement, signed in November 1985, required maximum co-operation between the RUC and the Garda Síochána that Larry Wren's animosity disappeared like snow off a ditch in springtime; his attitude towards me was as if the Dowra Affair had never been! If Dowra teaches us anything, it is that the expediencies of politics and politicians must be kept out of policing in order that the police service retains its integrity.

Notes

1 Captain Sean Feehan, *Operation Brogue* (Cork: Mercier Press 1983), extract published in *Irish Press*, December 1983.
2 Joe Joyce and Peter Murtagh, *The Boss (Charles J. Haughey in Government)* (Swords, Co. Dublin: Poolbeg Press 1983), p. 307.

14

COVER STORIES

The Terry Inquiry into Kincora, the RUC's joyful jubilee celebrations and even the Dowra Affair — everything in 1982 was overshadowed by a series of violent deaths towards the end of the year. On Wednesday, 27 October 1982 at 2.19 p.m., three police officers, Sergeant John Quinn, Constable Alan McCloy and Constable Paul Hamilton, were murdered in an IRA bomb attack at Kinnego Embankment outside Lurgan, County Armagh. Immediately before the bomb exploded, Jean and I were approaching Lurgan in a police car. We stopped momentarily at a roundabout. As we did so, we heard the explosion, and our driver pointed to the smoke and debris erupting on the skyline. A few minutes later, our observer had to respond to a radio call from Lurgan police station requesting our location. It transpired that the call was made in order to establish whether we had been the victims of the explosion. We were *en route* to Lurgan College, where it was Speech Day and I had to speak as chief guest, and Jean present the prizes.

Upon our arrival at the school, my driver telephoned RUC Headquarters and was told that three police officers had been injured. About forty minutes later, as I moved with Jean in the formal procession into the Assembly Hall, my driver whispered to me that the three officers had, in fact, been killed by a 1,000 lb bomb. As soon as the ceremonies were over, I left for the scene of the explosion, where I gave a brief interview to some waiting journalists. Afterwards, at Lurgan Station, I discovered that Kinnego Embankment had for some time been placed out of bounds to police and army patrols. It was only after a check by a police surveillance unit that local permission had been given to the three-man mobile patrol to visit the scene of a reported theft.

The murders of these policemen were subsequently to influence the minds of Deputy Chief Constable John Stalker and Detective Chief Superintendent John Thorburn of the Greater Manchester Police Force, in their investigation into three shooting incidents in which six unarmed people were killed by the RUC. Their investigation, and particularly the manner of it, resulted in much suspicion and damaging allegations of a 'Shoot to Kill' policy being operated by the RUC. It also caused much irresponsible comment by certain journalists and politicians.

Until the autumn, 1982 had been a relatively peaceful year by comparison to the bloody ones preceding it. By September, however, it became apparent that both of the republican terrorist organisations, the Provisional IRA and the Irish National Liberation Army (INLA), were hell-bent on stepping up their activities. They were in competition with one another, especially in the Armagh area, with the INLA being directed by a notorious terrorist called Dominic McGlinchey. Many attacks were made on individual members of the security forces and on civilians. Although good intelligence pre-empted some, others resulted in the tragic loss of several lives in County Armagh and along its border with the Republic of Ireland. The intensity of the terrorist competition in this area put the RUC and its Reserve under extreme pressure at that time.

Also in September, Assistant Chief Constable Bobby Killen had retired as head of Special Branch. I believe that Bobby's departure contributed indirectly to the events which were about to unfold. And likewise, I believe that if I had not been absent from mid-November into early December 1982, the general supervision of the police investigations into the shooting dead of the six unarmed men would have been much firmer at senior level than was the case.

Since Jean and I had had little or no respite for two years, we had decided to take an extended period of leave in the United States. We timed our holiday to coincide with a conference of the IACP (International Association of Chiefs of Police) in Atlanta, Georgia, from 13 to 18 November 1982. We also wanted to visit Barbara and Kevin in Florida, primarily to reassure ourselves that they were settling down happily into married life. Our arrangements were finalised, with departure booked from Dublin Airport early on 12 November and our return from Atlanta on 6 December.

On Thursday, 11 November, I attended an informal dinner at the home of an official in the Northern Ireland Office, while Jean stayed in the flat at Head-quarters to finish packing. If we were out late or had a very early engagement, we would have used the flat, rather than drive to or from home, down the Ards Peninsula. At approximately 11.30 p.m., I left the dinner to return to help Jean. As soon as I reached the car, my driver told me that a radio report had just been received saying that three people were dead in a shooting incident in County Armagh, but as yet it was unknown whether they were terrorists, civilians or members of the security forces.

Back at Headquarters, I learned that the dead were Sean Burns, Eugene Toman and James Gervaise McKerr, all known republican terrorists. I was told that they had broken through a police road-block, had been pursued by police officers, and shot. This shooting, which became known by the name of its location, just outside Lurgan, at Tullygally Road East, occurred about 10.30 p.m. on a dark road during extremely heavy rain and high winds. The officers involved reported that shots had been fired at them from the escaping vehicle. The area around the shooting was cordoned off until the arrival of police specialists. Details were scarce, but the pressure from journalists for information was mounting. An RUC press statement, based on available information, was issued some time later.

As my Deputy, Michael McAtamney, would be in charge during my absence, he and other operational chief officers were informed. I managed to snatch an hour or so of sleep before departing for Dublin and onwards to the United States. I was at that time satisfied that the three men were known terrorists, killed by police officers who had returned fire at their car, after it had failed to stop at a road-block.

During my twenty-six days' leave, a further twenty-four people died in Northern Ireland as a result of terrorism. There was undoubtedly great tension and fear throughout the community, with increasing demands on the security forces. In the midst of this, a second shooting incident occurred. RUC officers shot dead Michael Tighe and seriously wounded his companion, Martin McCauley, on 24 November. This incident also became identified by its location at an old hayshed beside Ballyneery Road North, again on the outskirts of Lurgan.

It was in the aftermath of this that Jean and I arrived back at Dublin Airport on the morning of 6 December. We were met by our usual RUC drivers in the official car, and had a Garda escort to the border. That day ended in horror, with seventeen dead in the 'Droppin' Well' explosion at Ballykelly.

The following days were taken up by reading myself in with intelligence briefs, reports of various kinds and Minutes of the regular RUC Command meetings. Amongst these documents were the preliminary reports about the Tullygally Road East incident of 11 November. I noted that the police officers involved were adamant that gunfire had been directed at them from the escaping car; they claimed to have seen flashes coming from its rear windows. Despite this, the most thorough search of the terrorists' vehicle and the road they had driven along had revealed neither weapons nor spent cases; in fact, there was no evidence at all of fire having been returned by the occupants of the car. Consequently, I immediately ordered that the Northern Ireland Forensic Science Laboratory be asked to examine this particular aspect of the incident.

Working with the RUC Technical Support Unit, the Laboratory carried out exhaustive tests under simulated conditions during the hours of darkness. Independent tests were also carried out by the Laboratory without RUC involvement. These tests established that, when shots were fired at a vehicle, no flashes were apparent during daylight hours, but flashes were clearly seen in darkness, and were also visible as soon as the light began to fade. The results of these tests were of considerable relevance in the subsequent trial of the three police officers most directly involved in that shooting incident. In his judgment at Belfast Crown Court, Lord Justice Maurice Gibson later addressed this very point:

> It was a dark wet November night and the forensic evidence satisfies me that bullets striking the rear window and other metal parts of the rear of the car would in such circumstances and conditions emit flashes which could readily be mistaken for the muzzle flashes of guns fired from the back of the car, especially after the rear window was broken, as it was.

Bearing in mind the information about the fugitives which the accused had and the furious efforts to escape which they were making, I have no doubt that it was a reasonable conclusion that the accused were being fired at.

The third shooting incident occurred in Armagh city, this time at a housing estate called Mullacreevie Park, on Sunday evening, 12 December. Two men, Seamus Grew and Roderick Carroll, were shot dead by the RUC, apparently after failing to stop at a vehicle check-point.

In all, six men had been shot dead by the police, and one seriously injured, in these three incidents. In the first and third, no weapons had been found in the possession of those killed. In the second, while rifles were found in the hayshed, they were old and had no ammunition. I was extremely irritated to learn that, although police investigations of these shootings were being diligently pursued at detective superintendent level, the investigations into the three different agencies involved were being inadequately co-ordinated at senior level. The agencies were Special Branch, which provided the intelligence on which police surveillance was based, the HMSUs (Headquarters Mobile Support Units), under Special Branch control, and thirdly, CID, which assumed responsibility for the investigations into all three shootings. I rectified this straight away, ordering that there should be close liaison to ensure a comprehensive investigation.

The HMSUs were sophisticated, highly trained police teams. The covert surveillance unit's strength lay in its ability to observe without being detected, thus enabling HMSUs to be placed in a position to intercept terrorists in possession of weapons or explosives. The primary aims of these reactive police resources were to intercept the terrorist and to gain sufficient evidence for prosecution to conviction. These aims are not helped by HMSU members having recourse to force, especially the use of firearms, because this is counter-productive to their main aims. These specially selected officers know this, and so recourse to firearms is, for them, the action of last resort. But they are trained in survival techniques, which, in very dangerous circumstances, have to be employed. These techniques include what has become a well-known description: the use of 'firepower, speed and aggression'. But firepower is justified only if they know, or honestly believe, that their lives are under an immediate and real threat, which is a justification recognised by law.

Death brought about by police action must, of necessity, always be the subject of the most careful scrutiny, and I believed I had taken the required corrective steps, but it was already too late. By then, cover stories to protect the sources of police intelligence underlying these security force operations in relation to the shooting incidents had been improperly incorporated into police statements. These were ultimately furnished to the Director of Public Prosecutions and the Coroner's Court.

Over the years of continuing terrorist activity in Northern Ireland, a routine police procedure had developed to prevent arousing the suspicions of terrorist organisations that their internal security had been breached. A cover story would be created to conceal the real reasons for the presence of the police, or other security forces, at the place where terrorists were apprehended or weapons and explosives seized. To be effective, such cover stories had sometimes to be included in a public statement given by RUC Headquarters to the media. Never were cover stories to be used for any purpose other than this, and most certainly they were never to be included in police statements or given as evidence.

It was in this latter respect that police procedures went so disastrously wrong in these fatal shooting incidents involving the RUC. On the directions of their immediate superior officers, and in order to protect the sensitive sources and methods by which their intelligence had been obtained, police officers concealed their true role as members of the Headquarters Mobile Support Units (HMSUs). Consequently, they were directed to state to CID officers investigating the deaths that they had been on routine preventive patrolling, albeit at a time of high risk, and had fortuitously intercepted these individuals during routine patrols. These lies ultimately resulted in consideration being given to charging some police officers with conspiracy to pervert the course of justice.

From the beginning, I was convinced that, while mistakes had occurred and wrong instructions had been given, no police officers had intended individually or collectively to break the law. No officer was directly involved in more than one of the incidents, and that was out of a unit of thirty or so. No conspiracy to kill, or to pervert the course of justice, would or could have been contrived or, if contrived, have been concealed by so many for so long.

What would ultimately be at issue was whether police intelligence — and indeed that of other security agencies — and the methods used to procure it should continue to be protected, as they had been for many years, or whether it was in the greater public interest that such vital information be revealed. In the police service generally, the cultivation of informants has long been a very necessary, albeit unpalatable, method of gleaning information. In Ireland in particular, the word 'informer' evokes the same repugnance and contempt as the word 'traitor'. Terrorists themselves recognise the intense threat posed by informers to the success of their cause, to the survival of their organisation, and to their own well-being. As a result, the punishment they mete out to an exposed informer is death after 'interrogation', for which one should read torture. The security forces and British intelligence agencies recognise their responsibility to protect informants, because of their very significant value in the defeat of terrorism.

Early in 1983, the police investigation file on the first shooting incident, in which James McKerr, Sean Burns and Eugene Toman died at Tullygally Road East, and that on the shooting dead of Michael Tighe and the injuring of Martin McCauley at Ballyneery Road North, were forwarded from CID to the Northern Ireland Director of Public Prosecutions, Sir Barry Shaw. A separate report on Martin McCauley was also prepared and submitted to the DPP, who subsequently approved recommendations that McCauley be prosecuted for his unlawful possession of firearms.

In April 1983, the police investigation file relating to the deaths of Seamus Grew and Roderick Carroll at Mullacreevie Park was received at RUC Headquarters Crime Department, where it was carefully studied. Problems emerged because aspects of the evidence given by the police officers involved in the shooting conflicted with the forensic evidence and, therefore, posed a doubt over the recommendation to be made to the DPP. In the absence of my Deputy, who was then in the United States on a sabbatical, the police file was referred directly to me, with an accompanying draft report for my consideration on the propriety of sending the case to the DPP. This was the only occasion while I was Chief Constable that I was asked personally to resolve an uncertainty over whether to prosecute a member of the RUC for a serious crime. Normally, any queries of that kind would have been resolved by the Deputy Chief Constable and, sometimes, discussed by him with me.

The draft report had been prepared by a highly competent and legally qualified chief superintendent. I discussed the file and its conclusions with him. His opinion was not founded on a belief that a police officer was guilty of murder, and so he had not recommended any specific charge. Rather, it was his view that the only way to decide the legality or illegality of the constable's action in shooting Grew and Carroll was to let the case go to trial.

I recommended, however, that there be no prosecution of the constable, because I had no doubt in my mind that he had not committed a crime. Never for a moment did I question the integrity of the information supplied to me in the police investigation file. I was greatly angered when subsequent events revealed that cover stories had been incorporated into this file, thereby giving an incomplete account of the circumstances surrounding the shooting incident.

Early in May 1983, Assistant Chief Constable Trevor Forbes — by then well established as head of Special Branch — and I met both the Attorney-General, then Sir Michael Havers, and Sir Barry Shaw, the DPP, in order to discuss the three police reports and their implications. I sensed at our meeting that serious consideration was being given to the prosecution of some police officers for murder. So concerned was I over the ultimate adverse effect of the proposed prosecutions that I told the Attorney-General I would be willing to resign to avoid this possibility, and the inevitable witch-hunt that would follow. I said specifically that if any of the prosecutions were undertaken, they would fail, but that the consequent propaganda would be unstoppable. My offer of resignation would not, I was informed, influence any decision regarding the prosecutions of RUC officers.

Directly after that meeting with the DPP and the Attorney-General, I had ordered that comprehensive intelligence briefs be prepared by all Special Branch officers concerned, including those in charge of the surveillance teams. On receiving them, I realised fully, for the first time, the extent to which the operational police officers had been instructed to conceal from the CID the very sophisticated counter-terrorist activities which had preceded the shootings on 11 November and 12 December. The failure to disclose this information to investigating CID officers, even after caution, had negatived the statements of the policemen concerned. This in turn had seriously damaged the credibility of the CID investigations.

After the forwarding of these briefs to the Director of Public Prosecutions, there at once followed detailed meetings between the DPP's senior staff and the heads of Special Branch and CID. These led to further investigations by CID, and further interviews with all police and army personnel directly or indirectly involved in the three shooting incidents. All of the resultant statements were passed to the DPP's office.

Within a few days, Sir Barry Shaw wrote to me to express his concern that the additional information provided to him was still not sufficient. He felt that I should appoint an officer at very senior level — with special and full responsibility — to co-ordinate all the investigations and reports, check for further possible evidence, and report to him as quickly as possible. Since Michael McAtamney had returned early from America and had been in command during the first two incidents, I appointed him to assume responsibility for the investigation of the matters which the DPP would identify. I directed Michael to detach himself from all other duties, and work directly with the DPP's office, keeping me advised of progress. With considerable skill, Michael and his assistant disentangled the complex circumstances surrounding the shooting incidents.

At the end of August 1983, Sir Barry ordered the prosecution of Constable John Robinson for the murder of Seamus Grew on 12 December 1982. This was followed by a direction in mid-September that three more police officers — Sergeant Montgomery, Constable Brannigan and another Constable Robinson — be prosecuted for the murder of Eugene Toman on 11 November 1982. The DPP's instructions were issued during my period of annual leave, and I was extremely upset to learn of them upon my return. My firm view, that these men were not guilty of murder, had been ignored. The preferring of criminal charges also had the effect of delaying any investigation into the disciplinary aspects of the behaviour of police officers in their well-intentioned, but wholly improper, use of cover stories to protect the providers of sensitive police intelligence.

With difficulty, and after two High Court applications, we secured the release into police custody of the four officers charged with murder. They were taken to a hastily created detention centre, where I had arrangements structured so as to provide for visits by wives and families, and to give the men access to adequate recreational facilities. Within existing Home Office guidelines, applications were made for legal aid to assist towards the men's defence.

Nevertheless, John Stalker would later write:

> Four . . . charged with murder, had been kept in custody for up to
> eighteen months in solitary confinement awaiting trial . . . They hoped for

some legal support — but it never came. A private fund contributed to by lower-ranking policemen paid for a barrister on a private basis. They seemed to me to have been abandoned and isolated by a police force that had identified a need for them, selected them, trained them, used them and then cut them adrift.[1]

The fact was that only Constable John Robinson, the first arrested and charged, was detained for twenty days in Crumlin Road Prison in Belfast. During this time, he was held in the hospital area of the prison, was visited frequently by a superintendent, and was never, even for those twenty days, in solitary confinement. When he and the other three officers were transferred into police custody, they had virtually unlimited visits from family and friends, and were allowed home occasionally. Moreover, the Police Authority met in full the legal fees incurred in the defence of the four officers.

Prior to the criminal trials of the four, I advised them to feel uninhibited in telling the whole truth, because it was their freedom, their careers and the well-being of their families which were at stake. Therefore, in April 1984, Constable John Robinson went on trial for the murder of Seamus Grew, and publicly revealed for the first time the involvement of two superintendents in concocting a cover story. Mr Justice MacDermott summed up the kernel of the problem for RUC officers in this trial:

> I would simply say that when an incident occurs the true facts should be ascertained, if that be possible, as quickly as possible and that a person who may have to face a charge of murder (or indeed any charge) should not be required to tell a false story.
>
> This accused like any other person who is cautioned should have been allowed to tell his story freely and without restrictions — if his statement contained secret or operationally important matters then arrangements for editing, if appropriate, could have been made. The matter having been approached as it was, the task of the investigating detectives must have been made extremely difficult . . .

His comments identified both the nature of the police misbehaviour, and the need to protect intelligence in a proper fashion.

Constable Robinson's revelations attracted excited, almost hysterical, attention from some journalists and politicians, resulting in a public outcry for a full independent investigation. Such was the hype stirred by Constable Robinson's evidence, and his subsequent acquittal, that I quickly realised that nobody would be satisfied with further RUC statements or internal investigations. Only an independent investigation would do.

The DPP had meanwhile written to me, formally requesting further investigations into matters revealed by my Deputy's inquiry. These related to the omission of relevant facts from some police officers' statements; to alleged factual matters included in their statements which were false or misleading; and to the possibility of any offence of perverting, or attempting or conspiring to pervert, the course of justice. I, therefore, asked one of Her Majesty's Inspectors of Constabulary, Philip Myers, to nominate a suitable senior police officer from Great Britain to conduct the independent investigation. As an HMI, Philip Myers's regional responsibilities included inspecting the RUC, although my first official meeting with him had been in 1972 when, as the Chief Constable of North Wales, he had been the Inspecting Officer at a Passing-Out Parade in Enniskillen, and I had been the RUC's Training Officer. I trusted his judgment implicitly.

Finally, the trial of the other three police officers for the murder of Eugene Toman commenced towards the end of May 1984, and was completed on 5 June. Lord Justice Maurice Gibson acquitted all three, and was highly critical of 'those who prompted this prosecution'. He also criticised:

> the prosecution's failure at the preliminary inquiry to disclose information at its disposal which by this failure had left the presiding magistrate . . . with a very partial picture, and I do not think I am putting this too far if I say a false picture, of the circumstances of the shooting.

The judge continued:

> I wish to make it clear that having heard the entire Crown case exposed in open court I regard each of the accused absolutely blameless in this matter. I consider that, in fairness to them, that finding ought to be recorded together with my commendation for their courage and determination in bringing the three deceased men to justice, in this case to the final court of justice.

I had been totally vindicated in my assertion — made to both the Attorney-General and the Director of Public Prosecutions — that no police officers would be prosecuted to conviction for murder. As I had also predicted, the unsuccessful prosecutions opened a veritable Pandora's box of ill-founded suspicions and criticism of me and of the RUC. I derived no pleasure whatsoever from the accuracy of my forecast.

Note
1 John Stalker, *Stalker* (London: Harrap 1988), p. 60.

15

STALKER: THE INVESTIGATION

Within the month, Philip Myers had contacted Sir Lawrence Byford, then Chief HMI, and it was proposed that the Deputy Chief Constable of the Greater Manchester Police Force should lead the investigation into the matters raised by the Director of Public Prosecutions. I had no knowledge at all of this police officer, not even his name — in fact, I noted him as 'Stocker' in my diary, and in a note to my Police Authority on 4 June 1984, I wrote:

> After close consultation with the HMI, an investigation is now in hand in relation to those allegations. Deputy Chief Constable Stocker of Greater Manchester Police Force, aided by a Detective Chief Superintendent and a number of other CID officers from his Force, is in charge of it and will report to me.

And so the Minutes of Police Authority meetings and formal letters to me continued with that spelling for several weeks, until his name was finally corrected to 'Stalker'. 'Stocker' was even adopted as the correct spelling by the local newspapers, and appeared in press reports about his appointment.

That simple error was not commented upon at the time and remained forgotten until, four years later, a journalist drew it to the attention of RUC Headquarters. He did so because of the very serious allegation made by John Stalker that, at our first meeting, I had handed him a flattened cigarette packet with a handwritten note on it.[1] The note was supposed to have outlined Stalker's family tree on his mother's side back to about 1900, and showed his Catholic ancestry. No such cigarette packet ever existed. Stalker himself could never produce it — although frequently pressed to do so — and my Senior Assistant Chief Constable, David Chesney, who remained with us throughout that lunch, certainly has no knowledge of it.

John Stalker knew little of the RUC or of me, if he really believed that I would have been party to 'a subtle way of letting [him] know' that, because of his mother's ancestry, he was 'vulnerable to allegations of Catholic minority bias'.[2] Catholic members of the RUC, from Peter Duffy, Deputy Commandant of the Depot during my initial training, and Sergeant Timoney, the instructor there, to senior officers, like my friends for many years, Michael McAtamney and Cahal Ramsay, greatly affected my life for the better, and improved my understanding of police work. So too had Jamie Flanagan, whose shrewdness and sureness of touch I envied and admired, and James O'Brien, my DI in Strabane, who epitomised for me what an RUC officer should be.

Not only was I uninterested in John Stalker's antecedents, but in truth I did not even know his proper surname when we first met. I had felt no need whatsoever to inquire into him, as I trusted Philip Myers's assessment of the man and accepted his nomination without question.

It was arranged that John Stalker and his deputy, Detective Chief Superintendent John Thorburn, would travel to Northern Ireland on 24 May 1984 to meet me at Headquarters. That initial meeting was relaxed and cordial, although Thorburn spoke little. John Stalker and I discussed the DPP's request for further investigations into the circumstances surrounding the three shooting incidents. I also gave him a draft of his Terms of Reference. While these fully embraced the matters identified by the DPP, Sir Barry Shaw, for further investigation, they also included two others which I had felt it necessary to add. First, I wanted Stalker to investigate the circumstances in which RUC officers might justifiably cross the border into the Republic of Ireland, and secondly, I wanted him to examine the difficulty created for officers when they act on intelligence which may not be disclosed, due to the need to protect its source(s). I included these two matters because they lay right at the core of the incidents which had led to Stalker's investigation, and, I believed, deserved to be examined because of public concern over the disclosures made by Constable Robinson in court.

I also explained that I had appointed Senior Assistant Chief Constable David Chesney to be John Stalker's direct point of contact at chief officer level, if he or his team of seven required advice or help of any nature. I assured him that he could himself come to see me on any occasion, if he felt it necessary. After that initial briefing, we were joined by David, and the four of us went for lunch at a golf club about twelve miles away. I regarded the lunch as a 'getting to know you' engagement, which was, as I recall it, enjoyable and without rancour and certainly without flattened cigarette packets! I wanted John Stalker and his team to feel that they had my support and that of my chief officers, because I fervently wished the controversial shooting incidents to be thoroughly investigated so that the myth of a 'Shoot to Kill' policy by the RUC could finally be laid to rest. Although I regarded Thorburn as somewhat taciturn, my first impressions of Stalker were entirely favourable. My view matched Philip Myers's positive opinion of him, and so I left that lunch convinced that I would have Stalker's full professional and energetic commitment to his investigation.

How wrong I was! Later, I deeply regretted my naïvety in accepting John Stalker's nomination without first asking questions about his qualifications. My tendency to trust the judgment of more senior police officers was a personal failing during my years in the RUC. Had I been more cautious, I would have checked John Stalker's police career and would never have accepted him as suitable for the inquiry, because of his lack of experience at both operational and senior command level. After only three years as a uniformed constable, he had joined CID, and remained there for nineteen years until 1980, when he became Assistant Chief Constable — or, in his words, 'an administrator, a desk policeman'.[3] Four years later, he was appointed Deputy Chief Constable of the Greater Manchester Police, and he commenced the RUC investigation only two months thereafter.

Be that as it may, following our first meeting, John Stalker wrote to me on 29 May 1984, agreeing the Terms of Reference which I had given him five days earlier. He also explained that he had already begun his investigation, and that he would make contact with me, from time to time, through David Chesney. As I confidently believed at this stage that Stalker's investigation would be the final one, I left it to him and put the matter from my mind in order to commit myself fully to my other duties as Chief Constable.

Regrettably my confidence in Stalker and his team soon weakened. Within three months, I began to receive reports from RUC members about John Thorburn's aggressive attitude during interviews. Feelings of anger and frustration were growing amongst experienced officers within Special Branch and our specialist anti-terrorist units. In the absence of any formal complaint, I ordered that the total co-operation of RUC officers should be maintained and said that I would consider only formal written complaints about the manner of the inquiry. I received none, nor did Michael McAtamney.

Stalker and Thorburn appeared to me to be content with the progress of their investigation, since I was not approached by either of them at any time during the seven months to the end of 1984. As for David Chesney, their Liaison Officer, he was never contacted at any time by John Stalker during his entire investigation. In retrospect, I recognise, and live painfully with, the fact that I was remiss from the outset in not ensuring that Stalker kept in periodic contact with me to brief me on his progress. The fact that I felt this unnecessary, because of my past experience of independent investigations into the RUC, is not a satisfactory excuse.

I later discovered that, after his first meeting with me and briefing by my chief officers, Stalker completely distanced himself from RUC Command. Weekly briefings with his team usually took place in Manchester, rarely in Northern Ireland. As the inquiry developed, a series of seemingly sensitive problems arose, and his team repeatedly had to request him to approach the RUC, the army or the intelligence services to resolve them.

Despite the public and media perception of his strong leadership and tight control of the inquiry, I am reliably informed by a member of his team that Stalker travelled fewer than twelve times to Northern Ireland, while his team spent approximately 150 days there, over a period of more than a year. In reality, therefore, it was Detective Chief Superintendent John Thorburn who was effectively and directly in charge of the investigation.

Some 300 people were interviewed by the team. Two hundred and one witnesses made statements, 65 people were interviewed with contemporaneous notes being recorded, and 22 people made statements under caution.

The same former member of his team claims that John Stalker was involved in only eight interviews, and conducted just three of them himself. None of the ten RUC officers who discharged bullets in the three separate incidents was interviewed by Stalker, nor were any of the RUC's CID officers who had conducted the initial police investigations. Equally surprising is the fact that Deputy Chief Constable Michael McAtamney was never approached by Stalker in relation to his 1983 investigation into the shootings. Since Michael had had overall responsibility for the RUC's internal investigation into the three shooting incidents, and since Stalker's Report was highly critical of him, it is hard to comprehend why Stalker thought it appropriate never to meet or interview him.

In September 1984, growing unease within the Force about the conduct of the Stalker team was intensified by the then Deputy Director of the Northern Ireland Forensic Science Laboratory. He wrote to a Senior Assistant Chief Constable, expressing concern over the manner in which his Laboratory staff were being treated by Stalker's inquiry team. One scientist, in particular, had been interviewed without prior notice, and had apparently been aggressively interrogated for several hours, during which time his investigative work and findings were challenged and criticised. In view of what turned out to be unjustified questioning of the totally independent discharge of the Laboratory's duties, the Deputy Director requested that, in future, such interviews should be properly arranged in advance with the Laboratory, when any scientist being interviewed would be accompanied by a superior. This serious complaint from the Forensic Science Laboratory was referred by letter to John Stalker, but no response was received.

In February 1985, John Stalker wrote to ACC Trevor Forbes requesting that his team be given access to particular areas of highly secret intelligence matters. In his letter Stalker had described the nature of the information he required. All of it had to do with the sophisticated surveillance techniques used not only by the RUC, but by the army and other British intelligence agencies. This request was followed almost immediately by Stalker making one of his rare visits to Northern Ireland. Trevor Forbes, quite properly, refused to divulge the extremely sensitive information that Stalker requested. Following the rebuff, John Stalker wrote directly to me, seeking the same information.

I told Stalker that, whether or not it frustrated his investigation, I myself would not make a decision which could jeopardise police intelligence sources. Much of the information about police informants which Stalker wanted had not even been disclosed to me, and I was determined that he should not have it, since I was not the controller of certain methods of intelligence gathering, but merely the custodian of them. Under no circumstances would I divulge anything about them to Stalker, or Thorburn, without the express approval of the Director of Public Prosecutions or, at his direction should he think it necessary, the Attorney-General. I viewed the matter as one of national security, which ultimately rested with the Prime Minister.

Giving additional reasons to sustain my decision, I also referred Stalker to article 6 (3) of the Prosecution of Offences Order (NI) 1972, by which I, as

Chief Constable, had a duty to furnish the DPP with such facts and information as might appear to him to be required for the discharge of his functions under the Order. I explained to John Stalker that, when I sent his Report to the DPP with my observations, the Director could within article 6 (3) call for any further information he considered necessary. I also informed Philip Myers, who was maintaining a 'watching brief' over the investigation, of my decision and the grounds for it, which he fully accepted.

Meanwhile, I became aware of further criticisms of the Stalker team, this time from high-ranking RUC officers. Things finally came to a head early in April 1985, when Michael McAtamney came hurriedly into my office, obviously extremely concerned. He explained that John Stalker had just phoned him from Manchester to request the immediate suspension of two RUC Detective Superintendents, Thomas George Anderson and Samuel George Flanagan. As Michael was unable to tell me the specific grounds on which Stalker had based his request, I was not prepared to approve, without clear justification, the suspension of any police officer, and in particular two such senior officers. Consequently, I asked Michael to tell Stalker that I wanted him to put his request for suspensions in writing, along with sound reasons to justify my acceding to it.

In a letter to me, dated 22 April 1985, Stalker did in fact request that Superintendents Anderson and Flanagan be suspended or removed from operational duty, and he set out information which he believed sustained his request. He also advised me that it would be some months before I received his full Report.

In the light of this first written request to me from Stalker for the suspension of two RUC officers or their removal from operational duties, I discussed the matter fully with Philip Myers. At the time, Superintendent Anderson was a fully operational Special Branch officer, while George Flanagan was an instructor at Bramshill Police College. The Bramshill College Commandant told me that he regarded Flanagan as probably his best instructor, and that he was very anxious to retain him on his staff. With the Commandant's agreement and that of Philip Myers, I permitted Flanagan to remain there. Again with the HMI's agreement, I transferred George Anderson from his operational post and gave him an administrative role at RUC Headquarters. I have never doubted that these decisions, fully supported by Myers, were the correct ones.

Impatient and irritated with the fact that this investigation was raising such procedural problems, I decided that it would be best to arrange a meeting with John Stalker, even though he had made no attempt to see me during the first eleven months of his inquiry. The meeting was arranged for 15 May 1985 at RUC Headquarters. I wanted to discuss with him an alternative approach, which I hoped might resolve our apparent impasse over 'sources' and intelligence-gathering techniques. I also hoped to raise with him the question of Thorburn's apparent truculence during interviews of RUC members, and our growing suspicion that someone within his team was leaking detailed information about the investigation to the media.

Such leaks had already resulted in a considerable loss of faith throughout the RUC in the independence of this particular inquiry, and stimulated mistrust and uncooperativeness towards the Stalker team. But nothing was proven — until, that is, January 1988. Then, along with thousands of other newspaper readers, I was made aware that my meetings with John Stalker, and other aspects of his investigation, had been embellished and contemporaneously leaked since 13 May 1985. The leaking was supposedly done by Stalker himself to the editor of the *Manchester Evening News*, Michael Unger, who kept a diary about the leaks for publication. This, of course, was an extremely serious breach of confidentiality.

The 'Unger Diary' was published in the *Guardian*, over a three-day period in late January 1988. Unger's record of the first phone call reads:

May 13, 1985.
John Stalker rings me early this morning at the office to talk about his inquiry into an alleged shoot-to-kill policy by the RUC. Stalker tells me that he is seeking some papers from Chief Constable Sir John Hermon that could show that RUC officers murdered members of the IRA. He is seeing Sir John tomorrow (*14 May*) to get the papers, and if he doesn't get them he will resign from the inquiry. He says that if the inquiry were conducted into a mainland police force then the problem wouldn't arise.

I ask Stalker why he is telling me this, because I hardly know him and the information, if published, would be extremely damaging.

Stalker says it helps him keep going — it forces him on — if he knows that someone outside the police force knows what is happening. If he begins to waver about the sensitivity of highlighting the problems of another police force then my knowledge will force him to carry on his investigations.

He also says that it is an insurance policy if anything happens to him.[4]

Neither my official diary for 1985 nor my weekly engagement sheet for the week commencing 13 May shows that I met Stalker on 14 May. On the contrary, I had lunch with Philip Myers, before meeting the General Officer Commanding and going with him to Stormont for a Security Policy Meeting with the Secretary of State, then Douglas Hurd, who had succeeded Jim Prior on 10 September 1984.

It was Wednesday, 15 May, when John Stalker arrived at my office, late. This was our first meeting since that of a year earlier, when we had had that pleasant lunch at the golf club. This second meeting took place against a background of continuing terrorist violence, with thirteen police officers already murdered since the beginning of the year.

My memory of the meeting is aided by brief notes, made immediately afterwards, and by certain actions which I took straight away, because I felt they were imperative. Naturally, the discussion embraced greater detail than I can now recall, but the thrust and serious content of it can still be outlined.

From the outset, I felt Stalker was ill at ease and tense. I began the meeting by explaining once again that, to the extent that the information he sought related to intelligence-gathering and surveillance techniques, I felt unable to assist him, since such information was highly classified. Before any of it could be disclosed to him, I emphasised that I required the authority of the DPP, who possibly needed the authority of the Attorney-General or even Prime Minister Thatcher.

Stalker's response both surprised and irritated me. Quite unexpectedly, he began to talk about a conflict of wills between us. With evident emotion, he expressed concern about my role as Chief Constable. He referred to us both as being strong-willed persons of high rank in the police service, who were used to making decisions and giving directions. I was further disconcerted when he voiced his worries about how I had obstructed his investigation. As I had given the Force a clear direction to co-operate fully with the Stalker inquiry, I felt this accusation was totally unjustified. His personal criticisms added to my annoyance. These included the suggestion that if I alone received the final Report of his investigation, there could be no guarantee that the complete file, as he had prepared it, would be delivered to the DPP.

Faced with such outrageous allegations, I displayed what I believe was remarkable constraint. Calmly and with care, I pointed out to Stalker that in light of the gravity of these charges, he should have been accompanied by a second and more senior officer in order to convey his comments in a proper manner. I made it plain that I considered them slurs on my professional integrity, and that I felt it necessary to advise the Secretary of State of the matter. Stalker was obviously unsettled by my response. I made terse remarks in response to his criticisms, so far as I understood them, and where I believed he had been in error. Surprisingly, he relaxed noticeably after this, and our discussion took a more realistic turn.

As intended, I went on to propose an alternative approach to break the stalemate between us over his request for access to intelligence. I suggested that we should ask an honest broker to examine the relevant areas raised by Stalker, and assess their relevance to his inquiry. Stalker agreed to my proposal, and so it was left to me to arrange a meeting between the three of us. He also agreed to complete his Report and forward it directly to me. The Report would be classed as an interim one, until a decision was made as to whether intelligence information — such as still existed — should be made available to him.

After Stalker left, I spoke personally that afternoon to Secretary of State Douglas Hurd by confidential telephone. I advised him fully of Stalker's criticisms of me, and assured him that I would keep him informed of any further developments. The next morning, John Stalker telephoned to withdraw his criticisms. I told him that I had already informed the Secretary of State of them and would now notify him of their withdrawal. Unknown to any of us at that time, Stalker it seems was busy describing events of these days to Michael Unger — in very dramatic terms, as can be gathered from the following extracts from the 'Unger Diary':

May 15, 1985.

Stalker rings again and says that he flew over to see Hermon. The conversation wasn't conclusive.

He says that his threat to resign and make the problem public is still there and he reads me his letter of resignation and the consequent press release. If he doesn't do this and it is seen that he isn't being allowed to carry on a normal police inquiry, he would lose his credibility within his own police force.

Sir John and Douglas Hurd (the Northern Ireland Minister) want the whole inquiry kept quiet because it is both a constitutional and legal issue. Stalker has tried appealing to the Government to get the necessary papers released but there was a 'deafening silence'. Stalker says that part of the problem is that if a big scandal broke in Northern Ireland then Hurd could fail in his ambition to become Foreign Secretary.

May 17, 1985.

Stalker has a 'hard-hitting' three hours with Sir John who has agreed to release the evidence 'provided the Army and MI5 agree'. Stalker says that, if this doesn't happen within two or three days, he will go ahead with his resignation as this would prove Sir John's provocation.

Stalker says he has been asking for these papers for months and getting nowhere.

'Policemen are committing murder and I am unable to get to them,' he says.

As it is a murder investigation he says that he has no option but to proceed or resign.[5]

On reading this account in early 1988, I was amused, yet appalled, that anyone could fantasise about such a situation involving a Chief Constable and the Secretary of State. To believe, in the face of the widespread media and political coverage, that Douglas Hurd and I wanted 'the whole inquiry kept quiet' was sheer nonsense. To read that John Stalker was supposed to have told a newspaper editor in 1985 that RUC officers were 'committing murder' was frightening.

On 4 June 1985, Stalker wrote a letter to me in which he set out his requirement regarding material evidence, which he believed still existed, and his grounds for requiring it. The letter was to be delivered to me by John Thorburn at Bristol. Jean and I had flown to London on 5 June, and were driven to Bristol so that I could attend a meeting of the Association of Chief Police Officers. The following day, Thorburn and I met in the foyer of our hotel. Although he was vaguely familiar to me in appearance, it was as if I were meeting a complete stranger. In truth, I had no mental picture of the man at all, since we had been in one another's presence so little. We had lunch together and I offered to buy him a drink. My recollection is that we both had a single beer. There was little casual conversation, and so I scanned the letter he had brought from John Stalker. Thereafter, John Thorburn and I discussed the forthcoming meeting arranged for Stalker and me with our honest broker in London on the 14th of the month. I also raised with him my need for specific assurances on two points.

First, I required a guarantee of total confidentiality from Stalker's team about the RUC investigation. Secondly, I wanted Stalker's agreement that once his Report was submitted, it would be processed to ensure access on a 'need to know' basis only, with every precaution taken to ensure its secrecy.

After our meeting, I made brief notes of our discussion and recorded one comment of Thorburn's. I had asked, 'Do you believe, irrespective of what offences or acts of indiscipline any of my officers may have committed, that any of them were guilty of murder?' Thorburn was visibly surprised by the question, and replied with some emotion that he did not.

The meeting arranged for 14 June took place, but unfortunately not with the success I had hoped for; instead of acting as honest broker, A's organisation did not want to become involved. While I cannot dwell on the meeting itself, since its location and participants — apart from John Stalker and me — are properly the subject of secrecy, I can record that it was not in any way acrimonious or intense. Because the impasse could not be resolved for us, it was accepted by Stalker that he would complete his Report, identifying in it those aspects of intelligence which he felt he still required, and that after careful study of it, I would forward it to the Director of Public Prosecutions. As we prepared to depart, 'A' cordially invited Stalker and me for lunch.

John Stalker's reply was greeted with disbelief. He nonchalantly explained that he could not join us, because he had already arranged to meet Peter Taylor, an investigative journalist for the BBC. I was well aware of Taylor's undoubted ability and, therefore, suggested to Stalker that it was perhaps not advisable for him to have such contacts immediately after such a sensitive meeting. But my advice did not appeal to John Stalker, and so he did not lunch with us.

On 17 June, I advised the DPP of the stalemate over intelligence materials. I also reiterated my refusal to release to Stalker any high-grade intelligence information which might still exist. The DPP was in possession of copies of the correspondence which had passed between Stalker and me on the issue, and was therefore fully *au fait* with my stance. Whether he agreed with it, he never revealed to me.

Towards the end of June 1985, Stalker again wrote to me, expressing his disappointment at my attitude and setting out his position as he saw it. He believed that there was missing evidence, relating to the shooting incident on 24 November in the hayshed, in which Michael Tighe had been killed. This was the only respect in which Stalker's investigation was not complete. He also advised me that, 'given a fair wind', he expected to have his Report with me by the end of July.

By August, Stalker's Report had still not arrived. Media interest was intense, and rumours were rife. I concluded from them that some people knew at least part of the content of the Report. Consequently, I wrote to Stalker, saying that we must address our minds to the manner in which he would deliver his Report, including its format, total number of copies and its classification. I marked my letter as copied to Philip Myers, by then Sir Philip as he had been knighted in the Queen's Birthday Honours List in 1985. In my letter I made it clear that the HMI would be kept fully informed of the progress of the Stalker Report, and of my final observations on it.

After a further exchange of letters, it was arranged that the Report would be delivered by Stalker to RUC Headquarters on 19 September. At the last minute, that date was changed by him to the 18th, a day on which I was fully engaged on an internal disciplinary inquiry. I, therefore, arranged for Deputy Chief Constable Michael McAtamney to receive the Report, before having lunch with Stalker and Thorburn. I hoped that at that stage I could join them, while the disciplinary hearing was in recess. The long-awaited Stalker Report was finally delivered to Headquarters around 11.30 a.m. on 18 September 1985. Immediately afterwards, Stalker and Thorburn went for a drive in County Down, instead of joining Michael for lunch and meeting me.

Notes
1 John Stalker, *Stalker* (London: Harrap 1988), p. 30.
2 *Op. cit.* pp. 30–31.
3 *Op. cit.* p. 19.
4 Michael Unger, 'Stalker Diary', *Guardian*, 28 January 1988.
5 *Ibid.*

16

THE TROUBLES OF 1985

At the beginning of 1985, Jean and I discussed the possibility of my retirement. I decided against it, because too much remained to be done without and within the RUC. The politicians had failed to resolve the Northern Ireland crisis, but in dealing with it they treated the Force as a bargaining counter. I also knew that both the Stalker Inquiry and the Dowra Affair still had to be concluded; in these circumstances, I felt it would have been totally wrong for me to leave before they were resolved. I determined, therefore, to carry on for as long as I had the ability and opportunity to contribute to the professional development of the RUC, and thereby increase its acceptance by the whole population of Northern Ireland.

We were visiting the United States when I was told by telephone on 28 February that the IRA had killed nine police officers in a mortar attack on the RUC station in Newry, County Down. We arranged to return at once, and by midday on 2 March were back in Belfast, where I received a detailed briefing on the incident. At 6.30 p.m. two days earlier, the station had been struck by the IRA's latest Mark 10 mortar bombs. There had been a direct hit on the canteen, which was then located in a temporary building in the station yard. A chief inspector, a sergeant, one constable, two women constables and four full-time members of the RUC Reserve had been killed, with many others injured. Temporary buildings within the complex had also been destroyed, and the station itself seriously damaged.

The first funerals were due to take place the afternoon we returned, and so I attended the funeral of a woman constable at 3 p.m. Immediately after the burial, I visited Newry and was shown the location of the parked lorry from which the mortars had been fired, beyond the perimeter fence at the rear. Without a clear view of the yard, I reckoned that the terrorists had selected the temporary buildings as the target and used the station's radio mast — with its red, helicopter navigational light — for directional purposes. Talking to the surviving police officers, I noted not only their grief and shock, but their intense resolve to carry on as normal.

The Divisional Commander briefed me on the attitude of the townspeople to the attack in Newry. When the multiple killing of the officers had become known, he explained, hundreds of local people had gathered silently in the side-streets near the station. They wished to convey their sympathy to the police and make a quiet protest at the killings, but were frightened to be seen doing so. A minority of the town's republicans, who gave their support to the IRA, intimidated those wishing to offer condolences. However, around eight o'clock on the evening of the attack, the Catholic nuns from the local convent had emerged and walked quietly along the street to the damaged station. As they did so, crowds of people had joined them from the side-streets. The nuns had apparently been very distressed by the carnage, and were determined to register their protest, despite the intimidation.

Before leaving Newry, I called at the convent and was introduced individually to each of its residents. I have a lasting memory of us all sitting in a large circle, talking and reminiscing about the past days in Newry and about police officers mutually known to us. The oldest resident, who was well over eighty years of age, was the daughter of a Royal Irish Constabulary constable, who had later joined the Royal Ulster Constabulary and had been stationed for many years in Springfield Road police barracks in West Belfast. Several others also had relatives in the RUC. I felt a oneness between us as we sat there together.

The following day, Sunday, 3 March, I planned to attend the Chief Inspector's funeral in the afternoon. About mid-morning, I was sitting in my office reading to catch up on developments which had taken place while I had been in America. In one corner of the room, an incident-monitoring television recorded 'All Quiet' within Northern Ireland. Suddenly, the screen flickered into life. The news was not good. Another Catholic police officer, an off-duty sergeant, had been shot by the IRA as he was about to go into mass with his family.

The multiple murder in Newry had a lasting effect on me. Photographs of the nine dead officers later appeared in the *Police Review*, and looking at their faces, pictured together on one page, disturbed me greatly. Nevertheless, I kept the magazine open in a drawer of my office desk until the day I retired and cleared out the office. (It still lies open at the same page in my study at home.) Seeing their faces, regularly staring back at me from the drawer, served as a constant reminder of the need to concentrate my energies, and those of the RUC, on the defeat of terrorism. Every murder of a police officer distressed me more than I could admit, even to Jean, but terrorist killings showed no signs of abating.

On 29 March, an off-duty, part-time Reserve constable was murdered by the IRA, and this was followed by the murder of another Reserve officer on 3 April. Both incidents occurred close to Newry. A few weeks later, on 20 May, two police cars, each containing four officers, travelled the short distance from Newry Station to the Killeen crossing point at the border with the Republic of Ireland. They were due to escort a vehicle, carrying bullion, from the border and through their area. As the cars moved to take up positions in front of and behind the armoured bullion vehicle, a massive bomb exploded at the roadside. The leading police car was blown to pieces, as were its four young occupants — an inspector, a constable, a woman constable and a Reserve constable — all died instantly.

Because it was an international frontier with customs posts on each side, it was normal practice for commercial lorries and trailers to be parked at the roadside just north or south of the crossing point. The 1,000 lb of explosives had been placed on a trailer, which was driven to the intended site of the explosion and parked, before the lorry unit drove away. The bomb had exploded at about ten o'clock in the morning.

My immediate concern was the anguish for the families involved, and the profound impact four more murdered officers would have on those left at Newry Station. Consequently, I decided to visit the scene of the explosion that afternoon. It had been declared 'out of bounds' by the army, which feared that secondary devices might have been placed by the IRA. The dismembered bodies and the mangled remains of the police car were scattered over a wide area, including a large field adjoining the road. Senior officers, who had already arrived, had defied the 'out of bounds' constraint in order to collect the larger portions of the bodies, which were clearly visible and easily retrieved. These were placed in large, black, plastic bags. Thereafter, a detailed search was required and this was being organised as I arrived. A line of police officers spread out across the field. They were carrying more large plastic bags for the remaining pieces of bodies, and smaller bags for bits which would be required for forensic or fingerprint examination.

I joined the line, to show common cause with the officers, and to demonstrate that I understood the traumatic nature of this terrible duty. I found their professionalism and calm demeanour most impressive. No unnecessary words were spoken. As the line of officers advanced very slowly up the field, examining the grass with meticulous care, the man on my left said to the supporting officers coming behind, 'Here's a hand. Fingerprint bag, please.' Another officer replied, 'I know that hand, it belongs to . . . ' and he proceeded to name the particular officer. He had recognised a ring on a finger. The officers then moved steadily forward again, their thoughts and emotions concealed.

After the search, I visited the bereaved families. Three of the murdered officers had been single, though the woman constable was engaged to be married. The Inspector left a widow and two very young boys. On the Wednesday and Thursday of that week, I attended three of the four funerals and felt depressed.

After detailed discussions with police officers in Newry Station, I stated publicly that I appreciated Taoiseach Garret FitzGerald's prompt offer of every help to track down and arrest those responsible. I also said that the RUC was 'satisfied that the explosives and the terrorists involved came from the Republic' to carry out the attack. It was firmly established that although the trailer had originally been hijacked in South Armagh, it had been driven to a place near Dundalk the previous day. There, the bomb had been loaded onto the trailer, and driven across the border by a DAF lorry tractor unit, before it drove away. The evidence came from the lorry itself. It had been fitted with a tachograph for the automatic recording of the speed and distance of travel with the date and duration of all journeys. It was a time of intense border activity by the terrorists, many of them living south of the border, especially in Dundalk. They worked along with fellow terrorists, who resided close to the border in the North. Logistically, republican terrorist resources were generally secreted in deep 'hides', often in remote rural areas of Ireland, and were brought to the North only when required for tactical operations.

My statement caused an instant outcry from the Irish Government and Garda Headquarters. They denied that there was any evidence to show the origin of the explosives or the perpetrators of the crime. At the time, I was intrigued by the vehemence of the verbal attack on me by the Irish Government and also by the Social Democratic and Labour Party. With hindsight I recognise that this was most probably due to their concern that the secret talks then taking place between the two Governments about the future of Northern Ireland might be compromised by my making an issue of the original location of the explosives.

It was already a very sensitive time in the North because of the recent election results, which reflected the volatility of the political scene. Sinn Féin, the political wing of the Provisional IRA, had participated in the district council elections for the first time. By winning fifty-nine council seats on 15 May, Sinn Féin gained representation on seventeen of the twenty-six councils. The subsequent presence of these particular members at council meetings caused considerable acrimony and physical, as well as verbal, confrontations with unionist councillors. Consequently, the RUC became involved in a convoluted peace-keeping role and, on occasions, in the eviction of disorderly councillors, and even members of the public.

With sectarian feelings already running high during April and May 1985, the widespread rumours of yet another loyalist strike only provoked further tension. Our Civil Emergency Plan was dusted down. In preparation for more protests and disruption, Mobile Support Units — already trained to a very sophisticated level — and uniformed officers underwent retraining on public order and anti-terrorist duties. Simultaneously, special teams of CID and Special Branch officers were created in border areas and South Londonderry to combat the increasing terrorist activity. Plans to reinforce police accommodation, particularly in view of its vulnerability to the IRA's Mark 10 mortars, were also taking shape at last, after unconscionable delays by the Police Authority and the British Treasury.

By mid-May 1985, the Force was fully prepared to address the smouldering problem of loyalist parades. Over almost a century, these had been given a special position in Northern Ireland and appeared to have acquired a sort of temporal sanctity. Participants believed they could parade almost wherever and whenever they chose. Their marches epitomised the right to civil and religious liberty, as long as the religion in question was Protestantism. By a process of evolution, the Orange Order, the Apprentice Boys and the Royal Black Institution had attained positions of privilege within the Protestant 'establishment' in Northern Ireland. At one time, no loyalist politician could aspire to government, or any position of public significance, unless he was a member of one or more of these organisations.

There was, however, no reciprocal right for Catholics; the equivalent Catholic organisations — namely, the Irish National Foresters and the Ancient Order of Hibernians — could not march other than in their own 'non-unionist' areas. They certainly could not have entered any area housing a sizeable number of Protestants without unleashing a vicious backlash of loyalist violence. I was not alone in believing that this superior attitude of the loyalists, in respect to their marches, had to be changed.

Consequently, our plans for dealing with parades were clearly understood at every level of command. In all cases, the RUC was to act from a position of strength, to avoid direct confrontation except when attacked, and — by all lawful means available — to maximise the number of culprits brought quickly before the courts. We would make full use of video recordings and photography, and deploy those local police who had a good knowledge of the demonstrators. All bands travelling from a distance would be accompanied by a local police officer, who knew most of the band members and camp-followers. As a condition of RUC approval for the parade itself to take place, the organisers were obliged to prevent unruly bands from participating. Where a tradition had grown up of midnight revelry immediately preceding the Twelfth of July, bandsmen who behaved offensively and aggressively could be refused permission to parade the following day. All of these reforms were hard pills for loyalists to swallow, as subsequent events illustrated.

During the summer of 1985, when notified parades were rerouted by the police, very serious confrontations arose between the RUC and loyalists. Our role was to give clear direction to parade organisers, and offer full co-operation to achieve an orderly march, but also to warn that those breaking the law would be prosecuted. In Cookstown, County Tyrone and Castlewellan in County Down, the loyalist violence was dealt with very firmly indeed by the police.

By this time, I had become more or less immune to criticism, accepting it as an unavoidable consequence of the office I held. I was determined to act as I thought was right and fair for the whole community in Northern Ireland, and not just the loyalist side of it. Regardless of the inevitable pressures and opposition provoked by our approach to loyalist marches, I knew that for the sake of long-term peace in the North, this nettle simply had to be grasped by the RUC.

Our emphasis on the need to identify and process offenders through the courts produced significant results. Throughout the marching season of 1985, the courts imposed severe financial penalties and made increasing use of suspended sentences or binding-over orders, whereby offenders had to keep the peace and be of good behaviour. In the more serious cases, involving assaults on police officers, terms of imprisonment were imposed. The attrition rate was surprisingly high, and the fines gradually escalated from around £25 to £400 for those convicted of a series of offences. Video recordings of attacks on the police, disorderly behaviour and other offences were made available at various police stations, together with the photographs of many culprits, so that they might be studied by police officers on duty at parades.

Unfortunately, the growing media speculation regarding the possible outcome of the secret talks between the British and Irish Governments over the future of Northern Ireland cast grave doubts on the integrity of the RUC's motives in trying to normalise the conduct of loyalist parades in mid-1985. Loyalist politicians repeatedly alleged that the RUC, and I in particular, were the instruments of the two Governments in this area, and suggested that our ultimate intention was to deprive the loyalists of their freedom to parade.

Throughout those summer months, the following possibilities were put to me time and again in seemingly casual conversations with senior civil servants attached to the Northern Ireland Office. What did I think of joint court systems in Ireland to deal with terrorist-related crime? What about local unarmed community policing to replace or augment the RUC? Would the police accompany all Ulster Defence Regiment patrols?

Rumours of such radical changes eroded the confidence of the loyalist community in its own British Government. They also made the RUC's control of loyalist parades much more controversial, even though the vast majority of parades continued to be conducted peacefully with increasingly close co-operation between the organisers, participants and police. The concentration of publicity on those few locations where violence erupted between the RUC and militant loyalists presented a very different picture to the outside world. All of that violence paled into insignificance compared with the events in Portadown, the town I used to refer to as 'the Vatican of Orangeism', because it always had such a strong Orange tradition.

During the 1970s, there had emerged a stridency among the loyalists of the Portadown area. Bitterness and hatred were reflected in the sectarian murders committed by extremists on 'both sides', within what became notorious as 'the murder triangle'. The Protestant paramilitaries, the Ulster Defence Association and Ulster Volunteer Force, vied with the Provisional IRA and the Irish National Liberation Army as perpetrators of atrocities, with the result that members of the security forces were constantly at risk.

By tradition, the loyalist parades in Portadown had traversed the so-called Tunnel/Obins Street route. Aware of the tension there, but unaware of the precise nature of the policing problems, I went along the parade route on several occasions by car and on foot. As mine was the final decision on rerouting or advising the Secretary of State to ban a march, I had to be fully informed about the area before reaching that decision.

From my point of view, the position in Portadown had been worsened in 1985 by the local police's last-minute rerouting of a Catholic band parade in the town on St Patrick's Day, 17 March. The band and the Catholic community had believed, with some substance, that the RUC would give approval to the traditional route, but it had not done so. Without a corresponding change of approach to loyalist parades in the town, I felt that the RUC would become increasingly alienated from the Catholic population.

Consequently, I discussed the situation in Portadown with representatives of the various churches, as well as with nationalist and loyalist bodies. I was impressed by the common sense of the Secretary to the Grand Orange Lodge; I found him both tactful and trustworthy. I was also extremely appreciative of the positive involvement of the Presbyterian Moderator, Dr Robert Dickinson, who accepted my assurance that I was not being influenced by political or Government pressures. His total commitment to law and order was critical at that time.

My experience of Cardinal Tomás Ó Fiaich, then the Catholic Primate of All Ireland, was somewhat different. I met him at 10.30 a.m. on 3 July to brief him about the RUC's approach to the forthcoming parades in Portadown. I also wanted to ask him if he might influence one or two of his local clergy, whose attitudes and comments were not helpful towards what I was seeking to achieve. I explained that it was my intention to reroute the Orange processions, on 12 and 13 July, away from the controversial Tunnel/Obins Street area, and to close it for future marches. He reacted with scepticism, doubting either the will or the ability of the Force to carry this out. Nothing I said seemed to convince him. The Cardinal remained doubtful even after I had outlined the general approach to be adopted by the RUC — sealing the entrance to the area with a strong barricade, with lines of armoured landrovers, and maintaining a substantial police presence.

Then, quite spontaneously, as I searched my mind for something to enlist his confidence, I added, 'Should there be an attempt to force an entry into the area through police lines, it'll not succeed as there will be a battalion of troops occupying the Tunnel and Obins Street.' This was literally a breath-stopper. His Eminence gasped, 'Do you mean that?' I confirmed that I did, even though I had at that stage no idea whether I could talk the General Officer Commanding into it! Again, I asked the Cardinal for his support and, this time, he agreed to do what he could.

Our conversation became more general and relaxed until, excusing himself for a moment, he returned with a transcript of an address he had recently given. He waited until I had studied it, and then, unexpectedly, he chided me for never commenting favourably on his statements, while I was regularly supportive of those made by Bishop (subsequently Cardinal) Cahal Daly. Extremely embarrassed, I replied rather lamely that it was something I had never considered. The meeting ended with a handshake.

Immediately thereafter, my most urgent action that day was to see the GOC, Bob Richardson, to ask him for a battalion of troops to be allocated to the Tunnel/Obins Street area on 12 July! Although it was contrary to all military logic, Bob did not appear surprised by my request and even agreed to it! Only after my retirement did I learn from the Colonel in charge of the 'battalion' on the day that only 250 soldiers had been allocated there. With vehicles and equipment in place, there was no room for more!

The major Twelfth parade was preceded by an exceptionally tumultuous church parade in Portadown on the preceding Sunday, 7 July, which put heavy pressure on those police officers on duty that day. Action was taken to thwart anticipated loyalist paramilitary involvement in the main event, but the omens for the Twelfth itself looked bad. In the event, on 12/13 July, RUC officers were violently attacked by loyalists in Portadown. Plastic bullet rounds had to be used from behind landrovers in order to restrain the rioters, and maintain a distance between them and the police. Despite violent disturbances, which spread throughout Portadown and caused much damage, the parade did not manage to penetrate the restricted area, nor did the army have to be committed for public order duties, although it provided a supportive reserve presence. All of this was made abundantly clear to the public through extensive television coverage, much of it recorded while the camera crews themselves were under attack from the rioters. During those two days, fifty-two RUC officers were injured, some seriously, and forty-three rioters were arrested, while many more were recorded by video and camera for later interview and prosecution.

On the evening of 12 July, I visited several of the police officers who had been detained in hospital. There I discovered that a full-time Reserve constable, who had been beaten and kicked unconscious by loyalists, had been prematurely discharged due to the pressure on medical facilities with so many casualties in the hospital that day. When I called at his home, I found him lying in extreme pain on a settee, being comforted by his wife. Before joining the RUC Reserve, he had been an international long-distance lorry driver and so it seemed natural in the circumstances to ask him about his future intentions. To my surprise, he replied that he wished to become a full-time RUC Traffic Branch officer. As I watched him passing out as a fully trained recruit the following year, I took great pleasure in the fact that his courage and determination had been duly rewarded.

It was ironic that four days after the loyalist violence on the Twelfth of July 1985, the triennial conference of the Imperial Orange World Council met in Belfast, with delegates attending from as far afield as Canada, Australia and West Africa. In light of the violence caused by their 'Brothers' in Portadown, I wondered what sort of message they really took back to their fellow Orangemen abroad.

The remainder of July and August brought further loyalist disturbances. However, tentative signs gradually emerged to suggest that the leaders of the Orange Order and the Black Institution were isolating extremist members by harnessing the weight of their moderates. Consequently, local police received much more positive and responsible co-operation in the organisation of loyalist parades. At their own request, I met Orange leaders in the autumn for discussions about their parades for the following year. The organisers of band parades adopted a policy of restricting participation to invited bands so that 'rogue' outsider bandsmen were, with police assistance, prevented from taking part.

Meanwhile, illegal or otherwise contentious parades by republican organisations and bands were also being dealt with firmly by the RUC. For the first time, Sinn Féin was actually giving local police formal notice of its parades, and complying with RUC directions about routes to be taken.

By mid-August 1985, I was content with our progress so far that year. As regards public order offences arising from parades and street disturbances, 468 loyalists and 427 republicans had been made amenable. Most prosecutions of republicans arose from disturbances in connection with the anniversaries of internment and the deaths of the ten hunger-strikers in 1981. I was confident that sensible political leadership within the unionist parties, careful discussion, and planning between parade organisers and RUC Command during the winter months would result in much further progress on loyalist parades in 1986. Subsequent political events were, however, quickly to dispel my satisfaction with the RUC's progress in controlling such parades.

Before these events unfolded, I had many other more pressing issues to pursue, not least enhancing the protection of most of our police stations, the vulnerability of which had been exposed with tragic results at Newry. There were still delays in our building programme, and seemingly no ability to provide us with fortified buildings capable of resisting the deadly Mark 10 mortars and large proxy bombs of the IRA. It took another four years, and the total commitment of a few companies within the Northern Ireland construction industry, before I could relax in the knowledge that police accommodation was being adequately strengthened. The RUC and the community undoubtedly owe these companies, and their courageous employees, an enormous debt of gratitude. They lived under constant threat because the IRA regarded them as legitimate targets for murder on account of the work they did for the security forces. A number of them were indeed killed.

In May 1985, I had renewed my efforts to persuade both the Secretary of State and the Police Authority of the necessity of a proper police training college. The enhanced strength and increasing sophistication of the police posted along the border resulted in temporary accommodation for specialist operational RUC units being provided in a military base close to Enniskillen. It was neither suitable nor adequate for this purpose, but Enniskillen Station itself was already grossly overcrowded.

To relieve the pressure on the existing Training Centre in Enniskillen, the Northern Ireland Office offered me facilities for recruit training in a police college in England. While I was prepared to locate advanced police training across in England, I wanted the recruits transferred to the recently acquired Garnerville complex on the outskirts of Belfast. It had been a residential domestic science training college and had facilities superior to those available at Enniskillen. I believed Garnerville would also be much safer for the recruits, whose security concerned me deeply. Most of them came from within a thirty-mile radius of Belfast, and yet every weekend they had to travel home from Enniskillen, and back to it again on Sunday evenings, in unprotected, private cars along miles of country roads, which were vulnerable to terrorist attack.

Although I managed to win agreement in principle that recruit training would be moved to Garnerville, there was no movement by the Police Authority or the Northern Ireland Office towards the purchase of land suitable for a college to suit all levels of RUC training. That state of affairs was to be

BELFAST TELEGRAPH

The Garda Síochána male voice choir sang at the Ulster Hall in October 1982 as part of the RUC's diamond jubilee celebrations. I am pictured here with the conductor of the choir.

BELFAST TELEGRAPH

With Larry Wren, Commissioner of the Garda Síochána, at the funeral of an RUC constable in Co. Donegal in June 1987.

With the GOC, Sir Robert Richardson (left), Princess Anne and
the Commander of RAF Aldergrove in May 1985.

Welcoming Princess Alexandra with Tom King,
the Secretary of State, in June 1987.

With Prince Andrew and Miss Sarah Ferguson and Jean at the annual RUC Sports Day in June 1986.

Welcoming the Queen Mother at Aldergrove.

The Duchess of Kent visiting RUC Headquarters in May 1989 to say farewell before I retired as Chief Constable.

BELFAST TELEGRAPH

Visiting Kinnego Embankment immediately after the explosion which killed three RUC officers on 27 October 1982. My good friend Bill Wilson is on the extreme left.

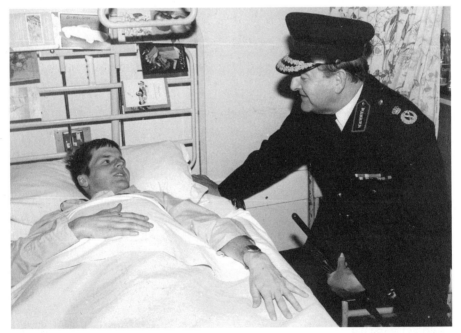

With an injured constable in hospital, after the 1987 Enniskillen Remembrance Sunday bombing.

At the press
conference when I
announced my
retirement in 1989.

Taking my last Passing-Out Parade
before retirement, accompanied by
Assistant Chief Constable Trevor
Forbes, on 14 April 1989.

Tom Rainey, then Chairman of the
Police Authority for Northern
Ireland, presenting me with its
'hairshirt' as a retirement gift
on 29 May 1989.

LEO CALLOW

Visiting the Keady joint Army/RUC base with Sylvia before Christmas 1988.

With Sylvia, Roy Webb and my sister, Belle, after receiving the Queen's Police Medal at Hillsborough.

BELFAST TELEGRAPH

With Sylvia outside St Anne's Cathedral, Belfast, to attend the Kegworth Memorial Service in February 1989.

Flying with the RAF in 1988.

Relaxing on my yacht on Strangford Lough in 1988

With Sylvia, Robert
(centre) and Thomas
in July 1996.

Happy in retirement
with Sylvia, Thomas,
granddaughter Katie,
Rodney, Barbara and
Robert leaning on the
newly created stone
walls, the results of my
'beach gardening'.

altered in dramatic fashion, in the autumn of 1985. Meanwhile, the catalogue of killings continued.

On 31 August, RUC Inspector Patrick Martin Vance was murdered at his home. I attended his funeral in Downpatrick, where the parish priest, Dr Joseph Maguire, publicly condemned his murder and said: 'Let all those who think of the wanton and cruel killing of this young officer consider that policing is an essential service in any civilised society.'

Bishop Cahal Daly presided at the mass. In deploring Inspector Vance's murder, Bishop Daly referred to the fact that it happened at a time when Catholic recruitment to the RUC had been on the increase. Later, at a mass for Seamus McAvoy, a successful businessman from Coalisland, who had been murdered in Dublin by the IRA because he had done work for the security forces, Bishop Daly again roundly condemned his murder and called upon Catholics 'to get out of the IRA'.

Only the previous day, 2 September 1985, Douglas Hurd was replaced by Tom King as Secretary of State for Northern Ireland. In my view, it was not the time for change at that level. About three months earlier, on 24 May, Bob Richardson had also been replaced as GOC by Sir Robert Pascoe. Jean had a particular liking for Maureen Richardson, and so we were both saddened to see them go. Fortunately, however, Bob Pascoe followed in the pattern of his two predecessors; I was thrice blessed with good GOCs.

On the morning of Wednesday, 4 September, the IRA launched a Mark 10 mortar attack on the RUC Training Centre at Enniskillen. Mercifully, the recruits had not yet been marched to the parade-ground for the routine morning inspection. If they had, many police officers would undoubtedly have been killed. As it was, thirty-five recruits and staff were injured, while the Training Centre and Police Divisional Headquarters within the station were both extensively damaged. The Mark 10's potential for devastation was so great that I became fully committed to moving all training as quickly as possible from Fermanagh to Belfast.

Despite an outcry from unionists generally, and especially from those in County Fermanagh, I directed that the first intake of recruits in 1986 would report to Garnerville, and that adequate training staff would be transferred from Enniskillen. The very new Secretary of State, Tom King, was upset, as the move was politically unacceptable at that time, and so I was subjected to a good deal of pressure from the Northern Ireland Office. Happily, after some initial argument, the Police Authority distanced itself from the NIO's stance, and gave me its support. The ultimate pressure point was, of course, finance, which the Northern Ireland Office advised would not be forthcoming. The Authority's response was that none would be required, since the money needed would be found from within its existing budget. The battle was won, to the advantage of police training and operational effectiveness, with Garnerville becoming the hub of preliminary RUC training.

By the end of that September, the focal point of the Protestant community's anger and apprehension had shifted from the RUC's control of its parades to the secret Anglo-Irish talks about Northern Ireland's future. Peter Robinson, the Deputy Leader of Rev. Paisley's Democratic Unionist Party, was reported as saying that any move to give the Republic of Ireland a political role in Northern Ireland would be seen by unionists 'as an act of war'. This was accompanied by media conjecture that officials from the Republic, possibly with diplomatic status, would be based in Belfast within some kind of consulate. The steadily rising number of IRA attacks did nothing to ease Protestant tensions and suspicions about the aspirations of the South.

In the middle of this highly sensitive time, I had to attend an international conference in Houston, Texas, to give an address on 'The problems of dealing with border terrorism'. Although I had a carefully prepared speech with me, I departed from it at points to elaborate on various matters, and it all passed uneventfully. Shortly after my return from America, I was startled to learn that certain aspects of this address had been misquoted by a Canadian journalist, and passed to *The Irish Times*. My remarks were supposed to have been derogatory of the Gardaí, and of the Irish Government's efforts towards defeating terrorism.

It was typical of the prevailing atmosphere in Northern Ireland that the remarks attributed to me resulted in a flurry of hysterical headlines, indignant statements in Dublin and rejoinders from Belfast. The *coup de grâce* was delivered by the President of the British Section of the International Police Association, a retired Assistant Chief Constable. The words of his letter came as poetry to my ears:

> Sitting as I was at the back of the room in Houston I had every opportunity to observe the reporter in question and his companion.
>
> They arrived late and spent most of the period talking to each other. One of them only made notes and then it seemed usually at the end of something you said. As he had been immersed in earnest conversation, he could not have heard fully what you had said and certainly not understood it completely.
>
> You undoubtedly need no support from me but I can most certainly confirm that you neither said nor implied what is alleged against you. But then I listened intently to what you had to say.
>
> This is as bad a case of misreporting as I have met and regrettably, I now realise, I saw it happening and could do nothing about it.

Events moved on so quickly that the fury and flurry over my misquoted remarks were soon eclipsed. On 2 November, around 6,000 members of the United Ulster Loyalist Front (UULF) and other loyalist extremists marched in Belfast. They included members of the Ulster Clubs, a new loyalist phenomenon, branches of which had sprung up throughout Northern Ireland. The Ulster Volunteer Force and the Ulster Defence Association had aided in the establishment of the UULF that summer, with the defeat of the Anglo-Irish talks as its stated objective.

On Tuesday, 12 November, I held a special meeting of all of my chief officers. Having been given a rather superficial briefing by the Northern Ireland Office, my knowledge of the intergovernmental talks and their outcome was limited, but I revealed everything I knew about them. I emphasised to the officers my firm view that any agreement between the two Governments would be a political matter, and was not to be the business of the RUC. Instead, our primary objectives would remain the protection of life and property, and the maintenance of stability within Northern Ireland.

The Anglo-Irish Agreement was signed in Hillsborough Castle on Friday, 15 November 1985, against a background of shouted protests from a sizeable, angry crowd of loyalists. They had been alerted the previous evening that the Castle, formerly the residence of the Governor of Northern Ireland and latterly that of the Secretary of State, was to be the venue for the signing ceremony. Many protesters filtered into the village during the early hours of the morning. The two Prime Ministers, Margaret Thatcher and Garret FitzGerald, senior officials and support staff arrived by helicopter. While the event was in progress, a young police constable was murdered and another seriously injured by a 300 lb IRA landmine at Crossmaglen, close to the border.

On the day after its signing, I received a copy of the Agreement, together with the accompanying statements. I studied the document closely, reading it several times, before formulating my personal opinion on it. Other than to Jean, I did not express that opinion for some months, and even then, did so with discretion.

The response of the vast majority of Protestants to the Anglo-Irish Agreement was, I think, epitomised by the reactions of a well-known Ulster couple. The husband, as Lord Lieutenant, was Her Majesty's representative for one of the six counties of Northern Ireland. At a social gathering, his wife asked me for my opinion of the Agreement. When I asked her if she had read it, she replied somewhat indignantly, 'Indeed I have not!' Quietly I replied that I had, and that I chose not to discuss it with her until she had. Later that evening, I asked her husband if he had read the Agreement. He declared quite angrily that he had not, but he was totally opposed to it!

The effect of the Agreement was dramatic. Amongst Protestants, the existing tension and indignation immediately intensified to a sense of rage and betrayal; even the most moderate of them rejected it out of hand. Sinn Féin and the IRA also rejected it, as did their avid republican supporters. For them it fell far short of their aspirations, and appeared to threaten their objective of total Irish unity. There was, however, a positive reaction to the Agreement from moderate Catholics throughout Northern Ireland, and they were encouraged by the enthusiastic support given to it by the SDLP.

Soon after 15 November, I had to listen to the worries of several senior civil servants, who came to me surreptitiously, seeking advice. As Ulstermen they felt deep anguish over the Anglo-Irish Agreement. Should they resign? They had been exhorted by unionist politicians and others to do so. What was my attitude to it? My advice? With considerably more irritation than sympathy, I gave it simply and directly, 'Do your duty, as I will mine.'

On Sunday, 17 November, I was infuriated to hear Taoiseach Garret FitzGerald state publicly on RTE radio that the Agreement was already bearing fruit in that *all* future Ulster Defence Regiment patrols would be accompanied by an RUC officer. Such a proposition had never been agreed by me with the Northern Ireland Office. I was silently critical of him for what I regarded as a totally erroneous claim. It was only years later, when reading his memoirs, that I realised that each of us had been misled by the British negotiators on this and other issues. 'There was *some* progress, although nothing like what had been promised, in the accompaniment of the UDR by the RUC on patrols.'[1]

By Saturday, 23 November, a massive loyalist rally had been organised in the centre of Belfast. Estimated to exceed 100,000 people from every part of the North, it was awesome in its anger. The loyalists' slogan became 'Ulster Says No'. They were implacably resolved to bring an end to the Anglo-Irish Agreement as quickly as possible by a variety of methods, including a boycott of all Ministers of State in the Northern Ireland Office; the latter were shunned for several years by loyalist politicians at local and national level. Local council business was also totally disrupted, as unionist councillors simply refused to take part, in protest against the Agreement. As for the fifteen unionist Westminster MPs, they declared on 16 November that they would resign *en masse* from their parliamentary seats in order to bring about by-elections, through which Protestants in Northern Ireland could express their rejection of the Agreement.

The dilemmas facing the RUC at that very volatile time were best summed up, in the House of Commons, by Sir Eldon Griffiths, a Conservative MP, who was then spokesman for the Police Federation of England and Wales, and that of the RUC:

> What happens to policing by consent if it is the clear and demonstrated majority will of those who live in Northern Ireland that the [A]greement shall not prevail? Police officers will face terrible dilemmas. There will be a professional dilemma. How do the police operate against the majority? I need not go into detail, because the House will understand what it means in real terms, but under our system of policing one cannot police against a majority.[2]

On 23 January 1986, the Unionist Parties increased their vote in the fifteen by-elections compared to that in the general election of 1983, but they also lost one seat — the Newry and Armagh constituency — to the SDLP.

It was widely suggested at that time, totally without justification, that my handling of loyalist parades earlier in 1985 was related to the Agreement, as was the RUC's introduction of a Code of Conduct. According to Paisley's Democratic Unionist Party, I was a quisling, an instrument of the Agreement, and a clamour arose yet again from them for my resignation. This tirade was to continue for almost a year.

Poor Jean, who had been shocked by the venom of the criticism levelled at me after my Houston speech, was caused further deep distress by the additional attacks on me after the signing of the Anglo-Irish Agreement. During the very difficult months following the Agreement, Jean and I still fulfilled many social engagements, with seldom a free evening or weekend. My time was devoted wholly to work, and I regarded social involvement as an essential part of that. I was so engrossed in it that I failed to recognise how profoundly the murder of so many police officers, and the grief of the bereaved families, had affected Jean. By the time I did notice her signs of stress and fatigue, I also realised that we had withdrawn from each other over those months. If fault there was, it lay with me.

In mid-November, Jean had mentioned that she was not feeling well and had visited her doctor. She told me that he had diagnosed a stomach upset, and had given her medication to treat it. It was then that my previous inclination to retire was discussed again. I told Jean that the RUC was about to face a more dangerous confrontation than it had ever before experienced, and that it was not the time for resignation. I knew in my heart that I had to see the Force through this very troubled period. Belatedly, I came to understand that I had failed Jean that year. It was a failure which soon became the source of great self-recrimination, but, at the time, pressures at work blinded me to it.

As part of the Agreement, it was expected that the Commissioner of the Gardaí and the RUC Chief Constable should attend meetings of the Anglo-Irish Conference. The first meeting was arranged for 11 December 1985. There was much public conjecture as to whether the Garda Commissioner and I would meet — or, rather, whether Larry Wren would meet me. The nonsense of the Dowra Affair was turned over again and again, with media predictions that the two of us would retire in the immediate future, at the behest of our respective Governments.

Such was the speculation that, on 29 November, I judged it necessary to issue a comprehensive statement to the Force, and also to the public. It stated in forthright terms that politics were not my business, nor that of the RUC, whereas policing was. Emphasising that operational responsibility would remain solely with me, I made it clear that I would remain free from political interference or direction. As far as the forthcoming Anglo-Irish Conference was concerned, I would attend when invited by the Secretary of State to discuss questions of security policy or security co-operation. I stressed that I would attend as a policeman, with police objectives in mind, since better cross-border co-operation was essential to the defeat of terrorism.

What, I often wondered, would be the effects on the RUC if it came into direct violent street conflict with the Protestant community, from which at least 90 per cent of its members came? Given the dangers, I knew very well that the Force must not be seen as either supporting or opposing the Agreement. I was fully determined to sacrifice the Force were it to succumb to loyalist violence on the streets. I was more committed to this stance than I could have revealed to anyone. I knew we had the resources, the manpower, the training, the strength and the firmness of Command to maintain law and order on the streets. The army would be there to give support, if we required it.

Consequently, early in December, I visited Dublin, where Larry Wren *did* meet me. We shook hands, and I found him at least as outgoing as when I had first got to know him nine years earlier; the Dowra Affair appeared to have been forgotten. Clearly, the Agreement had already achieved something positive! My reading of it convinced me that, whatever else, it provided the vehicle and the impetus for the Republic of Ireland to enhance its level of attrition against republican terrorists. Along with Larry Wren, I attended the first Anglo-Irish Conference meeting, which was held in Belfast on 11 December at Stormont Castle, behind formidable coiled, barbed-wire defences. The bitter loyalist protesters outside were easily contained by an intensive police presence.

To support the operation of the Agreement, a Joint Secretariat was established at Maryfield, near Palace Army Barracks at Holywood, just outside Belfast. From the outset, I was able to establish cordial relations with several of its staff. Together we enjoyed open and frank discussions on many matters, which was more than I could say about my relations by then with officials of the Northern Ireland Office and the Secretary of State. The latter seemed to have no realistic idea of the operational problems facing the RUC. Just four days after the signing of the Agreement, this was epitomised by an austere lofty civil servant from London, who greeted me at Headquarters with the remark, 'Oh, you're the Chief Constable who doesn't believe in financial management controls.' I replied, 'If you mean professional and realistic financial control, the answer is "No." If you mean objection to mindless demands for financial cuts to the detriment of operational effectiveness, the answer is "Yes."' The issue became one on which I fought with increasing personal bitterness until my retirement, and on which I once again proved to be the stormy petrel within the system.

Notes
1 Garret FitzGerald, *All in a Life* (Dublin: Gill & Macmillan 1992), p. 574.
2 Sir Eldon Griffiths, Hansard, 27 November 1985, p. 948.

17

THE HARDEST YEAR

Not only did I have the Anglo-Irish Agreement on my mind, but I had John Stalker's Report, delivered only two months earlier on 18 September 1985. The Stalker Report comprised twenty volumes in book form, as well as an album of photographs and maps; in all, it totalled 3,609 pages. It did not in any way follow the recognised and established format of files prepared for the Director of Public Prosecutions (NI); most notably, it was not indexed for easy reference and was difficult to read. It also failed to make recommendations on the two crucial matters which I had included in John Stalker's initial Terms of Reference.

Following its receipt, I directed that it should be studied by two experienced Detective Chief Superintendents, neither of whom had been involved in the original RUC investigation into the three shooting incidents. Within a week, both of them were expressing grave concern about its content. Given this initial analysis of such a lengthy Report, I decided to augment the study team to include a legally qualified Assistant Chief Constable and the RUC's internal legal adviser. Their thorough study of the Stalker Report required more than four months.

As the Report contained many sharp criticisms of Michael McAtamney's previous investigation in 1983, and of the Northern Ireland Forensic Science Laboratory's Report into the shooting incidents, I felt it necessary to ask each of them to answer those criticisms. Their detailed responses were not received until early February 1986, by which time our internal analysis of the Report was also complete.

However, the four-month delay at RUC Headquarters before the Report was referred to the Director of Public Prosecutions raised doubts, if not suspicions, in the DPP's office and the Northern Ireland Office. In addition, the Anglo-Irish Agreement, signed right in the middle of this period, served only to increase the political sensitivities already surrounding the Stalker Report. I found myself on a lonely course, with my Police Authority also exerting pressure to receive more and more information about the Report's content, together with explanations for the delay in our analysis of it.

By 1986, I was one year into what was to be the most stressful and traumatic four-year period of my professional and private life — a period more tragic than I, or anyone else, could have imagined possible. Although satisfied that I coped as best I could, I realise with hindsight that the events of those years have permanently scarred me psychologically. However, an inherent resilience and tenacity developed over many years, coupled with a chance meeting in 1987, have had a remarkably therapeutic effect on me.

By the time I received our comprehensive analysis of Stalker's Report in the February of 1986, I had very limited time to spend on it, due mainly to the problems created by the widespread loyalist violence following the signing of the Agreement. As the ACC and his team had done a painstaking and thorough analysis of the Report, I was content to accept their conclusions and recommendations. Consequently, I forwarded it, along with the Report, to the DPP, stressing my acceptance of the analysis and the overall recommendation that no further prosecutions were justified. I also added severe criticism of the Stalker Report, particularly its failure to produce the evidence needed to sustain its conclusions.

Within a month, and after consultation between the DPP and the Attorney-General, I was given authority by the latter to make available to John Stalker certain specifically identified, classified documents. Under the Prosecution of Offences Order (NI) 1972, I also received a request from the DPP for further inquiries to be undertaken into one aspect of the Ballyneery Road shooting incident in the hayshed.

At last, the decision to give Stalker access to this highly sensitive information had been made at the level which I considered necessary, and so responsibility for any future unauthorised disclosures to the media would rest there too. In mid-March 1986, I wrote to Stalker advising him of the Attorney-General's decision, and the DPP's request for further inquiries; I asked him to call on me to receive the documents, which at my insistence had been specifically listed by the DPP. I also made it plain that I wished to discuss certain elements of his Report. I believed it was time for me to make it absolutely clear that any future inquiries by him were to be conducted in strictest confidence.

But I heard nothing from Stalker until 27 April, when I was about to leave for Malta for four days to attend an Interpol conference on international terrorism. I was told that he intended to call at RUC Headquarters on 30 April in order to collect the relevant documents. In the car *en route* to the airport, I wrote a directive to my Staff Officer that Stalker should be advised that I wished to talk to him *before* he recommenced his inquiry, and that I would meet him on his next visit. When Stalker and Thorburn came on 30 April, during my absence, they were received by Assistant Chief Constable Trevor Forbes, and given the documents.

In mid-May, my office was informed that Stalker and Thorburn would return to Northern Ireland on the 19th. However, on Friday, 16 May, John Stalker phoned me unexpectedly to say that he and his team would not be coming on that date. As for our meeting before he recommenced, he said that he thought John Thorburn could carry out initial routine inquiries. I had to emphasise that I wished to see him before any investigations began, and so it was eventually agreed that he would come over on the 21st of the month to see me.

Two days after that phone call, on Sunday, 18 May, Sir Philip Myers rang me and began his conversation by saying that the Chief Inspector of Constabulary, Sir Larry Byford, had received a complaint from Stalker about a row he had had with me on the telephone on the previous Friday. Sir Philip explained that he would see Sir Larry at a conference in Scarborough the next day, Monday 19th, and would be in touch with me thereafter. He added that I might have to fly to Speke Airport in Liverpool to meet him on Tuesday or Wednesday, 20/21 May, when he could explain what was happening, because it was not possible for him to do so by telephone.

Already mystified, I was further puzzled when Sir Philip disclosed that he and an unnamed Chief Constable would be seeing Sir Barry Shaw, Secretary of State Tom King, and Sir Robert Andrew, the Permanent Under Secretary at the Northern Ireland Office. His final comment, that Douglas Hurd, then British Home Secretary, was '*au fait* with developments', left me intrigued — and rather irritated that I was not being kept equally well informed.

The following day, Stalker again phoned me, but this time it was to say he would not after all be coming to Northern Ireland on 21 May as arranged. He offered no explanation for this sudden change of plan. Instead, we finally agreed that, subject to my seeing John Thorburn before he commenced his investigations on the 26th, I would meet Stalker at RUC Headquarters on 2 June. Later that same day, Sir Philip Myers did ring as he said he would. He explained only that he and Colin Sampson, then Chief Constable of West Yorkshire Police, would fly to Northern Ireland the next day to talk to Sir Barry Shaw, Robert Andrew and me about Stalker.

I remember clearly that Tuesday, 20 May 1986 was stormy with heavy rain. Sir Philip and Colin Sampson had already seen the other two men by the time they arrived at my office at 2.25 p.m. They were due to catch the 3.15 plane from Belfast Harbour Airport, and so there obviously was not much time to talk. I found what they had to say utterly shocking.

They revealed that John Stalker had been under secret investigation by the Greater Manchester Police for several months. A two-page document, both sheets slightly smaller than A4 size, was produced. In it was listed a series of matters of an extremely serious nature. They explained that the possibility of Stalker's involvement in them was currently being investigated. I listened with increasing disbelief and dismay. When offered a copy of the document to keep, I handed it back with revulsion, and ill-concealed annoyance; I wanted nothing whatsoever to do with it. They left soon afterwards, without making clear what was to happen next.

A week later, on the morning of Tuesday, 27 May, I left Headquarters at 6.20 a.m. to travel to Paris for an International Association of Chiefs of Police symposium on violent crime and terrorism. Being away offered no respite from affairs back home. That evening, Sir Philip Myers rang me at my hotel to brief me on developments. He explained that, on the following day, the Wednesday, he and Colin Sampson would see James Anderton, then Stalker's Chief Constable at the Greater Manchester Police, and they would meet the Chairman of Stalker's Police Authority on the 29th, the Thursday. At 10 a.m. on the 30th, Stalker would be given the choice of annual leave or suspension from duty. I was stunned by this, and told Philip Myers at some stage during our conversation that Stalker had already arranged to travel to Northern Ireland on Monday, 2 June to meet me. Sir Philip stressed that Stalker would not be coming.

Afterwards, I clearly recollect that I phoned RUC Headquarters to tell Michael McAtamney that there was a question mark over Stalker, because he was under investigation. Without having been told specifically, I must, nevertheless, have connected Colin Sampson with the investigation into Stalker's activities, because I do remember saying to Michael that I would not like Sampson to take over Stalker's RUC inquiry too. Sampson had been investigating Stalker for activities totally unconnected with the RUC, but I felt most strongly that appointing Sampson to handle both would inevitably mean that the two would become linked together in the minds of many people. Michael rang me back, the next morning, with the message that it was 'too late': Colin Sampson's likely appointment to continue the Stalker inquiry had already been leaked to journalists in Northern Ireland!

I returned to Belfast from Paris early on 30 May, and to a busy schedule of meetings and briefings. Late that afternoon, I rang Philip Myers, who informed me that John Thorburn would travel to Northern Ireland on 2 June to recommence the investigation. I insisted that he should not, as I was most unhappy about the developments in Manchester, and wanted to assess their effects on the RUC. I was also concerned about the obviously inspired rumours that Colin Sampson would be taking over the RUC inquiry, while at the same time pursuing the Greater Manchester Police's investigation into Stalker's activities there.

During the morning of 31 May, I again spoke to Sir Philip about Thorburn's imminent return. He agreed to discuss this with Colin Sampson, and later phoned back to say that it would be postponed for a week. At an urgently convened working lunch that afternoon, I discussed the position with my own Police Authority Chairman, Sir Myles Humphreys, its Secretary, and Michael McAtamney. We felt that to have Colin Sampson replace John Stalker, whom Sampson was simultaneously investigating, would be quite disastrous for the RUC. To have Sampson retain Stalker's own team under John Thorburn would be even more unfortunate.

That evening, I phoned Permanent Under Secretary Robert Andrew, to convey my deep anxiety at the possibility of Colin Sampson assuming control of the RUC investigation. My own position, I felt, had been compromised by the premature disclosure to the media of Colin Sampson's probable appointment to replace Stalker. How could I object to his appointment, once his name was out? To have done so would have been misinterpreted as Hermon obstructing another chief officer's investigation into the Force.

My cryptic notes made at the time reflected my anger and sense of frustration, even bitterness, that the RUC was once again going to become embroiled in controversy. I scribbled in my diary, 'Clearly collusion between PM/RA/CS and DPP. I must hold the line.' Those initials referred to Philip Myers, Robert Andrew, Colin Sampson and the DPP, Barry Shaw. I felt extremely angry that I had not been consulted at an early stage about Sampson's appointment, but in retrospect, I know that there was no such 'collusion'. The fact remains, however, that I was not consulted, reflecting at best a breach of etiquette, but at worst a lack of trust in me.

News of Stalker's removal from duty within the Greater Manchester Police and from the RUC inquiry broke on Saturday, 31 May, and continued to gather momentum over that weekend. The official confirmation that Colin Sampson would assume control of the investigation into the RUC only exacerbated the whole sensitive situation. It was at this point, I am convinced, that a conspiracy theory was conceived regarding Stalker's sudden removal from the 'Shoot to Kill' inquiry. Although wholly without substance, the notion of a conspiracy between the RUC, the Greater Manchester Police and even senior members of the British Government and civil service, was seized upon avidly. The other notion that Freemasons within both police forces had conspired to get rid of Stalker was equally fantastic! I was so angered by the baseless conspiracy theories that I obtained the Police Authority's agreement that financial assistance would be considered in suitable cases for RUC members who felt libelled by reports of their involvement in such conspiracies.

Ironically, it was Peter Taylor who, in a later BBC *Panorama* programme, totally destroyed the myth that there had been any kind of conspiracy to have Stalker removed from the RUC inquiry. Taylor also established beyond doubt that Stalker had been secretly under investigation within his own Force for most of the time he was engaged in our inquiry. Throughout June of 1986, the 'Stalker Affair', as it became known, attracted an incredible amount of vehement and irresponsible journalistic comment.

It quickly became apparent that John Stalker had not known of the long investigation into his own conduct, until after his removal from duty. The shock to him must have been considerable, as was reflected in his television interviews, where he looked and sounded devastated by his enforced leave of absence. He too seized upon the notion of a conspiracy against him. Whether he did so innocently or not, I have never been able to decide. The obvious distress caused to him, and his immediate family, met with sympathy from the public, which in general found the conspiracy theory extremely attractive.

Yet, despite all the media hype, I have to admit that the Stalker Affair was not at that time my greatest concern. Instead, as recorded in the Foreword to my Annual Report:

> 1986 was a most extraordinarily difficult time for this Force and the community.
>
> The combination of factors and events was indeed formidable. Deep-seated opposition to the Anglo-Irish Agreement and the continuing political impasse; massive public order problems, outbreaks of sectarian

murder, attacks and intimidation; confrontation with the police and attacks on their homes and families, community alienation and division, and pervading all, the unceasing threat to life from terrorist organisations.

Although it was not top of my list of problems, I knew that matters outstanding from Stalker's inquiry still had to be resolved. John Thorburn, with his previous team of detectives, resumed the investigation on 9 June, in advance of Colin Sampson's involvement. From within his own Force, Sampson selected Assistant Chief Constable Donald Shaw to assist the remaining inquiry team. It was Shaw's task to control the day-to-day running of the investigation, with Thorburn acting as his deputy.

I met Colin Sampson in London on Friday, 13 June. I scarcely knew the man, having had only the most casual of exchanges at conferences of the Association of Chief Police Officers over the previous few years. I undertook to provide him with background papers, which he might find of assistance in achieving a fuller understanding of his investigation. On 28 June, I despatched those papers to him, together with press cuttings which were causing us great anxiety, as they revealed leaks to the media. I also wrote to the Chief Constable of Greater Manchester, asking him to secure the assurance of the team serving under Sampson that it would comply with the regulations governing communications to the media. John Thorburn had, meanwhile, assured me that neither he nor any member of his team was responsible for certain newspaper reports attributed to them.

Despite the fact that the leaks were generating an air of suspicion within the Force, I instructed RUC members to give Colin Sampson total co-operation and support in his investigation. As the Attorney-General had given approval for the full disclosure of certain intelligence material, I was able to grant Colin access to this, without reservation.

Early in July, Colin Sampson wrote to me requesting that Superintendents Anderson and Flanagan be immediately suspended from duty. I knew that the inclusion of false cover stories in statements of evidence should never have been allowed, let alone directed by the Superintendents, and that I had no alternative but to accede to his request.

By July 1986, Sampson had completed his inquiries so far as the outstanding aspects of the shooting incidents were concerned. Thereafter, he directed his attention to the three chief officers against whom Stalker had levelled criticisms amounting to serious breaches of police professionalism. The three were Assistant Chief Constable Trevor Forbes, Deputy Chief Constable Michael McAtamney and myself.

On 8 September, Colin Sampson interviewed me after caution and after written questions had been presented to me. My replies to his questions were robust and somewhat disparaging. At DPP and Attorney-General level, my responses to the criticisms of me by both Stalker and Sampson must have been accepted without adverse comment or query, as I was never again asked to address them.

By this time, I felt isolated and under tremendous pressure. I was very concerned about the continuing terrorist activity, and about the violence displayed by loyalists in protest against the Anglo-Irish Agreement. But beyond all else, I was terribly worried about Jean's fast-deteriorating health, which necessitated her sudden admission to hospital on 19 October 1986.

On the next day, 20 October, the Attorney-General, Sir Michael Havers, wrote to inform me that I would shortly be receiving the first volume of Colin Sampson's Report, and that he had asked Sampson simultaneously to send an identical copy directly to the Director of Public Prosecutions (NI). Obviously, the time we had taken to study and analyse Stalker's voluminous and unorthodox Interim Report had been neither forgiven nor forgotten!

When I did receive Sampson's Report, and had studied it, it seemed to me that he had not brought a fresh, clinical eye to the whole investigation, but had in effect taken over from where Stalker and Thorburn had left off. I, therefore, personally drafted a carefully considered response to the Sampson Report, signed it on 18 November, and forwarded it to the DPP. I shall never forget the date. Jean had died the day before, just a month after she had gone into hospital.

November 17, 1986 changed the way of life I had known for almost forty years. Jean had gone, and I was beset by problems. It was my hardest year, which had even begun badly, with two RUC officers murdered by a booby-trap bomb in Armagh, within the first few minutes of 1986. Their murders had incensed the loyalists who had been wending their way in a protest march against the Anglo-Irish Agreement. They had left Derry on New Year's Eve and were due to arrive at the Joint Secretariat at Maryfield on Saturday, 4 January. The mood of the loyalists was far from friendly towards any representatives from the Republic of Ireland, regarded by many as the main hiding-place for republican terrorists. Since the RUC had primary responsibility for the protection of Maryfield, I was determined that its occupants should be totally secure from any attack. I, therefore, ensured that additional police resources were maintained within the nearby army barracks, in order to augment, if necessary, those RUC officers already protecting the principal Maryfield entrance.

On the Saturday, many hundreds of demonstrators arrived, and by this stage, the crowd had been infiltrated by members of the Ulster Defence Association (UDA) and the outlawed Ulster Volunteer Force (UVF). The police were viciously attacked. Twenty-five officers were injured — some quite seriously — the entrance gates were badly damaged, and two police vehicles were overturned, before being set on fire. Numerous men wearing Balaclavas were amongst the angry mob, and were instrumental in orchestrating the violence. The demonstrators were motivated by a genuine sense of betrayal by their own British Government, in its clandestine partnership with the Irish Government. Together, the two were seen as having plotted secretly to propel the loyalists into a situation whereby the Irish Government had secured an increasing involvement in the affairs of Northern Ireland, while the North's

constitutional position within the United Kingdom was correspondingly
eroded.

In the face of the vehement loyalist 'Ulster Says No' campaign, RUC
members had to maintain even greater personal vigilance, because violence
was coming at them from both republican terrorists and bitter loyalists. I placed
special emphasis on making regular informal visits throughout the Force.
During my formal inspections of Subdivisions, I also directly ensured that all
RUC members fully understood their role and duties.

Nevertheless, at this most sensitive time, Alan Wright, still the Chairman of
the RUC's Police Federation, began making public statements which had
serious political connotations. He declared:

> No doubt the Chief Constable and the Army's GOC will make their
> operational plans — but my members are in the thick of it. The police are
> between the devil and the deep blue sea . . . The Government is being
> totally unrealistic in its policy of putting the emphasis of security on to
> the police. It's unfair to put this continual burden on the police. It is
> ridiculous. We are not soldiers . . . [1]

I immediately suspended the Force Regulation which permitted RUC
representative associations to comment publicly on matters of 'welfare and
efficiency'. A short time later, in defiance of this, Alan Wright gave a press
conference. As soon as I was informed of this, I directed a disciplinary
investigation into the matter. I knew I would be criticised for being too
authoritarian and suppressive, but I was committed to curtailing, once and for
all, his propensity to make public statements on matters far beyond the remit of
the Federation.

On this occasion, local journalists were less than sympathetic towards him,
and recognised that the Federation could 'raise controversial issues with the
Chief Constable, the Police Authority or the Secretary of State orally or in
writing':

> But the Federation, through its Chairman, Mr Alan Wright, has insisted
> that its concern with 'welfare and efficiency' gives it a wide brief to
> pronounce on police policy . . . But someone has to lead — often on the
> basis of intelligence that cannot be known to the rank and file — and it is
> not denying free speech to insist that any criticism should be channelled
> direct to those who made the decisions, rather than through the media.[2]

After mediation by the HMI, Sir Philip Myers, the Federation agreed that,
except for statements about welfare and efficiency, 'no member of the Force
may give an interview or make a statement or contribute an article to the press,
radio or television on any subject connected with police work, or
administration, the administration of justice, operational security, or of a
political nature without the prior approval of the Chief Constable' (Force
Information Bulletin, No. 60, 1 September 1987).

In mid-February 1986, the Federation called a formal meeting, which was attended by approximately 400 police members. Within a routine agenda, the Anglo-Irish Agreement was raised for discussion. A member tape-recorded parts of this discussion, including the comments of two sergeants, whose criticism of the Agreement elicited much boisterous applause. One of them, in his final remarks, asked the Federation Chairman to convey to the Police Authority, the Chief Constable and their 'political masters' not only the complete disgust the Police Federation had for them, but the view that the RUC had become a political puppet in the eyes of the population of Northern Ireland.

Following this meeting, Rev. Ivan Foster, a colleague of Rev. Ian Paisley's, was given a copy of the tape recording. Foster played it at a specially convened press conference in early March, but in the continuing pressures of the time, this particular issue was submerged, and greater emphasis was placed upon the need for increased, not decreased, contact with the Federation.

The main pressure, in the early spring of 1986, still came from the loyalists. They announced that if Prime Minister Margaret Thatcher failed to meet unionist demands about the Agreement, opposition to it would be channelled into a one-day protest strike with mass demonstrations across Northern Ireland. This was scheduled for Monday, 3 March. As the day approached, the turmoil and apprehension within the community mounted steadily. Yet another loyalist Workers' Committee was formed, comprising a divergent group of individuals and some politicians. While it is truly impossible to convey the awful sense of foreboding, which permeated the community as a whole, I can describe one simple incident which reflected the depth of fear and distrust of loyalists at that time. About the third week in February 1986, as Jean was about to go to bed, she had locked the two doors which gave access to our flat from the main RUC Headquarters building. This was something she had never done before. Locking the doors revealed how deeply concerned she was for my personal safety. I calmly unlocked them, saying, 'I'll never do that. There's nothing to worry about here.'

On Friday evening, 14 February, I had met the leaders of the two unionist parties, Mr James Molyneaux of the Ulster Unionists, and Rev. Ian Paisley of the Democratic Unionists. They came at their request to my office, both men sombre and subdued. Jim Molyneaux, whom I always found stable and responsible, expressed their concern for the future of Northern Ireland, and their fears for the RUC in the face of increasing loyalist rejection of the Agreement. Ian Paisley complained that 'the book' was being thrown at loyalists, who were being prosecuted for public disorder and associated offences. Immediately after our meeting, I recorded it as having been 'low-key and amicable'!

A fortnight later, I had a meeting with my chief officers and Divisional Commanders, and was impressed by their phlegmatic attitude. The Civil Emergency Plan was being fully implemented, with all police leave cancelled and maximum resources gradually being built up. We also undertook close liaison with all public service facilities throughout Northern Ireland.

Following that meeting, I issued a statement simultaneously to the media and the Force. In it, I recognised the democratic right of people to protest peacefully and declared that, since the politics of the present situation were not the business of the RUC, our policy would be to liaise with demonstration organisers to ensure that all forms of protest were peaceful and within the law. It was a comprehensive and conciliatory statement to members of the public, offering them our total co-operation, provided we had theirs. A twenty-four-hour information service was also created to facilitate such interaction and to minimise loyalist propaganda. I knew I was demanding the impossible of my officers; on the one hand, I required that they be relaxed and positive in dealing with local demonstrators, and on the other, I required them to respond immediately in strength to violence and intimidation of the general public.

We were determined that maximum attention would be given to the Catholic community, which was extremely apprehensive and fearful of what 3 March would hold in store for it. Police officers were heavily deployed throughout the evening and night of Sunday, 2 March, but so too were small groups of loyalist protesters. It was a 'cat and mouse' game during the hours of darkness. When people began travelling to work, there were several sharp confrontations. At some trouble spots, the police were not present in sufficient strength to ensure that roads were kept open to enable traffic to flow freely. As well as some extremely violent scuffles between the police and loyalists, there were some incidents where the police failed to respond with the necessary firmness; in a number of wholly or predominantly Protestant areas, I believed that several Subdivisional Commanders might have made more effective use of the available resources. Some Commanders were to say quite candidly to me that they had begun softly by persuading, but to no avail, and so by lunchtime they had moved to the strict application of the law.

The problems of operational command on the ground had been made even more difficult by our strategy of keeping predetermined roads open, to allow those who were resolved on going to work to do so safely. This strategy meant that some less important roads remained closed by the protesters; we needed to concentrate all our resources on keeping open the main arterial routes until after any workers had gone home. It was only then that the police were able to deal more robustly with the remaining road-blocks. By evening, a steady escalation of street disturbances placed increasing demands on police manpower, as did the growing level of attacks on, and intimidation of, Catholics.

The next morning, I received a detailed report of all incidents. Mercifully, there had been no deaths. The police had borne the brunt of the injuries, with 47 wounded to varying degrees, while few, if any, civilians had been injured. Of more than 1,000 road-blocks, 441 had been swiftly cleared by police. The Force had policed 84 protest demonstrations with minimum violence, but with some traffic disruption. There were 329 reported cases of damage to property, including buildings and vehicles, and 237 strong complaints of intimidation. Police vehicles had been petrol-bombed, and civilian cars hijacked and burned. In all, 65 baton rounds had been fired to control the rioters, with four determined gunfire attacks by loyalists on the police, involving 40 to 50 shots being fired.

There had also been 132 complaints alleging police inactivity. Amongst them was an extremely angry letter from a Senior Secretary within the Northern Ireland Civil Service, an Ulsterman and a Catholic. He complained bitterly that he and many others had been delayed by road obstructions for over two hours in the thirty-mile journey from his home to the office. I wrote reminding him of the problems and challenges faced by Mr Christian in *The Pilgrim's Progress*. A month later, I received his penitent reply: 'I am sorry to have written to you about the Day-of-Action. When I see the abuse your people are taking I am ashamed that I should have allowed myself to be irritated by a more than usually tedious journey to work.' It was indeed a generous, albeit belated, recognition of the Force's contribution on that potentially horrendous day.

With 3 March 1986 over, the gloom and immense foreboding of the previous weeks lifted. The impossible task which I had set the RUC of being chameleon-like — co-operative with the demonstrators, and then switching to firm policing as circumstances warranted — had in the main achieved remarkable success. Many nationalists, however, felt that we had failed them, while loyalists felt we had been a suppressive tool, used by the British and Irish Governments to compel their acceptance of the Agreement. From the RUC's point of view, I reckoned that this was about the best we could expect, as we endeavoured to remain impartial.

On later reflection, I regarded that day as the turning-point; it marked the emancipation of the RUC from the yoke, whether real or imagined, of unionist/loyalist influence. To break that yoke, I had been quite prepared for the Force to withstand even more extreme and prolonged violence than had actually occurred on 3 March.

With fifteen attacks on police officers' homes on that day alone, rehousing such families was a fast-growing problem for us. Temporary accommodation at police stations was only a partial solution, as was the provision by the army of some of their unoccupied houses. With another marching season drawing closer, and my policy of regulating parades and bands made much harder by the intense loyalist resistance to the Agreement, I knew that a reserve of homes for police families would be required. Therefore, at a national meeting of the Association of Chief Police Officers, I requested that any available police houses within their Forces should be identified for the sake of RUC families forced out by loyalists. I quickly received pledges of several hundred houses throughout Great Britain, particularly in London. Fortunately, this contingency plan never needed to be implemented.

In the aftermath of the loyalist Day-of-Action, an Anglo-Irish Conference was hurriedly arranged for Belfast on 11 March. Security was much reduced around Stormont Castle, but maintained at the Maryfield Secretariat, where we believed there was a real possibility of a serious loyalist attack. In the event, there were vociferous protests at both Maryfield and Stormont, but less physical violence than at previous meetings. Three Democratic Unionist Party councillors were arrested as they endeavoured to cut their way through the protective fencing at Stormont, and they were subsequently charged with disorderly behaviour and criminal damage.

With so much happening early in 1986, I saw little of Jean except at social events and travelling to and from them. My inquiries as to her health were always answered with reassurances that she felt well. Towards the end of March, we managed to take a six-day holiday in Cyprus, where we stayed in a good hotel and relaxed by driving around the Greek-occupied territory. I was guided by what Jean preferred to do, regarding the holiday as her break from the pressures of being part of my job.

It was in that hotel that I was first made starkly aware of how my exposure to television as Chief Constable had greatly reduced my anonymity. With one or two frosty exceptions, the hotel residents recognised me and were anxious to chat and socialise in the evenings. This recognition was highlighted one evening, as we returned to our room in the lift. A rather tetchy old Englishman asked me how long I had been coming to the hotel. My explanation that this was our first visit obviously irritated him greatly: 'Well, I've been coming here for years and you're known by far more residents than I am'! Little did he realise that such recognition also meant lack of privacy and constant vigilance on my part.

After our return, I discovered that my involvement at meetings of the Anglo-Irish Conference was fast becoming a sensitive issue for me. Although I never had any personal or professional qualms about attending, I found it difficult on occasions to keep a strictly impartial stance. The integrity of my role and that of the RUC had been clearly enunciated in my various public statements, not just for the benefit of the whole community, but for the enlightenment of the Secretary of State and the British Government too!

The Anglo-Irish Agreement itself recognised my independence, in that article 9 (b) stated:

> The Conference shall have no operational responsibilities; responsibility for police operations shall remain with the heads of the respective police forces, the Chief Constable of the RUC maintaining his links with the Secretary of State for Northern Ireland and the Commissioner of the Garda Síochána his links with the Minister for Justice.

In my view, 'links with the Secretary of State' did not mean that I was to be the subject of direction or control by him; the Police Authority for Northern Ireland was specifically established to ensure there was no political or governmental influence on my command of the RUC.

Other articles within the Agreement did, however, give rise to difficulties. The fact that article 2 listed 'security and related matters' as ones which could be dealt with by the Anglo-Irish Conference put me on guard lest my operational responsibility be eroded.

It was article 9 (a) of the Agreement which ostensibly set the most practical and achievable objective for the Commissioner and me, and our respective Forces. It provided that:

> With a view to enhancing co-operation on security matters, the Conference shall set in hand a programme of work to be undertaken by the Chief Constable of the RUC and the Commissioner of the Garda Síochána and, where appropriate, groups of officials in such areas as threat assessments, exchange of information, liaison structures, technical co-operation, training of personnel and operational resources.

To my mind, it was article 9 (a) which completely justified my attendance at Anglo-Irish Conference meetings. I believed it gave us the opportunity to attack terrorist crime in all its forms, and from all directions. My senior officers examined those areas designated in the article. Working Parties were created, with equal representation and total commitment from both Forces. Certainly, relationships between the participants were excellent. I again felt that trusting, co-operative relationship with the Gardaí which I had personally experienced through the 1950s at local level across the border from Victoria Barracks and Strabane.

Our initiatives, however, required acceptance and realistic commitment by the Irish Government; they would have involved major restructuring and expansion of specialist units within the Garda Síochána. Consequently, many of the positive proposals advanced by the Joint Working Parties were never approved at Conference level.

I soon recognised that the Westminster and Dublin Governments had divergent priorities and objectives for the Agreement, and its Conference meetings. The British were motivated by a series of economic, political and diplomatic reasons to minimise — if not eradicate — as quickly as possible the republican terrorist threat to Northern Ireland and Great Britain. The 'Irish problem' had become an international embarrassment to the British Government, which viewed success against terrorism as an imperative in encouraging loyalist politicians towards political progress within the North.

By contrast, the Irish Government regarded as its priorities the political progress in Northern Ireland, the redress of inequalities facing the Northern Catholic minority, and a greater involvement by Dublin in the North's internal affairs. Without these, the Irish Government knew it would experience difficulty, and some danger, in enhancing its own attrition rate against republican terrorism; it had to ensure that Sinn Féin and the IRA did not attract political or sympathetic support from extremists within the Republic of Ireland.

I drew comparisons with the draconian action taken by the Irish Government in 1961, following the decisive general election in September of that year, when Sinn Féin failed to gain any representation in the new Dáil. The new Government, under Taoiseach Sean Lemass, dramatically reintroduced the Special Criminal Court, consisting of five army officers, to try terrorist-type crimes under the Offences Against the State Act. Punitive sentences, coupled with remarkable successes by the Gardaí during this period, contributed substantially to the IRA's five-year campaign being terminated on 26 February 1962, only five months after the Irish general election.

But 1986 was not 1961. By 1986, the Republic could not resort to such short-term severe measures, except in the wake of a successful political initiative in Northern Ireland, which achieved whole-hearted acceptance throughout Ireland, and had the support of both sovereign states. It was patently clear that the Anglo-Irish Agreement did not fall into this category.

During 1986, I found that at Conference meetings there was an increasing tendency to raise operational policing matters. On such occasions, I felt it incumbent upon me to stress that such matters were my responsibility as Chief Constable, citing article 9 (b) of the Agreement. At one particular meeting in June, when my objection to such interference had not had the desired effect, I quietly left the Conference. Outside, I waited in the foyer of Stormont Castle, until the meeting adjourned for lunch, and then I returned to the meeting in the afternoon.

About a month later, on 10 July 1986, the *Belfast Telegraph* became aware of the incident, and declared in large headlines, 'Hermon Riddle, Abrupt Exit from Pact Talks'. Publicity about my walk-out was a shot across the bows for future Conference participants, and was not, I have to admit, entirely fortuitous!

The next evening, the 11th, I went to Stormont to advise the Northern Ireland Office of my decision about the route for the Portadown march on the Twelfth of July. I explained that the Orange parade would be rerouted away from the Obins Street/Tunnel area. Limited use of the Garvaghy Road would, however, be permitted in order that local Orange lodges and bands could parade along it — under strict conditions — on the Twelfth morning. I was immediately taken aback by the intensity of the opposition by those present to the use of Garvaghy Road. As I gathered my street plans and papers together, I kept my temper and explained that I had requested the meeting at Stormont to communicate to the Secretary of State my decision about routing the Portadown parade on the Twelfth; I had not come to discuss it.

Perhaps I had been expected to adopt the same approach to Portadown as taken earlier that year, when the Apprentice Boys gave notice of a march through Portadown on Easter Monday, 31 March. Their proposed route included the Tunnel/Obins Street areas and was, therefore, totally unacceptable. I had no hesitation in recommending to Secretary of State Tom King that it be banned; he agreed. I decided that the police would divert contingents of Apprentice Boys from Portadown, and turn bands back to their own localities. Severe violence was inevitable. At least fifty people were seriously injured, including thirteen police officers. Loyalist mobs deliberately obstructed ambulances taking RUC casualties to hospital. RUC officers' houses in the town were stoned, and shots fired at some. Catholic houses, businesses and schools were also attacked. Since reporting was becoming more objective, loyalists and their conduct were increasingly being criticised by journalists, while the RUC's position received considerably more sympathy and understanding.

Again, Sir Eldon Griffiths, spokesman for the Police Federation, put the position of the RUC in perspective when he warned that the British Government should be careful not to strain the loyalties of the RUC too far:

> The crux of the matter is that the RUC is now being required to police against the demonstrated will of a majority in Northern Ireland while simultaneously waging a war, for which it is neither trained nor equipped, against an international terrorist offensive . . . The wonder is that the RUC has not cracked under the strain of being shot in the back by the IRA and being spat at, or intimidated out of the police houses, by mobs of loyalist hooligans.[3]

Yet, the British Government did not take care; it caused serious problems for me in relation to the RUC's Code of Conduct. I had initiated action on the Code by creating a Study Group early in 1985, months before the signing of the Anglo-Irish Agreement on 15 November. I had included in my Group five very competent members of the Police Authority. Then, in the immediate aftermath of the Agreement, unionist members had withdrawn from Police Authority meetings, in accordance with their party's policy. However, as 1986 passed, some began drifting back to attend general and sub-committee meetings, albeit with discretion, even secrecy. They were responsible Protestant people, who genuinely supported the RUC, but also wished to ensure that its members maintained the highest standards through the introduction of a proper Code of Conduct. If I had not been able to convince them that the Code had been initiated by me, without any direct or indirect involvement from the Republic of Ireland, the unionist members of the Study Group would have withdrawn at once from its preparation, and doubtless also from the Police Authority itself.

To prevent the two Governments from making political mileage out of the Code, I had it issued through the Library at the House of Commons. 'As a result,' wrote Garret FitzGerald, 'none of the impact we had hoped for from this development was achieved.'[4] I was intrigued to discover from Garret FitzGerald's autobiography that he had been given British undertakings on the RUC's Code of Conduct and the Chief Constable's operational integrity, amongst other matters. These undertakings were of no substance, since I had either refused to consider them, or they had never been referred to me formally and firmly.

Amidst all of this wheeling and dealing between the British and Irish Governments, I felt irritated and disillusioned. I was committed to seeing the Agreement evolve within the democratic process, rather than perish like the power-sharing Executive of 1974, and so I despised nonsense which portrayed the Force as anything other than impartial.

For these and many other reasons, I recognised that I had to be seen to be firmly in control operationally, and also in control of the Force as a whole.

Towards this end, I gave more and more television and radio interviews, because they were the most instant and direct means of communication. On 3 April, when interviewed on a popular local television programme, I revealed that RUC intelligence had made us aware that the banned Apprentice Boys' parade intended for Portadown on Easter Monday had been at the centre of an extreme loyalist plot to spread violence throughout Northern Ireland. Armalite rifles, handguns and explosives had been seized from loyalist sources. Violence was planned to spread from Portadown to Protestant and Catholic interfaces in Belfast, Derry and other areas where there were sufficient loyalist paramilitary members to create it. However, the vast majority of the Apprentice Boys and their families were unaware that the parade was to be infiltrated by loyalist paramilitaries with a hidden agenda to cause as much mayhem as possible for the police.

The day of that particular interview, poor Jean had been visiting some police families who had been attacked. While she was at one home in Lurgan, an angry group of loyalists gathered outside, and threw eggs and tomatoes at her as she emerged. It was an ugly scene, but police were at hand to escort her, shaken but uninjured, from the area. She continued her visits and I did not see her until early evening, when she reassured me that she had suffered no ill effects. 'I was surrounded by four RUC constables and taken to my car,' she explained, 'I felt as safe as if I were in a castle.' That night fourteen more police homes were attacked by loyalists throwing bottles and stones.

Throughout that summer, Jean maintained an almost daily routine of visiting such homes and initiated a series of actions from Headquarters to alleviate some of the problems. Although I noticed evidence of fatigue, she dismissed my inquiries lightly, saying that we both needed a break and might have a long holiday in the autumn. Since mid-1985, we had drawn apart in our own private lives. Jean frequently complained of tiredness, and whenever possible would retire to bed early. For the first time, there was, not a barrier, but a distance between us, and even our conversation had lost its personal intimacy. When I snatched time for walking, something which we had always enjoyed together, Jean no longer chose to accompany me. It was the only form of exercise I had time for in 1986, and she felt I benefited more from it by walking alone.

Jean was to suffer another blow before the end of June, with the news that Maureen Richardson, Bob's wife, had died of cancer. Even though we knew that she had been unwell for some time before Bob's retirement as General Officer Commanding, neither of us was prepared for this news. The funeral was arranged for Monday, 30 June at Cannongate Kirk in Edinburgh, the Regimental church of the Royal Scots Regiment, of which Bob was Colonel-in-Chief. We flew on the Monday in a military Beaver aircraft from Aldergrove to Turnhouse Airport, Edinburgh. The old aircraft was noisy and slow, giving us an unpleasant trip. Jean was apprehensive and felt unwell but was, nevertheless, determined to attend. It was the saddest of occasions. The Kirk was filled to overflowing, and Bob looked totally devastated. His normally cheerful face was granite-like, with his jaw locked and protruding even more than usual. I felt terribly sad for him, as I sensed the grief within his huge frame and impassive face.

Maureen's death was followed within weeks by the tragic death of Dean Sammy Crooks of St Anne's Cathedral, Belfast. He had died as the result of a horrible car crash. Sammy had been a close friend of ours, and had officiated at Barbara and Kevin's wedding. Before his retirement, I had been committed with an interdenominational group of business and professional people to raising money for 'Sammy's' cathedral. Affectionately nicknamed 'The Mafia', we raised about £95,000 to remove the debt, left after the restoration of the cathedral's roof. Sammy's wife, Isobel, was one of Jean's favourite people, one whom she much admired, and so, again, Jean took this death badly.

It was after Sammy's Thanksgiving Service in the cathedral, on 25 August, that Jean and I invited the 'Mafia' charity committee members back to Headquarters. As they were departing, I suddenly noticed her standing apart in our lounge, and was shocked by her drawn and frail appearance. Her natural defence had dropped for only a few moments. When alone, I asked anxiously if she was well. Composed and back in control, she reassured me that it was tiredness and that our forthcoming holiday in September would give her the relaxation and rest she needed.

Notes

1 *Belfast Telegraph*, 24 January 1986.
2 *Belfast Telegraph*, 'Viewpoint', 4 February 1986.
3 *Irish News*, 2 April 1986.
4 Garret FitzGerald, *All in a Life* (Dublin: Gill & Macmillan 1992), p. 553.

18

'BUT I UNDERSTOOD, JACK'

During the preceding months, it had become obvious that within the loyalist population, the division was deepening between the vast majority, who abhorred violence, and the vociferous minority, who used it aggressively. Protestant church leaders and leaders within the Orange and Black Institutions publicly condemned violence, as did the leadership of the Unionist and Alliance Parties.

As for the Apprentice Boys, they gave notice of yet another defiant and provocative parade, again in Portadown. The lead-up to the parade, scheduled for 5 May, brought increasingly violent attacks on police officers' homes, with the mother of a constable having her clothes set on fire during one such incident. I gave a press conference and put on public display those weapons already seized from loyalist organisations.

When the Apprentice Boys cancelled their proposed Portadown march, I felt that a shaft of light had appeared, albeit at the end of a long tunnel. This, I believed, was the first sign of moderation. At that time, I also gave a comprehensive interview to the *Belfast Telegraph* on the theme, 'Why I am at the Conference'. The questions addressed to me by Barry White, an experienced and respected journalist, were blunt and direct. My responses were the same. Published in unedited form on 1 and 2 May, the articles, I believed, succeeded in identifying the true role of the RUC and its Command in relation to the Anglo-Irish Agreement. The public response to this interview was extremely reassuring, as is reflected in the following extract from a letter subsequently published in the *Belfast Telegraph*:

> the ability, and willingness, to give frank and forthright answers to a series of searching questions was clearly evident.
>
> What a salutary lesson for many of our political spokesmen who seem incapable of giving a straight answer to a straight question, often employing all the tricks of the trade to avoid doing so. Indeed, one can't help feeling that the two articles . . . should be compulsory reading for more than one loyalist politician.
>
> The Chief Constable made it clear . . . that he was stating his position as a policeman, with no political connotations whatsoever. This came across loud and clear. Nevertheless, in the second interview, in response to a question by Barry White dealing with the possible reasons for the

recent spate of attacks on the homes of Catholics and police personnel, he made a point that goes very near the heart of the problem, when he said among other things, 'their ascendancy is being eroded . . .'.

When will our hard-liners recognise the reality that as far as Northern Ireland is concerned the era of ascendancy politics has run its course?[1]

This was indeed the case, as was evidenced at the Twelfth celebrations that year. After the quite serious disturbances at the church parade in Portadown on 6 July, when Orange marchers attacked the RUC and a riotous group overturned a police landrover with the crew inside, I reckoned that the Twelfth of July itself, which fell on a Saturday, would see sustained and violent disturbances.

My personal decision to permit eight local Orange lodges, accompanied by six bands, to traverse the Garvaghy Road on the Twelfth morning had, as I anticipated, caused much irritation. My decision on the issue meant there was neither an outright winner nor an outright loser. Garvaghy Road was a main road with three sizeable housing estates, two Catholic and one Protestant, in close proximity to it. The eight lodges had formally approached the police cordon at Obins Street and, after serving a protest letter, had marched peacefully in a dignified manner along Garvaghy Road around 7 a.m. By agreement, they did not return by that route in the evening.

My reasons for approving Garvaghy Road were first that it was a main thoroughfare, and secondly that the three estates, particularly the two Catholic ones, were set back some distance from the road, so the residents did not have to view the parade from close range. Above all, I knew that the location of the district's local Orange Hall made Garvaghy Road a natural route for them to march. Provided their behaviour and that of the bands were good, and did not give offence to residents within hearing distance, it could well be maintained as the route for the future. It was a decision which pointed the way forward as I saw it, where mutual respect and consideration had, by necessity, to be shown by all.

On the Twelfth night, loyalist mobs stoned Catholics in Portadown. The police intervened to protect those people from attack, and then found themselves attacked with petrol bombs from both sides. That night, 150 baton rounds were fired, and twenty-eight police officers were injured across Northern Ireland, half of them in Portadown. The widespread disturbances quickly subsided, except in Portadown, where animosity towards the police smouldered on. There followed four more nights of rioting by extreme loyalists in the town, with shots being fired at the police, and a car bomb detonated, while police were in the vicinity.

The SDLP, and especially those members from Portadown, were greatly upset by my decision to allow the Garvaghy Road parade, and made their views abundantly clear. The Ulster Unionist Party and Orange Order held their own public inquiry, and accused the RUC of provoking disorder and resorting to indiscriminate brutality.

Personally, I was satisfied with the outcome. Most certainly no decision of mine on Portadown could ever have received general acceptance. The fact that it was condemned by all sides again suggested to me that it had been the correct decision. The independence of the police had clearly manifested itself. The Secretary of State rounded it off by declaring publicly that my decision had been even-handed, and that operational matters were the total responsibility of the Chief Constable.

In this, I was soon reassured by the stance of some loyalist leaders. Credit is due in particular to the Royal Black Institution, widely regarded as comprising the more responsible and stable members of the Orange Order. The Black parade organised through Portadown on 14 July followed a non-contentious route, approved by the police. Although a rabble of loyalists sought to redirect the parade, the Blackmen literally fought them off with their rolled umbrellas, which formed part of their meticulously correct dress of dark suits, bowler hats, and sashes.

In the midst of the turmoil which followed the signing of the Anglo-Irish Agreement, yet another problem arose — from a wholly unexpected direction. The system of using informers, or 'supergrasses' as they had become known, was running into trouble. Shortly after my appointment as Chief Constable in January 1980, the supergrass system had been initiated to deal with an IRA activist in Derry; he had grown completely disillusioned with the continuing violence of his own organisation, and wished to start a new life for himself and his family. He freely made statements implicating not only himself but his fellow terrorists in many serious crimes. There was no doubt that the first 'converted terrorist', a description I preferred, was sincere in his concern for his family's future well-being, and in his desire to escape from the viciousness surrounding him.

Like Special Branch and CID, I was taken aback by this new development, and hasty discussions were initiated with the DPP's office on how best to handle the phenomenon. The complexities and sensitivities of using converted terrorists were enormous, as were the administrative procedures necessary when arresting and interviewing many hardened terrorists. Laborious though it was, a system of processing such cases developed during the early 1980s, and 'supergrasses' kept emerging. Many dramatic trials — each of long duration and vehemently contested by those accused — took place, with very positive results in terms of convictions and sentencing. From the beginning, I had recognised the benefits of the system of converted terrorists, and was eager to see it continue. I was satisfied that the proper procedures were followed, with all steps monitored and approved by the DPP.

At successive Anglo-Irish Conferences, and through the media, the Irish Government managed to raise its opposition to the 'supergrass' system to an international level. While the opposition to its use grew, the Attorney-General, then Sir Michael Havers, stated publicly that such trials would continue with the full support of the British Government:

the use of such evidence is perfectly legitimate and it is indeed the duty of the Director of Public Prosecutions for Northern Ireland to have recourse to it whenever he considers that . . . it is in the public interest that a prosecution should be instituted and pursued on that basis. I make it clear that he has my full authority and support for his practice in this respect.[2]

There is no doubt that republican and loyalist terrorist organisations were thrown into disarray by 'supergrasses'. Consequently, the terrorists resorted to threatening the lives of their families and relatives. There were several cases of close relatives being kidnapped, with the threat of execution if the 'supergrass' did not withdraw his evidence. Some did. Others went on giving evidence in court. The Provisional IRA continued to execute men whom it believed to be 'informers'.

It was in 1986 that the whole issue of supergrass evidence, and the legal issue of corroboration, came to a head. Many appeals were heard against convictions based solely on the uncollaborated evidence of supergrasses. The procedures themselves ultimately proved to be inadequate, because insufficient consideration had been given to the complex, intricate web of evidence produced; it relied almost wholly on the ability of the supergrass to give very detailed evidence accurately time and again against very many defendants. Without contemporary notes, it was extremely difficult for supergrasses to be certain beyond reasonable doubt about numerous dates, times, places, and the exact duration and depth of their involvement with fellow activists, with whom they plotted and committed heinous crimes. The limitations in intellect, accurate recall and articulation of certain supergrasses had not been realised; proper guidance and protection were not given to help them to meet the awesome ordeal of exposure to the courts and the media, nor were their families sufficiently protected from violence, threats and intimidation. The DPP and prosecution lawyers were, I believe, also too ambitious or insensitive to the frailties of witnesses, and the confusion they would inevitably experience in the hands of capable and seasoned defence counsel, who were fully briefed by the defendants.

The immense political and religious pressures also contributed to the failure of the supergrass system. Initial enthusiasm within British political and legal circles for the system to succeed in fighting terrorism swung full circle, ending up with rejection. Spurred on by political expediency to make the Anglo-Irish Agreement appear to produce results, British support for the supergrass system waned dramatically in 1986. Yet, before my retirement, the circle turned again and I received signals that, if further informers were to emerge, the RUC would receive support. These overtures fell on my sceptical, if not deaf, ears!

Despite the twists and turns of events within Northern Ireland, I had a quiet confidence that the Force had acted, and would continue to act, impartially and with a high level of success, and that the work of years of building it up was bearing fruit. Events then suddenly took yet another unexpected turn.

On the afternoon of 6 August, all security force personnel were alerted to the threat that loyalists were intending to invade Catholic areas in Northern Ireland. That evening there were unusual and intensive movements of vehicles and loyalists known to be involved in disruptive activities. Our top priority was to prevent incursions of vulnerable Catholic areas, and so throughout the evening and well after midnight, numerous groups of vehicles were stopped and searched by the police and army. On becoming aware of the intensive security activity, the majority of vehicles withdrew and went home. It was estimated that many hundreds of vehicles and thousands of people, almost exclusively Protestant men and youths, were involved. I remained at RUC Headquarters to monitor the progress and outcome of events in case there turned out to be some unknown, vicious dimension to it all.

Two serious incidents did occur. One was in Swatragh in County Londonderry, where several loyalists entered the village and set up vehicle check-points. Some openly carried firearms, and shots were fired during the evening. When the RUC arrived, the loyalists hurriedly dispersed, and, in their stead, local Catholic youths began stoning the police.

It was undoubtedly the other incident which attracted most publicity, as it involved the incursion by a group of loyalists into the Republic of Ireland, where they 'occupied' Clontibret, in County Monaghan. This village was probably 30 per cent Protestant. In any event, it boasted two public houses, one Protestant and one Catholic church, as well as about two dozen houses. The loyalist group — estimated in size from 100 to 1,000 — attacked the Garda station, painting 'Ulster is Awake' on its outer wall. Two uniformed, unarmed Garda officers were pulled from their car, kicked and punched. Locals were intimidated and terrified. When plain-clothes Gardaí arrived, one man was arrested. The man taken into custody was Peter Robinson, Deputy Leader of Paisley's Democratic Unionists.

The next day, I issued a detailed statement to the public and the Force, in which I directed that the intensive level of police and army patrolling would continue until 11 August. I also ordered the immediate withdrawal not just of police protection from Peter Robinson's home in Belfast, but of his police escort of two constables in an armoured car. As Robinson was a Westminster MP, I came under extreme pressure to restore his protection. I refused. When asked what the Secretary of State would do if Robinson were murdered, I replied sharply, 'He would blame me!' Peter Robinson's protection was not, in fact, restored until I gave a personal direction several years later, just before I retired; by that time, he had proven his stability again.

Despite all the disturbances and pressures of the spring and summer of 1986, a high level of stability and normality prevailed throughout the population by the autumn. Sure that the worst was over, I decided to link a holiday with an Interpol conference in Belgrade. My final remark to Michael, my Deputy, was 'Keep it tight.' I departed on leave with a quiet confidence that all was under control, with RUC policies and strategies fully understood and firmly grasped.

On 12 September, Jean and I arrived in Rijeka, where our hotel room had a double balcony overlooking the harbour and the town. Jean was exhausted, but thrilled at the expectation of a few weeks' relaxation abroad.

During that first week, she retired early and breakfasted late. By contrast, I rose around 6 a.m., jogged for about a kilometre to an excellent beach and bathed, before jogging back for breakfast. In the daytime, we walked and were at ease with one another. Before retiring for the night, I wrote a diary of the holiday, a habit I had developed over the years. As Jean still felt weary after our first seven days, we were glad we had arranged to hire a car. Jean's tiredness persisted, and although the hotel food was well prepared, she ate little.

As the days passed, she began to feel and look better, which reassured both of us. With the car, our itinerary became more varied, as our mornings and afternoons were spent driving around the area. In the late evenings, we listened to music or sat out on the balcony, chatting together and quietly enjoying our own company. Jean was content, and insistent that I should relax, rather than worry about her. By the 25th, she seemed much better, even energetic, and we spent a pleasant day shopping in the town. My diary records my relief, as well as the fact that I found a copy of the previous day's *Times*, which we both read avidly.

The paper carried news of the acquittal of a notorious IRA terrorist. My mind began then to dwell on the problems of the last couple of years — the violent loyalist reaction to the Anglo-Irish Agreement, the Stalker Affair, and the controversial rerouting of parades. I felt dejected and depressed, but concealed my innermost feelings from Jean.

The next morning, we departed and travelled along the coast, where the scenery could only be described in superlatives. Our evening in Zagreb was idyllic, too, with a fortunate choice of restaurant for dinner, and a humorous waiter, who spoke fluent English. Jean appeared to blossom. We were serenaded by an excellent group of minstrels, who sang in both English and the local dialect. To our amusement and pleasure, they sang, 'My Bonnie Lies Over the Ocean'. Despite a considerable walk back to our hotel, Jean remained happy. Hand in hand, we talked over what had been a thoroughly enjoyable day.

Our journey the next day to Dubrovnik compared very badly with it. Although Jean complained of being weary, she was anxious to explore the old part of the city, which we intended to make the focal point of our holiday. However, we became hopelessly lost and miserable, as we drove round and round in circles. Eventually, we managed to reach the white-walled city, but could not find a parking space anywhere. I was already feeling totally frustrated, when Jean urgently asked for something to drink, but insisted that only mineral water would do. The heat was overpowering, and she was obviously distressed. My diary faithfully records just how I felt at that time:

> For the first time, unsure of routes and no parking, Stalker, that terrorist, Jean unwell and always so tired. I'm afraid I just snapped. What a bloody

way to get rid of fatigue, pressures and strain. Literally snapped! Maybe it was there all the time. Maybe having read in the *Times* that 'H' was acquitted, the underlying strain which surfaced. I don't know, it was a frightening lesson and one I'll never forget. I hope Jean does forget. Being Chief Constable for so long demands its price. I suspect I have yet still to make some final payments . . . Took an hour or so to settle, had got water for Jean who with it took her usual tablets. Just sat along the road, profoundly shaken. Apologised to Jean. She remained calm and almost seemed to have expected it. I'd relaxed too much and accepted (erroneously) that all was now well.

Back into Dubrovnik but I felt disorientated, in hotel I had two large stiff whiskeys — definitely not me! Watched from veranda fishing boats, 20–30 in gathering dark, the black 'cardboard' hills, flickering lights, a steamer leaving, the background noises of boat engines, no breeze for sails, sipped my Johnny Walker BL, felt more relaxed and desperately tired. Dressed up (tie, blazer and all) and thought, what the hell anyway. Jean had a sherry, I had a brandy and in to dinner.

Very, very tired, got Jean tea in bed and she too must have been shocked at my 'temper'. It wasn't temper. It was utter frustration and despondency. I asked her forgiveness. She replied, 'There's no need.' Settled down and to bed. I slept immediately.

Despite Jean's continuing problems with food and weakness, the next five days were almost perfect. I was relaxed and caring towards her, content to keep to her pace of walking and to abide completely by her wishes. Although reluctant, Jean was persuaded to see a doctor. He spoke English, and I remained while Jean outlined her symptoms. He explained that there was a virus in the area, which caused stomach upsets, diarrhoea and sickness. He believed Jean had caught it, and the severity of its effects had aggravated her tiredness and lack of appetite. She was prescribed a suitable medicine. Plainly relieved, Jean insisted on carrying on with our sightseeing, and rejected any suggestion that we should return home.

During those last few days, I took many happy photographs of Jean, and with the aid of a timing device on the camera, I also took some of the two of us together. On our final night in Dubrovnik, Jean looked very well. At the restaurant, a surprise awaited us — we were the chief guests that evening. In attendance were the managers of the restaurant, and the hotel and district managers, along with other selected guests. The meal was superb, with Jean's choice of courses beautifully prepared. We were fêted by all present, and Jean basked in the unexpected gesture. Much later, I discovered that it was our Ulster travel agent who had arranged it all.

On Saturday morning, we departed early and drove all day in brilliant sunshine through mountain forests, over tortuous corkscrew but well-surfaced roads to Sarajevo. Our journey was one of the rarest experiences of my life for the sheer beauty of it. We arrived in Sarajevo in the early evening. Jean was tired and after dinner she wished to retire. On her insistence, I walked into the town, visiting the city centre, the old town, and thinking and finding myself praying silently for Jean and her recovery to good health. I thought remorsefully of the pressures of the past two years, and indeed of the past twenty years; there was a reawakening of what we had lived through.

Early the next morning, I sought a doctor, but in vain. Instead, I found a chemist shop open, and outlined the background to Jean's present condition, and the Dubrovnik doctor's diagnosis. The chemist agreed with the prescription, and advised that she should continue to take the same medicine.

Afterwards, we drove to Belgrade through enchanting, yet completely different, countryside. At the Hotel International, we saw familiar faces arriving for the Interpol conference, which began the next day. Many of the members, who had met her at previous conferences, immediately realised that Jean was unwell. A further medical opinion accorded with that of the doctor in Dubrovnik. However, her loss of weight over the previous week was so obvious that I again tried to persuade her to return home with me on the first available flight. She would have none of it; she found the hotel comfortable, and was happier staying there than she would be terminating her break and my conference. She merely confined her movements to the hotel and its grounds, and rested more. I travelled alone in a taxi into Belgrade to do some shopping for Jean. The driver spoke remarkably good English, and the conversation remains with me because of its absurdity:

DRIVER: You are English?
SELF: No, I am not.
DRIVER: You speak the English!
SELF: I am Irish.
DRIVER: Ah, Irish. I love the Irish. I love the IRA.
SELF: Quite. And why do you love the IRA?
DRIVER: They fight the English. I hate the English. They are the suppressors of people. Their Empire, they suppress many people. I hate the English.
SELF: That is not true now. There is no Empire. England has no wish to suppress people. Why do you hate them?
DRIVER: Ah. But the English are still English!

A pause. 'Here is a man with firm views,' I thought, and I decided to pursue the conversation.

SELF: You have many German tourists in your country. How do you feel about them?
DRIVER: The Germans, they come here in war, they pay dearly. They come as tourists. They pay dearly.

At that I thought it best to let sleeping dogs lie, and fell silent in the back of the taxi.

During the conference, Jean's only engagement was a dinner hosted by the then Commissioner of the Hong Kong Police. She and I sat at opposite ends of the table, our eyes met frequently and I felt a steadily deepening concern. It had been our habit over the years to establish eye contact at formal events, when I would respond if she wanted me to be at her side. That night, from a distance, I saw the stark transformation in her face, which was gaunt and strained. There was a haunted, sad look in her eyes. She made little conversation. A group of singers entered, and by sheer coincidence they too rendered, 'My Bonnie Lies Over the Ocean'. With that, Jean and I smiled, both knowing that our minds were back to our evening meal some days earlier. For those few minutes, a silent empathy existed between us, to the exclusion of everyone else at the table. On our final night, I discovered that I was to be proposed for the Interpol Executive Council, but I decided not to tell Jean, who seemed to have no stamina for new challenges, and given how poorly she was, it was of little relevance to me too.

Back home, I unpacked on Tuesday, 14 October, while Jean remained in bed. Although I wanted to call our doctor straight away, she insisted on resting for a few days, before going to see him. On Friday, she did go with Belle. Blood and other samples were taken, and Jean was asked to return to the surgery on Monday for the results. I went with her this time. A doctor explained that Jean had to go immediately for further tests. The doctor was clearly upset, though well under control. My eyes caught hers squarely, and she looked away. In that moment, I had a dreadful premonition that Jean was going to die.

Travelling home, we sat quietly in the car, Jean took my arm and held it tightly. As we approached a junction close to Headquarters, we had to turn left. Across the road was a church, with its doors ajar, but without anyone in sight. A hearse sat empty and unattended outside. The raised hatch-door yawned open. It looked stark and menacing. I flinched inwardly. We arrived at RUC Headquarters moments later, and in the privacy of the flat, Jean began to cry softly. I held her in my arms, reassuring and comforting her.

Two phone calls and an hour later, I took her to a private clinic, much against her personal wishes. It was her acute fear of losing personal, or rather bodily, privacy which motivated her resistance to going. I had been aware, understanding and sympathetic of her need for privacy during the greater part of our married life. She was always fastidious about what she ate, and what she wore, and I wanted an environment where her surroundings and her food would be absolutely as she would have wished. The private clinic provided all of that. But more than anything, I wanted to remain by her side, because I had an overwhelming sense of having failed her.

Jean's cancer was quickly diagnosed. The initial prognosis was that she had a less than 10 per cent chance of survival beyond a year. I had to grasp this terrible situation as a whole. I had been absent from Northern Ireland for four weeks. Much had happened in my absence and there were many policing matters requiring my attention. I worked long hours, but found time for frequent short visits to the clinic.

Jean settled quickly into her world, which was her room. Television and radio were of no interest to her, and so I provided a stereo with her favourite cassettes. A bond, richly forged between us, meant that little needed to be said. Occasionally, during those first few days I would walk her along the corridors and back to her room. Holding my arm, she walked slowly, but showed quiet contentment at our being together and being seen together.

When I tried to voice my regrets and to apologise for my concentration on work to the detriment of our family and her, she interjected, 'But I understood, Jack.' Two other remarks revealed her true, silent and private nature. Once, when I expressed my love for her, she replied, 'I was always so proud of you, Jack,' and again, when I commented on our marriage and life together, she said, 'I've seen so many marriages of friends and acquaintances, of celebrities and others, but ours was special, Jack.' I found much comfort from those three simple statements.

Precisely two weeks after her admission to the clinic, Jean was transferred to Belvoir Park Hospital, which specialised in cancer treatment of the most serious types. Radiotherapy treatment began on Tuesday, continued on Wednesday and Thursday. On the first day, Jean walked for her treatment, on the second she travelled by wheelchair, and on the third by stretcher. There was no further treatment. The specialists, when I met them, were sombre but pragmatic. I telephoned a good friend, a renowned and skilled surgeon. I wanted the stark facts, the truth about Jean's condition. Only he, I believed, understood that. He gave me the truth — Jean had no hope of surviving and would be dead before Christmas.

Thereafter, Barbara arranged the earliest flight home from Florida. Rodney was already close by and Jean's father, then eighty-six, was being looked after by Belle. I prepared all four of our small, close-knit family for Jean's death. I thought four out of five was all I could prepare.

When I had all our holiday photos developed, Jean and I spent much of our time together looking at them, reminiscing and reliving much of it. For her it had been our finest holiday. If she had had any suspicion that she was dying, it never revealed itself. I explained to her that her illness was serious, but that when she recovered, I would retire and we would enjoy life together to the full. I think she believed me implicitly, because she wished to, and that was enough.

On those occasions when I left Jean's private room, while medical staff attended to her, I noticed various Catholic priests visiting the private ward adjoining hers. I inquired after the patient, and found out that he was a young priest in his thirties, who was also suffering from cancer. He asked if he might visit Jean, and she gladly agreed, finding his company and spiritual reassurances comforting. He and our own local rector ministered to her, and I know both contributed to her feeling of tranquillity and serenity.

Jean died on the evening of Monday, 17 November 1986, with Barbara, Rodney and me present. She had lapsed into unconsciousness several hours earlier. She died with dignity, and without suffering. The nursing staff, doctors and specialists were beyond compare, and understood my concern that Jean should retain her sense of privacy and self-respect.

However my life evolved, it could never again be the same. With all my experiences over many years, I only then began truly to understand and appreciate what ultimate grief was. Sadness I had felt many times, but only with Jean's death did I plumb the desperate depths of grief.

So much more to say, to explain, to reveal, of that time, but no more. My life had to go on. 'My bonnie lies over the ocean, Oh bring back . . . ' rang in my head at night-time, and was sung in a muted voice during the long months ahead as I lay awake, alone in the flat at Headquarters. So too was Acker Bilk's 'Stranger on the Shore'. It was always Jean's special tune, one we had played often as we sat together in the clinic.

I was totally bereft without her. She had been part of me and my life for almost forty years, and suddenly she was gone. Key members of my staff at Headquarters were so worried at the time that they placed a protective shield around me. The RUC's Press Officer, Bill McGookin, and Bill Wilson, my closest friend, skilfully shielded me from the media, and also brought a degree of balance to my life. They did this so subtly that I scarcely saw — and certainly failed fully to appreciate — their sympathy and loyalty. As its first Press Officer, Bill McGookin had, from 1969, loyally and steadfastly served five successive Chief Constables and was the continuous link between us, during those most traumatic years in the history of the RUC. In November 1987 the two Bills were there — very discreet and always tactful — as a sort of buffer for me.

Jean's funeral took place on 20 November. I returned to duty the following Monday, and sought refuge in work. As 1986 drew to its close, my own health, or rather my state of mind, was my main priority. I was stricken with guilt and remorse over Jean's death, but I concealed it from everyone. My own private assessment was that I needed a period of at least three months to recover. There was, however, going to be a new and inexperienced Police Authority Chairman as of the New Year, and the Stalker Affair was at its most contentious.

With many other serious problems and criticisms surrounding the RUC as it headed into 1987, I did not wish to be the weak link. Nevertheless, I did not regard myself as indispensable, and increasingly wondered whether the pressures I had already endured since becoming Chief Constable were such that it was time for a change. But . . .

> But I have promises to keep,
> And miles to go before I sleep,
> And miles to go before I sleep.

('Stopping by Woods on a Snowy Evening', Robert Frost.)

Notes
1 *Belfast Telegraph*, 'Letters', Gerry O'Grady, Londonderry, 15 May 1986.
2 Hansard, House of Commons Debates, 19 March 1986.

19

THE AFTERMATH OF STALKER

It was March 1987 when I received Colin Sampson's second Report. To analyse it thoroughly took time, and so it was towards the end of June 1987 before I forwarded its analysis to Sir Barry Shaw. After months of deliberation — and, presumably, consultation with the Attorney-General — Barry wrote to me on Friday, 22 January 1988, giving his conclusions. Having taken into consideration all the relevant circumstances surrounding the three fatal shooting incidents, he had decided not to direct any prosecutions.

On the following Monday, 25 January, the Attorney-General, Sir Patrick Mayhew, made a statement in the House of Commons at Westminster about the Stalker/Sampson investigations. He said he agreed with the DPP that no further prosecutions would be warranted in respect of the three shooting incidents. While the DPP had concluded that there was 'evidence of the commission of offences of perverting or attempting or conspiring to pervert the course of justice, or of obstructing a constable in the execution of his duty', both Sir Patrick and the DPP were satisfied that it would not be in the public interest to institute criminal proceedings in respect of these. The Attorney-General also announced that safeguards would be made to ensure that, in the future, facts and information reported to the DPP 'are in all respects full and accurate, whether or not any security interest is involved.'

Irish politicians found his statement so 'astounding' that the Dublin Government called for an early meeting of the Anglo-Irish Conference. Loyalists, of course, regarded this as clear evidence, if any were needed, of the Republic meddling in the internal affairs of Northern Ireland.

The simultaneous revelations in the 'Unger Diary', published in the *Guardian* on the Thursday, Friday and Saturday of that same week of January 1988, did little to alter the generally sympathetic mood towards John Stalker. Even though they indicated that he had consistently leaked information to a newspaper editor during his RUC investigation, the public still perceived him as a good man, who had been removed from the RUC inquiry in suspicious circumstances. The newspaper coverage throughout February and March, eulogising Stalker and condemning the decisions of the DPP, was unprecedented. Reaction was voluminous, with press cuttings on these two subjects reaching a depth of seven inches for the period from the end of January to St Patrick's Day!

However, the police service at senior level throughout the United Kingdom was shocked by John Stalker's behaviour. The Association of Chief Police Officers issued a statement condemning the revelations in the 'Diary', while Colin Sampson wrote to me personally expressing his concern about them. So too did members of the Stalker team, in particular Detective Superintendent Simons, who wrote on 19 February 1988:

> I am aware that you and other members of the Royal Ulster Constabulary have, for some considerable time, considered that we may have been responsible for leaking information to the press. Indeed, I have been present during interviews when Royal Ulster Constabulary Officers have overtly expressed that opinion. You will be aware that we have strenuously and consistently denied any conduct of the kind.
>
> We now wish to take the opportunity to disassociate ourselves from any involvement in the material recently published in a national newspaper under the title 'Unger Diaries' and attributed to Mr Stalker.
>
> We are astounded by these newspaper articles, and hope that you accept that our duty of confidence to the enquiry is intact. As a matter of general principle we do not support the publication of any books on matters that would be regarded as classified information.

Stalker had in fact retired prematurely from the Greater Manchester Police on Friday, 13 March 1987, before the inquiry into the RUC had been completed by Colin Sampson. Within months of his retirement, he became a public figure, and was in constant demand for television and radio interviews. Being personable, articulate and persuasive, his appeal was remarkable. The extensive publicity which had followed the Attorney-General's controversial statement ensured that when *Stalker* was published in London two weeks later, on 8 February 1988, it quickly became a bestseller, read avidly by a public intrigued by alleged murder, mystery, and hints of conspiracies. John Stalker described his book as 'a story not so much of terrorism as of ambition and professional and political survival'. Just whose ambition and survival are unclear.

In a television interview for the BBC *Newsnight* programme on 18 February 1988, John Stalker was to claim: 'The book is the result of very meticulous and careful research. It is true. I stand by everything in it.' He portrayed himself as having been totally immersed in, and in control of, what he described as 'undoubtedly the most important investigation ever that's been conducted by one policeman into another'.

I must admit that when I first read *Stalker*, I flung it across the room, so incensed was I by its innuendoes and false statements. Some passages within it were deeply offensive to me, especially those which related to the fictitious cigarette packet. I was intrigued and extremely disappointed that neither the Secretary of State, the Northern Ireland Office nor the British Government ever criticised the massive distortions contained in *Stalker*, and serialised in the *Daily Express*.

Police Constable Ian Westwood, a member of the Greater Manchester Police, who was an elected Federation representative for his Force, made the following comments in his review of *Stalker*:

> Both Sir John Hermon and Mr James Anderton say that the book contains errors, inaccuracies, and is misleading. They would, wouldn't they? Or at least that is what many people would like us to believe. But I can quite clearly state that it is inaccurate, at least in part, where I have first hand knowledge of what was said or done . . .
>
> . . . two occasions that this reviewer can use personal knowledge of the circumstances and on each of those occasions they are erroneous. These instances tend to show Mr Stalker in a more favourable light, or those he sees as his past adversaries in a less favourable light. If both are as inaccurate as I am convinced they are then it certainly leaves a large question mark in my mind over the rest of the content of the book. I for one do not believe it can be taken at face value. Like any witness shown to be wrong in part of their evidence the credibility of the whole must be doubted . . .
>
> The book to my mind is written out of bitterness and that in itself is its failing.[1]

After the publication of *Stalker* on 8 February 1988, I established a team to examine the book's contents. The team's findings confirmed those of PC Westwood, and led to the following initial RUC statement of 10 February being issued to the public:

> The RUC wishes to comment, briefly at this stage, on some matters arising from the publicity given to Mr Stalker's book.
>
> 1. Both in his book and in public statements Mr Stalker has made it clear that he found no evidence of a 'shoot-to-kill' policy. Let it therefore be stated once and for all: there was no such policy and Mr Stalker's comments and the Attorney General's recent statement support what the RUC has repeatedly said.
>
> 2. It has been suggested that the RUC had a hand in Mr Stalker's removal from his Northern Ireland inquiry. This is untrue. The RUC had no involvement. Recent revelations in the '*Guardian*' newspaper confirm that even Stalker himself did not believe it at the time. As far back as the beginning of June 1986 he is reported as saying that he didn't think an RUC 'dirty tricks' department was involved. It has now been alleged that the Chief Constable of the RUC attended a meeting at Scarborough with Her Majesty's Chief Inspector of Constabulary at which Mr Stalker's situation was apparently discussed. This again is untrue. Sir John Hermon was not at Scarborough.

3. Mr Stalker claims that in the course of his investigation he was obstructed from the outset by the RUC and suffered lack of co-operation. This was not the case and the RUC rejects this unjustified complaint.

4. There are many other matters pertaining to Mr Stalker's book and his utterances which the police do not accept as being accurate and the RUC clearly wishes to register this point. (Force Information Bulletin No. 73)

Not least amongst the inaccuracies in *Stalker* was his account of receiving from me his Terms of Reference for the RUC investigation, the vital starting-point.

On reading these, he claimed he 'began to feel the first pangs of irritation' at what he saw as 'an attempt to circumscribe' his inquiries.[2] The Terms of Reference encompassed entirely the DPP's requirements for a further investigation after Michael McAtamney's. The other two additional matters — concerning hot pursuit by RUC officers across the border into the Republic, and the protection of intelligence sources — were so central to the circumstances surrounding the fatal shootings that I felt compelled to include them. When I showed Stalker these Terms at our first meeting he at no time alluded to 'pangs of irritation' about them. Nor was I advised by John Stalker that he had, for some unknown reason, extended his Terms of Reference to include an investigation of the Kinnego bomb, which had killed three RUC officers on 27 October 1982. However, in *Stalker* he recounted his investigations into Kinnego.

Not only that, but throughout his inquiry, Stalker never once contacted David Chesney, the Senior Assistant Chief Constable whom I had appointed as his Liaison Officer and whom he had met at our first lunch. However, in his book, he claimed, 'The RUC provided two drivers and a liaison officer — a detective sergeant . . . I was never able to obtain the services of someone with more clout within the RUC'.[3]

Much else was incorrectly written in *Stalker* about the RUC's methods of protecting informants. For example, he complained that when his team put requests to Special Branch:

Again, they would neither confirm nor deny that an informant was involved. They refused to give me details, despite my clear responsibility to examine the difficulties associated with the use of informants in Northern Ireland and to look at the circumstances of RUC incursions into the Irish Republic.[4]

Since it was strongly suspected at that time that someone within the Stalker team was leaking information to the press, how could RUC officers trust the team enough to reveal highly sensitive details about informants? Stalker also referred frequently in his book to secret tape recordings and alleged transcripts. All aspects and methods of intelligence gathering, in relation not only to terrorism but to non-terrorist crimes, are protected. There is ample precedent to establish that it is Government policy that the consent of the Attorney-General and Director of Public Prosecutions should be obtained in respect of Special Branch intelligence, as in the case of the national intelligence services. Certainly, the RUC has always recognised and followed this principle. John Stalker was well aware of this, and should not have misinterpreted my refusals for access to such information as 'obstruction'. The truth of the matter is that I insisted it was for the Director of Public Prosecutions, the Attorney-General, or possibly the Prime Minister herself to grant Stalker access to intelligence information.

When Stalker was told on 28 May 1986 that he was under investigation by the GMP, he said: 'I knew then, as powerfully as it is possible to know, that what was happening to me was rooted firmly in my enquiries in Northern Ireland. It was no secret that I was within a couple of days of obtaining the vital tape, and of interviewing the highest policemen in the RUC.'[5] The revelations in the 'Unger Diary' entry of Stalker's reported discussions with Michael Unger four days later, on 1 June, are devastating. It reads:

Stalker says that he is due to go to Belfast the next day — Monday — to get the documents that Hermon refused to give him the previous year and to interview Hermon, his deputy and Assistant Chief Constable Forbes. He says that the documents are top-secret surveillance material which proves that the RUC went in to the hayshed without warning and shot dead Tighe (the survivor always claimed this and that Tighe, 17, was shot in the face at point-blank range from the window of the barn. The survivor had a policeman stand over him with a gun and another say: 'Finish the bastard off').

The policemen involved weren't told that the hayshed had been under secret surveillance by the police and MI5. In fact, the left hand didn't know what the right hand was doing.

Hermon has tapes of the incident and always refuses to release them, says Stalker. The Government doesn't want them released as two cabinet ministers (Hurd and King) might feel obliged to take responsibility and resign if the tapes reveal a cover-up of murder and the operation of a shoot-to-kill policy. The Anglo-Irish accord would fail . . . Stalker's suspension could have been triggered last week because he was due to go to Belfast tomorrow to ask these pertinent questions. Sir Philip Myers, HM Inspector of Constabulary, knew he was going and the sort of questions to be be [*sic*] asked.

. . . Myers and Hermon are very close friends, with Hermon often going over to Colwyn Bay to stay with Myers. Stalker says this is well known because of the extra policing required in Colwyn Bay.

Stalker says that he doesn't think that an RUC 'dirty tricks' department is behind the 'suspension': he thinks that Greater Manchester police have stumbled across something and then used this as 'manna from heaven' to get him off the RUC inquiry.[6]

Stalker has not admitted the accuracy of Michael Unger's account of their conversations, nor, to my knowledge, has he denied it. I can only say that what was revealed to Michael Unger was grossly distorted. The documents I had originally refused to give Stalker were not 'top-secret surveillance material', but intelligence documents later approved by the Attorney-General for release to Stalker's inquiry team. Nothing in those documents 'proves that the RUC went in to the hayshed without warning and shot dead Tighe', or that 'The survivor had a policeman stand over him with a gun and another say: "Finish the bastard off"'.

The allegation in the 'Diary' entry that 'Hermon has tapes of the incident and always refuses to release them' is wholly untrue. The truth is that I never had any such tapes in my possession, nor had I ever sight of them in November 1982 or since. Moreover, the suggestion that 'Myers and Hermon are very close friends, with Hermon often going over to Colwyn Bay to stay with Myers' is a travesty of the truth. Jean and I stayed only twice at the Myers's home: the first time was a weekend from 19 to 22 August 1982, and the second on 16 and 17 February 1985. The only other time I stayed at the Myers's home was overnight on 11 June 1987, seven months after Jean's death. We were professional associates, each with his own independence of role and, I believe, with respect for the other.

These are but a few examples of the many inaccuracies scattered throughout *Stalker*. Nevertheless, in an interview on Radio Ulster's *Good Morning Ulster* programme on 11 February 1988, John Stalker still maintained that his book was 'the result of careful research and careful notes and careful legal opinion and I regard it as being accurate'.

Unfortunately, the inaccuracies like the notions of conspiracies, invoked throughout *Stalker*, are hard to put right so long after the events which gave rise to them. At least the detailed research by the journalist Peter Taylor completely debunked the myth of a conspiracy to remove Stalker. This was finally confirmed at Government level by a lengthy answer to the House of Commons on 4 April 1990, by the then Home Secretary, Mr David Waddington. He was compelled to make the statement after John Stalker's fanciful suggestion of possible involvement by officials at Cabinet and Home Office level in his removal from the RUC inquiry. This arose early in 1990, because Stalker had somehow obtained typed copies of manuscript notes from my personal diary for the period 16 May–2 June 1986. There, I had recorded for 30 May 1986 (two days after Stalker was placed on extended leave), 'Expressed concern regarding structure of enquiry. Clearly collusion between PM/RA/CS and DPP. I must hold the line.' 'PM' referred to Philip Myers, the Inspector of Constabulary. 'RA' of course referred to Sir Robert Andrew, Permanent Under Secretary at the Northern Ireland Office, not Sir Robert Armstrong, then Private Secretary to Margaret Thatcher. The initials 'CS' stood for Colin Sampson, and the 'DPP' referred to Sir Barry Shaw. In other words, there was no Cabinet Office involvement in what I suspected was 'collusion' about the appointment of Colin Sampson to the RUC inquiry, and my comments had nothing whatsoever to do with having Stalker removed from it.

Stalker also chose to distort my earlier diary entry for 18 May 1986. In it, I had recorded notes of a phone call from Sir Philip Myers, and they read: 'Mentioned a CC seeing BS RA TK and that DH was au fait with developments'. The 'CC' referred to 'a Chief Constable', as then unknown to me, going to see (future tense) Barry Shaw, Robert Andrew and TK, Tom King, then Secretary of State for Northern Ireland, and DH referred to Douglas Hurd, then British Home Secretary. This phone call gave me my first hint that something, of which I had no knowledge, was wrong and that something was about to happen, but Sir Philip felt unable to talk to me about it on the telephone. As the Home Secretary, Mr Waddington, explained in the Commons, it was regrettable that:

> Mr Stalker misquoted Sir John Hermon's diary entry so as to make it refer to Sir Philip Myers telling him that 'a Chief Constable *has* seen BS RA and TK and that DH was au fait with developments', with a clear implication that the entry referred to events that had already taken place. In fact, Mr Sampson had at that time seen none of the persons to whom Sir John was referring.[7]

I found the Home Secretary's statement of 4 April 1990 straightforward and supportive, in stark contrast to the British Government's overall approach at the actual time of the publication of *Stalker*, two years earlier. Then, even though the Attorney-General's statement of 25 January 1988 made it clear that there were to be no more prosecutions of RUC officers arising from the shooting incidents, I felt that some had already been found guilty, albeit only in the public mind. I did not, and do not, believe that there was 'evidence of the commission of offences of perverting or attempting or conspiring to pervert the course of justice, or of obstructing a constable in the execution of his duty'. As with the murder charges, I remain totally convinced that, on the evidence presented by John Stalker and Colin Sampson, no charges of conspiracy or obstruction would have succeeded in a court.

As for the two suspended officers, Superintendents Flanagan and Anderson, the Police Authority had accepted, on the basis of professional medical advice, that they should be retired from the Force on the grounds that they were permanently disabled for the purpose of police duty. The pressures, especially of prolonged suspension, had had their effects on both men. They, like so many others, were casualties of the traumatic events in Northern Ireland.

As for 'the role played by senior officers', it was announced in the House of Commons on 17 February 1988 by Secretary of State Tom King that the Police Authority for Northern Ireland, as the disciplinary body for those ranks, had to consider Sampson's observations in relation to Michael McAtamney, Trevor Forbes and me. The HMI, Sir Philip Myers, was required to make available to the Authority relevant material for its consideration.

I regarded my being the subject of such an investigation as completely unjustified, and so I had no concern about its outcome. My written response to

Sir Philip was little other than a reiteration of the written observations I had already made to the DPP, when forwarding Stalker's and Sampson's Reports to him, and my written responses to the questions addressed to me, after caution, by Colin Sampson. The fact that this fresh inquiry into my role became sensationalised by the press, and sparked off renewed demands for my resignation, came as no surprise. It was other pressures, personal ones and the prolonged exposure to the rigours of the office of Chief Constable, which left me stressed and somewhat embittered. I too had become a casualty of the 'Troubles'.

Within a short time, the new Chairman of the Police Authority, Tom Rainey, asked Michael, Trevor and me to attend a meeting at the Police Authority's Headquarters in Belfast to be advised of the outcome of its inquiries. We arrived and were seen separately, without any prior discussions. After interviewing us, the Police Authority issued the following statement on 29 June 1988:

> On the basis of its examination of the matter and in the light of the advice received, the Authority concluded by a majority of one that it was not necessary to appoint an investigating officer to enquire further into Mr Sampson's observations and resolved that no disciplinary proceedings needed to be taken in any of the three cases. *It should be stressed that the point at issue for the Authority was not that of culpability but of further possible investigation.* [emphasis added]

That last sentence in effect made clear that no breach of RUC Regulations or Discipline had been found, and hence no further investigation was justified on the facts. However, the disclosure of the narrowness of the Authority's voting, without more elucidation, served to fuel speculation that we three had only just escaped formal investigation. Our interpretation of the statement was quite different; we felt that it did in fact exonerate all three of us from any fault. Hence, our own joint statement, issued the next day, reflected our confidence: 'We welcome the statement of the Police Authority for Northern Ireland. We always knew that we had nothing to fear from any investigation. Nevertheless, we are pleased that the Police Authority has vindicated our position.'

While that rounded off the inquiry into the role of the most senior RUC officers, two other matters were outstanding. First, the criticisms identified in the Sampson/Stalker Reports about shortcomings in operational and administrative matters within the RUC became the subject of a special inspection by one of HM Inspectors of Constabulary, Mr Charles McLachlan. His Report I accepted, and his recommendations were quickly implemented. Secondly, I invited Mr Charles Kelly, Chief Constable of Staffordshire Police Force, to oversee the disciplinary investigation arising from the Stalker/Sampson Report. With considerable wisdom he appointed a new team from within his own Force and, after a thorough inquiry, he delivered his Report to RUC Headquarters towards the end of July. He recommended a series of disciplinary charges against twenty RUC officers, ranging in rank from constable to chief superintendent. By this time, I had also selected Sir Kenneth Oxford, then Chief Constable of Merseyside, to preside over the disciplinary hearings, as I knew him to be strict but fair, with many years of experience at the highest rank.

In accordance with RUC Disciplinary Regulations, all the police officers charged were entitled to be legally represented, and each availed of that right. The hearings were scheduled to commence on Monday, 13 March 1989, and were expected to run for several weeks. However, they were unexpectedly ended the next day. There had been discussions between the lawyers, acting on behalf of the accused officers, and the Presenting Officer (so called because, on my behalf, he presented the evidence to sustain the charges).

When news of this sudden development reached me, I called Bill McGookin, the RUC Press Officer, and Deputy Chief Constable Michael McAtamney to my office. After we obtained precise details of the outcome, the following Force Bulletin No. 105 was prepared, with a view to sending it out directly to all stations:

> Following an investigation by Mr Charles Kelly, Chief Constable of Staffordshire, a Disciplinary Board was held in Belfast yesterday and today, presided over by another mainland Chief Constable.
>
> Twenty officers appeared before the Board charged with breaches of Force Disciplinary Regulations. The outcome was as follows:
>
> Eighteen officers were reprimanded.
>
> One officer was cautioned.
>
> Charges against one officer were dismissed.

At my direction, the Bulletin was held until copies of it were delivered to the Police Authority and the Northern Ireland Office. Fifteen minutes later, I ordered the release of the Bulletin to the media. This had the effect of simultaneously informing the community and all members of the RUC of the facts, thereby pre-empting any unauthorised leaks. Despite the waves of opposition and bitter criticism during the previous six and a half years, my firm belief in the integrity of my officers had finally been sustained.

Notes
1 *Manchat*, GMP's Federation Magazine, April 1988.
2 John Stalker, *Stalker* (London: Harrap 1988), p. 29.
3 *Op. cit.* p. 32.
4 *Op. cit.* p. 53.
5 *Op. cit.* p. 109.
6 Michael Unger, 'Stalker Diary', *Guardian*, 28 January 1988.
7 Home Secretary David Waddington's statement in the House of Commons, 4 April 1990.

20

A FORLORN AND UNCERTAIN YEAR

After Jean's death in November 1986, I spent a sad Christmas and lonely New Year, the bleakness exaggerated by a dull, depressing winter. I felt forlorn and isolated, as if I occupied some sort of void. With a sense of detachment and numbness, I remained within an invisible cocoon, watching myself behave apparently quite naturally. For the first time in my life, I felt totally desolate. I realised very quickly the considerable contribution Jean had made to the welfare of the Force generally; hers had not been a cosmetic involvement, but one of genuine commitment. I was anxious to ensure that this caring side of the responsibilities of Command should continue.

However, in the early months of 1987, I found it so distressing to attend the funerals of murdered officers that I decided that, in future, I would be represented at such funerals by a senior assistant chief constable, while I continued with my personal visits to the families in their homes. Often, I wished I might lift their grief and shoulder it myself. Throughout that year, I heard comments of great sadness, which remain with me. When I asked one particular widow if there was anything I could do to help, she looked into my face and asked calmly, 'Can you bring him back?'

On another occasion, I found it necessary to intervene on behalf of the parents of a policeman who had been murdered four years earlier. Because of a rare failure in the RUC's welfare system, they had suffered enduring distress and had asked for a personal interview with me. Even with their deep Christian faith, I found them both disorientated, extremely bitter, and struggling to cope. I eventually resolved the problem. Later, while attending a Police Federation garden party, I was handed a small parcel from the couple. It contained a Bible, beautifully and painstakingly adorned with the inscription: 'Praying you will know the help of God at all times in the great responsibility that is yours'. On the opposite cover was Psalm 145, verse 18: 'The Lord is nigh unto all them that call upon Him, to all that call upon Him in truth.' That verse remains a challenge, one I too often fail.

After Jean's death, I began going to church with great regularity. Invariably, I attended Holy Communion at 8.15 a.m., walking the short distance to St Columba's, where Jean's funeral service had been held, and returning by a circuitous route for exercise, before breakfast. That early service was simple, without music and without singing. For someone like me, who is not devout, it was the bottom line; there was no escape from one's conscience, and from an uncomfortable awareness of one's own frailties.

To lift my spirits, I decided to set myself three personal objectives. With retirement in mind, and a commitment to remain in Northern Ireland, I first began searching for a house. Since I expected Rodney, Belle and Roy — Jean's widowed father — to live with me, I wanted a house that would allow each of us privacy. Finding such accommodation was not as easy as I imagined!

My second target was to look for a sensible boat, which would present a challenge and foster my interest in single-handed sailing. My seventeen-foot yacht no longer tested even my 'shamateurish' abilities. My knowledge of sailing was confined to what I had acquired by trial and error, and a minimal amount of studying books on the subject.

The third objective followed naturally from the second, and it was to take a basic sailing course, before buying a new boat. The course was also intended to serve as a brief holiday for the year, and provide useful experience. With the help of an acquaintance in the Isle of Wight, I found myself aboard a yacht, bound for what I believed would be proper professional sailing instruction. The first weekend I spent with several others on a basic course for crew. I was not impressed by the 'skipper', nor by the loss of privacy from having to live on board with strangers. On our second evening, I tried to convince the 'skipper' that if he anchored overnight on the location he had selected, we would beach before low tide. My endeavours were to no avail. We were grounded on the ebb tide!

Mercifully, the following five-day cruising course was a different matter. There were four others in addition to a 'skipper', an academic who had abandoned a teaching career in sheer frustration over the changes being perpetrated in education by the Conservative Government. He owned his own yacht, and was very competent. Of the remaining crew, there was a girl in her teens, a 'yuppie'-type stockbroker and a young married couple. I reckoned that my age was more than the combined ages of any two of them. I appreciated the relaxed, friendly atmosphere generated between us.

Having initially given an assumed name, I did feel rather deceitful in maintaining it with these particular crew members. I, therefore, decided to disclose my true identity, and declared that I was 'Sir John Hermon, Chief Constable of the Royal Ulster Constabulary, known to my friends as Jack'. Their response was one of complete indifference! Frankly, I found it very difficult to accept that, even though I had been at the centre of a maelstrom of publicity over the Stalker Affair and the RUC's handling of loyalist opposition to the Anglo-Irish Agreement, no one on that yacht seemed to have been previously aware of my existence!

Instead, I was expected to share all the chores of cooking, washing up, and keeping the boat shipshape. I even took pride in the fact that I managed to cook an excellent breakfast for everyone, while bracing myself against the best efforts of a lively sea to destroy it. In the evenings, we usually moored for the night and adjourned to the nearest pub. We also shared the experience of all-night sailing in a very fresh wind with a rather turbulent sea.

That sailing course had an extremely therapeutic effect upon me, but it was short-lived because my other objectives were less easily achieved. It became obvious that a suitable house for my diverse relatives was not available in an area where I could live safely. After diligent searching and much frustration, I decided upon a building site, with a view to designing and building a home to suit my family's needs. What began as a challenge and distraction from my increasingly controversial role as Chief Constable became a real burden, involving unnecessary delays, escalating costs and unpleasant confrontations with the architect and the workmen.

The purchase of a yacht also proved troublesome. One drawn to my attention by a police officer in a *Belfast Telegraph* advertisement seemed ideal for my purposes. It could be sailed single-handed, but for me to do so would require new skills and expertise on my part. It was owned by a certain gentleman called 'John Christian', who described himself to me as a Canadian businessman, and who told me he had been sailing with his wife and two young children on a planned 'lifetime experience' holiday.

Through an intermediary, I purchased the yacht in September 1987. Within a matter of months, a storm of publicity broke about how the RUC Chief Constable had bought a boat from a fraudster. The implication of one particular newspaper report was that if John Stalker had been suspended from the Greater Manchester Police for allegedly consorting with known criminals, why should Sir John Hermon be allowed to remain in charge of the Royal Ulster Constabulary? 'John Christian' turned out to be an international confidence trickster with a list of aliases, and several previous convictions! Fortunately, all receipts and information were available to prove that I had bought the boat innocently believing the man to be whom he professed. After his return to the south of England, 'John Christian' was sentenced at Canterbury Crown Court on 26 May 1988, and jailed for two years on fraud and deception charges.

Episodes like this were deeply offensive to me. Down through the years, I sometimes felt dogged by false charges — concerning my acquisition of the yacht, the fluorescent light in my locker in Hastings Street, and even the reception for Barbara's wedding. I was able to refute all of them without any difficulty, but with great personal annoyance that they had been raised in the first place.

By early 1987, the nature of the allegations against me was very different. It was argued that, as Chief Constable, I had discriminated against a number of women police Reservists. A legal action had resulted from my refusal to renew the three-year contracts of full-time RUC women Reservists, while at the same time renewing those of the men. A test case had been taken by a Mrs Johnston, and supported by the Equal Opportunities Commission for Northern Ireland. With EEC legislation on equal treatment for men and women invoked in support of her case, it had been referred by the local Industrial Tribunal to the European Court of Justice in Luxembourg for a preliminary ruling. This laborious process lumbered on until a final hearing was fixed for March 1987, back in Belfast before the Industrial Tribunal.

I was not prepared for the unusual experience of several days in the witness-box. To me, this case was the unjustified outcome of a correct decision, which I had taken in the early 1980s. I had directed that the contracts of the women Reservists should not be renewed at that time, because the RUC was below strength and also under considerable pressure from terrorism and street violence. With excessive overtime having to be performed, I desperately needed male officers, who could carry firearms and perform riot duties. No women police officers in the UK were then trained to carry firearms on duty, or to perform front-line public order duties.

Throughout the Tribunal's hearing, I had a sense of unfairness about it all. I understood that, at the relevant time, a certificate had, in fact, been issued giving the RUC exemption from the equality legislation on the grounds of public security. I still regret having been persuaded, by the Police Authority and the Northern Ireland Office, to agree to a settlement. It had, after all, been a test case before the European Court of Justice, which for the first time had been invited to resolve the conflict between two fundamental principles of Community law. Which had precedence: public security or equality of employment opportunities for men and women? In the event, the European Court had remained neutral, leaving the local Tribunal to determine the issue. With an agreed settlement, whereby compensation was paid to the women involved, the Tribunal was deprived of the chance to decide on the facts. Despite my feelings of injustice, the case indirectly changed my life.

On 27 September that year, I received a document entitled 'Goliath against the Girl Davids', a description which had been used by a lawyer involved in the *Johnston* case. The document emanated from the Law Faculty of Queen's University, Belfast, and had been written by a lecturer whose speciality was European Community law. Apparently, it was intended for publication in the *Northern Ireland Legal Quarterly*. The author was identified by an accompanying letter as Miss Sylvia Paisley, and she was seeking my views on her article before its publication. I immediately took exception to the flamboyant title, and also found myself irritated by some of its content.

Quite spontaneously, I telephoned the university and was connected to the appropriate extension. 'Who's speaking?' a precise female voice inquired. When I identified myself, I was bemused to hear her sharp reply, 'Pull the other leg! I'm busy.' Further exchanges followed, as I tried to prove that my phone call was not a hoax. Finally, she appeared to accept that I was the Chief Constable, and that I wished to discuss her article.

It was to be 27 November before Miss Paisley found a gap in her diary for an appointment at my office. As she entered (late) around 11 a.m., I saw a rather prim and stern-looking woman, whose face changed as soon as she caught sight of a J.B. Vallely painting on the wall behind the door. I was intrigued by the fact that she appeared so knowledgeable about his work. Anyone familiar with it will know that the exact subject-matter of his paintings is certainly not always readily identifiable. I concluded that she obviously had interests outside the Law Faculty.

She eventually gave me an opportunity to outline the complete background to the *Johnston* case, and a lively discussion ensued, before she agreed to note my points of view and some, at least, of my criticisms. At that stage, I was not to know that the only thing she would change in her original article was its title, so that it was published under the heading, 'Arms and the Man: *Johnston v. RUC Chief Constable*'.[1]

Our discussion was interrupted by my Staff Officer, who reminded me that I was already late for lunch at Garnerville Training Centre, where there would be a Passing-Out Parade later in the afternoon. Hurriedly, I asked Miss Paisley to accompany me to lunch. She reluctantly agreed. I failed to comprehend why eating her own wheaten bread and cheese sandwiches alone in her office seemed to have greater appeal than having lunch as my guest at Garnerville! On our arrival, I was extremely surprised to discover that she was already well known there, having given a series of lectures on the Inspectors' Development Courses. It seemed appropriate, therefore, to ask the Commandant to arrange a suitable lunch for her, as the catering staff were used to her vegetarian preferences. I quickly left her in order to join the visiting Chief Constable.

Straight after lunch, the guests and the Inspecting Officer went outside for the Passing-Out. With a visiting chief officer, it was my habit not to attend the ceremony itself, and so I remained in the large dining-room to relax with coffee and an unfinished brandy. I thought I was alone. Then, I saw Miss Paisley sitting at a distant table. I had completely forgotten she was there and that her car was still at RUC Headquarters! We began to talk.

I was interested to learn that after her mother's early death, her father had brought up his four young daughters so that each would have her own career and independence. Beyond law, Sylvia was interested in the arts, in walking and in wildlife. I detected that she suffered from a fair degree of stress, much of it brought on by the nature of life in Northern Ireland. She had been deeply distressed by the callous murder of one of her young colleagues, Edgar Graham, in the street just outside the room where she had been lecturing. Several other tragic deaths in the following months, and also an outbreak of shingles, had not helped her frame of mind. She struck me as a lonely figure, who hid her loneliness in dedication to her work. As we parted that day, I did not expect our paths to cross again.

The year 1987, like that conversation with Sylvia, stands out in my memory because it was dominated by death and coping with the consequences of sudden death. After six terrorist murders in January and February, the next three months recorded a total of forty-one killings, including eight police officers, three Ulster Defence Regiment soldiers and twenty-nine civilians.

Amongst the civilians killed were Lord Justice Maurice Gibson and his wife, Cecily, who were blown up in their car by a huge IRA bomb at Killeen, near the border, as they travelled north from Dublin on 25 April, after a holiday abroad. He had been a prime target for the IRA, particularly after his comments describing Sean Burns, Eugene Toman and James McKerr as having been brought to 'the final court of justice' when they were fatally shot by RUC officers.

The Gibson murders greatly aggravated the political situation within Northern Ireland, still tense after the signing of the Anglo-Irish Agreement. Attempts by unionist politicians unfairly to cast suspicion on — if not attribute blame to — the Gardaí for the lapse in the Gibsons' security were mischievous, to say the least. I was quick to refute such suggestions, when it was discovered that the couple had themselves revealed their true identities when booking the holiday. Earlier that month, I had actually recorded a personal note that Garda members were displaying considerable activity in the Republic, seizing weapons, ammunition and explosives.

After the defeat of Fine Gael in the Irish general election in February, Charles Haughey was returned as Taoiseach. With the subsequent resignation of Garret FitzGerald from the leadership of Fine Gael, one of the main architects behind the Anglo-Irish Agreement had left the stage. Whilst in Opposition, Haughey's personal antipathy towards the Agreement had been well known. Consequently, his return to power gave rise, initially at least, to uncertainty and tension between the British and Irish Governments.

It was my experience that, in times of upsurges of terrorism or severe public disorder, the British Government tended to be helpful in providing, or at least promising us, additional finance and resources. But as soon as the immediate pressure receded, and the situation in Northern Ireland became less volatile politically, calls for cut-backs in expenditure quickly resumed.

The only time I had met with an instant and favourable response was towards the end of 1983, when police resources were under stupendous pressure, and help had come from a totally unexpected quarter. The Prime Minister visited Northern Ireland on 23 December, making several public appearances. As was customary, I was present for her arrival at Aldergrove Airport, and again when she left. During a fifteen-minute period before she boarded the aircraft, the RAF staff had provided a cup of tea, and Margaret Thatcher took the opportunity to chat with those present. In casual conversation, she asked me if there were any particular problems which I wished to raise. I said there was — I needed a further 500 RUC officers. 'Are you satisfied you need them?' was all she asked. I confirmed that I was. Signalling to the Secretary of State, then James Prior, she called, 'Jim, come over here.' When he joined us, she simply declared, 'The Chief Constable needs 500 officers. See that he gets them!'

However, the Prime Minister's immediate and confident response had unfortunate consequences. In the following years, all of my reasonable requests for additional manpower were delayed, and challenged again and again, before being turned down without adequate explanation. I was advised that in both the Treasury and the Home Office, feathers had been ruffled by the Prime Minister's spontaneous decision at Christmas 1983, or perhaps it was the perceived temerity of my direct response to her inquiry.

I, therefore, felt extremely annoyed and disappointed that undertakings for additional resources to combat terrorism, given in April 1987 at Secretary of State level, were apparently forgotten. Instead, I was advised that no further vehicles were to be ordered, and no further contracts for much-needed fortified buildings were to be approved — despite serious delays on most current building projects because of the IRA's murder of, and threats to, building contractors and their work-forces.

1987 was one of those years when we were under pressure continually to make savings, despite the spate of killings that year. Amongst those killed were nine men who died together in particularly traumatic circumstances on Friday, 8 May. During the evening, an IRA terrorist unit of eight men launched a vicious attack on Loughgall police station in County Armagh. Security forces lay in ambush, and every member of the unit was shot dead, as was an innocent motorist. This was the largest group of republican casualties to die together since the early 1920s. The effect reverberated throughout the community, and well beyond.

Loughgall had been identified by very careful analysis as the most likely target for an IRA attack. An appearance of normality was maintained at the station, with two volunteer policemen performing routine duties, but army units were also secretly deployed in the area. At the same time, the IRA had implemented its plan by taking two local families hostage in their homes. A mechanical dumper was seized, as well as a big van with a sliding side-door. A large bomb was then placed in the dumper's bucket, before it was driven through the village towards the police station. It smashed through the protective fence, and was driven up against the station wall, where the driver ignited the short fuse on the bomb, before running off to make his escape. In the meantime, the van had conveyed seven heavily armed terrorists to the station. As soon as the bomb exploded, they rushed out of the van with their guns blazing, and charged at the station.

Their plan was executed so quickly that it caught those on duty within the station by surprise. Consequently, they did not escape injury. Part of the first floor and wall of the station collapsed on top of two police officers, grievously injuring one and causing serious injuries to the other. Although the small number of soldiers concealed inside the station had been briefly disconcerted by the speed of the attack and the massive explosion, they soon opened fire. Other soldiers, hidden in positions outside the building, also opened fire on the terrorist unit. The driver of the digger had died on the station fence, still holding the cigarette lighter which he had used to ignite the fuse of the bomb.

The following day, I visited the two constables in hospital, before going to the badly damaged station. The villagers of Loughgall were still stunned by what had happened. The weapons used by the terrorists were ballistically connected to a series of murders and attempted murders. One revolver had been taken from the body of a police officer murdered at Ballygawley Station in County Tyrone, in a bomb and gun attack in December 1985. Since then, it had been used in the murder of three more people.

At his funeral, one of the terrorists was described from the pulpit as 'an upright and truthful man', who had lost his life in a 'most brutal way'.[2] Such eulogies do the Catholic clergy no credit, when it is recalled that this same 'upright man' had died as he and his comrades were doing their utmost to kill injured police officers, who lay trapped below the debris of their bombed station.

I could not help but contrast this with the words of a Catholic bishop, two months earlier. Gerard Logue, an IRA volunteer, had killed himself with the accidental discharge of a weapon. He was buried on 24 March, in Derry. The family had given assurances to the local RUC that there would be no paramilitary display at the funeral. The police distanced themselves from the mourners, but a volley of shots was fired at the graveside. Martin McGuinness, a senior member of Sinn Féin, rejected the RUC statement, asserting that no such guarantee had been given to the police. Because the gunmen had desecrated church property and were applauded by mourners for doing so, the Catholic Bishop of Derry, Dr Edward Daly, immediately banned the bodies of paramilitary members from Catholic churches in the city during requiem masses at their funerals; if the family so wished, requiem mass could be celebrated independently of the burial service. 'We cannot permit our church-grounds to become battlegrounds for anyone,' he said. Referring to the IRA, the Bishop said, 'They are not freedom fighters. They are not engaged in a struggle for freedom. They are engaged in a ruthless and unprincipled campaign for power through murder, terror and intimidation . . . They have repeatedly demonstrated that they respect neither God nor man.'[3]

There is no doubt that Catholic families whose loved ones had been killed as the result of their involvement in violent crime were sometimes manipulated by terrorist godfathers, wishing to exploit the funerals in order to provoke violence against the RUC. But of course, a minority of those families did harbour hatred towards the Force, and willingly agreed to a military-type IRA funeral.

Only a few weeks after Logue's funeral, this sensitive problem arose again on 6 April 1987, when the coffin of Laurence Marley, an IRA man murdered by loyalist terrorists, was draped in a tricolour and carried from his home in North Belfast. Scuffles broke out between police officers and Sinn Féin stewards, and the coffin was brought back to the house and kept there for three days. During this time, demonstrations were organised on the street outside, and the family appealed to Cardinal Tomás Ó Fiaich and Bishop Cahal Daly to ask the police to withdraw. By the time the funeral eventually took place, Sinn Féin and IRA propaganda had ensured that the RUC's handling of events was viewed in a very poor light.

Yet, I knew that those directly involved in policing the funeral had performed their duties conscientiously, and with all the sensitivity that was possible, given the awkward circumstances. For us it was a no-win situation: if we stood back and tolerated the paramilitary 'display', we were criticised by loyalists; if we refused to tolerate it, we were in confrontation with Sinn Féin sympathisers. I was deeply concerned about the damage being done by such funerals to the quiet, steady improvement of RUC relations with the Catholic community throughout the 1980s, as evidenced most clearly in our crime detection statistics.

Surprisingly, the IRA issued a statement after Marley's funeral saying that it would 'no longer fire volleys of shots over dead members' coffins in church grounds'. Although this signalled a clear gain for the Catholic church, whose authority was being recognised by republican terrorists, in its statement the IRA reserved its right to 'pay tribute to its dead . . . outside the church precincts'.

Bishop Cahal Daly stated publicly that 'The RUC must rethink their policy in respect of funerals of paramilitaries.' Referring to the 'inordinately difficult task' faced by the RUC, he continued properly and positively by saying that 'a funeral was not the occasion for the display of police and military strength — nor for a paramilitary propaganda coup'.[4]

In a newspaper interview I gave twelve days later, I said that I was examining the recent suggestions by Bishop Cahal Daly on how to handle paramilitary funerals. He had recommended that the RUC should formulate conditions which it expected mourners to observe, and which should be announced publicly in advance. I thought this procedure was eminently sensible, and in line with police statements relating to individual funerals in the past. Consequently, in my interview I was able to declare that 'We will be influenced very much by the Bishop's utterances and . . . [those] of other responsible clergy of any denomination.'[5] Nevertheless, I emphasised that the RUC would take all necessary action where weapons and paramilitary uniforms were displayed at funerals. I believed Bishop Cahal Daly had established a clear understanding that the Catholic church would make the funeral arrangements only with the immediate family or undertakers, never with paramilitary organisations, and the priests of the parish would insist that there should be no flags, emblems, political banners or paramilitary displays in the church or its precincts. The Bishop had stressed that the church could have no control over what happened on public roads or in cemeteries, as this was the duty of the police. I responded by saying, 'I find those regulations governing funerals, set by the Catholic Church, would be very close indeed — and probably identical — to our desired approach towards funerals, regardless of the manner of death of the deceased.'[6]

I gave instructions that specific proposals be prepared at once about the RUC's manner of policing paramilitary funerals, and that they should then be announced. On 9 May, the day following the Loughgall attack, our announcement was published in prominent advertisements in the three most popular local daily newspapers. The subsequent funerals of the eight Loughgall terrorists were firmly policed, and passed without any serious confrontation.

The problem, however, had not been laid to rest. The following October, two men were killed by the premature detonation of a bomb, which they were transporting by car through Derry. The IRA quickly claimed that both men were 'volunteers on active duty'. A paramilitary funeral was held at the church, where the clergy had to yield under protest 'to avoid any unbecoming scenes'. Afterwards, as the funeral made its way to the cemetery, shots were fired in the air by a masked gunman, who emerged unexpectedly from the crowd. The regulations of church and state were thus defied in a direct challenge, orchestrated by Sinn Féin and IRA activists. Clashes ensued between the police and the mourners; again the IRA tried to exploit the situation in order to make the RUC appear oppressive and insensitive at a funeral.

It was common knowledge at this time that the total failure of Sinn Féin's political thrust in the Republic in 1987, and its poor showing against the Social Democratic and Labour Party in the local council elections in Northern Ireland, caused disputes and confrontation within its political and military wings. Members were also concerned that the Anglo-Irish Agreement, if successful, would seriously damage Sinn Féin's ultimate goal of a united Ireland.

The IRA was, therefore, seeking to minimise the effects of these political setbacks by using the funerals of its members to demonstrate its continued presence and defiance. This was done despite the fact that the local police in Derry had reached agreement with each of the bereaved families that the funerals would be properly conducted. Two public statements were issued explaining that the Force had followed its declared policy on paramilitary funerals, and adding that the police had tried at all times to deal sympathetically with the wishes of the families, the church and public representatives.

Since the RUC emerged with considerable credit for its handling of these two funerals, I felt it was only a question of time before the IRA joined battle with us again over this issue. I could never have envisaged how much more savage the battle would become before it was resolved.

In early September, I had been satisfied to learn from a review of the Protestant marching season, between April and the end of August, that out of almost 2,000 parades, there had been only 36 illegal ones. I had no need to request that the Secretary of State ban any parades, and only eleven route changes were imposed by the police. I felt that this rumbling problem had at last been substantially resolved. A more responsible, mature approach by loyalist organisations seemed to have emerged, along with a return of the desire to co-operate with the RUC.

That said, the suggestion in one of my Annual Reports that 'responsibility for decisions on the holding and routing of parades should rest with an independent tribunal' appeals to me even more strongly nowadays, as it would remove the RUC completely from the accusation of making political decisions in its rerouting of marches. The creation of a tribunal would air fully the difficulties surrounding parades, including any blatant sectarian behaviour of participants, bands and local residents. Comprising able representatives of all law-abiding sections of our community, it could identify routes well in advance of a parade, and thus be distanced from the pressures and emotions of the moment. The police, whose views should still be taken into account, would then act in accordance with the tribunal's decision. No such tribunal was established in my time as Chief Constable.

With hindsight, I am sure that my aggressiveness over financial constraints in 1987 did not win me many supporters amongst those in the Northern Ireland Office, or at Cabinet level. Nevertheless, I felt betrayed in a way; the RUC had endured so much in the wake of the Anglo-Irish Agreement, and still its efforts were going unrecognised by the Conservative Government. I began to sense a growing lack of trust in my abilities from both the Police Authority and the Northern Ireland Office. I sensed them too from London, and from the Prime Minister herself.

Since being appointed Chief Constable, I had felt that Margaret Thatcher, a robust and dynamic Prime Minister, had an understanding of Northern Ireland and its problems. I believed that I could confidently continue to serve while she was in office. However, my encounter with her at the Chequers meeting, in May 1981, about the republican hunger-strikers had revealed a much more tempestuous and abrasive side to her than I could have imagined. Since 1985, I had been noting her increasingly strident and swingeing approach to many public issues, and the way she seemed to seek refuge from domestic difficulties by stepping up her involvement in international affairs. I read these as signs of strain from being too long in office.

With some amusement, I privately drew personal comparisons between the two of us: I too was beginning to feel the strain of being in office, having endured unremitting pressures since 1980. With the strain came the doubts in my own ability to carry on. This self-doubt was a previously unknown experience for me while Chief Constable, but grew fairly rapidly after Jean's death. I did not wish to acknowledge, especially to myself, how much I missed her. Perhaps, my own doubts made me believe that others, including Margaret Thatcher, had also lost confidence in my ability. She and I were to meet again in 1987, at a time of great sorrow and anger.

On Sunday morning, 8 November 1987, I received a call from Force Control. There had been a large explosion during the open-air Remembrance Day ceremony at the war memorial in Enniskillen, County Fermanagh. A number of people were believed killed, and large numbers of spectators injured. There was nothing further to report at that time. All necessary action was being taken. I could only wait.

Later that day, I went alone to Enniskillen. Journalists and cameramen were there in strength. Already, there were hints that the RUC and army had been neglectful in not examining the semi-derelict building in which the IRA bomb had been placed. I visited the scene, and afterwards held an in-depth debriefing session in the local station. After receiving a full description of the measures taken by the security forces before the ceremony, I called a press conference and described their preparations in order to rebut the suggestion of possible negligence on their part in not locating the bomb. Later efforts by a few newspapers to sustain such allegations withered away.

Of the eleven people killed in the explosion, the majority were elderly, retired spectators at the service. Of the sixty-three injured, many would suffer for the rest of their lives. Feelings ran high, and cries of outrage reverberated throughout the island of Ireland. That Sunday evening, the RUC in Belfast intercepted a 1,200 lb bomb being transported by the IRA to the city centre, prior to detonation. The following day, another 150 lb bomb was discovered about twenty miles from Enniskillen, in the small village of Tullyhannon on the border with the Republic. A memorial service had also been held there the day before — the obvious inference was that the IRA had attempted a simultaneous massacre in Enniskillen and Tullyhannon, but one of the bombs had failed to detonate.

In these dangerous circumstances, a visit by the Prince and Princess of Wales to Enniskillen was deferred for security reasons until 16 November. Even at the time, there was considerable conjecture about difficulties within their marriage. I found this disturbing, as I liked them both and disliked gossip of a marital rift. In the hospital, I did notice how they kept a distance apart, and this concerned me, especially as television cameras had been given controlled access to the wards. I, therefore, suggested to a member of their entourage that he should manoeuvre the royal couple into sitting at each side of a bed, where they would be seen talking to the same injured person. This was done, and I hoped that somehow the projection of togetherness on television screens might help to reduce the damaging speculation about their marriage. As time has shown, the rift between them was much deeper than I had believed.

On Sunday, 22 November, a second Remembrance Service took place in Enniskillen, to commemorate not only the dead of two World Wars, but the eleven others who had been murdered only two weeks before. Margaret Thatcher arrived by helicopter at St Angelo Airport, just outside Enniskillen. It was a bleak day, with intermittent rain showers and a cold wind blowing. I thought the PM was somewhat on edge and rather detached, showing no warmth of personality — something which struck me as most unusual, given the reason for her attendance. A cup of tea was provided, while she asked to be briefed about the procedures to be followed at the war memorial.

I shall never forget how a senior civil servant used a plate of assorted biscuits to identify the memorial and the positions of celebrities in relation to it. My mind flashed to the film *The Four Feathers*, where the retired general, in laying out a dining-table as a battlefield, had used a pineapple to identify his position, and a variety of nuts for all the others involved. Keeping a judicious distance away, I could not help but notice that in this particular case Prime Minister Thatcher was represented by a chocolate cream!

Notes
1 [1987] *Northern Ireland Legal Quarterly*, p. 252.
2 *Belfast Telegraph*, 11 May 1987.
3 *Belfast Telegraph*, 27 March 1987.
4 *Belfast Telegraph*, 10 April 1987.
5 *Belfast Telegraph*, 22 April 1987.
6 *Ibid.*

21

'DEATH IS A FEARFUL THING'
(SHAKESPEARE'S CLAUDIO)

My relations with Tom Rainey, who in January 1987 succeeded Sir Myles Humphreys as Chairman of the Police Authority, were at first excellent. Tom's zeal for the job was impressive, as was his apparent ability to grasp the intricacies of the roles of the Authority and the RUC itself. Since we felt that there was too much formality in the relationships between our respective organisations, the two of us used to meet weekly to discuss issues of mutual concern. At first, we found our meetings of considerable benefit. Gradually, Tom Rainey's attitude changed, and I came slowly to realise that the 'honeymoon' relationship with the new Chairman had in fact ended, to be succeeded by a strained, even difficult, one.

By comparison, Garda/RUC relationships continued to demonstrate a high level of co-operation and trust, even after the change of Garda Commissioner in 1987. The aftermath of the Remembrance Day bombing of 8 November of that year overshadowed my meeting with the new Garda Commissioner, Eamon Doherty, who succeeded Larry Wren. Having known Larry since the mid-1970s and having got on well with him, I was unhappy that the Dowra Affair had soured our friendship. Certainly, I never felt that his refusal to meet me after Dowra in 1982, until the Anglo-Irish Agreement in 1985, was his personal decision. In the event, he departed his office without any formal recognition from me or my Command, basically because I feared a further rebuff, which would have been embarrassing and hurtful. It remains a source of regret, however, because — whatever else — Larry Wren was a professional and dedicated officer, whom I liked.

Eamon Doherty, who had been one of Larry's deputies, was shrewd and gregarious, with a great sense of humour. His appointment came as a breath of fresh air to those RUC officers involved with the Garda Síochána, especially as the three years after Dowra had been difficult and sensitive for both Forces. The fact that Eamon visited RUC Headquarters on 10 November, immediately after his appointment, was a good portent of our future relationship, and indeed we worked extremely well together.

One particular event presented both of us with a major and potentially lethal problem. On 1 November 1987, the *Eksund*, a small French coaster, had been seized off the western coast of France *en route* to Ireland. It was manned by an Irish crew, and contained an estimated 150 tons of explosives, including

Semtex, rifles, rockets, ammunition and other weaponry, procured in Libya.

It was believed that similar cargoes had been landed earlier on the west coast of Ireland and distributed between a series of large, carefully prepared underground 'hides' in the remote rural areas of the Republic. The IRA had not committed any of these fighting materials before the interception of the *Eksund*. Obviously, this was to protect its source of supply, until it had, in its mind, 'milked the Libyan cow dry'.

Within days, the Gardaí launched a massive and unprecedented search in the Republic, involving some 4,500 Garda officers and 2,500 troops. The RUC gave them maximum support from the northern side of the border, and I personally contacted the Commissioner to offer total co-operation in every way open to us.

Media criticism of the Irish Government for giving public notice of this search was, I thought, unjustified. Such an effort could not properly have been launched without some warning. In explaining why the search would last for at least a week, the Irish Minister for Justice, then Mr Gerry Collins, declared that:

> no state can tolerate a situation where arms of the volume and power we are talking about are held by any group other than the lawful security forces . . . the cargo of the *Eksund* which included surface-to-air missiles threatened the lives of Irish people and the very safety and security of the state. The power of those highly sophisticated weapons to maim, destroy and kill was on a scale we have never before encountered.[1]

In the event, the Irish State had to tolerate this situation, because the bulk of the unintercepted munitions remained under IRA control.

More than any other item, Semtex gave the IRA its most dangerous weapon, one which it used with devastating results in Northern Ireland and Britain. In July 1987, the IRA had also introduced another extremely deadly weapon in the form of a sophisticated grenade, known as the 'drogue bomb', with the ability to penetrate even heavily armoured vehicles. By April 1988 there were seventy-nine IRA attacks using these grenades, with one RUC member killed and thirty-four persons injured — fifteen police officers, two soldiers and seventeen civilians. Urgent steps were, therefore, taken to alter police and army patterns of patrolling, especially in urban areas, in order to minimise the threat. I felt it necessary to advise the public that 'The drogue bomb is a lethal weapon which endangers the lives of the security forces and members of the public. The security forces are entitled in law to resort to firearms to combat grenade attacks.'[2]

At a press conference, one particular reporter was very critical of me for directing the Force to use firearms against people throwing drogue bombs. I immediately outlined a scenario where he, his wife and children were driving their car along a street, when a terrorist stepped out and prepared to throw a drogue bomb at their car. If an RUC officer, armed with a rifle, observed the terrorist, would the reporter prefer the officer to shoot the terrorist or allow him to throw the bomb? While there was some applause from the other journalists present, the man snapped that it was an unfair question.

Changes which the British Government had undoubtedly hoped for in the Garda's fight against the IRA's continued ability to hide such bombs and weapons in the Republic, after the Anglo-Irish Agreement, did not materialise. Much of this, the Irish Government could not afford, either financially or politically. The creation of a 'Border Zone' on the northern side of the frontier with the Republic caused further serious tensions between the two Governments. The objective was to create an additional designated Brigade area, within which the British army would exercise primacy over the RUC in decision-making.

Although my relations with the General Officer Commanding, by then Sir Robert Pascoe, had been cordial and trusting since his appointment on 24 May 1985, I was never certain where he stood concerning the Border Zone, nor did I ask. My discreet inquiries about its origins were never fully answered. It was delegated, via the Northern Ireland Office, to Bob Pascoe and me to refine the details of the Zone between ourselves, and then implement them. I was mindful that Bob would require the approval of his superiors at the Ministry of Defence, before ultimate acceptance and institution of the Border Zone. It was at the end of May that the Joint RUC/Army Directive was signed, giving approval for the operational implementation of the much-diluted plan for the Zone.

It was my good fortune to have had Bob Pascoe involved in the establishment of the Zone, because he was a sensitive and intelligent soldier, and between us we were able to minimise the effects of the initiative, without the serious conflict which would have occurred had I rejected it out of hand or, conversely, had I approved its implementation as originally presented. To my satisfaction, this unfortunate and ill-conceived project was to be dismantled within a year of its introduction.

Lieutenant-General Sir John Waters assumed command of the army on the day of Bob Pascoe's departure, 1 June 1988. Sadly, John Waters and I could never form a working relationship such as I had enjoyed with his three predecessors. As my relations with the new General Officer Commanding grew uneasy, I also felt, with good reason, that I was losing much of the support of my Police Authority. At the same time, political pressures, arising from the Anglo-Irish Agreement, had caused me to become guarded and withdrawn towards Secretary of State Tom King, in order to ensure that the RUC was not dragged into the volatile and abrasive arena of that divisive political scene. My isolation was not, however, total.

My brief acquaintance with Sylvia Paisley at the end of November 1987 was unexpectedly renewed in amusing circumstances, during an encounter in a Belfast theatre, where she was clearly embarrassed to be seen in my company. She telephoned over Christmas, however, and we arranged to go walking together and, later, sailing. I was intrigued to discover that, although she had been to places like Russia and India, she had not in fact taken the time to see

Northern Ireland properly. I, therefore, set about correcting this, being far more familiar than she with the local countryside.

I found it a pleasant opportunity to have her accompany me on what would otherwise have been lonely, nostalgic walks. Almost without exception, we were driven in my official car, and always, for purposes of security, a policeman chaperoned us. Gradually, Sylvia became a regular visitor to RUC Headquarters, where she met staff at all levels and also Belle, Rodney, Barbara, and Roy. I was greatly reassured by the noticeable friendship and rapport that quickly grew between them.

I began taking her to some social functions, where I would have felt isolated, even vulnerable, on my own. I did so not only to end the loneliness and vulnerability, but to end the gossip. In February 1988, unfounded rumours had linked me with a widow, whom Jean and I had known for several years and of whom we were very fond. As the lady in question was a public figure in her own right, those rumours became embarrassing to each of us. With Sylvia to accompany me publicly, that gossip was laid to rest, as were the tentative 'match-making' endeavours of some well-intentioned acquaintances. During this time a strong bond of love and affection developed between Sylvia and me.

In stark contrast to my personal circumstances, those of many others continued to be ruined by violent death, as was recorded in my Foreword to the Chief Constable's Annual Report that year:

> The perception of 1988 is one of terrorist atrocity followed by terrorist atrocity . . . A total of 93 persons died as a result of violence arising from terrorism. Of the 54 civilians who were killed, 28 were regarded as known terrorists. . . . 33 members of the Army lost their lives. . . . Six members of the RUC and Reserve were murdered by terrorists . . .

Of the five deaths through terrorist activity in February 1988, three victims were members of the Ulster Defence Regiment, and two were IRA members, killed instantly on 29 February by their own bomb. Again I was anxious to neutralise the ability of Sinn Féin and the IRA to use these funerals for propaganda purposes against the RUC. Consequently, the local police sought the co-operation of the Catholic clergy, the bereaved families and Mr Seamus Mallon, Deputy Leader of the Social Democratic and Labour Party, and the Westminster MP for South Armagh, the constituency in which the funerals would take place.

The RUC's planning was meticulous. One of our primary concerns was to distance the police from the mourners, in order to minimise the risk of officers being killed or injured in gun attacks by assailants hiding in the crowd. An RUC officer visited Cardinal Ó Fiaich to explain our strategy and obtain his help towards ensuring order. The Northern Ireland Office and the Police Authority Chairman were fully briefed as to our approach, details of which were also made public. The RUC repeatedly stated that it did not seek conflict or confrontation with any section of the community and least of all on the occasion of funerals. That remains the RUC's position.

The funeral chosen by the IRA to embarrass the RUC was that of Brendan Burns. He was a notorious terrorist, to whom over twenty-five murders had been attributed, and whom the IRA described as 'one of its bravest and most dedicated volunteers'. The emergence of a colour-party of masked and uniformed men at Burns's graveside resulted in a physical confrontation between the police and some of the more militant mourners.

Meanwhile, an oration delivered at the graveside of the other man promised that the IRA would avenge the deaths of both. The two funerals had been such emotionally charged occasions, where bitter animosity towards the RUC could very easily have turned into violence, that I was extremely relieved that the security forces had sustained no casualties. A post-analysis of the events concluded that it had been of substantial benefit to announce publicly our intentions about policing the funerals. Violent deaths, and more violent funerals, were to follow.

The day after those funerals, 6 March 1988, three IRA terrorists were shot dead in Gibraltar by the Special Air Service (the SAS). Neither Mairead Farrell, Daniel McCann nor Sean Savage was armed when shot. They were immediately claimed by the IRA as the members of one of its units on 'active service'. The British Foreign Secretary, then Sir Geoffrey Howe, announced in the House of Commons, very soon afterwards, that the SAS members believed they had no alternative but to shoot the three dead, in case one of them detonated the bomb which he said was hidden in a nearby car. He revealed that the IRA unit had planned to carry out a bomb attack to kill and maim members of the local garrison of British soldiers, whilst on parade. However, after the three were shot, no bomb was found in the car. These events attracted enormous publicity world-wide, and became a source of much controversy.

Before their bodies were brought back from Gibraltar, RUC Headquarters issued a formal statement to the media to emphasise that the police had no wish to intrude on the grief of the bereaved families, and to ask that the funerals take place in a lawful manner without the necessity for any RUC involvement, apart from traffic control. It was also stressed that the police can not stand by and allow terrorists to flaunt their criminality with weapons and paramilitary persons, the same weapons and the same people involved in continuing murder and destruction in the community.

On 14 March, black flags were prominently displayed along the route as the coffins were driven north from Dublin Airport. At the border, RUC officers were present in strength, and the three hearses were separated, each being escorted by a strong police contingent on the remaining part of the journey to Belfast. In the west of the city, dozens of black flags and thousands of people lined the anticipated routes.

In the darkness of the evening, at a temporarily erected shrine in West Belfast, four masked and uniformed IRA activists fired three rifle volleys. The IRA then issued a statement saying, 'The IRA has now paid its honour to its fallen volunteers. We wish the bereaved families of Mairead, Sean and Dan peaceful and dignified funerals.' About the same time, and also in West Belfast, Kevin McCracken was shot dead by soldiers, as he prepared to shoot at them; yet another grief-stricken family, and another contentious funeral.

Throughout Northern Ireland, the atmosphere became extremely tense, as the community waited for retaliation from the IRA. There was rioting by republican elements in Belfast and Derry City. During these difficult hours, it was drawn to my attention that Thames Television and Ulster Television had both publicly apologised for the broadcast interview in which the Rev. Ian Paisley had managed to call me 'a liar' several times in the course of a few minutes. That personal victory was completely overshadowed by my anxiety about the funerals of 'the Gibraltar three' on the 16th.

Police plans involved a massive presence of security forces in West Belfast in order to prevent disturbances and paramilitary displays, including more volleys being fired at the graveside. The public was kept fully informed of our intentions. Church leaders, politicians and other persons of influence within the Catholic community were approached for assistance in maintaining calm, and avoiding confrontation during the funerals.

I viewed the situation with growing concern. The police themselves, and their families, were becoming increasingly apprehensive about their vulnerability at such funerals, and I feared the possibility of deaths, even multiple deaths, of police officers in the narrow city streets.

I discussed all options with my senior Command. During the nights before the funerals, I thought long and hard. I prayed too, because the final decision on policing them would be mine. On 15 March, I made it: there would be no security forces whatsoever in the immediate vicinity of the three-hearse cortège. Instead, the whole area would be sealed off, and traffic diverted well clear of the route to Milltown Cemetery. Army helicopters, with their highly sophisticated television equipment, would be hovering overhead, and the procession would be viewed on monitor screens at RUC and Army Headquarters. Adequate resources would be held on stand-by to meet any requirement that might arise.

What influenced me more than anything else was the IRA's action on the evening of the 14th. By firing volleys and publicly wishing 'the bereaved families of Mairead, Sean and Dan peaceful and dignified funerals', the IRA had chosen its position, and, with journalists and camera crews from around the world present, it would be seen by millions whether the organisation could adhere to it. I was convinced that any violence, however contrived, in proximity to the funerals would be attributable to the IRA alone.

Early on Wednesday, 16 March 1988, Sinn Féin members were out on the streets preparing for the funerals. They appeared perplexed at the total absence of police officers. Crowds and crowds of mourners assembled on the footpaths. After the church services, the three hearses travelled abreast along the city streets, with family mourners leading an estimated 19,000 to Milltown Cemetery.

That same morning, an unprepossessing individual, named Michael Stone, had embarked on a mission. He had left the centre of Belfast carrying two loaded handguns, with additional ammunition, and a number of grenades concealed in his clothing. Along with other passengers, he had taken a black taxi to West Belfast, and attended the funeral service of Sean Savage and Daniel McCann. Sinn Féin leaders, Gerry Adams, Danny Morrison and Martin McGuinness, were among those in the packed chapel, with many other Sinn Féin members. Afterwards, Stone had walked with the funeral procession to Milltown Cemetery. He positioned himself only a short distance from the grave. Around 10,000 mourners had managed to enter the cemetery to pay their last respects. That was not why Stone was present.

The graveside ceremonies progressed peacefully at first. The coffins of Mairead Farrell and Daniel McCann had already been interred. That of Sean Savage was being solemnly lowered into the grave, as a priest intoned a prayer. Just then, Michael Stone began throwing grenades and firing indiscriminately into the crowd. He appeared to have no particular targets, just the mourners in general. Absolute panic ensued. People threw themselves to the ground, or cowered behind headstones, or fled for their lives. In the turmoil, three people died, and more than fifty were injured. Describing Stone, an eyewitness said: 'He was laughing. He was really sick. He was shooting at us and throwing grenades, and laughing.' As Stone backed away from the graveside, he continued to throw grenades and fire his two handguns at random.

Panic and terror in the cemetery turned within minutes to outrage and remarkable courage. Scores of mourners, screaming with anger, charged at Stone, forcing him to run wildly towards the M1 motorway, a few hundred yards away. Even then, he managed to throw his last grenades at them, and, in full flight, reloaded to fire his remaining shots. On the motorway, two Traffic Branch RUC officers in a single police vehicle had been on duty for several hours. Their task that day was to prevent pedestrians taking a short cut, via the busy motorway, to and from the cemetery for the funerals, and to prevent cars stopping or slowing down just to observe the funerals, thereby creating traffic hazards. At about 1.22 p.m. the officers heard explosions and gunfire, before a yelling, frantic crowd stampeded towards them. They did not understand what was happening, but realising that they were grossly outnumbered, they radioed for police resources to come to the scene at once, and then drove away.

Michael Stone climbed over the motorway perimeter fence, but was caught by his pursuers and knocked to the ground, where he was kicked and beaten. Just as he was being bundled into a hijacked vehicle, the police resources arrived, but only a few. They stood a short distance from the mob. A uniformed inspector bravely advanced on foot, with only one constable in support. Demanding the release of the now semi-conscious Stone, the Inspector led him back to his vehicle, and the police left the scene. If they had not arrived and acted so promptly, Stone would almost certainly have been brutally beaten and killed.

The ensuing hurricane of publicity, conjecture and recrimination, both nationally and internationally, focused on Stone's grenades and bullets in the cemetery. Vociferous demands for my resignation quickly followed. Entirely overlooked were the facts that the actual funerals of 'the Gibraltar three' had passed off peacefully, and that any suggestion of 'suppressive' policing of republican funerals had been averted. I reacted calmly to the storm of criticism, because I was sure that my decision on policing the funerals had been wholly correct.

Again, I pay tribute to Bishop Cahal Daly, who, that day, stated that he believed the police action at the 'Gibraltar three' funerals to have been correct, and that the murderous behaviour of Michael Stone could not have been anticipated. Stone later revealed that he had, for some years, been engaged as a 'contract killer' for loyalist terrorist organisations, and he admitted to three murders in different parts of Northern Ireland. With surprising openness, he also disclosed that he had long harboured a consuming hatred of republican terrorists, a hatred he extended to Catholics generally. Ultimately, he was charged with, and convicted of, six murders and other serious crimes. I was convinced that Stone would have carried out his kamikaze-style attack regardless of a police presence.

The subsequent funerals of Kevin McCracken and others — including one of Stone's victims at Milltown Cemetery — passed off peacefully; again, in accordance with my decision, the police stood clear. Then, on Saturday, 19 March, two more of Stone's victims, John Murray and Kevin Brady, were to be buried. John Murray, who had no associations with republican terrorism, was buried first, and his funeral was dignified. That of Brady was potentially contentious, since he had been claimed by the IRA as a 'volunteer'.

From the outset of Kevin Brady's funeral, it was clear that Sinn Féin was adopting a different stance. Its marshals were wearing arm-bands, and many had hand-held radios in order to control events tightly and contain the mourners, who lined the footpaths. Some of these marshals were also in evidence at the deceased's home and along the route. Large numbers of black taxis had been assembled by Sinn Féin, and were used to 'police' the crowds. Obviously, the political wing of the IRA was intentionally assuming the role of the constabulary. It seemed equally obvious to me that the local Catholic clergy and SDLP councillors were unable to exercise much influence, if any, over the manner in which the funeral cortège was conducted through the streets.

I knew it was not possible to change the RUC's 'stand clear' tactics, since any close involvement at that stage would have resulted in conflict. Our overall plan for Brady's funeral was the same as for those immediately preceding it, with the police and army held back from the cortège. All security forces had, as previously, been fully briefed, and no member was permitted to approach the funeral route without prior approval. Instead, the entire proceedings were under close surveillance from cameras in the helicopter hovering overhead. The helicopter's recordings, broadcast on monitors at Army and RUC Headquarters, had become known as 'heli-tele'.

Suddenly, 'heli-tele' showed a saloon car coming along a side-street and driving slowly between the lines of mourners. When some of them tried to stop the car, it abruptly accelerated away. When others obstructed it by standing on the road, it reversed very quickly. The car endeavoured to drive away, but found its route intentionally and effectively blocked by a number of the black taxis 'policing' the funeral.

With the memory of Michael Stone's attack in Milltown Cemetery so fresh in everyone's mind, it is understandable that the mourners at Kevin Brady's funeral were extremely fearful and suspicious of this mysterious car weaving in amongst them. Nevertheless, what followed is not easily explained. The crowd simply erupted with anger. People surged round and over the car like wasps on jam. With frightening, unbelievable speed, the car was submerged by a screaming, violent mob. Some attempted to tear it apart with their bare hands, while others used metal bars to break through the windows and roof. The driver suddenly opened his window, thrust out a hand that held a pistol, and fired a shot. The mob panicked and momentarily scattered. The two men quickly tried to climb out of the car, but did not fire at their immediate assailants, nor into the thronging crowd.

There was to be no escape for either man. They were grabbed, kicked and beaten to the ground, and their clothes stripped from them. Within a minute, Sinn Féin marshals ordered that the two — scarcely conscious — were to be removed from the street and thrown over a spiked wall. After falling several feet, the men appeared to be unconscious, but were nevertheless bundled into a black taxi and driven off at speed. On waste ground a mile or so away, they were dragged from the car.

As the journalists had been left behind, only 'heli-tele' was able to record their final, awful moments. Amazingly, the two captives emerged from the taxi still putting up a fight, but were overcome at once. Both were then shot. The taxi sped off. An RUC Mobile Support Unit, with a military escort, had already been alerted, and arrived at the scene of the shooting in less than four minutes. A short time later, both victims were identified as having been off-duty British soldiers.

Corporals Derek Wood and Robert Howes were members of the Signals Regiment, whose daily duties included carrying out routine maintenance of army radio communications systems. Corporal Wood, a veteran of four years' service in Northern Ireland, was to have been transferred the following week. Corporal Howes was to have been his replacement. Exactly why they were in the vicinity of Kevin Brady's funeral has never been fully explained. One suggestion was that Wood was initiating his successor into his duties, and showing him the dangerous areas in Belfast. Another was that, for some reason, they had not been briefed on the precise details of the funeral and the prohibition on security force members' entering the area until it was over.

The Catholic church and its people were shattered by the brutality displayed. The *Irish News* referred to the

sense of collective guilt that all decent citizens in the nationalist sector are now experiencing . . . almost within the protective shadow of a Catholic church, an uncontrolled blood-lusting mob unleashed a diabolical ritual of human killing that was recorded for the world's television and its printing presses. The participants in the brutal orgy may well have formed part of the congregation that had just celebrated the ritual of the Sacred Liturgy.[3]

The fact that people were able to sit at home and watch on television the horrific recordings of the Milltown killings and those of the two corporals caused immense shock and distress. The impact of 'heli-tele' was unprecedented. Yet, viewers had been spared the worst details, which I had to watch when the full confidential 'heli-tele' recordings were played over to me. I shall never forget the callous shooting of Howes and Wood, nor the devilish triumphalism of the man who pulled the trigger, before passing the gun to others, who delivered the *coup de grâce*: a bullet in each of their heads. Contentious republican terrorist funerals had spiralled into a major political and sectarian issue, with the RUC in the eye of the whirlwind. My action to extricate the Force from the dangerous and demoralising role of close-quarter policing at funerals had itself been successful, but at a terrible price.

The following Force Bulletin (No. 85) was, therefore, issued on 23 March 1988:

> Regrettably, experience has shown that the influence of clerics and others in the community, however well-intentioned, is not enough to curb the behaviour of paramilitary organisations. Experience has also shown that the maintenance of the law and the prevention of outrages will only be guaranteed through the firm presence of the police and the army. Whilst the precise tactics of the police and the army in any respect on any occasion will always be determined by the known circumstances, it must be clearly understood for the future that the police will not countenance breaches of the law or the usurpation of the police function.

The final decisions regarding the policing of republican funerals that week had been mine. As I bore sole responsibility for our 'stand clear' policy, the appalling manner of these killings caused me deep anguish and much soul-searching. Gradually, a balanced view evolved in my mind. I examined my reasons for those decisions. My experience of close-quarter policing of republican funerals in 1987, and my awareness of the intelligence information about the IRA's deadly intentions towards the police, strengthened my belief that my decisions had been the right ones in the known circumstances. The unrelenting pressures from clergy and politicians to change the RUC's approach to policing such funerals, and not least the intolerable strains and risks to which police officers were exposed during them, also served to convince me that I had acted judiciously. Michael Stone's attack in the cemetery, and the inexplicable intrusion by two off-duty soldiers upon a republican terrorist's funeral, were simply not events that anyone could have foreseen. Nevertheless, I recognised that violent deaths, whoever the victims, were becoming increasingly difficult for me to bear.

Notes

1 *Belfast Telegraph*, 23 November 1987.
2 RUC Information Bulletin No. 86, issued 22 April 1988.
3 *Irish News*, 21 March 1988.

22

A JOURNEY'S END AND A NEW BEGINNING

It was something of a surprise to me when I realised how compatible Sylvia and I were, and how each of us had grown to depend on the other for companionship and friendship. Never could I have foreseen myself marrying again after Jean's death. Nonetheless, despite the disparity in our ages — something which worried me but not Sylvia — we agreed to marry. 1988 was, after all, a leap year! We became engaged at the end of July 1988, but it was essential, from a security point of view, that our engagement be kept secret; otherwise, she would have been a very easy target. We had the total support of our respective families. Sylvia's presence had restored sparkle and vitality to my life, and indeed to RUC Headquarters.

Our marriage was fixed for Saturday, 31 December 1988, as a new year seemed an ideal time to begin a new life, and it also suited the holiday plans of certain family members, who lived overseas. As for my retirement from the RUC, it would be sometime in 1989. Several weeks after I had tentatively mentioned to Police Authority Chairman Tom Rainey that I was considering retirement, I was amused to learn that a senior English member of the Northern Ireland Office (and a friend) had been heard to say that they had had 'enough of truculent Ulstermen! We will have an Englishman' as the next RUC Chief Constable.

On Monday morning, 16 May 1988, I had my routine meeting with Tom Rainey. The following day, he unexpectedly arranged to visit me again. I saw him for only a short time, because it was a day already crowded with official engagements. Tom was plainly uncomfortable. His request was simple. He wished me to retire six months later, on 22 November 1988, the day before my sixtieth birthday! I remember little else of our brief conversation that day, except that I felt I should be very cautious. I guessed that Tom was merely the messenger doing his master's bidding. Although the major role of the Police Authority, since its creation, had been to protect the RUC from political interference, I believed that Tom Rainey's words on that Tuesday indicated political direction at its most blatant.

After he left my office, I was inclined to stand firm. Yet, I had to consider carefully my own future and evolving family circumstances. I was under no illusions as to the effects on me of the events of the past few years. That day, I decided that my retirement date would be one of my own choosing, and that it would not be until well into 1989. With my decision made, I asked Tom Rainey to see me on Wednesday, 18 May. Again, the conversation was a brief one. My diary entry for that day reads:

> Would go 31 May 1989 — see Stalker clear. I have outlived my stay so far as PA [Police Authority], NIO [Northern Ireland Office] and HO [Home Office] concerned.

These blunt, cynical comments reflected my feelings of the time, and my sense that I was being done a gross injustice. Yet, I also realised that so long as I continued as Chief Constable, the roles of the RUC, the Police Authority and the British Government must be recognised, sustained and supported by me, and could not be allowed to suffer because of my personal feelings. I was all too well aware of the backgrounds to the retirements of most of my predecessors, from 1969 onwards. Unlike them, I would control my own retirement, and retain my self-respect.

The uncertainty caused within the Force by growing speculation about my imminent departure bothered me considerably. On 22 June, I arranged a press conference about security matters, but before it commenced, a reporter asked me when I intended to retire. I suggested that he should keep that query for the conference itself. He did so, giving me the opportunity publicly to disclose my intention to retire in 1989, on a date of my choosing. This public comment was primarily for the benefit of Tom Rainey, the Northern Ireland Office and the British Government.

With a trusted friend from the Northern Ireland Office, I tentatively touched on my public announcement to retire in 1989. From behind his thick lenses, he looked me straight in the eye, as he warned, 'Take care . . . you have made your contribution.' I felt a chill in my spine. His words were clearly ones of caution, rather than advice to a close friend. Despite them, I knew I had already set my course, and would hold to it in direction and timing.

On 28 September, I wrote to Tom Rainey. I told him:

> You are aware of my intention to retire from the Royal Ulster Constabulary in 1989.
>
> In recent discussions between us and recognising the implication of my retirement for the Police Authority and my own personal circumstances we agreed a mutually suitable date to be the 31st May, 1989.
>
> Accordingly I now formally notify you of my intention to retire with effect from the 31st May, 1989.
>
> In requesting your acceptance of my retirement I wish also to record my appreciation of the understanding of you and your Authority in this matter and of the conditions you have outlined to me relating to my retirement, as agreed by your Authority.

That day, I also wrote to the Secretary of State, Tom King, as follows:

> You are already aware of my intention to retire as Chief Constable in 1989.
> I wish formally to advise you that I have today tendered my resignation to the Chairman of the Police Authority to take effect from 31 May, 1989.

The change in attitudes towards me within the Police Authority, the Northern Ireland Office and the army was exacerbated by my growing personal cynicism about the integrity of each of these organisations, with which I had to work closely. After Lieutenant-General Sir John Waters had taken over as GOC on 1 June 1988, the difficulty of maintaining the cordial relations I had enjoyed with his predecessors soon became apparent. Co-operation between the RUC and the army began to suffer. At one stage, this resulted in a meeting being called by Prime Minister Thatcher at 10 Downing Street. There, it was obviously intended that everyone should be seated before the Prime Minister entered, but I had been unexpectedly delayed outside in a corridor by a senior member of the intelligence services. I was, therefore, the last to arrive, which clearly irritated the PM.

My briefcase subsequently added to her irritation. It was a somewhat dilapidated, slimline leather case with a zip-fastener along the top, but without a locking device. My personal briefing file consisted of no more than two foolscap pages. As the meeting ended, I pointed out that I had not been given a highly secret document, which had been circulated to the others present. Margaret Thatcher immediately offered me her copy. She then noticed my briefcase, and complained that it was not secure. She promptly handed the document to the person on my left and ordered him to carry it for me, since he had a sophisticated case with a conspicuous locking system. My thoughts raced ahead to the bullet-proof cars, the Metropolitan Police Close Protection Unit and the plain-clothes military escorts, who would be accompanying us to Northolt Airport, and with all that in mind, I enjoyed the nonsense of Mrs Thatcher's fuss over my briefcase!

That meeting confirmed my impression of a growing stridency in the voice and attitude of the Prime Minister, as well as a tendency not to listen to the opinions of others. I found generally that Denis Thatcher, on the other hand, remained surprisingly frank and relaxed, with a philosophical attitude to life, both as a businessman and as the husband of the Prime Minister. I suspect that he contributed infinitely more to his wife's remarkable political career and reputation than will ever be recognised.

By the end of 1988, GOC John Waters and I had worked out a mutually acceptable procedure for coping with disagreements between our respective organisations. However, one major issue, the multiple deaths of soldiers in Northern Ireland, put considerable strain on that procedure, and exacerbated our uneasy relationship. During the first five months of 1988, four regular soldiers had been murdered. Their deaths attracted a far higher level of publicity in Great Britain than the killing of two RUC and seven Ulster Defence Regiment members in the same period. The death of even one British soldier was a sensitive political issue at Westminster; multiple deaths evoked considerable emotion and extreme anger on the part of Prime Minister Thatcher.

On Wednesday evening, 15 June 1988, a 'fun run' was held in Lisburn, a provincial town about ten miles west of Belfast. Since Army Headquarters was based there, some British soldiers were permitted to participate. A group of them arrived in Lisburn in a van and parked it in a civilian car park, despite the fact that it could easily have been properly protected at Army Headquarters, less than a mile away. During the 'fun run', the IRA booby-trapped the vehicle. As the soldiers drove away afterwards, it exploded in the street, within yards of the car park. Six soldiers were killed outright, and civilians in the vicinity were injured. The fact that a 'fun run' had been turned into an opportunity to commit such cold-blooded murders caused an immediate wave of revulsion throughout the country, and beyond. It was patently obvious that a grievous breach of military security had occurred, not only in the way the soldiers parked their vehicle, but in their failure to check it thoroughly before moving off.

More criticisms were raised a week later, when an army helicopter was attacked by IRA gunfire and forced to land. A stringent tightening of army security followed, but another horrendous killing of soldiers took place on the evening of Saturday, 20 August. A number of off-duty soldiers were returning from leave. While travelling from Aldergrove Airport to Omagh Army Barracks in County Tyrone, their civilian bus was attacked by the IRA at Ballygawley; a massive bomb had been hidden at the side of the road. Eight soldiers died, and others were very seriously injured.

Fierce criticism was again directed at the army's lack of security and at the GOC, particularly when it became known publicly that the road taken by the bus had been placed out of bounds for the security forces, as a result of RUC intelligence information.

This led senior army Commanders at their Lisburn Headquarters to place even more intense pressure upon my operational chief officers, who were concerned by the anxiety within army circles to place blame elsewhere for this breach of security. All of this troubled me deeply, because I was painfully aware that the harmony I had enjoyed with three successive GOCs had gone. What made the situation even more disturbing was the knowledge that I had little time to repair the damage in our relations, since I would be leaving midway through 1989.

So seriously did Prime Minister Thatcher view the situation that a meeting at 10 Downing Street was hurriedly arranged for the evening of Saturday, 20 August, immediately following the murder of the soldiers at Ballygawley. GOC John Waters and Secretary of State Tom King accompanied me. With some cynicism, I felt that the flurry of meetings, and the publicity accorded them, were more for political and cosmetic purposes than for any operational benefit.

Such was the clamour of public opinion after the soldiers' murders that a debate on capital punishment, the fifth in ten years, took place in the House of Commons. I was pleased to learn that, on a free vote, a motion for its introduction was soundly defeated. In the debate, I had agreed to be quoted by a Government minister as being totally opposed, on purely pragmatic grounds, to the introduction of capital punishment in Northern Ireland. That evening, at its annual conference, the RUC Federation's Chairman made a public statement crying out for the reintroduction of internment north and south of the border. I remained strongly opposed to this too, realising that without a significant political development in Northern Ireland, the Republic of Ireland could not support internment. If it were imposed unilaterally in the North, internment would be counterproductive, and would create even greater problems for the security forces.

By sheer coincidence, that same week it was announced that I had been awarded the Queen's Police Medal, the only Queen's award dedicated solely to the police service of the United Kingdom. It may be awarded to a police officer of any rank from constable to chief constable. Although conferred primarily for conspicuous gallantry, it may also reward 'a specially distinguished record' in various fields of policing, including 'dealing with serious or widespread outbreaks of crime or public disorder'. Frankly, I have forgotten what particular aspect of policing entitled me to be a recipient. However, after a decade of almost constant criticism from Northern Ireland politicians, the media, and — sometimes — British Government ministers, I may be forgiven for feeling that 'conspicuous gallantry' of a unique type might have been relevant! Whatever the grounds, it was a pleasure for a 'truculent Ulsterman' to receive it, and a pleasure to have it bestowed on the Queen's behalf at Hillsborough Castle, with Sylvia, Belle and Roy present, and with a number of other RUC officers being similarly honoured.

Sylvia had resigned from her post at Queen's University, and, in her own unorthodox way, began making virtually all the wedding arrangements herself, including baking the cake. The location and timing of our marriage, however, were kept closely guarded secrets right up to the last minute — literally! Apparently, as I chatted to some guests outside the church in Donaghadee, County Down, I was recognised by a woman living in a house opposite. She immediately contacted her brother, who happened to work for a local radio station, and so instead of emerging to the sound of the sea beside the church, Sylvia and I were greeted by the click, click, click of cameras.

Television crews and reporters were totally unexpected and unwanted, but in fairness to them, they took their photos only at the church and then left us alone to enjoy a small party at RUC Headquarters. Remaining unorthodox to the end, Sylvia refused to change into her going-away outfit, preferring instead to wear her wedding dress until midnight, as 31 December 1988 was the only day she would wear it. We left Headquarters around 7 p.m. and travelled to the border, where we transferred to a Garda car and went to begin our honeymoon in Dublin — probably the last place anyone would have expected us to go!

Sylvia and I continued our honeymoon in the United States. It was her first visit to the country, and from the outset, she was captivated. With some initial encouragement, she revealed an unsuspected talent for jogging, and also for navigating, as we zigzagged our way across Florida and Georgia in a series of hired cars. Our idyllic honeymoon contrasted sharply with the situation awaiting us back home.

Very soon after our return, we realised that the secrecy of our quiet, family wedding on New Year's Eve had not been well received by the Northern Ireland Office and other 'establishment' figures. In our absence, there had been initiated from within the Police Authority what was described to me as a 'witch-hunt' over our wedding arrangements. Who paid for the party? Who paid for the wedding-cake? Who paid for the flowers? My office staff were startled and upset by these lines of inquiry, as were the catering staff, all of whom had fully respected our request for total secrecy. The reception had been properly arranged with the RUC's caterers, and paid for entirely by Sylvia and me. It was not only intensely annoying for us to come home to find staff unnecessarily upset, but extremely offensive to have suspicions cast upon our integrity behind our backs. This behaviour only reinforced my desire to leave behind the job, the Police Authority and all the trappings of office.

Back in mid-November 1988, an advertisement for the post of RUC Chief Constable appeared in newspapers in Britain and Northern Ireland. The closing date for applications was fixed for 22 December. Within a few weeks, I had been reassured to learn that there were thirteen applicants, including my three Senior Assistant Chief Constables. On 30 January 1989, it was announced that the candidates for head of the RUC had been short-listed to four; two were English Chief Constables, and the other two were senior officers from the London Metropolitan Police Force. With these four, it was plain that there was going to be no risk of another Ulsterman following me. None of the three Senior Assistant Chief Constables from within the RUC was short-listed. The Force generally was very surprised by their exclusion, as these men were highly respected for their operational experience, management skills and command abilities. They were, however, men of independent mind, who, like me, held strong views about the role of the RUC, including its essential independence. The fact that not one of them had been put on the short list was, I thought, an omission of crass stupidity.

It was felt that the four short-listed candidates should have an opportunity to see around the Chief Constable's flat in Headquarters, since the new man would be required, as part of his terms of appointment, to live there. Sylvia and I found it a very interesting experience to chat to each candidate, while showing him round. We were particularly intrigued to learn that only one of them had actually studied the Anglo-Irish Agreement, before applying for the post of RUC Chief Constable. Anyone intending to take on the job should have regarded it as essential preparation! On 23 February 1989, Hugh Annesley, an Assistant Commissioner in the Metropolitan Police, was chosen to succeed me.

Amidst the fuss and demands created by my impending retirement, political pressures continued and had to be resisted. I experienced a sense of hopelessness about the ongoing pressures for further financial savings. These had resulted in my ordering the closure of six limited-opening police stations and five police posts, and the reduction of Traffic Branch by fifty officers, Community Relations Branch by twenty and Crime Prevention by ten. A deep cut of 25 per cent was also made in our 'Neighbourhood Policing Programme'. When I announced these decisions publicly, they considerably upset the Police Authority and the Northern Ireland Office, which had expected the savings to be made in administrative, rather than operational, costs. After the stringent cuts of the previous year, I had warned them of my intentions to make operational savings, but I doubt if they believed me.

Political interference was to raise its ugly head again, this time in relation to a visit by the Duchess of Kent to Northern Ireland, scheduled for Tuesday, 23 May 1989. I was told about it less than three weeks beforehand and was irritated by this, because I would normally have been informed six to eight weeks in advance of a royal visit, to allow for adequate planning. My annoyance must have been obvious to the official who notified me, as he immediately urged me to accept the short notice, since the Duchess was coming specifically to say farewell to the RUC Chief Constable! Later, I learned that the Northern Ireland Office had asked the proper channels at Buckingham Palace to postpone her visit to coincide with the Secretary of State's annual Hillsborough garden party later in the summer, but the Palace had insisted that the Duchess would come on 23 May. In the circumstances, I saw it as a generous and thoughtful gesture by the Royal family. The Duchess of Kent, in particular, had been a frequent visitor to Northern Ireland, and had displayed genuine compassion and concern for members of the Force, its widows and injured officers. Her visit turned out to be a most enjoyable and memorable farewell, unlike the previous evening, when I had been dined out by the Secretary of State at Hillsborough Castle.

Amongst Tom King's guests were the Director of Public Prosecutions, Sir Barry Shaw, the Chairman of the Police Authority, Tom Rainey, and his lady Deputy. It was on this occasion that she revealed to me that she had been a child of eight living in Ardmoulin Street at the time of the Divis Street riots in 1964. Her views about the RUC's riot control then were less than complimentary, to put it mildly! Such was her conduct later that evening that she had to be escorted from the room and taken home. Although I felt very strongly that her opinions of the RUC made her unsuited to continue as Deputy Chairperson of the Police Authority, the Northern Ireland Office allowed her to remain as such until January 1990.

After that particular dinner at Hillsborough, it seemed highly appropriate that a few days later, the Police Authority presented me with a very curious retirement present — a coarsely knitted wool shirt, mounted within a picture frame. Having a Police Authority was, as I had described it, like 'a hair shirt on a frosty morning; necessary but bloody uncomfortable!' Despite inevitable differences over financial and other issues, I was never in any doubt about the need for my Authority. I also recognised the sincerity, courage and commitment of its members towards the maintenance of an acceptable police force in Northern Ireland. For that and many other reasons, I fear lest the Authority's functions be passed to Government, with the appointment of chief officers resting with the Home Office or, in the case of Northern Ireland, the Secretary of State. My experience of the attempts by politicians and civil servants to influence Chief Constables on matters of policing convince me that I am right in this.

My fears of Government meddling were reinforced when I read the first three-year 'Review of the Working of the [Intergovernmental] Conference', published on 24 May 1989. That day, Tom King announced that he had placed in the Library of the House of Commons a document compiled by the British Government on 'Developments Since the Signing of the Anglo-Irish Agreement'. Not only did this document smack of self-justification, but it claimed credit for certain unrelated changes in policing, and totally disregarded the adverse 'developments' arising from the Agreement. Not least amongst these were the street violence, and the vicious attacks on police officers' homes. I was so incensed by the inaccuracy of this review of the Agreement's 'success', but so proud of the RUC's endeavours towards policing it impartially, that I responded as follows in my last Force Bulletin, No. 106:

Anglo-Irish Agreement: A Message from the Chief Constable

1. Arising from current publicity in respect of the Anglo-Irish Agreement I feel it is necessary to restate the position of The Royal Ulster Constabulary as originally set out in a statement dated 29 November 1985.

2. It has been inferred from time to time that developments within the Force have taken place as a result of the Agreement or through political influences being brought to bear on the Force. Any such inferences are misleading and without foundation. For example, the introduction of our Professional Policing Ethics (or Code of Conduct) was entirely an RUC initiative and had no political origin whatsoever.

3. Decisions taken by the RUC have been impartial, professional police decisions unrelated to the Anglo-Irish Agreement. Our decisions on parades and public order and our policy in accompanying military patrols, insofar as our manpower enables us to do so, have been matters determined by the leadership of the RUC.

At all times I have been committed to preserving the integrity of the RUC and ensuring that it is free from political interferences or direction. In this I have been fully supported by my Chief Officers and the command of the Force at large. It was for this purpose also that the Police Authority was brought into being.

4. The people of Northern Ireland have a right to expect that police decisions are indeed police decisions and that the RUC will at all times be apolitical and impartial in its policies and actions.

As I retire I draw great satisfaction from knowing that the Force at all levels is fully committed to this professional approach to its duty.

I felt strongly that this particular Force Bulletin should be made public, and it was on 30 May. Although this caused some irritation to both the British and Irish Governments, I was happy that I would be retiring with the record put straight on the role of the RUC under my command since the Anglo-Irish Agreement; it was my final shot across their bows.

The next day, Sylvia and I vacated the flat at RUC Headquarters by mid-afternoon, because Hugh and Elizabeth Annesley were due to arrive around 6 p.m. My last day of office began early with headlines in the local newspapers, not about my statement on the Anglo-Irish Agreement, but announcing that our first baby was due in the late autumn! Given our respective ages and our mutual desire to have children, Sylvia's pregnancy so soon after our marriage was the answer to many prayers. I must say we were both very touched by the obvious delight of Headquarters staff and our families at this happy news. Added to this was Bishop Cahal Daly's wonderful blessing on us and our unborn child. He had come to Headquarters on my last morning, to say 'farewell' personally. Such a gesture was typical of this fine man.

After his departure, Sylvia and I hosted a buffet lunch for our drivers and Command Secretariat staff at all levels. Bill Wilson, then head of the Secretariat, was there, but his health was more precariously poised than any of us could have guessed. Having given formal notice of my retirement, I had asked Bill to make preparations for my successor, by carefully recording notes on all important and sensitive policing issues which would affect him. Although Deputy Chief Constable Michael McAtamney was highly experienced and competent, he had distanced himself from me, and become so guarded that I preferred to work with Bill on these notes. On several occasions, Bill had privately told me that he wished to retire when I did, because he felt he was too set in his ways to change under a new Chief Constable. Nevertheless, at my request, he agreed to remain in post for a short while after my departure, primarily to help my successor.

Although the lunch was full of good humour, our departure was inevitably tinged with personal sadness at leaving these people, who were not only staff, but our friends. Soon we were on board the ferry *en route* to Oban in Scotland, and a new beginning. We both wondered how the staff would find their new Chief Constable. Would he understand their Ulster ways? Would he appreciate their humour and their loyalty, as well as the sacrifices and pain so many had experienced, directly and indirectly?

Tragically, my plan that Bill Wilson should assist Hugh Annesley was not to be. When we phoned from Oban, it was obvious from Bill's voice that he was becoming weaker. Sylvia and I were, therefore, relieved when he went into hospital, as we were confident that with a proper diagnosis and the necessary treatment, he would recover his strength and his sense of fun. Our first visit, after returning to Northern Ireland, was to see him in Dundonald Hospital. I hoped that our faces did not reflect the shock we both felt at seeing the massive deterioration in his health, since we had last seen him on 31 May. I was so concerned that I immediately contacted two medical specialists at the hospital, to find out exactly what was wrong with Bill. When they advised me that nothing could be done for his condition, I felt utter despair and frustration at the cruelty of it.

Bill died peacefully on 18 July 1989. He had been my protector from my own impetuosity and my frailties; I had been his, in turn. I wept bitterly for the loss of the man who for many years had been, without a doubt, my best friend. Within seven weeks of my leaving office, Bill had died, and with him had gone our many plans about what we could do together in the future. I was especially sorry that he never saw one particular letter, from Strabane, County Tyrone, amongst the dozens I received to wish me well in retirement. The 'Strabane letter' reflected many of my thoughts about leaving the police. It was typed exactly as follows:

Dear Sir John,

I am writing to wish you all the best in your forthcoming retirement from the RUC.

As a Catholic living in a town with tremendious terrorists and subsequint social problems I have observed the overwhelming majority of the Police conduct in their duties in a professional and caring manner.

Certainly the massive floods which Strabane experienced bear witness to the work which your men did, and, I can assure you the people of Strabane were glad of their help.

I am sure at times you found your job as Chief Constable very frusting amidst all the pressures of the media, and, whilst i did think you could have handled some situations better, we are all entitled to make mistakes and i believe you did your best.

23

SUING AND BEING SUED

My level of stress throughout my last years as Chief Constable was considerably heightened by the fact that certain false and irresponsible media comments, arising from the Stalker Affair, compelled me to take legal actions. I was particularly irritated by the serious and mischievous allegations that I was a Freemason and that there had been Masonic conspiracy to remove Stalker, which were wholly untrue. The libel proceedings were time-consuming and distasteful to me but resulted in the following apology, which appeared in the *Manchester Evening News* (Final) on 17 September 1987:

> In our edition of 25 July 1986, under the heading 'The Masonic Connection', we published an article in which we reported that Sir John Hermon, the Chief Constable of Northern Ireland, was a member of a masonic lodge in Northern Ireland.
>
> In the same article we reported that a number of those connected, directly or indirectly, with the enquiry in Manchester into the alleged professional misconduct of Manchester's Deputy Chief Constable, were also freemasons.
>
> The *Manchester Evening News* recognises that this article could have been interpreted as suggesting that Sir John was involved in an improper attempt by freemasons to achieve Mr Stalker's removal from the Northern Ireland enquiry, and to influence the enquiry in Manchester into Mr Stalker's alleged misconduct.
>
> It accepts without reservation that there was and is no truth whatever in such an interpretation, and that Sir John Hermon was never at any time a freemason or member of any associated or similar organisation and that he did not seek to instigate or promote allegations against Mr Stalker in order to bring about Mr Stalker's removal from the Northern Ireland enquiry or to influence the Manchester enquiry in any way.
>
> We are glad to take this opportunity to correct any misunderstanding which there might have been, and wish to apologise unreservedly to Sir John that such an interpretation was possible of what appeared in this newspaper on that day.
>
> We have agreed to pay Sir John Hermon damages and his legal costs as a demonstration of our sincerity and are happy to publish this apology in order to vindicate his reputation with those who may have misinterpreted our article.

Despite the success of these proceedings, the pernicious niggling by certain sections of the media continued. The Dublin *Sunday Independent*, for example, ill-advisedly published a letter from a reader in Greystones, County Wicklow, who claimed:

> John Stalker makes it clear in his book that before he was unceremoniously pulled off his enquiry that he had informed his superiors that he intended to interview the Chief Constable, Sir John Hermon, and Deputy Chief Constable McAtamney under caution on charges relating to conspiracy to murder and interfering with the course of justice. . . .
>
> There can be little doubt that had he been allowed to do so and been given access to the evidence which was deliberately withheld from him charges would have resulted.[1]

After our libel actions had been initiated, the newspaper made informal overtures to me, claiming that the publication of the letter had been an error of judgment on the part of a member of staff. Although I felt some sympathy, I determined to maintain my view that legal action was the only avenue available to force some degree of responsibility for accuracy and truthfulness upon certain sections of the press. I pursued my action. In any event, since Michael McAtamney was pursuing his, I had little option, as the interpretation of my not doing so would have been quite appalling. The action was conceded by the *Sunday Independent*, without final recourse to the courts, but with all costs and substantial damages paid and a generous apology published.

By comparison, the comments published in *Private Eye*, 5 September 1986, were much more insulting. An article was written about John Stalker's suspension, in which it was claimed that 'a familiar reaction' to his removal was that it 'would make little difference to the course of his inquiry, into murder, bribery and corruption in the Royal Ulster Constabulary', because, as was being 'said on all sides', as long as John Thorburn was there, 'the work will get done and the guilty will be brought to book'. It continued:

> Chief Supt John Thorburn was, in many ways, even more of a pain in the neck to the bully-boys in the RUC than was Stalker. To start with, the RUC thought they could contain Stalker. At his first meeting, RUC Chief Constable Sir John Hermon told Stalker that his boys had 'checked you out'. 'We hear your mother was a Catholic and your father a Protestant,' he went on, 'That will do us.' In fact, as Sir John knew, Stalker's paternal grandfather had been an officer of the Orange Lodge. Though Stalker himself remains a Catholic, his religion is not strong, and he has certainly never seen the problems of Northern Ireland in religious terms.[2]

While I felt that the whole tenor of the article was gratuitously offensive to the RUC, I was particularly incensed by the false remarks attributed to me regarding my conversation with John Stalker when we first met. My legal advisers were satisfied that it contained libellous remarks, and again the Police Authority willingly supported me. Preparations for my libel action duly went ahead.

Meanwhile, on 19 February 1988, *Private Eye* repeated its libel of 5 September 1986, and exacerbated it by quoting the references to the notorious, albeit non-existent, cigarette packet as published in *Stalker*. The article also stated:

> It may well be that Sir John Hermon's interests in suing for libel may have been diverted by Mr John Stalker's recent book, most of which was taken up with showing how members of the Royal Ulster Constabulary (especially the Special Branch) were involved in murdering people named to them as IRA men by informers who were paid (out of public funds) many thousands of pounds; and how Mr Stalker's inquiry into these matters was systematically and obstinately obstructed.[3]

My solicitors, in a letter to *Private Eye*'s solicitors, identified eleven defamatory comments, and made it clear that I would argue that the publication of 19 February 1988 had compounded the magazine's earlier libel.

While the legal posturing and manoeuvring moved on through 1988, I was preoccupied with other pressing operational matters within the RUC. Then, on 13 January 1989, *Private Eye*'s solicitors unexpectedly advised mine that they intended applying for an adjournment of the action from the agreed commencement date of 13 February 1989. The reason they gave was that John Stalker and John Thorburn would not be available on the date originally agreed. A compromise date for the action was agreed; it would be listed for the week beginning 17 April. Since it was widely known that my retirement from the RUC was to become effective from 31 May 1989, I wanted the case disposed of before I left office. But now, with battle lines drawn, I was faced with the totally unexpected.

The political furore over the investigation of Stalker's behaviour within his own police Force and the alleged conspiracy to remove him from the RUC inquiry had caused serious embarrassment to relations between the British and Irish Governments. The British side certainly wanted the whole matter laid to rest; any residual stigma that attached itself to the RUC seemed to be of little concern, except to the Force and to me. This attitude, and a series of other issues, left me feeling isolated, and more bitter than I realised. Even so, I was not prepared for what lay ahead.

There were a number of chief officers from other Forces whom, I felt, were potential witnesses on my behalf in my forthcoming libel action. Accordingly, I made personal approaches to them, identifying the specific matters on which they could give evidence. I studiously avoided any matter of a confidential nature, which might compromise the offices they then held. Without exception, they expressed a willingness to attend, if required by a 'friendly subpoena'. However, when subpoenas were served, my solicitors received a letter from the Crown Solicitor. It requested my solicitors to identify the matters about which they would 'wish them to give evidence and the respect in which [they would] consider that such evidence would be relevant to the issues in the action'. My solicitors explained that the action involved 'matters of sensitivity and considerations of public interest with regard to such matters'. The Crown Solicitor responded by claiming that some of my potential witnesses 'feel strongly that they should not become involved and it would be entirely inappropriate for them to give evidence in these circumstances'. He 'respectfully' suggested that the decision to call them as witnesses 'be carefully reconsidered'.

The British Government and the Northern Ireland Office knew very well of my anger about the effects of Stalker's removal from duty, about his Report, and about the flow of distorted leaks to journalists. They knew of my several requests for an inquiry into the leaks, and knew that all such requests had been rejected. They knew too of the damage being done to the reputation of the RUC by lies like *Private Eye's* reference to the 'bully-boys in the RUC', and especially the Special Branch being 'involved in murdering people named to them as IRA men by informers'. In the face of all this knowledge, neither the Government nor the NIO made any effort to assist me in defending the reputation of the Force. On the contrary, efforts were made at very senior level to try to 'persuade' me to abandon my legal action.

On the date agreed for the hearing, 17 April 1989, it became apparent that *Private Eye* was keen to settle out of court. Substantial damages — undisclosed, at the magazine's insistence — and payment of all costs of my action were agreed, as was a statement of apology, which was to be read out in court. I initially rejected the apology as inadequate, because it did not specifically withdraw Stalker's allegations regarding the flattened cigarette packet. However, I was persuaded by counsel that my success was as complete as a civil action could be.

Private Eye itself refused to publish the apology; it would not go beyond the statement being read out in court. I dismissed this as irrelevant, and asked my Staff Officer to arrange for a media presence at the court. Cameramen and reporters duly turned out in strength to hear the following apology being read out at Belfast Crown Court on Monday, 17 April 1989:

> *Private Eye* acknowledges that the article published on the 5th September, 1986, contained material inaccuracies of a defamatory nature. *Private Eye* wish to record publicly that it was never the intention to suggest in that article that Sir John Hermon obstructed John Stalker's inquiry or that the Chief Constable acted in a bigoted or sectarian fashion. *Private Eye* accepts that the plaintiff acted in a professional and honourable manner and apologises for any distress or embarrassment caused to him and have agreed to pay him damages and costs.

By coincidence, at 4 p.m. that day, a Security Policy Meeting took place, with Tom King, the Secretary of State, as usual in the chair. Under agenda item 'Any other business', I took devilish pleasure in advising Tom King and the others present of the successful outcome of my libel action earlier in the day! I was right not to have been 'persuaded' to abandon it.

Within two months, I had retired. Thereafter, a clean break seemed the best course, and so, with some reservations, I decided not to pursue legal proceedings against Harrap and Penguin, the publishers of *Stalker*. In retrospect, I suspect that had I done so, those actions would have been successful and the many other inaccuracies in *Stalker* exposed. The total truth concerning the travesty of Stalker's inquiry was not to be laid bare until a wholly unexpected event.

In November 1989, I became aware that Yorkshire Television (YTV), with a company called Zenith Films, intended to produce a drama-documentary film about certain events in Northern Ireland between late 1982 and mid-1986. The film would be entitled *Shoot to Kill*. I wrote expressing my anxiety that the reputation of the RUC and my own as Chief Constable be protected. I emphasised that much that was false or grossly distorted had been published in the past, and had been redressed by a series of successful legal actions.

Two weeks later, on 15 December, I received a response from the Director of Programmes at YTV stating:

> If your concern is that our film will be a sensationalisation of events in Northern Ireland, may I assure you that that is not our intention. The drama is based entirely on known facts and is in our opinion, a responsible piece of programme making.

With this, I believed I had my reassurance and YTV's commitment that its film would be a factual one without sensationalism. Consequently, I was content to await the outcome, especially with the additional assurance that John Thorburn had, after his retirement, acted as consultant to Yorkshire TV in producing the film, and so I expected that it would be accurate.

In May 1990, I was invited by YTV to RUC Headquarters for an advance viewing of *Shoot to Kill*, which was to be shown throughout the UK on the independent television network in two episodes on 3 and 4 June. Having accepted the invitation, I contacted Headquarters to make the necessary arrangements. That was followed by a telephone call informing me, with considerable embarrassment, that I had been refused permission to attend. When I asked who had made such a ridiculous decision, I was told it was the Deputy Chief Constable, Michael McAtamney, in the absence of the Chief Constable. I requested that it be referred back to the Chief Constable, then Mr Hugh Annesley. After a brief delay, I was given approval to attend Headquarters, but only on condition that I come unaccompanied, without any legal representative. (I had not even thought of, much less raised, the idea of being legally represented during the screening!) I was also asked to arrive on time and to depart immediately afterwards, without any discussion about the film.

On 21 May, I attended the viewing. Arriving precisely on time, I was escorted to the office of the RUC Press Officer, where, as I recollect, there were six others present: the Deputy Press Officer, a superintendent well known to me, a senior Special Branch officer, the civilian legal adviser for the RUC, a sergeant to operate the video equipment, and Keith Richardson of YTV, who scarcely spoke. I felt I was an unwelcome stranger there, and sensed the embarrassment caused by my presence. RUC Headquarters suddenly seemed to me like an alien environment, where the wealth of friendly, relaxed and humorous conversation, which I had always enjoyed and often fostered, had vanished.

After a ten-minute delay of uncomfortable silence, broken by a rare comment, Michael McAtamney appeared. After a curt nod from him towards me, the screening immediately commenced. It continued for more than three hours. I was shocked by the nature and content of the film. I seemed to be the only one making notes. At its end, and without discussion or comment, Michael McAtamney left the room. I was promptly escorted back to the main door, and left Headquarters. I could not help but notice the frequent, spontaneous smiles and greetings from staff in the walk along corridors to and from the screening. Not all of the old order had changed!

The following day, I contacted the Northern Ireland representative of the Independent Television Commission to express my criticisms of the proposed screening of the film. My views, when relayed, appeared to have no effect. However, not all were as unimpressed. Shortly afterwards, Ulster Television stated publicly that the two-part film would not be shown in Northern Ireland. Ostensibly, this action was taken because the Coroner's inquests into the fatal shootings portrayed in the film were still pending. The film could, therefore, be seen only on the east coast of the Republic of Ireland, where ITV broadcasting could be picked up from the west coast of Great Britain.

I had done what I could to stop the screening of the film, and felt sure that Chief Constable Hugh Annesley would, after taking into account the views of those who attended the viewing, make strong representations to YTV, and possibly even serve an injunction to stop the public screening of the film. The innuendo that named RUC officers, behaving like foul-mouthed bully-boys, had unlawfully embarked on a campaign of murdering republican terrorists was utter nonsense. The representation of police procedures, practices and training was also totally divorced from fact.

Although I firmly believed that the majority of scenes in which I was portrayed were libellous, I felt constrained at first to stand back, regarding it as the responsibility of RUC Command to challenge the film. Ten days passed before I learned that Headquarters did not intend to take any action. I was angry and very disappointed by this stance being taken over such a disgraceful portrayal of the RUC.

By 31 May, I had decided I had no alternative but to issue a personal statement to the media via the Press Association. In its wording, I carefully tried to avoid in any way compromising Chief Constable Hugh Annesley's position or that of the RUC. Quoting the reassurance given to me by Yorkshire TV on 15 December 1989, I declared that the film had most certainly not been based 'entirely on known facts', but instead 'contains many inaccurate or totally false portrayals of past events'. I rejected it as 'neither an objective nor factual portrayal of the shooting incidents to which the film refers, or of the subsequent investigations', and I rejected as totally false several scenes relating to me as Chief Constable. My statement concluded with a refusal of a YTV invitation to participate in a discussion programme arranged to run immediately after the broadcast of the second part of *Shoot to Kill*; I would have no part in a discussion programme about a film which I completely rejected and abhorred.

The following day, 1 June, RUC Headquarters belatedly issued its own statement, in which it roundly condemned the YTV production. The title of the drama was described as inaccurate, unjustified and offensive to the RUC. The statement continued:

> the Drama should not be seen as representing a factual account of events in County Armagh in 1982 and subsequent investigations. On the basis of what the RUC has previewed and of reports in the news media there are inaccuracies, distortions and misrepresentations. The RUC, therefore, takes strong exception to a broadcast which is unjustifiably damaging to the Force.
>
> In particular, the RUC takes exception to an inference, which has been widely reported, that the lives of three police officers were sacrificed in order to save an informant. This is a lie and a despicable one at that . . . There is a solemn obligation on the part of the RUC to do all in its power to safeguard its members . . .

This Headquarters statement included criticism of John Thorburn for acting as consultant to the producers of the film. The RUC also rejected YTV's invitation to participate in the discussion programme, 'on the ground that it [the RUC] refuses to give any credence or legitimacy to a flawed, offensive production. To associate ourselves with Yorkshire Television would be to condone the harm wrongly inflicted on this Force.'

Shoot to Kill was broadcast, as scheduled, in two parts on the evenings of Sunday, 3 and Monday, 4 June 1990, but only in Great Britain. The assertion that the film was factually accurate was stressed by its director, Peter Kosminski, in the discussion programme shown live, late in the evening of 4 June. When asked by the interviewer if there was anything in the programme which did not happen, Kosminski replied, 'Absolutely nothing.' He explained that 'We prepared a research brief that ran to something like 150 pages, plus appendices, and then we presented that brief to an experienced writer who turned it into drama.'

However, after the showing of the film, the Stalker inquiry team — minus John Stalker and John Thorburn — issued the following statement:

The Greater Manchester Police wish to draw attention to a recently screened television drama documentary entitled *Shoot to Kill.* Each of the serving Greater Manchester Police Officers who comprised the enquiry team in Northern Ireland and referred to by name in the credits of the programme wish to make it clear they have had no involvement with its production and disassociate themselves from any implied connection.

They also wish to point out that the programme contained many significant inaccuracies and in every way grossly overexaggerated the personal involvement of Mr Stalker, the former Deputy Chief Constable of Greater Manchester Police.

The Greater Manchester officers wish to stress that the Stalker/Sampson Enquiry found no evidence of a 'Shoot to Kill' policy.

The inference in the televised programme that RUC officers murdered on the Kinnego Embankment, Armagh in October 1982, were 'sacrificed' to protect the involvement of an informant is wildly misleading. This was never the conclusion drawn in any of the reports submitted to the RUC and ultimately to the Director of Public Prosecutions for Northern Ireland.

The officers also wish to point out that they have throughout maintained a duty of confidence to the enquiry and as a matter of general principle they do not support the publication or production of any material that would be regarded as classified information.

The team's statement intensified the media hype already generated by the film. Immediately after its broadcast, I received a constant stream of requests for interviews from both radio and television. Consequently, Tuesday, 5 June was hectic. It began at 7.30 a.m., when I gave a recorded interview at home for BBC television. I then did an interview with John Suchet in Belfast, to be broadcast by Independent Television for the *ITN News* at 1 p.m. I made clear that 'scenes within the film which portrayed Stalker and I meeting are not at all factual. The film is so flawed with inaccuracies and untruths as to be totally without credibility.'

Afterwards, I flew to London, for a dinner engagement that evening, and yet another interview. At the television studios, I was introduced to Jon Snow, the presenter of Channel 4 *News* broadcast at 7 p.m. It was our first meeting and, in a relaxed manner, we briefly discussed the film. He outlined his intended line of questioning. I felt quite at ease, but not for long.

Jon Snow opened his live interview by stressing my condemnation of the film because of its inaccuracies. An excerpt from it was screened, showing the actor T.P. McKenna, portraying me as bullish and arrogant, during a conversation with the actor playing John Stalker. When I rejected the portrayal as untrue, Snow proceeded to press me repeatedly on whether I proposed to sue. Since I had not yet thought about this, let alone taken legal advice, I was naturally ambivalent about answering 'yes' or 'no'. He then asked me if I was saying that John Thorburn's account of events, which the film seemed to follow, was flawed. Exasperated with this persistent line of questioning, I replied:

Yes, I am. And I may say this, that I have said that the whole investigation was flawed and faulted and one of the reasons was that they totally transcended their Terms of Reference which were laid down by the Director of Public Prosecutions. Secondly, they came to a subjective conclusion, without evidence at all, that the RUC, having lost three officers murdered, set about on a 'Shoot to Kill' policy. Stalker and Colin Sampson have both identified there was no 'shoot to kill' policy but this programme identified one other issue of which I have no knowledge, and that is a suggestion, an implication that the Royal Ulster Constabulary sacrificed three of their officers to murder by the terrorists to protect a source. Now we find that totally offensive, totally untrue . . . To identify a 'Shoot to Kill' where none existed and also to have a hidden agenda, not previously revealed, that three police officers were sacrificed by their own Force, their own officers, to protect a source is deeply offensive to the Royal Ulster Constabulary, every member of it, and to the community as a whole.

That spontaneous and angry response to Jon Snow's question had serious repercussions later. In my diary for that day, I recorded, 'A bad and nasty interview . . . but seemingly it turned out well.' The latter comment sprang from the fact that, immediately afterwards, many RUC officers and others conveyed their appreciation that I, as a lone voice, had spoken out and defended the RUC from the consequences of a notoriously poor piece of 'investigative' journalism.

After serious discussion and thought, I decided that, in the interests of the Force, and to protect my own professional integrity, I should obtain legal advice. Thereafter, my solicitors wrote to Yorkshire TV, identifying as defamatory the implications in the film that I had been involved:

    (a) in a conspiracy to carry out the unlawful killing of suspected terrorists;

    (b) in conspiracies to falsify evidence;

    (c) in conspiracies to pervert the course of justice;

and also the implications that I had:

    (d) presided over and directed 'a Police Force which knowingly allowed three serving members to be lured to certain death in order that the credibility of an intelligence source could be protected';

    (e) been responsible for 'bugging' the offices of the Stalker/Sampson investigation team;

    (f) conspired with others to make false accusations of corruption against John Stalker.

After an exchange of correspondence, the television company replied that any proceedings served would be vigorously defended, and public statements by me about the film would be scrutinised with a view to a possible counter-claim.

Since my legal advice was that I had a good case, I sought financial support from the Northern Ireland Police Authority for my costs in the libel action I intended to take. Other RUC officers, who felt libelled in the film, also asked the Authority for financial backing. We were all refused. The others decided that they could not risk the massive costs of a contended libel action. If I went ahead, I knew I would go it alone. What should I do for the best?

Already the pressures on Sylvia and me, since our marriage, had been considerable. Her eldest sister had been killed in a tragic car accident in July 1989, just three months before our first son, Robert Paisley, named after his grandfather, was born. Within a few weeks of his birth, we learned that Sylvia's youngest sister had cancer, and that the prognosis for her at that time was bleak, to say the least. On top of all this, we moved into our new home, in an unfinished state, and encountered ever more acrimonious arguments with the builders and the architect. Given these difficult circumstances, I agonised over inflicting on both of us the additional anxiety and hassle of fighting a libel action against a powerful television company. Nevertheless, I knew better than anyone the extent of the injustice being done to the RUC by the film going unchallenged. I knew the feelings of those officers portrayed in it, their frustrations and anger, and their subsequent bitterness at the Police Authority's decision about withholding its support.

It was during this critical time that we were invited to a charity concert, organised privately by a police constable, with the RUC Silver Band providing the music. With some connivance on Sylvia's part, the band dedicated to me its playing of 'My Way', the song made famous by Frank Sinatra. So often I had behaved like a stormy petrel, and done it my way! I was deeply moved by the spontaneous and sustained applause which followed the tune. It was just the spur I needed to forge ahead with my libel action.

Sylvia's attitude to it was soundly based on her legal training. While recognising my commitment towards redressing, as far as possible, the unjustified criticisms of the RUC and the libellous way in which I had been portrayed in the film, she was well aware of the vagaries of the legal process and the inevitable financial consequences of failure — or even qualified success, where costs were not awarded. With notable courage and, I suspect, secret fears, she expressed her complete support for my decision.

Early in August 1991, I became aware that RTE in Dublin was planning to screen *Shoot to Kill* later that month. Having always enjoyed a good working relationship with RTE, I contacted its Northern Ireland representative to advise him of my legal action against Yorkshire TV. If RTE were to show the film, I stressed, I would have no alternative but to take similar proceedings against it, although I had no wish to do so. RTE very wisely cancelled its proposed screening.

Then, wholly unexpectedly, John Thorburn issued a libel writ against me for certain comments I had made in the Channel 4 *News* interview with Jon Snow about eleven months earlier, on 5 June 1990. The firm of London solicitors which represented Yorkshire Television in my action against it also acted for John Thorburn in his action against me. Being engaged in fighting two libel actions simultaneously proved to be one of the most complex and stressful periods of my life. I personally spent day after day contacting potential witnesses, obtaining statements, analysing the film scene by scene, and discussing both cases with two sets of lawyers, one in London, the other in Belfast.

Twice, I had to go to the High Court, regarding access to specific documents, and twice I won. In the first instance, I, as the plaintiff against Yorkshire TV, sought discovery of the producer, Peter Kosminski's, 150-page research file. Mr Justice Carswell ruled, *inter alia*, that the existence of any memorandum, letter or other document relating to the compilation and production of the film should be disclosed. In the second case, as defendant in Thorburn's action, I rejected his claim for discovery of certain intelligence documents. In fact, the *Times* 'Law Report' cited *Thorburn* v. *Hermon*[4] as a leading new case on public interest immunity for access to documents which Government ministers refuse to disclose in the interests of national security.

Early in 1992, my opponents' solicitors began to make overtures towards a settlement. Without explanation, in the final stages of coming to an agreed statement of apology, Yorkshire TV broke off the discussions. I was unmoved by the loss of this 'near victory', having privately developed a desire to see both John Stalker and John Thorburn exposed to expert cross-examination in the face of the evidence of the many witnesses I could assemble. This, above all, was what I wished to achieve through these libel actions.

It was not to be. In June 1992, Yorkshire TV and John Thorburn simultaneously agreed to settle. All costs incurred were met by my opponents, including all expenses of the two earlier applications to the High Court for the discovery of various documents. While the damages agreed by Yorkshire TV were substantial, it was the apology which meant much more to me. It was read out on my behalf by my QC at Belfast High Court on Tuesday, 23 June 1992. It declared that:

> Yorkshire Television acknowledge that between 1980 and 1989 Sir John Hermon, as Chief Constable of the RUC, carried out his duties in a committed, honourable and professional manner and that he was at all times motivated solely by a desire to ensure the proper administration of justice for all the people of Northern Ireland.
>
> Yorkshire did not at any stage seek to denigrate the integrity of Sir John, or the manner in which he carried out his difficult duties as Chief Constable of the RUC, and it sincerely regrets any hurt and distress occasioned to Sir John, his family and the RUC, through the broadcast of the programme *Shoot to Kill* on June 3 and 4, 1990.
>
> The defence has agreed to make proper amends to the plaintiff to vindicate his good name.

I did indeed feel totally exonerated by this statement, and was particularly pleased to see that, even though a libel action is by its very nature a personal one, Yorkshire TV did regret not only my distress but 'any hurt and distress occasioned to . . . the RUC' by its film. My pleasure was further enhanced by the statement agreed with John Thorburn, as the plaintiff, issued when he announced the withdrawal of his libel action. It read:

> Mr Thorburn and Sir John Hermon have now reached a settlement of their dispute. *The Plaintiff wishes to take this opportunity to state publicly that he is satisfied that the RUC did not pursue a 'shoot to kill' policy in 1982, and specifically that the Defendant did not authorise or condone any deliberate or reckless killings by his officers or the sacrifice of three of his serving officers to preserve the secrecy of a police informer.* In his turn, the Defendant accepts that the Plaintiff as a professional policeman carried out his work for the Stalker Inquiry in a committed manner and was motivated by a proper desire to ensure that the investigation achieved its objectives. The Defendant did not intend any imputation on the Plaintiff's integrity as a serving police officer and withdraws any such imputation as there may have been . . . [emphasis added]

Both these statements were welcomed by the RUC generally as a vindication of its own professionalism and integrity. To those retired and serving police officers, in particular Stalker's inquiry team, and those civilians who were prepared to stand up and be counted as witnesses for me, I remain enormously grateful. Since embarking on the libel action against Yorkshire Television, I had suffered bouts of depression and intense anxiety about the welfare of my family had I failed, because the financial consequences of failure were so horrendous. Even with both actions settled in my favour, the consequences of the mental stress lingered long afterwards, and no amount of financial damages could ever properly compensate me for those hidden scars.

Notes
1 *Sunday Independent*, 28 August 1988.
2 *Private Eye*, Colour Section, 5 September 1986.
3 *Private Eye*, Colour Section, 19 February 1988.
4 *The Times*, 21 February 1992.

24

BOYS, BEACHES AND BOATS

On 11 April 1992 our second son, Thomas Rowan, was born. Our joy was complete — two healthy boys, who provide Sylvia and me with much fun and entertainment, and great happiness. It is said that 'everyone's goose is a swan', and our two are undisputedly swans! This lively pair keep me busy and feeling young even in my late sixties. It is such a delight to have that most valuable of commodities, spare time, to spend with them as children, time that I never had while Barbara and Rodney were growing up; life then was so hectic, compared to today's pace.

Thomas and Robert are, therefore, very much the focus of our lives, as we revolve around them. The same is true of Belle, as she remains happily integrated with the four of us by living in a flat within our home. Roy Webb, Jean's father, also lived with us for several years, but in his ninety-fifth year he was suffering from such acute senile dementia that he went into permanent residential care in an excellent nursing home, about twenty miles away. Every time I visit him, I come away saddened, having seen the cruel effects of dementia on this fine man, who had once been much closer to me than my own father, and who had been meticulous in all that he did. Sadly, he no longer knows where I fit into his past life, nor is he able to recognise his only grandchildren, Barbara and Rodney. Both of them remain in regular contact with us, although we see too little of them on account of their own lives having changed and developed, beyond Northern Ireland.

During the summer of 1996, Barbara remarried, a quiet American this time, after divorcing Kevin in 1990. Even before this, she had made America, or more precisely Florida, her home, where she and Peter seem well settled and content with life. Meanwhile, Rodney married Patricia, a young Catholic teacher, and moved to Manchester, where they now have three lovely young daughters, Katie, Clare and Anne. Despite the passage of time and the miles that separate us, Sylvia and I strive to retain a close-knit family.

Friends were genuinely concerned that after my retirement I should keep mentally active and become involved in various activities, rather than stop working completely. But I was tired; and I had grown to loathe paperwork. Therefore it was with considerable reluctance that I followed their advice. To begin with I worked part-time as a consultant to a security company and later, in 1993, I accepted the presidency of a professional security association but have also retired from that.

Then during 1994 and 1995 there was an unexpected development in my involvement in the business world; the 'good Samaritan' who had so kindly helped us with the completion of our house needed someone to promote his construction business in the Middle East. I agreed to help, and found it an enjoyable and fulfilling experience to gain an insight into Arab culture, and the convoluted problems of the Middle East. However, my frequent business trips became too disruptive of family life, particularly for the boys, and so, by November 1995, I decided it was time to retire from this too.

Having gradually withdrawn from these various commitments, I have instead been able to develop my pleasure in boating, and have also acquired a keen interest in what I call 'beach-gardening'. This began in 1990 when I needed to be alone to unscramble the tumult in my head over the libel action involving Yorkshire TV and the constant hassle with the workmen because of the slow completion of our house in Donaghadee. I began shifting the big granite and basalt rocks on the foreshore, fifty yards from our home, and used them to build a retaining wall to prevent land erosion, and another one out into the sea; I was curious to learn if this would encourage sand to come in to form a reasonable beach. Breaking big rocks and then wheeling barrowfuls of them to construct dry stone walls became a passion. It was something of a standing joke that I would leave the house, saying to Sylvia, 'I'll be up in half an hour,' and she would make a mental note not to start preparing the next meal for at least three hours! Local recognition as being something of a 'retired oddity' has its advantages!

I have no doubt that the RUC guards (we have had a rotation of eight, in squads of two, for twenty-four hours every day, since we moved to Donaghadee) considered it a little strange, to say the least, that their former Chief Constable was utterly dismissive of their frequent suggestions that I should get a mechanical digger down to do the job for me. A digger was the last thing I wanted, because shifting stones gave me great mental relaxation, useful physical exercise, and constant satisfaction, as I watched a sandy beach develop, where none had been before. The inevitable consequence was that when Thomas and Robert were toddlers, neither was interested in buckets and spades to build the usual sandcastles. Instead, they too wanted to carry stones in their plastic wheelbarrows! We three looked comical, but our sense of achievement in our creations was enormous. In more recent times, the three of us have used the beach for launching the rowing-boat for outings to and around the Copeland Islands, and fishing expeditions in our smaller dinghy. Age has certainly not diminished my love of being out at sea, and indeed the companionship of Robert and Thomas has only enhanced it; with the yacht and a small motorboat, we enjoy many picnics and outings along the coast.

Having been central to the development of the RUC during the most turbulent and violent years of Northern Ireland's history through to the continuing political impasse, it is inevitable that I maintain a deep interest in events as they occur. I have concerns as to the ultimate effects of that continuing impasse and the resulting violence from terrorist activity and grave public disorder. The Provisional IRA's cease-fire of 31 August 1994 and the subsequent one by the loyalist paramilitary groupings gave rise to tremendous hope of being able to live in Northern Ireland without fear of being murdered or maimed. The much-vaunted 'Peace Process' was begun. In my view, the peace process was a psychological creation and cover for the efforts of both the Irish and British Governments to pursue their respective objectives within those historically unique documents, the Anglo-Irish Agreement of 15 November 1985 and the Downing Street Declaration of 15 December 1993.

Too many of the initiatives emanating from those agreements have each had aspects which might rightly be dubbed as a 'bridge too far' for the divergent political groupings, and equally divergent constitutional and political aspirations of the people of Northern Ireland. I believe the mantle of 'peace-at-any-price' which has cloaked the Agreement and Declaration has done those documents, and thereby the people of Northern Ireland, a grave injustice. True and lasting peace must be diligently pursued and, if necessary, fought for, if placed in jeopardy by terrorist groupings. Certainly, it should never become a weapon of convenience for terrorists to use against governments, or the people they respectively govern. When the RUC is regarded as part of 'the problem' in Northern Ireland, the temptation is for political interference to make it part of the solution. During my tenure as Chief Constable, I had to strive constantly to keep the RUC clear of political manipulation.

I identify with, and indeed find comfort and solace from, a quotation attributed to the late Theodore Roosevelt:

> The credit belongs to the man who is actually in the arena, whose face is marred with sweat and dust and blood; who strives valiantly; who errs and comes short again and again; who knows great enthusiasm, the great devotions and spends himself in a worthy cause; who, if he wins, knows the triumph of high achievement and who, if he fails, at least fails while daring greatly, so that his place shall never be with those cold and timid souls who know neither victory nor defeat.

I believe I held the line.

INDEX